Public Administration
For UGC-NET/SLET/JRF

Paper I, II and III

Previous Years' Papers with Key

Atlantic Research Division

Published by

ATLANTIC

PUBLISHERS & DISTRIBUTORS (P) LTD

7/22, Ansari Road, Darya Ganj,
New Delhi-110002
Phones : +91-11-40775252, 23273880, 23275880, 23280451
Fax : +91-11-23285873
Web : www.atlanticbooks.com
E-mail : orders@atlanticbooks.com

Branch Office
5, Nallathambi Street, Wallajah Road,
Chennai-600002
Phones : +91-44-64611085, 32413319
E-mail : chennai@atlanticbooks.com

ISBN 978-81-269-1956-7

Printed in India at Nice Printing Press, A-33/3A, Site-IV,
Industrial Area, Sahibabad, Ghaziabad, U.P.

Preface

The University Grants Commission (UGC) conducts National Eligibility Test (NET) on various subjects twice every year, once each in June and December, to determine eligibility for college and university level lectureship and for award of Junior Research Fellowship (JRF), for Indian nationals in order to ensure minimum standards for the entrants in the teaching profession and research.

The book contains previous years' solved papers (objective type questions) on the subject of Public Administration, from June 2005 to December 2013. It covers all three papers (Paper I, II and III). In Paper I (General Paper on Teaching and Research Aptitude), and Paper II (Elective), solved papers have been included from June 2005. In Paper III (Core and Elective), solved papers of objective type questions have been included from June 2012, conforming to the existing UGC-NET pattern. In addition, three sets of Mock Tests for Paper I, II and III have been included in the book under Practice Papers. Answers have been given at the end of each set for self-check.

It will be useful for those preparing for UGC-NET/SLET/JRF in the subject of Public Administration. It will give them a feel of the type of questions asked in NET in this subject, i.e. Multiple-choice, Matching type, True/False, Assertion-Reasoning type, etc. The papers included in this book will enable the students to judge their own level of competence besides adding to their knowledge. It will also help them revise the important questions in the entire syllabus and enhance their self-confidence. Suggestions for further improvement of the book are, however, welcome.

Atlantic Research Division

Contents

DECEMBER–2013

Note: This paper contains Sixty (60) multiple-choice questions, each question carrying two (2) marks. Candidate is expected to answer any Fifty (50) questions. In case more than Fifty (50) questions are attempted, only the first Fifty (50) questions will be evaluated.

PAPER–I

1. The post-industrial society is designated as
   (a) Information society
   (b) Technology society
   (c) Mediated society
   (d) Non-agricultural society

2. The initial efforts for internet based communication was for
   (a) Commercial communication
   (b) Military purposes
   (c) Personal interaction
   (d) Political campaigns

3. Internal communication within institutions is done through
   (a) LAN (b) WAN
   (c) EBB (d) MMS

4. Virtual reality provides
   (a) Sharp pictures
   (b) Individual audio
   (c) Participatory experience
   (d) Preview of new films

5. The first virtual university of India came up in
   (a) Andhra Pradesh
   (b) Maharashtra
   (c) Uttar Pradesh
   (d) Tamil Nadu

6. Arrange the following books in chronological order in which they appeared. Use the codes given below:
   (i) Limits to Growth
   (ii) Silent Spring
   (iii) Our Common Future
   (iv) Resourceful Earth

   Codes:
   (a) (i), (iii), (iv), (ii)
   (b) (ii), (iii), (i), (iv)
   (c) (ii), (i), (iii), (iv)
   (d) (i), (ii), (iii), (iv)

7. Which one of the following continents is at a greater risk of desertification?
   (a) Africa (b) Asia
   (c) South America (d) North America

8. "Women are closer to nature than men." What kind of perspective is this?
   (a) Realist (b) Essentialist
   (c) Feminist (d) Deep ecology

9. Which one of the following is not a matter a global concern in the removal of tropical forests?
   (a) Their ability to absorb the chemicals that contribute to depletion of ozone layer.
   (b) Their role in maintaining the oxygen and carbon balance of the earth.
   (c) Their ability to regulate surface and air temperatures, moisture content and reflectivity.
   (d) Their contribution to the biological diversity of the planet.

10. The most comprehensive approach to address the problems of man-environment interaction is one of the following:

(a) Natural Resource Conservation Approach
(b) Urban-industrial Growth Oriented Approach
(c) Rural-agricultural Growth Oriented Approach
(d) Watershed Development Approach

11. The major source of the pollutant gas, carbon mono-oxide (CO), in urban areas is
(a) Thermal power sector
(b) Transport sector
(c) Industrial sector
(d) Domestic sector

12. In a fuel cell driven vehicle, the energy is obtained from the combustion of
(a) Methane (b) Hydrogen
(c) LPG (d) CNG

13. Which one of the following Councils has been disbanded in 2013?
(a) Distance Education Council (DEC)
(b) National Council for Teacher Education (NCTE)
(c) National Council of Educational Research and Training (NCERT)
(d) National Assessment and Accreditation Council (NAAC)

14. Which of the following statements are correct about the National Assessment and Accreditation Council?
1. It is an autonomous institution.
2. It is tasked with the responsibility of assessing and accrediting institutions of higher education.
3. It is located in Delhi.
4. It has regional offices.

Select the correct answer from the codes given below:

Codes:

(a) 1 and 3 (b) 1 and 2
(c) 1, 2 and 4 (d) 2, 3 and 4

15. The power of the Supreme Court of India to decide disputes between two or more States falls under its
(a) Advisory Jurisdiction
(b) Appellate Jurisdiction
(c) Original Jurisdiction
(d) Writ Jurisdiction

16. Which of the following statements are correct?
1. There are seven Union Territories in India.
2. Two Union Territories have Legislative Assemblies.
3. One Union Territory has a High Court.
4. One Union Territory is the capital of two States.

Select the correct answer from the codes given below:

Codes:

(a) 1 and 3 only
(b) 2 and 4 only
(c) 2, 3 and 4 only
(d) 1, 2, 3 and 4

17. Which of the following statements are correct about the Central Information Commission?
1. The Central Information Commission is a statutory body.
2. The Chief Information Commissioner and other Information Commissioners are appointed by the President of India.
3. The Commission can impose a penalty upto a maximum of ₹ 25,000
4. It can punish an errant officer.

Select the correct answer from the codes given below:

Codes:

(a) 1 and 2 only (b) 1, 2 and 4
(c) 1, 2 and 3 (d) 2, 3 and 4

18. Who among the following conducted the CNN-IBN – The Hindu 2013 Election Tracker Survey across 267 constituencies in 18 States?
    (a) The Centre for the Study of Developing Societies (CSDS)
    (b) The Association for Democratic Reforms (ADR)
    (c) CNN and IBN
    (d) CNN, IBN and The Hindu

19. In certain code TEACHER is written as VGCEJGT. The code of CHILDREN will be
    (a) EKNJFTGP (b) EJKNFTGP
    (c) KNJFGTP (d) None of these

20. A person has to buy both apples and mangoes. The cost of one apple is ₹ 7 whereas that of a mango is ₹ 5. If the person has ₹ 38, the number of apples he can buy is
    (a) 1 (b) 2
    (c) 3 (d) 4

21. A man pointing to a lady said, "The son of her only brother is the brother of my wife". The lady is related to the man as
    (a) Mother's sister
    (b) Grand mother
    (c) Mother-in-law
    (d) Sister of Father-in-law

22. In this series
    6, 4, 1, 2, 2, 8, 7, 4, 2, 1, 5, 3, 8, 6, 2, 2, 7, 1, 4, 1, 3, 5, 8, 6, how many pairs of successive numbers have a difference of 2 each?
    (a) 4 (b) 5
    (c) 6 (d) 8

23. The mean marks obtained by a class of 40 students is 65. The mean marks of half of the students is found to be 45. The mean marks of the remaining students is
    (a) 85 (b) 60
    (c) 70 (d) 65

24. Anil is twice as old as Sunita. Three years ago, he was three times as old as Sunita. The present age of Anil is
    (a) 6 years (b) 8 years
    (c) 12 years (d) 16 years

25. Which of the following is a social network?
    (a) amazon.com (b) eBay
    (c) gmail.com (d) Twitter

26. The population information is called parameter while the corresponding sample information is known as
    (a) Universe
    (b) Inference
    (c) Sampling design
    (d) Statistics

Read the following passage carefully and answer questions 27 to 32:

Heritage conservation practices improved worldwide after the International Centre for the Study of the Preservation and Restoration of Cultural Property (ICCROM) was established with UNESCO's assistance in 1959. The inter-governmental organisation with 126 member states has done a commendable job by training more than 4,000 professionals, providing practice standards, and sharing technical expertise. In this golden jubilee year, as we acknowledge its key role in global conservation, an assessment of international practices would be meaningful to the Indian conservation movement. Consistent investment, rigorous attention, and dedicated research and dissemination are some of the positive lessons to imbibe. Countries such as Italy have demonstrated that prioritising heritage with significant budget provision pays. On the other hand, India, which is no less endowed in terms of cultural capital, has a long way to go. Surveys indicate that in addition to the 6,600 protected monuments, there are over 60,000 equally valuable heritage structures that await attention. Besides the small group in the service of Archaeological Survey of India, there are only about 150 trained conservation professionals. In order to overcome this severe shortage the emphasis has been on setting up dedicated labs and training institutions. It would make much better sense for conservation to be made part of mainstream research and engineering institutes, as has been done in Europe.

Increasing funding and building institutions are the relatively easy part. The real challenge is to redefine international approaches to address local contexts. Conservation cannot limit itself to enhancing the art-historical value of the heritage structures, which international charters perhaps overemphasise. The effort has to be broad-based: It must also serve as a means to improving the quality of life in the area where the heritage structures are located. The first task therefore is to integrate conservation efforts with sound development plans that take care of people living in the heritage vicinity. Unlike in western countries, many traditional building crafts survive in India, and conservation practices offer an avenue to support them. This has been acknowledged by the Indian National Trust for Art and Cultural Heritage charter for conservation but is yet to receive substantial state support. More strength for heritage conservation can be mobilised by aligning it with the green building movement. Heritage structures are essentially eco-friendly and conservation could become a vital part of the sustainable building practices campaign in future.

27. The outlook for conservation heritage changed
    (a) after the establishment of the International Centre for the Study of the Preservation and Restoration of Cultural Property.
    (b) after training the specialists in the field.
    (c) after extending UNESCO's assistance to the educational institutions.
    (d) after ASI's measures to protect the monuments.

28. The inter-government organization was appreciated because of
    (a) increasing number of members to 126.
    (b) imparting training to professionals and sharing technical expertise.
    (c) consistent investment in conservation.
    (d) its proactive role in renovation and restoration.

29. Indian conservation movement will be successful if there would be
    (a) Financial support from the Government of India.
    (b) Non-governmental organisations role and participation in the conservation movement.
    (c) consistent investment, rigorous attention, and dedicated research and dissemination of awareness for conservation.
    (d) Archaeological Survey of India's meaningful assistance.

30. As per the surveys of historical monuments in India, there is very small number of protected monuments. As per given the total number of monuments and enlisted number of protected monuments, percentage comes to
    (a) 10 percent (b) 11 percent
    (c) 12 percent (d) 13 percent

31. What should India learn from Europe to conserve our cultural heritage?

(i) There should be significant budget provision to conserve our cultural heritage.
(ii) Establish dedicated labs and training institutions.
(iii) Force the government to provide sufficient funds.
(iv) Conservation should be made part of mainstream research and engineering institutes.

Choose correct answer from the codes given below:
(a) (i), (ii), (iii), (iv) (b) (i), (ii), (iv)
(c) (i), (ii) (d) (i), (iii), (iv)

32. INTACH is known for its contribution for conservation of our cultural heritage. The full form of INTACH is
(a) International Trust for Art and Cultural Heritage.
(b) Intra-national Trust for Art and Cultural Heritage.
(c) Integrated Trust for Art and Cultural Heritage.
(d) Indian National Trust for Art and Cultural Heritage.

33. While delivering lecture if there is some disturbance in the class, a teacher should
(a) keep quiet for a while and then continue.
(b) punish those causing disturbance.
(c) motivate to teach those causing disturbance.
(d) not bother of what is happening in the class.

34. Effective teaching is a function of
(a) Teacher's satisfaction.
(b) Teacher's honesty and commitment.
(c) Teacher's making students learn and understand.
(d) Teacher's liking for professional excellence.

35. The most appropriate meaning of learning is
(a) Acquisition of skills
(b) Modification of behaviour
(c) Personal adjustment
(d) Inculcation of knowledge

36. Arrange the following teaching process in order:
(i) Relate the present knowledge with previous one
(ii) Evaluation
(iii) Reteaching
(iv) Formulating instructional objectives
(v) Presentation of instructional materials
(a) (i), (ii), (iii), (iv), (v)
(b) (ii), (i), (iii), (iv), (v)
(c) (v), (iv), (iii), (i), (ii)
(d) (iv), (i), (v), (ii), (iii)

37. CIET stands for
(a) Centre for Integrated Education and Technology.
(b) Central Institute for Engineering and Technology.
(c) Central Institute for Education Technology.
(d) Centre for Integrated Evaluation Techniques.

38. Teacher's role at higher education level is to
(a) provide information to students.
(b) promote self learning in students.
(c) encourage healthy competition among students.
(d) help students to solve their problems.

39. The Verstehen School of Understanding was popularised by
(a) German Social Scientists
(b) American Philosophers
(c) British Academicians
(d) Italian Political Analysts

40. The sequential operations in scientific research are
(a) Co-variation, Elimination of Spurious Relations, Generalisation, Theorisation.

(b) Generalisation, Co-variation, Theorisation, Elimination of Spurious Relations.
(c) Theorisation, Generalisation, Elimination of Spurious Relations, Co-variation.
(d) Elimination of Spurious Relations, Theorisation, Generalisation, Co-variation.

41. In sampling, the lottery method is used for
(a) Interpretation
(b) Theorisation
(c) Conceptualisation
(d) Randomisation

42. Which is the main objective of research?
(a) To review the literature
(b) To summarize what is already known
(c) To get an academic degree
(d) To discover new facts or to make fresh interpretation of known facts

43. Sampling error decreases with the
(a) decrease in sample size
(b) increase in sample size
(c) process of randomization
(d) process of analysis

44. The principles of fundamental research are used in
(a) action research
(b) applied research
(c) philosophical research
(d) historical research

45. Users who use media for their own ends are identified as
(a) Passive audience
(b) Active audience
(c) Positive audience
(d) Negative audience

46. Classroom communication can be described as
(a) Exploration
(b) Institutionalisation
(c) Unsignified narration
(d) Discourse

47. Ideological codes shape our collective
(a) Productions (b) Perceptions
(c) Consumptions (d) Creations

48. In communication, myths have power, but are
(a) uncultural. (b) insignificant.
(c) imprecise. (d) unpreferred.

49. The first multi-lingual news agency of India was
(a) Samachar
(b) API
(c) Hindustan Samachar
(d) Samachar Bharati

50. Organisational communication can also be equated with
(a) intra-personal communication.
(b) inter-personal communication.
(c) group communication.
(d) mass communication.

51. If two propositions having the same subject and predicate terms are such that one is the denial of the other, the relationship between them is called
(a) Contradictory (b) Contrary
(c) Sub-contrary (d) Sub-alternation

52. Ananya and Krishna can speak and follow English. Bulbul can write and speak Hindi as Archana does.

Archana talks with Ananya also in Bengali. Krishna can not follow Bengali. Bulbul talks with Ananya in Hindi. Who can speak and follow English, Hindi and Bengali?
(a) Archana (b) Bulbul
(c) Ananya (d) Krishna

53. A stipulative definition may be said to be
(a) Always true
(b) Always false

(c) Sometimes true, sometimes false
(d) Neither true nor false

54. When the conclusion of an argument follows from its premise/premises conclusively, the argument is called
(a) Circular argument
(b) Inductive argument
(c) Deductive argument
(d) Analogical argument

55. Saturn and Mars are planets like the earth. They borrow light from the Sun and moves around the Sun as the Earth does. So those planets are inhabited by various orders of creatures as the earth is. What type of argument is contained in the above passage?
(a) Deductive (b) Astrological
(c) Analogical (d) Mathematical

56. Given below are two premises. Four conclusions are drawn from those two premises in four codes. Select the code that states the conclusion validly drawn.
Premises:
(i) All saints are religious. (major)
(ii) Some honest persons are saints. (minor)
Codes:
(a) All saints are honest.
(b) Some saints are honest.
(c) Some honest persons are religious.
(d) All religious persons are honest

Following table provides details about the Foreign Tourist Arrivals (FTAs) in India from different regions of the world in different years. Study the table carefully and answer questions from 57 to 60 based on this table.

Region	**Number of Foreign Tourist Arrivals**		
	2007	**2008**	**2009**
Western Europe	1686083	1799525	1610086
North America	1007276	1027297	1024469
South Asia	982428	1051846	982633
South East Asia	303475	332925	348495
East Asia	352037	355230	318292
West Asia	171661	215542	201110
Total FTAs in India	5081504	5282603	5108579

57. Find out the region that contributed around 20 percent of the total foreign tourist arrivals in India in 2009.
(a) Western Europe
(b) North America
(c) South Asia
(d) South East Asia

58. Which of the following regions has recorded the highest negative growth rate of foreign tourist arrivals in India in 2009?
(a) Western Europe
(b) North America
(c) South Asia
(d) West Asia

59. Find out the region that has been showing declining trend in terms of share of foreign tourist arrivals in India in 2008 and 2009.
(a) Western Europe
(b) South East Asia
(c) East Asia
(d) West Asia

60. Identify the region that has shown hyper growth rate of foreign tourist arrivals than the growth rate of the total FTAs in India in 2008.
(a) Western Europe
(b) North America
(c) South Asia
(d) East Asia

ANSWERS

1. (a)	2. (b)	3. (a)	4. (c)	5. (d)
6. (c)	7. (a)	8. (b)	9. (a)	10. (d)
11. (b)	12. (b)	13. (a)	14. (b)	15. (c)
16. (d)	17. (c)	18. (a)	19. (b)	20. (d)
21. (d)	22. (c)	23. (a)	24. (c)	25. (d)
26. (d)	27. (a)	28. (b)	29. (c)	30. (b)
31. (b)	32. (d)	33. (c)	34. (c)	35. (b)
36. (d)	37. (c)	38. (b)	39. (a)	40. (a)
41. (d)	42. (d)	43. (b)	44. (b)	45. (b)
46. (d)	47. (b)	48. (c)	49. (c)	50. (c)
51. (a)	52. (c)	53. (d)	54. (c)	55. (c)
56. (c)	57. (b)	58. (d)	59. (a)	60. (c)

PAPER–II

Note: This paper contains fifty (50) objective type questions, each question carrying two (2) marks. All questions are compulsory.

1. "Public Administration is the Art and Science of Management applied to the affairs of the State." Who of the following made this statement?
   (a) Herbert Simon
   (b) F.M. Marx
   (c) Dwight Waldo
   (d) L.D. White

2. Which of the following is the common feature of New Public Administration and Development Administration?
   (a) Ecological perspective
   (b) Effective coordination
   (c) Change oriented
   (d) To serve the organisational interests

3. Which one of the following is favoured by Urwick and Gulick?
   (a) Organisation headed by plural bodies
   (b) Commission type organisation
   (c) Decentralised organisation
   (d) Single top executive

4. **Assertion (A):** Principle of unity of command cannot be strictly observed in practice in an organization.
   Reason (R): Employees are often subject to dual control technical and administrative.
   Codes:
   (a) Both (A) and (R) are correct and (R) is the correct explanation of (A).
   (b) Both (A) and (R) are correct, but (R) is not the correct explanation of (A).
   (c) (A) is true, but (R) is false.
   (d) (A) is false, but (R) is true.

5. The statement that 'Organisational objective should reflect manifestation of individual goals' is advocated by:
   (a) Chester Bernard
   (b) Elton Mayo
   (c) Chris Argyris
   (d) Peter Drucker

6. The term "Grapevine" is associated with
   (a) Supervision
   (b) Control
   (c) Communication
   (d) Command

7. Match List I with List II and select the correct answer from the codes given below:
   List I (Author/s)
   A. Eva Etzioni
   B. Fredrick Herzberg
   C. Ernest Dale
   D. E.N. Gladden
   List II (Book)
   i. An Introduction to Public Administration
   ii. Management: Theory and Practice

iii. Work and Nature of Man
iv. Bureaucracy and Democracy: A Political Dilemma

Codes:	A	B	C	D
(a)	i	ii	iii	iv
(b)	iii	ii	i	iv
(c)	i	iii	ii	iv
(d)	iv	iii	ii	i

8. Which of the following is not a correct match with the views of M.P. Follett?
   (a) Constructive Conflict – not warfare, but is only appearance of differences
   (b) Integration – dealing with conflict through compromise
   (c) Depersonalizing order – law of situation
   (d) Obstacle to Integration – people's habit of enjoyment

9. Which one among the following is not a principal category of classification of public personnel?
   (a) Service (b) Group or Class
   (c) Post (d) Grade

10. Behavioural Approach is subject to criticism on which of the following grounds?
   (i) Inadequate conceptual framework to explain the organization phenomena.
   (ii) It takes an autonomous view of administrative system.
   (iii) It offers definite suggestions to improve decision making.
   (iv) It adopts idealistic view to explain human behaviour.
   Select the correct answer by using codes given below:
   Codes:
   (a) (i) (ii) (iii) (iv) (b) (i) (ii) (iii)
   (c) (i) (ii) (iv) (d) (i) (iii) (iv)

11. Independent Regulatory Commissions in U.S.A. are regarded as:
   (i) The arms of the Congress
   (ii) Islands of autonomy
   (iii) The fourth branch of the Government
   (iv) Headless
   Select the correct answer from the codes given below:
   Codes:
   (a) (i) (ii) (iii) & (iv)
   (b) (i) (ii) & (iv)
   (c) (iii) (ii) & (i)
   (d) (ii) & (iii)

12. The sequential order of motivational model developed by Laurie J. Mullius is:
   (i) Driving Force
   (ii) Desired Goals
   (iii) Needs or Expectations
   (iv) Fulfilment
   Codes:
   (a) (ii) (iv) (iii) (i) (b) (iv) (iii) (ii) (i)
   (c) (i) (ii) (iii) (iv) (d) (iii) (i) (ii) (iv)

13. Put the following in the descending sequential order:
   (i) Division (ii) Department
   (iii) Wing (iv) Section
   Codes:
   (a) (i) (ii) (iii) (iv) (b) (i) (iii) (ii) (iv)
   (c) (iv) (i) (iii) (ii) (d) (iv) (iii) (ii) (i)

14. The factors leading to the systematic study of CPA in the USA were:
   (i) New developments in scientific and technological fields.
   (ii) Emergence of large number of new nations on the world scene.
   (iii) Dissatisfaction of scholars with the culture bound traditional Public Administration.
   (iv) Desire of scholars to develop this subject into an independent discipline.
   Select the correct answer from the codes given below:

Codes:
(a) (i) and (iv)
(b) (i), (ii) and (iii)
(c) (ii), (iii) and (iv)
(d) (i), (ii), (iii) and (iv)

15. Which of the following trends are not associated with Comparative Public Administration?
(i) Normative to Empirical
(ii) Ideographic to Nomothetic
(iii) Prismatic to Fused
(iv) Traditional to Structural – functional
Select the correct answer from the codes given below:
Codes:
(a) (i) & (ii) (b) (ii) & (iv)
(c) (iii) & (iv) (d) (i) & (iii)

16. In which of the following countries, the law passed by Parliament cannot be declared unconstitutional by the judiciary?
(a) U.K. & India
(b) U.S.A. & India
(c) India only
(d) U.K. only

17. Who of the following said that "Growth is the result of human efforts"?
(a) J.N. Khosla
(b) Merle Fansod
(c) W.A. Lewis
(d) Irving Swerdlow

18. Ira Sharkansky refers to three characteristics of bureaucracies in more developed countries: These include:
(i) Bureaucracies are large, having numerous sub-units with specialized employees.
(ii) Bureaucracy accepts directions from other legitimate branches of government.
(iii) Bureaucracy is considered to be professional—a sign of specialization among bureaucrats.
(iv) Widespread discrepancy between form and reality.
Select the correct answer by using codes below:
Codes:
(a) (ii) (iii) and (iv) (b) (i) (ii) and (iv)
(c) (i) (ii) and (iii) (d) (i) (iii) and (iv)

19. Which among the following is not a feature of Agraria model as developed by Fred W. Riggs?
(a) Predominance of universalistic, specific and achievement norms.
(b) Stable local groups and limited spatial mobility.
(c) A deferential stratification system of diffuse impact.
(d) Relatively simple and stable occupational differentiation.

20. The United Nations Development Programme (UNDP) constructed a framework to measure States comparative ability to provide for citizens well-being. It is known as
(a) Millennium Development Goals (MDG)
(b) Human Development Index (HDI)
(c) Human Development Goals
(d) None of the above

21. The Aitchison Commission recommended classification of Civil Services in India into
(i) The Imperial Civil Service
(ii) The Indian Administrative Service
(iii) The Provincial Civil Service
(iv) The Subordinate Civil Service
Select the correct answer by using codes given below:
Codes:
(a) (i) (iii) (iv) (b) (ii) (iii) (iv)
(c) (i) (ii) (iii) (d) (i) (ii) (iv)

22. **Assertion (A):** The judicial reforms in India should be aimed at increasing access

by reducing delays and arrears in the system and enhancing accountability through structural changes and by setting performance standards and capacities.

Reason (R): No major steps for judicial reforms in India have been taken so far.

Codes:

(a) Both (A) and (R) are correct and (R) is the correct explanation of (A).
(b) Both (A) and (R) are correct, but (R) is not the correct explanation of (A).
(c) (A) is true, but (R) is false.
(d) (A) is false, but (R) is true.

23. Which of the following institutions is not involved in policy making in India?
(a) Prime Minister's office
(b) National Development Council
(c) Planning Commission
(d) Central Social Welfare Board

24. **Assertion (A):** Parliament has overseeing functions in relation to the Executive in India.

Reason (R): Comptroller and Auditor General of India is the eyes and ears of the Parliament.

Codes:

(a) Both (A) and (R) are correct and (R) is the correct explanation of (A).
(b) Both (A) and (R) are correct, but (R) is not the correct explanation of (A).
(c) (A) is true, but (R) is false.
(d) (A) is false, but (R) is true.

25. Which of the following statements about Central Secretariat in India is not correct?
(a) It is both a policy-making and executive agency in certain cases.
(b) It is a policy-advisory body.
(c) It is headed by the Cabinet Secretary.
(d) It is collective name for all the Secretariat departments of the Government of India.

26. "The Civil Service should be manned by the most promising young men of the day by a competing (Literary) examination on a level with the highest description of education in this country." This statement is made in
(a) The Macaulay Report
(b) The Northcote-Trevelyan Report
(c) The 1st Administrative Reforms Commission Report
(d) The Appleby Report

27. Consider the following about Prime Minister's office:
(i) It is a think-tank of the Prime Minister.
(ii) It is an extra-constitutional body.
(iii) It was given status of a Department under the Government of India Transaction of Business Rules.
(iv) Administratively it is headed by the Cabinet Secretary.

Select correct answer using the codes given below:

Codes:

(a) (i) and (ii)
(b) (i) (ii) and (iii)
(c) (i) (iii) and (iv)
(d) (i) (ii) (iii) and (iv)

28. The tenure of the members of Public Accounts Committee of Indian Parliament is:
(a) One year (b) Two years
(c) Three years (d) Five years

29. The district has been placed under the charge of district officer who is empowered to promulgate orders to prevent any danger of breach of public peace. While doing so, he/she is performing the duties as a
(a) District Collector
(b) Administrative Officer
(c) Coordinator
(d) District Magistrate

30. Which of the following is not the recommendation of 2nd ARC to

modernize the office of the District Collector?
(a) Establishment of Management Information System
(b) Establishment of Computerized District Grievance Cell
(c) Establishment of Vigilance Committee in the office of the District Collector
(d) Establishment of a Forum to interact with civil society group and media

31. The Cantonment Boards are classified into how many categories?
(a) One (b) Two
(c) Three (d) Four

32. "Only a committed bureaucracy could bring about social transformation envisaged in the Five-Year Plans and in progressive legislations." This statement was made by
(a) Jawaharlal Nehru
(b) V.P. Singh
(c) Chandrashekhar
(d) Indira Gandhi

33. Which of the following statements about the functions of Kotwal under Moughal administration is not correct?
(a) He was the supreme authority in magisterial matters in the administration of a town.
(b) He exercised police powers at the municipal level.
(c) He was responsible for managing financial matters.
(d) He had regulatory role in educational affairs at the municipal level.

34. "Corruption may help in assimilating new groups into the system and thus serve as a substitute for reform." This statement belongs to
(a) Samuel Huntington
(b) Myron Weiner
(c) K. Santhanam
(d) Ralph Braibanti

35. **Assertion (A):** Specialists are not fit for the post of Secretary of Government department.
Reason (R): Specialists possess a narrow vision.
Codes:
(a) Both (A) and (R) are correct and (R) is the correct explanation of (A).
(b) Both (A) and (R) are correct, but (R) is not the correct explanation of (A).
(c) (A) is true, but (R) is false.
(d) (A) is false, but (R) is true.

36. "Science begins with observation and must ultimately return to observation for its final validation." Who among the following made this statement?
(a) P.V. Young
(b) Nels Anderson
(c) William J. Goode & Paul K. Hatt
(d) Robert K. Merton

37. When the universe is heterogenous and too large, the best sampling method which can be adopted is
(a) Random Sampling
(b) Stratified Sampling
(c) Multi-stage Sampling
(d) None of the above

38. In which way theory is a tool of science?
(i) It defines the major orientation of science.
(ii) It offers conceptual scheme.
(iii) It summarizes facts into empirical generalizations.
(iv) It does predict facts.
Select the correct answer by using codes given below:
Codes:
(a) (i) and (ii) (b) (iii) and (iv)
(c) (i) (ii) and (iii) (d) (i) (ii) and (iv)

39. Which one of the following names is not associated with random numbers used for sampling process?

(a) L.H.C. Tippett
(b) William J. Goode
(c) M.G. Kendall
(d) B. Babington

40. **Assertion (A):** Welfare State is criticised as too expensive.
Reason (R): Financing the services has become a burden and the cost has to be borne by the middle and upper middle classes through the instrument of progressive taxation.
Codes:
(a) Both (A) and (R) are correct and (R) is the correct explanation of (A).
(b) Both (A) and (R) are correct, but (R) is not the correct explanation of (A).
(c) (A) is true, but (R) is false.
(d) (A) is false, but (R) is true.

41. As per the Memorandum of Articles of Central Social Welfare Board
(i) In each of the participating States/ UTs there has to be a State Social Welfare Board.
(ii) The State Board is to perform such functions as are entrusted to it by the Ministry of Social Welfare.
(iii) More than half the members of the State Social Welfare Board are to be nominated by State Governments/ UTs.
(iv) The Chairman of the Board is preferably a woman social worker.
Select the correct answer by using codes given below:
Codes:
(a) (i) and (ii) (b) (ii) and (iii)
(c) (iii) and (iv) (d) (i) and (iv)

42. Which one among the following is not an example of Public-Private Partnership (PPP)?
(a) BOT – Built, Operate & Transfer
(b) BOLT – Built, Operate, Lease & Transfer
(c) BLOT – Built, Lease, Operate and Transfer
(d) BOOT – Built, Operate, Own and Transfer

43. **Assertion (A):** National Livelihood Mission is a part of social welfare in India.
Reason (R): National Rural Health Mission aims at the development of physical infrastructure in rural areas.
Codes:
(a) Both (A) and (R) are correct and (R) is the correct explanation of (A).
(b) Both (A) and (R) are correct, but (R) is not the correct explanation of (A).
(c) (A) is true, but (R) is false.
(d) (A) is false, but (R) is true.

44. Which one of the following is the incorrect distinction between Functional and Policy-making Boards of Public Enterprises?

	Functional Boards		Policy-Making Boards
(a)	Small in size	–	Comparatively large in size
(b)	Only specialists members	–	Both specialists and generalists members
(c)	Generally selection of members from within the enterprise	–	Generally selection of members from outside the enterprise
(d)	Members are generally part-timer	–	Members are generally full-timer

45. Which of the following should be the functions of the District and Metropolitan Planning Committees according to the 2nd ARC?
(i) Integration of spatial economic development.
(ii) Concerted rural and urban planning.

(iii) Advice and assistance to local bodies in the preparation of development plans and their effective implementation.
(iv) Advice to the Planning Commission in the preparation of Five Year Plans.

Select the correct answer by using the codes given below:

Codes:

(a) (i) (ii) and (iii) (b) (i) (iii) and (iv)
(c) (ii) (iii) and (iv) (d) (i) (ii) and (iv)

46. 'In case of a Metropolitan Corporation, a separate Ombudsman should be constituted.' This recommendation is made by
(a) National Commission on Urban Affairs
(b) P.C. Hota Committee
(c) Veerappa Moily Committee
(d) First Administrative Reforms Commission

47. 'Government of India should draft and place before Parliament a Framework law for local governments.' This recommendation was made by
(a) National Law Commission
(b) Second Administrative Reforms Commission
(c) Justice Panchhi Commission
(d) Sarkaria Commission

48. Which of the following statements about the composition of Ward Committee in a municipal area is not correct?
(a) Composition and the territorial area of a Ward Committee may be provided by the Law of State Legislative.
(b) State Legislative may also make a provision regarding the manner in which the seats in a Ward Committee should be filled.
(c) In case of multiple-wards, the Chairman of the Ward Committee shall be elected by the members of the Ward Committee.
(d) In case of two or more wards, the Chairman of that Ward Committee shall be nominated by the State Government.

49. The State Finance Commission is provided for in which of the following provisions of the Constitution?
(a) Art. 243(H)
(b) Art. 243(I)
(c) Art. 243(M)
(d) Art. 243(O)

50. Which of the following has defined "Panchayat as an association of village people for doing administrative, judicial or the other public works"?
(a) Jai Prakash Narain
(b) John Mathai
(c) Mahatma Gandhi
(d) A.S. Altekar

ANSWERS

1. (c)	2. (c)	3. (d)	4. (a)	5. (c)
6. (c)	7. (d)	8. (b)	9. (c)	10. (c)
11. (a)	12. (d)	13. (b)	14. (d)	15. (c)
16. (d)	17. (c)	18. (c)	19. (a)	20. (b)
21. (a)	22. (c)	23. (d)	24. (b)	25. (c)
26. (b)	27. (b)	28. (a)	29. (d)	30. (c)
31. (c)	32. (d)	33. (d)	34. (a)	35. (a)
36. (c)	37. (b)	38. (c)	39. (b)	40. (b)
41. (b)	42. (c)	43. (c)	44. (d)	45. (a)
46. (c)	47. (b)	48. (d)	49. (b)	50. (b)

PAPER–III

Note: This paper contains seventy five (75) objective type questions of two (2) marks each. All questions are compulsory.

1. "In simplest terms administration is determined action taken in pursuit of a conscious purpose." This statement is given by:
   (a) Z.A. Vieg
   (b) Pfiffner
   (c) Nigro
   (d) Marshall E. Dimock
2. Of the three distinctions made by Simon between Public and Private Administration, which one of the following is not among them?
   (a) That public administration aims at social welfare, while private administration is profit oriented.
   (b) That public administration is bureaucratic, while private administration is business like.
   (c) That public administration is political whereas private administration is non-political.
   (d) That public administrtion is characterized by red tape from which private administration is free.
3. Which of the following is not a feature of a formal organization?
   (a) Legal status
   (b) Permanence
   (c) Primacy of structure
   (d) Shared values and common standards of behaviour
4. Which one of the following is not correct about Woodrow Wilson?
   (a) He was a professor of Political Science.
   (b) He was the President of USA.
   (c) He was the first comparativist in Public Administration.
   (d) He was the Chairman of the American Society for Public Administration.
5. Match List I with List II and select the correct answer from the codes given below:

   List I (Book)
   A. The Administrative State
   B. Administrative Theories and Politics
   C. The Elements of Administration
   D. Principles of Public Administration

   List II (Author)
   i. L. Urwick
   ii. F.W. Willoughby
   iii. Dwight Waldo
   iv. Peter Seef

Codes:	**A**	**B**	**C**	**D**
(a)	i	ii	iii	iv
(b)	iii	iv	i	ii
(c)	ii	i	iv	iii
(d)	iv	iii	ii	i

6. **Assertion (A):** M.P. Follett can be considered as a link between the classical and behavioural theories.
   Reason (R): M.P. Follett developed certain principles and their universality as well as stressed on the importnace of emotions.
   Codes:
   (a) Both (A) and (R) are correct and (R) is the correct explanation of (A).
   (b) Both (A) and (R) are correct, but (R) is not the correct explanation of (A).
   (c) (A) is true, but (R) is false.
   (d) (A) is false, but (R) is true.
7. 'A process of fusion of individual aspirations with organisational goals, individual skills with organizational position and individual conduct with organizational role' is advocated by
   (a) Chester Bernard (b) Rensis Likert
   (c) Chris Argyris (d) Kurt Lewin

8. Co-existence of formally differentiated structure of a diffracted society with undifferentiated structure of fused society has been described by F.W. Riggs as
   (a) Heterogeneity
   (b) Formalism
   (c) Overlapping
   (d) Poly communalism

9. Valence Expectancy, as an alternative theory of motivation was propounded by
   (a) Paul Hersey and Keneth H. Blackchard
   (b) Black and James Mouton
   (c) Victor H. Vroom
   (d) Hobhouse

10. **Assertion (A):** Leadership is defined by result, not attributes.
    Reason (R): The productivity of work is not responsibility of worker, but of the manager.
    Codes:
    (a) Both (A) and (R) are correct and (R) is the correct explanation of (A).
    (b) Both (A) and (R) are correct, but (R) is not the correct explanation of (A).
    (c) (A) is true, but (R) is false.
    (d) (A) is false, but (R) is true.

11. In the context of the New Public Management theory, the administration is apparently moving
    (i) from rule to result orientation
    (ii) from system to enterprise
    (iii) from the duties of administration to the rights of citizens
    (iv) from decentralisation to centralisation.
    Select the answer by using the codes given below:
    Codes:
    (a) (i) and (iv)
    (b) (iii) and (iv)
    (c) (i), (ii) and (iii)
    (d) (ii), (iii) and (iv)

12. "Organization is the form of every human association for the attainment of a common purpose." This statement is given by
    (a) J.D. Mooney
    (b) L.D. White
    (c) John M. Gaus
    (d) Luther Gullick

13. According to Chester Bernard an organisation:
    (i) is not a leviathan.
    (ii) is pejorative sense of bureaucracy.
    (iii) is a figure of organisation man.
    (iv) is an impersonal system of coordinated human effort.
    Select correct answer using the codes given below:
    Codes:
    (a) (i) and (iv)
    (b) (i), (ii) and (iii)
    (c) (ii), (iii) and (iv)
    (d) (iii) and (iv)

14. Match List I with List II and select the correct answer from the codes given below:
    List I (Theory)
    A. Classical Approach
    B. Human Relations Approach
    C. Systems Approach
    D. Socio-Psychological Approach
    List II (Thinker)
    i. Chester Bernard
    ii. Douglas McGregor
    iii. Henry Fayol
    iv. Elton Mayo

Codes:	**A**	**B**	**C**	**D**
(a)	i	iii	iv	ii
(b)	iii	ii	i	iv
(c)	iii	iv	i	ii
(d)	iv	iii	ii	i

15. Nicholas Henry classified various models of policy formulation and implementation

into three broad groups. Which one among the following is not correct?
(a) Exclusion/Consumption Paradigm
(b) Incrementalist Paradigm
(c) Rationalist Paradigm
(d) Strategic Planning Paradigm

16. Comparative Public Administration emphasises that
(i) organizations must be viewed as embedded in specific cultures and political settings.
(ii) both the study and practice of administration are pervasively value-loaded.
(iii) the principles of public administration are seriously inadequate.
(iv) any proper discipline must have complimentary micro and macro aspects.
Select the correct answer by using codes given below:
Codes:
(a) (i), (iii) and (iv) (b) (i), (ii) and (iv)
(c) (ii), (iii) and (iv) (d) (i), (ii) and (iii)

17. Comparative Administrative Group (CAG) was
(i) established in the year 1963.
(ii) initially funded by Ford Foundation.
(iii) initially chaired by Fred. W. Riggs.
(iv) established in U.S.A.
Select the correct answer from the codes given below:
Codes:
(a) (i), (ii)
(b) (ii), (iii) and (iv)
(c) (i), (ii), (iii) and (iv)
(d) (i) only

18. Arrange the following institutions of local government in U.K. in descending order. Use the codes given below:
(i) Metropolitan District
(ii) Metropolitan County
(iii) Parish
(iv) Shire
Codes:
(a) (i), (iv), (iii) and (ii)
(b) (ii), (i), (iv) and (iii)
(c) (ii), (iii), (iv) and (i)
(d) (iv), (i), (ii) and (iii)

19. The City Manager as a Chief Executive in council-manager form of local government in USA is
(a) appointed by the State Governor
(b) appointed by the Council
(c) elected by the Council
(d) appointed by the Mayor

20. "The Development Administration is primarily concerned with the tasks and process of formulating and implementing the four P's." This statement was made by
(a) Donald C. Stones
(b) F.W. Riggs
(c) Weidner
(d) Luther Gullick

21. Who of the following expressed the view that "administration in the developing countries is imitative rather than indigenous"?
(a) Ferrel Heady
(b) David McClelland
(c) T.N. Chaturvedi
(d) Hahn Been Lee

22. Which of the following scholars is not correctly matched with the meaning of development given by him?
(a) Colm and Geiger – Change plus growth
(b) F.W. Riggs – Nation building and socio-economic progress
(c) T.N. Chaturvedi – Transformation of society

(d) Hahn-Been Lee – Achievement of progressive political, economic and social objectives

23. Arrange the following publications in a correct sequence and select the correct answer from the codes given below:
(i) The Frontiers of Development Administration.
(ii) Approaches to Development, Politics, Administration and Change.
(iii) Political Order in Changing Societies.
(iv) Cultural Hurdles in Development Administration: Concepts and Problems.

Codes:
(a) (iv) (ii) (iii) (i) (b) (i) (ii) (iii) (iv)
(c) (iv) (iii) (i) (ii) (d) (ii) (iv) (i) (iii)

24. Development administration is a process for carrying out planned change in the economy, in agriculture or industry or capital infrastructure supporting either of these, and to a lesser extent, in the social service of the State."
Who has given this statement?
(a) Milton J. Esman
(b) J. Montgomery
(c) Edward W. Weidner
(d) F.W. Riggs

25. The Cabinet in India is
(i) A Constitutional body
(ii) Part of the Council of Ministers
(iii) Institutionalised by usage
(iv) Policy making institution at highest level

Select the correct answer by using codes given below:
Codes:
(a) (i) and (ii) (b) (ii) and (iii)
(c) (ii) and (iv) (d) (ii), (iii) and (iv)

26. **Assertion (A):** Under the colonial raj, the predominant nature of administration was regulatory and maintenance of law and order.
Reason (R): As a matter of deliberate policy strategically sensitive positions in the Government were entrusted to British officers.

Codes:
(a) Both (A) and (R) are correct and (R) is the correct explanation of (A).
(b) Both (A) and (R) are correct, but (R) is not the correct explanation of (A).
(c) (A) is true, but (R) is false.
(d) (A) is false, but (R) is true.

27. Arrange the following reports in the chronological order. Select the correct answer from the codes given below:
(i) Gopala Swamy Ayyangar Report
(ii) Appleby Report (First)
(iii) Gorwala Report
(iv) First Administrative Reforms Commission Report

Codes:
(a) (i) (ii) (iii) (iv) (b) (i) (iii) (ii) (iv)
(c) (iv) (iii) (ii) (i) (d) (i) (iv) (iii) (ii)

28. Which of the following is not correctly matched?

List I (Prime Minister)	List II (Secretary/Principal Secretary/Minister of State in PMO)
(a) Lal Bahadur Shastri	L.K. Jha
(b) Indira Gandhi	P.N. Haksar
(c) Rajiv Gandhi	A.N. Verma
(d) P.V. Narsimha Rao	Bhuvnesh Chaturvedi

29. Match List I with List II and select the correct answer from the codes given below:

List I (Commissions/Committees)
A. Economic Administration Reforms Commission
B. The Commission on Centre-State Relations

C. Committee on Prevention of Corruption
D. Railway Corruption Enquiry Committee

List II (Chairperson)

i. J.B. Kripalani ii. K. Santhanam
iii. L.K. Jha iv. R.S. Sarkaria

Codes:	A	B	C	D
(a)	i	ii	iv	iii
(b)	iii	iv	ii	i
(c)	i	iii	iv	ii
(d)	iv	ii	iii	i

30. Which one of the following is not a report of Second Administrative Reforms Commission?
(a) Unlocking Human Capital: Entitlements and Governance—A Case Study
(b) Social Capital—A Shared Destiny
(c) Capacity Building for Conflict Resolution
(d) Efficient Conduct of State Enterprises

31. Which of the following statements regarding All India Services are correct?
(i) New All-India Services may be created only if Council of States declares to do so by a majority resolution.
(ii) New All-India Services may be created if it is necessary or expedient in the national interest.
(iii) All-India Services may be created by a law passed by the Parliament.
(iv) All-India Judicial Service may also be created by Parliament by law.

Select the correct answer by using codes given below:

Codes:
(a) (i), (ii) and (iii)
(b) (ii), (iii) and (iv)
(c) (i), (iii) and (iv)
(d) (i), (ii), (iii) and (iv)

32. Before independence, the appointments to the All India Services were made by
(a) Governor-General-in-Council
(b) Secretary of State for India
(c) East India Company
(d) Cabinet Secretariat

33. "On the whole experience seems to show that the interests of the tax payers cannot be left to the spending departments." This statement is made by
(a) First Hoover Commission
(b) Donoughmore Committee
(c) Haldane Committee
(d) Eleventh Finance Commission

34. Which of the following statements about the institution of C.A.G. in India is correct?
(a) It is a colonial legacy.
(b) It is an innovation of Independent India.
(c) It performs auditing and accounting functions.
(d) It is an executive agency of the Government of India.

35. Match List I with List II and select the correct answer from the codes given below:

List I (Author)

A. K.L. Handa B. M.J.K. Thavraj
C. Robert Presthus D. P.K. Wattal

List II (Books)

i. Parliamentary Financial Control
ii. Programme and Performance Budgeting
iii. Public Administration
iv. Financial Administration of India

Codes:	A	B	C	D
(a)	iv	ii	iii	i
(b)	iii	ii	iv	i
(c)	i	iii	ii	iv
(d)	ii	iv	iii	i

36. **Assertion (A):** The Finance Ministry exercises financial control over all the administrative ministries.

Reason (R): It is responsible for the formulation and exemption of the budget.

Codes:

(a) Both (A) and (R) are correct and (R) is the correct explanation of (A).
(b) Both (A) and (R) are correct, but (R) is not the correct explanation of (A).
(c) (A) is true, but (R) is false.
(d) (A) is false, but (R) is true.

37. Which of the following is not a feature of a good sample?
(a) Sample should be big in size.
(b) Sample should be representative of the universe.
(c) Sample should be reliable.
(d) Sample should be measurable by known probability sampling design technique.

38. Science is defined as
(i) an accumulation of systematic knowledge.
(ii) a method of approach to the entire empirical world.
(iii) an approach which aims at the finding of ultimate truth.
(iv) a mode of analysis that permits the scientist to state propositions.

Select the correct answer with the codes given below:

Codes:

(a) (i) and (ii) (b) (iii) and (iv)
(c) (i), (ii) and (iii) (d) (i), (ii) and (iv)

39. Which one of the following is not a limitation of scientific method?
(a) Scientific explanation is never complete.
(b) It eliminates arbitrary and ambiguous opinion.
(c) Conclusions are never final.
(d) It is very difficult to oppose established opinion.

40. Which one of the following is not a limitation of Questionnaire method?
(a) Less expensive
(b) Problem of response
(c) Unsuitable for deeper study
(d) Less possibility of complete information

41. According to Goode and Hatt simple observation is most useful for which of the following?
(a) Exploratory Studies
(b) Descriptive Studies
(c) Diagnostic Studies
(d) Experimental Studies

42. Decentralization of functions and powers of headquarters to the field offices is known as
(a) Geographical decentralization
(b) Political decentralization
(c) Administrative decentralization
(d) Functional decentralization

43. **Assertion (A):** The plurality of organisations and departments at the District level has created many problems.

Reason (R): District Administration, in order to be effective, must have a unity of purpose and singularity of approach which is often found missing.

Codes:

(a) Both (A) and (R) are correct and (R) is the correct explanation of (A).
(b) Both (A) and (R) are correct, but (R) is not the correct explanation of (A).
(c) (A) is true, but (R) is false.
(d) (A) is false, but (R) is true.

44. Which of the following is not correct regarding developmental role of District Collector in India?
(a) He has a directive role in the scheme of Panchayati Raj.
(b) His position in relation to Panchayati Raj varies from State to State.

(c) He takes initiative to take up need based development programmes.
(d) He performs the role of coordinator and extends help in implementing development programmes.

45. Protection of natural environment in India is
(i) the responsibility of the State under the Constitution.
(ii) the fundamental duty of every citizen of India.
(iii) mandatory function of the NGOs.
(iv) the legal responsibility of the National Capital Region Planning Board.
Select the correct answer from the codes given below:
Codes:
(a) (i), (ii), (iii) and (iv)
(b) (i), (ii) and (iii)
(c) (i) and (ii)
(d) (iii) and (iv)

46. Which of the following programmes are being implemented through the watershed development approach?
(i) Drought Prone Areas Programme
(ii) Desert Development Programme
(iii) Integrated Wasteland Development Programme
(iv) Integrated Rural Development Programme
Select the correct answer from the codes given below:
Codes:
(a) (i) and (ii)
(b) (i), (ii) and (iii)
(c) (i), (ii) and (iv)
(d) (i), (ii), (iii) and (iv)

47. Which of the following is the rationale of privatisation/disinvestment in PSEs?
(i) Release of the large amount of public resources locked up in non-strategic PSEs.
(ii) Stemming the further outflow of the scarce public resources for sustaining the unviable nonstrategic PSEs.
(iii) Reducing the public debt.
(iv) Beneficial effect on the capital market.
Select the correct answer by using the codes given below:
Codes:
(a) (i), (ii), (iii) and (iv)
(b) (i), (ii) and (iii)
(c) (ii) and (iii)
(d) (iii) and (iv)

48. "The growth of rural settlements which have acquired urban characteristics is very slow." This observation about the process of urbanization in India was made in:
(a) 10th Five Year Plan
(b) 11th Five Year Plan
(c) National Sample Survey
(d) National Development Council

49. Match List I with List II and select the correct answer from the codes given below:
List I (Committees/Commissions)
A. Haldane B. Plowden
C. Mesterman D. Hoover
List II (Reports)
i. Report on Control of Expenditure
ii. Organisation of Executive Branch of Government
iii. Report on Budgeting and Accounting Political Activities of the Civil Servants
iv. Report of Machinery of Government Committee

Codes:	**A**	**B**	**C**	**D**
(a)	iv	iii	ii	i
(b)	iv	i	iii	ii
(c)	i	iv	iii	ii
(d)	ii	i	iv	iii

50. Which Five Year Plan has stressed upon the involvement of voluntary organization

and specifically to supplement Government effort to offer the rural people choices and alternatives?
(a) Sixth Five Year Plan
(b) Seventh Five Year Plan
(c) Ninth Five Year Plan
(d) Eleventh Five Year Plan

51. Which one of the following is optimal model of policy-making according to Y. Dror?
(a) Pure Rational Model
(b) Incremental Model
(c) Economically Rational and Extra-rational Model
(d) Pure Rational and Economically Rational Model

52. **Assertion (A):** Public administration theorists, instead of political scientists, dominate the rationalist approach to policy-making and implementation.
Reason (R): New Public Management lays emphasis on the deeper role of public agencies in managing and delivery of public services.
Codes:
(a) Both (A) and (R) are correct and (R) is the correct explanation of (A).
(b) Both (A) and (R) are correct, but (R) is not the correct explanation of (A).
(c) (A) is true, but (R) is false.
(d) (A) is false, but (R) is true.

53. Put the following stages of rational policy planning process in the sequential order:
(i) Appraisal
(ii) Formulation of alternative courses of action
(iii) Discerning problem
(iv) Review
Select the correct answer by using codes given below:
Codes:
(a) (ii) (i) (iii) (iv) (b) (iii) (iv) (ii) (i)
(c) (iii) (i) (iv) (ii) (d) (i) (ii) (iii) (iv)

54. Which of the following are the definitional elements of public policy?
(i) Declaration of goals
(ii) Proposed course of action
(iii) A declaration of general purpose
(iv) An authoritative decision
Select the correct answer from the codes given below:
Codes:
(a) (i), (ii), (iii) and (iv)
(b) (i), (ii) and (iii)
(c) (ii), (iii) and (iv)
(d) (i) and (ii)

55. Which one of the following makes provisions for social security?
(a) Indian Contract Act
(b) Maternity Benefit Act
(c) Indian Industries Act
(d) Indian Companies Act

56. Policy analysis is concerned with
(a) Finding out the impact of policy
(b) Intuitive judgments about the effects of policy
(c) Prescription of policy rather than explanation of policy
(d) Finding out the contents of policy rather than the search for their causes and consequences

57. **Assertion (A):** The role of the national planning agency in the formulation of fundamental social and economic policies is gradually diminishing.
Reason (R): Policies are now taking shape in a greater degree from debates in Parliament and from the play of new social and political forces within the community.
Codes:
(a) Both (A) and (R) are correct and (R) is the correct explanation of (A).
(b) Both (A) and (R) are correct, but (R) is not the correct explanation of (A).

(c) (A) is true, but (R) is false.
(d) (A) is false, but (R) is true.

58. Which is not a part of the Telecom Sector reforms in India?
(a) Corporatisation of telecom services.
(b) Grant of autonomy to Bharat Sanchar Nigam.
(c) Introduciton of regulation.
(d) Adjusting to intellectual property regime.

59. Which one of the following is correct regarding 'economic and social planning'?
(a) It is included in Union List.
(b) It is a part of the State List.
(c) It is incorporated in Concurrent List.
(d) It is not in any of the above stated lists.

60. Which of the following is known as the third sector of Indian economy?
(a) Public Sector (b) Co-operatives
(c) Private Sector (d) Joint Sector

61. Global Constitutionalism has impacted India's economic policy in which of the following ways?
(i) It has led to liberalisation of trade.
(ii) It led to the introduction of competition in both the public and private sectors of economy.
(iii) It led to encouragement to FDI.
(iv) It led to adoption of the policy of privatisation.

Select the correct answer by using the codes given below:

Codes:
(a) (i) and (ii)
(b) (i), (ii) and (iii)
(c) (i), (ii), (iii) and (iv)
(d) (iii), (iv) and (ii)

62. The Panchayati Raj Divas (Day) in India is celebrated on
(a) 21st April (b) 24th April
(c) 2nd October (d) 14th November

63. Lord Ripon's Resolution on 'Local-Self Government' was adopted on
(a) 18th April, 1882
(b) 18th June, 1882
(c) 18th May, 1882
(d) 18th December, 1882

64. Which one of the following is not included in Eleventh Schedule of Constitution of India?
(a) Planning for economic and social development
(b) Non-conventional energy sources
(c) Poverty alleviation programme
(d) Technical training and vocational education

65. Which of the following is/are the recommendations of P.K. Thungon Committee?
(i) Fixed term of 5 years for Panchayati Raj Bodies.
(ii) The Panchayati Raj Bodies should not remain superseded for more than six months.
(iii) District Collector should be made the CEO of the Zila Parishad.
(iv) Setting up of State Finance Commission.

Select the correct answer from the codes given below:

Codes:
(a) (i), (ii), (iii) and (iv)
(b) (i), (iii) and (iv)
(c) (iii) and (iv)
(d) (iv) only

66. Which one of the following has prescribed a local Government led, community wide and participatory effort to establish a comprehensive action strategy for environmental protection, economic prosperity and community well being in the local jurisdiction?
(a) UN Millennium Development Goals
(b) Local Agenda 21

(c) World Urbanisation Prospects 2001
(d) An Urbanizing World: Global Report on Human Settlements

67. **Assertion (A):** Civil society organisations promote participative democratic practices.
Reason (R): The salient feature of participative democracy is the presence of a large number of voluntary agencies.
Codes:
(a) Both (A) and (R) are correct and (R) is the correct explanation of (A).
(b) Both (A) and (R) are correct, but (R) is not the correct explanation of (A).
(c) (A) is true, but (R) is false.
(d) (A) is false, but (R) is true.

68. MNREGA is a programme that is
(i) open to social audit
(ii) implemented by the Gram Panchayat at the village level
(iii) implemented by the village development officer and Gram Panchayat at the village level
(iv) meant for all unskilled able bodied persons desirous to seek work
Select the correct answer from the codes given below:
Codes:
(a) (i), (ii) and (iii)
(b) (i) and (ii)
(c) (i), (ii) and (iv)
(d) (i), (ii), (iii) and (iv)

69. **Assertion (A):** Rural Development Programmes suffer from lack of effective monitoring and evaluation.
Reason (R): Rural Development Administration is deficient in professionalism and have multiplicity of authorities.
Codes:
(a) Both (A) and (R) are correct and (R) is the correct explanation of (A).
(b) Both (A) and (R) are correct, but (R) is not the correct explanation of (A).
(c) (A) is true, but (R) is false.
(d) (A) is false, but (R) is true.

70. Arrange the following in a chronological order:
(i) Rural-Urban Relationship Committee
(ii) National Commission on Urbanisation
(iii) Taxation Inquiry Committee
(iv) Local Finance Inquiry Committee
Select the correct answer from the codes given below:
Codes:
(a) (ii) (i) (iv) (iii) (b) (i) (iii) (ii) (iv)
(c) (iv) (iii) (i) (ii) (d) (iii) (ii) (iv) (i)

71. Rural Development means:
(i) Provision of social services
(ii) Improving infrastructure facilities
(iii) Providing economic help to the individuals and groups for self employment
(iv) Capacity building of rural local government
Select the correct answer from the code given below:
Codes:
(a) (i), (ii), (iii) and (iv)
(b) (i), (ii) and (iii)
(c) (i) and (iii)
(d) (iii) and (iv)

72. Arrange the following programmes for rural development in a sequence and select the correct answer from the codes given below:
(i) Intensive Area Development Scheme
(ii) Tribal Area Development Programme
(iii) Drought-prone Area Programme
(iv) Command Area Development Programme
Codes:
(a) (i), (ii), (iii) and (iv)
(b) (ii), (i), (iii) and (iv)

(c) (iv), (iii), (i) and (ii)
(d) (ii), (iv), (i) and (iii)

73. National Capital Region Planning Board is
(a) Statutory Body
(b) Created by an executive order
(c) Established by the Planning Commission
(d) Created by the Ministry of Urban Development under judicial direction

74. The Community Development Programme was started on the recommendation of
(a) Krishnamachari Committee
(b) Project Appraisal Committee
(c) Planning Commission
(d) Balwantrai Mehta Committee

75. Which of the following statements are correct about the rural cooperatives?
(i) They are schools of social dialogue and democracy.
(ii) They are based on the values of self-help and self-responsibility.
(iii) They can transform survival type of activities into legally protected and productive work.
(iv) Their members are generally both producers and beneficiaries.

Select the correct answer by using the codes given below:

Codes:
(a) (i) and (ii)
(b) (i), (ii) and (iii)
(c) (ii), (iii) and (iv)
(d) (i), (ii), (iii) and (iv)

ANSWERS

1. (a)	2. (a)	3. (d)	4. (d)	5. (b)
6. (a)	7. (c)	8. (c)	9. (c)	10. (a)
11. (c)	12. (a)	13. (a)	14. (c)	15. (a)
16. (d)	17. (c)	18. (b)	19. (b)	20. (a)
21. (a)	22. (b)	23. (a)	24. (b)	25. (d)
26. (b)	27. (b)	28. (c)	29. (b)	30. (d)
31. (b)	32. (b)	33. (c)	34. (a)	35. (d)
36. (a)	37. (a)	38. (d)	39. (b)	40. (a)
41. (a)	42. (a)	43. (b)	44. (c)	45. (c)
46. (b)	47. (a)	48. (b)	49. (b)	50. (b)
51. (c)	52. (c)	53. (c)	54. (a)	55. (b)
56. (a)	57. (a)	58. (d)	59. (c)	60. (b)
61. (c)	62. (b)	63. (c)	64. (a)	65. (a)
66. (b)	67. (b)	68. (c)	69. (a)	70. (c)
71. (a)	72. (b)	73. (a)	74. (a)	75. (d)

JUNE–2013

Note: This paper contains Sixty (60) multiple-choice questions, each question carrying two (2) marks. Candidate is expected to answer any Fifty (50) questions. In case more than Fifty (50) questions are attempted, only the first Fifty (50) questions will be evaluated.

PAPER–I

1. Which one of the following references is written as per Modern Language Association (MLA) format?
   (a) Hall, Donald. Fundamentals of Electronics,
   New Delhi: Prentice Hall of India, 2005
   (b) Hall, Donald, Fundamentals of Electronics,
   New Delhi: Prentice Hall of India, 2005
   (c) Hall, Donald, Fundamentals of Electronics,
   New Delhi: Prentice Hall of India, 2005
   (d) Hall, Donald. Fundamentals of Electronics.
   New Delhi: Prentice Hall of India, 2005

2. A workshop is
   (a) a conference for discussion on a topic.
   (b) a meeting for discussion on a topic.
   (c) a class at a college or a university in which a teacher and the students discuss a topic.
   (d) a brief intensive course for a small group emphasizing the development of a skill or technique for solving a specific problem.

3. A working hypothesis is
   (a) a proven hypothesis for an argument.
   (b) not required to be tested.
   (c) a provisionally accepted hypothesis for further research.
   (d) a scientific theory.

Read the following passage carefully and answer the questions (4 to 9):

The Taj Mahal has become one of the world's best known monuments. This domed white marble structure is situated on a high plinth at the southern end of a four-quartered garden, evoking the gardens of paradise, enclosed within walls measuring 305 by 549 metres. Outside the walls, in an area known as Mumtazabad, were living quarters for attendants, markets, serais and other structures built by local merchants and nobles. The tomb complex and the other imperial structures of Mumtazabad were maintained by the income of thirty villages given specifically for the tomb's support. The name Taj Mahal is unknown in Mughal chronicles, but it is used by contemporary Europeans in India, suggesting that this was the tomb's popular name. In contemporary texts, it is generally called simply the Illuminated Tomb (Rauza-i-Munavvara).

Mumtaz Mahal died shortly after delivering her fourteenth child in 1631. The Mughal court was then residing in Burhanpur. Her remains were temporarily buried by the griefstricken emperor in a spacious garden known as Zainabad on the bank of the river Tapti. Six months later her body was transported to Agra, where it was interred in land chosen for the mausoleum. This land, situated south of the Mughal city on the bank of the Jamuna, had belonged to the Kachhwaha rajas since the time of Raja Man Singh and was purchased from the then current raja, Jai Singh. Although contemporary chronicles indicate Jai Singh's willing cooperation in this exchange, extant *farmans* (imperial commands) indicate that the final price was not settled until almost two years after the mausoleum's commencement. Jai Singh's further cooperation was insured by imperial orders issued between 1632 and 1637 demanding that he provide stone masons and carts to transport marble from the mines at Makrana, within his "ancestral domain", to Agra where both the Taj Mahal and Shah Jahan's additions to the Agra fort were constructed concurrently.

Work on the mausoleum was commenced early in 1632. Inscriptional evidence indicates much of the tomb was completed by 1636. By 1643, when Shah Jahan most lavishly celebrated the 'Urs ceremony for Mumtaz Mahal', the entire complex was virtually complete.

4. Marble stone used for the construction of the Taj Mahal was brought from the ancestral domain of Raja Jai Singh. The name of the place where mines of marble is
   (a) Burhanpur (b) Makrana
   (c) Amber (d) Jaipur

5. The popular name Taj Mahal was given by
   (a) Shah Jahan
   (b) Tourists
   (c) Public
   (d) European travellers

6. Point out the true statement from the following:
   (a) Marble was not used for the construction of the Taj Mahal.
   (b) Red sand stone is non-visible in the Taj Mahal complex.
   (c) The Taj Mahal is surrounded by a four-quartered garden known as Chahr Bagh.
   (d) The Taj Mahal was constructed to celebrate the 'Urs ceremony for Mumtaz Mahal'.

7. In the contemporary texts the Taj Mahal is known
   (a) Mumtazabad
   (b) Mumtaz Mahal
   (c) Zainabad
   (d) Rauza-i-Munavvara

8. The construction of the Taj Mahal was completed between the period
   (a) 1632 – 1636 A.D.
   (b) 1630 – 1643 A.D.
   (c) 1632 – 1643 A.D.
   (d) 1636 – 1643 A.D.

9. The documents indicating the ownership of land, where the Taj Mahal was built, known as
   (a) Farman
   (b) Sale Deed
   (c) Sale-Purchase Deed
   (d) None of the above

10. In the process of communication, which one of the following is in the chronological order?
    (a) Communicator, Medium, Receiver, Effect, Message
    (b) Medium, Communicator, Message, Receiver, Effect
    (c) Communicator, Message, Medium, Receiver, Effect
    (d) Message, Communicator, Medium, Receiver, Effect

11. Bengal Gazette, the first Newspaper in India was started in 1780 by
    (a) Dr. Annie Besant
    (b) James Augustus Hicky
    (c) Lord Cripson
    (d) A.O. Hume

12. Press censorship in India was imposed during the tenure of the Prime Minister
(a) Rajeev Gandhi
(b) Narasimha Rao
(c) Indira Gandhi
(d) Deve Gowda

13. Communication via New media such as computers, teleshopping, internet and mobile telephony is termed as
(a) Entertainment
(b) Interactive communication
(c) Developmental communication
(d) Communitarian

14. Classroom communication of a teacher rests on the principle of
(a) Infotainment
(b) Edutainment
(c) Entertainment
(d) Enlightenment

15. ________ is important when a teacher communicates with his/her student.
(a) Sympathy (b) Empathy
(c) Apathy (d) Antipathy

16. In a certain code GALIB is represented by HBMJC. TIGER will be represented by
(a) UJHFS (b) UHJSF
(c) JHUSF (d) HUJSF

17. In a certain cricket tournament 45 matches were played. Each team played once against each of the other teams. The number of teams participated in the tournament is
(a) 8 (b) 10
(c) 12 (d) 14

18. The missing number in the series 40, 120, 60, 180, 90,?, 135 is
(a) 110 (b) 270
(c) 105 (d) 210

19. The odd numbers from 1 to 45 which are exactly divisible by 3 are arranged in an ascending order. The number at 6th position is
(a) 18 (b) 24
(c) 33 (d) 36

20. The mean of four numbers a, b, c, d is 100. If c = 70, then the mean of the remaining numbers is
(a) 30 (b) $\frac{85}{2}$
(c) $\frac{170}{3}$ (d) 110

21. If the radius of a circle is increased by 50%, the perimeter of the circle will increase by
(a) 20% (b) 30%
(c) 40% (d) 50%

22. If the statement 'some men are honest' is false, which among the following statements will be true. Choose the correct code given below:
(i) All men are honest.
(ii) No men are honest.
(iii) Some men are not honest.
(iv) All men are dishonest.

Codes:
(a) (i), (ii) and (iii)
(b) (ii), (iii) and (iv)
(c) (i), (iii) and (iv)
(d) (ii), (i) and (iv)

23. Choose the proper alternative given in the codes to replace the question mark.
Bee – Honey, Cow – Milk, Teacher –?
(a) Intelligence (b) Marks
(c) Lessons (d) Wisdom

24. P is the father of R and S is the son of Q and T is the brother of P. If R is the sister of S, how is Q related to T?
(a) Wife
(b) Sister-in-law
(c) Brother-in-law
(d) Daughter-in-law

25. A definition put forward to resolve a dispute by influencing attitudes or stirring emotions is called
(a) Lexical (b) Persuasive
(c) Stipulative (d) Precisions

26. Which of the codes given below contains only the correct statements?

Statements:

(i) Venn diagram is a clear method of notation.
(ii) Venn diagram is the most direct method of testing the validity of categorical syllogisms.
(iii) In Venn diagram method the premises and the conclusion of a categorical syllogism is diagrammed.
(iv) In Venn diagram method the three overlapping circles are drawn for testing a categorical syllogism.

Codes:

(a) (i), (ii) & (iii)
(b) (i), (ii) & (iv)
(c) (ii), (iii) & (iv)
(d) (i), (iii) & (iv)

27. Inductive reasoning presupposes
(a) unity in human nature
(b) integrity in human nature
(c) uniformity in human nature
(d) harmony in human nature

Read the table below and based on this table answer questions from 28 to 33:

Area under Major Horticulture Crops

(in lakh hectares)

Year	Fruits	Vegetables	Flowers	Total Horti-culture Area
2005-06	53	72	1	187
2006-07	56	75	1	194
2007-08	58	78	2	202
2008-09	61	79	2	207
2009-10	63	79	2	209

28. Which of the following two years have recorded the highest rate of increase in area under the total horticulture?
(a) 2005–06 & 2006–07
(b) 2006–07 & 2008–09
(c) 2007–08 & 2008–09
(d) 2006–07 & 2007–08

29. Shares of the area under flowers, vegetables and fruits in the area under total horticulture are respectively:
(a) 1, 38 and 30 percent
(b) 30, 38 and 1 percent
(c) 38, 30 and 1 percent
(d) 35, 36 and 2 percent

30. Which of the following has recorded the highest rate of increase in area during 2005-06 to 2009-10?
(a) Fruits
(b) Vegetables
(c) Flowers
(d) Total horticulture

31. Find out the horticultural crop that has recorded an increase of area by around 10 percent from 2005-06 to 2009-10.
(a) Fruits
(b) Vegetables
(c) Flowers
(d) Total horticulture

32. What has been the share of area under fruits, vegetables and flowers in the area under total horticulture in 2007-08?
(a) 53 percent (b) 68 percent
(c) 79 percent (d) 100 percent

33. In which year, area under fruits has recorded the highest rate of increase?
(a) 2006-07 (b) 2007-08
(c) 2008-09 (d) 2009-10

34. 'www' stands for
(a) work with web
(b) word wide web

(c) world wide web
(d) worth while web

35. A hard disk is divided into tracks which is further subdivided into
(a) Clusters (b) Sectors
(c) Vectors (d) Heads

36. A computer program that translates a program statement by statement into machine language is called a/an
(a) Compiler (b) Simulator
(c) Translator (d) Interpreter

37. A Gigabyte is equal to
(a) 1024 Megabytes
(b) 1024 Kilobytes
(c) 1024 Terabytes
(d) 1024 Bytes

38. A Compiler is a software which converts
(a) characters to bits
(b) high level language to machine language
(c) machine language to high level language
(d) words to bits

39. Virtual memory is
(a) an extremely large main memory.
(b) an extremely large secondary memory.
(c) an illusion of extremely large main memory.
(d) a type of memory used in super computers.

40. The phrase 'tragedy of commons' is in the context of
(a) tragic event related to damage caused by release of poisonous gases.
(b) tragic conditions of poor people.
(c) degradation of renewable free access resources.
(d) climate change.

41. Kyoto Protocol is related to
(a) Ozone depletion
(b) Hazardous waste
(c) Climate change
(d) Nuclear energy

42. Which of the following is a source of emissions leading to the eventual formation of surface ozone as a pollutant?
(a) Transport sector
(b) Refrigeration and Airconditioning
(c) Wetlands
(d) Fertilizers

43. The smog in cities in India mainly consists of
(a) Oxides of sulphur
(b) Oxides of nitrogen and unburnt hydrocarbons
(c) Carbon monoxide and SPM
(d) Oxides of sulphur and ozone

44. Which of the following types of natural hazards have the highest potential to cause damage to humans?
(a) Earthquakes
(b) Forest fires
(c) Volcanic eruptions
(d) Droughts and Floods

45. The percentage share of renewable energy sources in the power production in India is around
(a) 2-3% (b) 22-25%
(c) 10-12% (d) < 1%

46. In which of the following categories the enrolment of students in higher education in 2010-11 was beyond the percentage of seats reserved?
(a) OBC students
(b) SC students
(c) ST students
(d) Woman students

47. Which one of the following statements is not correct about the University Grants Commission (UGC)?
(a) It was established in 1956 by an Act of Parliament.
(b) It is tasked with promoting and coordinating higher education.
(c) It receives Plan and Non-Plan funds from the Central Government.

(d) It receives funds from State Governments in respect of State Universities.

48. Consider the statement which is followed by two arguments (I) and (II):

Statement: Should India switch over to a two party system?

Arguments: (I) Yes, it will lead to stability of Government.

(II) No, it will limit the choice of voters.

(a) Only argument (I) is strong.
(b) Only argument (II) is strong.
(c) Both the arguments are strong.
(d) Neither of the arguments is strong.

49. Consider the statement which is followed by two arguments (I) and (II):

Statement: Should persons with criminal background be banned from contesting elections?

Arguments: (I) Yes, it will decriminalise politics.

(II) No, it will encourage the ruling party to file frivolous cases against their political opponents.

(a) Only argument (I) is strong.
(b) Only argument (II) is strong.
(c) Both the arguments are strong.
(d) Neither of the arguments is strong.

50. Which of the following statement(s) is/are correct about a Judge of the Supreme Court of India?

1. A Judge of the Supreme Court is appointed by the President of India.
2. He holds office during the pleasure of the President.
3. He can be suspended, pending an inquiry.
4. He can be removed for proven misbehaviour or incapacity.

Select the correct answer from the codes given below:

Codes:

(a) 1, 2 and 3 (b) 1, 3 and 4
(c) 1 and 3 (d) 1 and 4

51. In the warrant of precedence, the Speaker of the Lok Sabha comes next only to

(a) The President
(b) The Vice-President
(c) The Prime Minister
(d) The Cabinet Ministers

52. The black-board can be utilised best by a teacher for

(a) putting the matter of teaching in black and white
(b) making the students attentive
(c) writing the important and notable points
(d) highlighting the teacher himself

53. Nowadays the most effective mode of learning is

(a) self study
(b) face-to-face learning
(c) e-learning
(d) blended learning

54. At the primary school stage, most of the teachers should be women because they

(a) can teach children better than men.
(b) know basic content better than men.
(c) are available on lower salaries.
(d) can deal with children with love and affection.

55. Which one is the highest order of learning?

(a) Chain learning
(b) Problem-solving learning
(c) Stimulus-response learning
(d) Conditioned-reflex learning

56. A person can enjoy teaching as a profession when he

(a) has control over students.
(b) commands respect from students.
(c) is more qualified than his colleagues.
(d) is very close to higher authorities.

57. "A diagram speaks more than 1000 words." The statement means that the teacher should
(a) use diagrams in teaching.
(b) speak more and more in the class
(c) use teaching aids in the class.
(d) not speak too much in the class.

58. A research paper
(a) is a compilation of information on a topic.
(b) contains original research as deemed by the author.
(c) contains peer-reviewed original research or evaluation of research conducted by others.
(d) can be published in more than one journal.

59. Which one of the following belongs to the category of good 'research ethics'?
(a) Publishing the same paper in two research journals without telling the editors.
(b) Conducting a review of the literature that acknowledges the contributions of other people in the relevant field or relevant prior work.
(c) Trimming outliers from a data set without discussing your reasons in a research paper.
(d) Including a colleague as an author on a research paper in return for a favour even though the colleague did not make a serious contribution to the paper.

60. Which of the following sampling methods is not based on probability?
(a) Simple Random Sampling
(b) Stratified Sampling
(c) Quota Sampling
(d) Cluster Sampling

ANSWERS

1. (d)	2. (d)	3. (c)	4. (b)	5. (d)
6. (c)	7. (d)	8. (c)	9. (a)	10. (c)
11. (b)	12. (c)	13. (b)	14. (b)	15. (b)
16. (a)	17. (b)	18. (b)	19. (c)	20. (d)
21. (d)	22. (b)	23. (d)	24. (b)	25. (b)
26. (b)	27. (c)	28. (d)	29. (a)	30. (c)
31. (b)	32. (b)	33. (a)	34. (c)	35. (b)
36. (d)	37. (a)	38. (b)	39. (c)	40. (c)
41. (c)	42. (a)	43. (b)	44. (d)	45. (c)
46. (a)	47. (d)	48. (c)	49. (a)	50. (d)
51. (c)	52. (c)	53. (d)	54. (d)	55. (d)
56. (b)	57. (c)	58. (c)	59. (b)	60. (c)

PAPER–II

Note: This paper contains fifty (50) objective type questions, each question carrying two (2) marks. All questions are compulsory.

1. The major concerns of Public Administration discipline is/are
(i) Absorption of the principles of democracy.
(ii) Policy sensitivity
(iii) Innovative, proactive and risk taking administration
(iv) Coping capacity of administration and government to face modern challenges.
Select the correct answer by using the codes given below:

Codes:
(a) (ii) only (b) (i), (ii), (iii)
(c) (ii), (iii), (iv) (d) (i), (ii), (iii), (iv)

2. Frederick Taylor noticed a phenomenon of workers, purposely operating below their capacity and called it
(a) Skiving
(b) Lack of standards of work
(c) Unscientific decision making
(d) Failure of management to design jobs

3. A formal organization
(i) grows and expands
(ii) is deliberately impersonal
(iii) forces the members of the group to observe the common rules
(iv) relationship created by the organization structure are to be honoured by everyone.

Select the correct answer by using the codes given below:

Codes:
(a) (i), (iii) and (iv) (b) (i), (ii) and (iv)
(c) (i), (ii) and (iii) (d) (ii), (iii) and (iv)

4. Arrange Elton Mayo's experiments in a chronological sequence. Select the correct answer from the codes given below:
(i) First Inquiry
(ii) Human Attitudes and Sentiments
(iii) The Great Illumination
(iv) Absenteeism in the Industries
(v) Social organisation

Codes:
(a) (i), (iv), (v), (iii) and (ii)
(b) (i), (iii), (iv), (ii) and (v)
(c) (i), (iii), (ii), (v) and (iv)
(d) (i), (ii), (iii), (iv) and (v)

5. Which of the following statements about Simon's view of rationality is correct?
(a) Rationality is uni-dimensional.
(b) Simon propounds the concept of total rationality.
(c) Every decision maker has unlimited knowledge about alternatives.
(d) Rationality is limited by the skills, values, purpose and knowledge levels of the decision maker.

6. Which one of the following concept is not developed by Peter Drucker?
(a) Generic Management
(b) The concept of Transactional Influence
(c) Management by Objectives
(d) Knowledge Worker

7. Who among the following rejected the principle of unity of command?
(a) Elton Mayo (b) F.W. Taylor
(c) Henry Fayol (d) Presthus

8. Which of the following is not a characteristic of Job-centric supervisor in the scheme of Rensis Likert?
(a) He exerts heavy pressure on worker for work.
(b) He shows confidence in subordinates.
(c) He allows little freedom to subordinates.
(d) He helps subordinates when mistakes occur.

9. Which one is not among the four systems of management or leadership styles given by Rensis Likert?
(a) Exploitative authoritative
(b) Benevolent authoritative
(c) Constructive
(d) Participative (Democratic)

10. Which theory considers personality, motives, values and skills as attributes of leadership?
(a) Trait theory
(b) Behavioural theory
(c) Situational theory
(d) Contingency model

11. Yehezkel Dror refers 'Meta Policy' as
(a) Policy on policy making system
(b) Master policy
(c) Super policy
(d) Integrated policy

12. Which of the following is the part of executive office of the U.S. President?
(a) White House staff and office of Management and budget.
(b) White House staff and office of Personnel Management
(c) Office of Management and Budget and Federal Labour Relation Authority
(d) Office of Management and Budget and Office of Personnel Management

13. Who said the following words about comparative Public Administration "the theory of public administration applied to diverse cultures and national settings and the body of factual data by which it can be examined?"
(a) Robert A. Dahal
(b) Ferral Heady and S.L. Stokes
(c) William J. Siffin
(d) Dwight Waldo

14. Match List I with List II and codes given below:
List I (Authors)
A. J.S. Mill B. Thomas Carlyle
C. Dewey D. Vablan
List II (Comments)
i. Continental nuisance
ii. Professional Governors of government
iii. Trained incapacity
iv. Occupational Psychosis

Codes:	**A**	**B**	**C**	**D**
(a)	ii	i	iv	iii
(b)	iii	ii	i	iv
(c)	ii	i	iii	iv
(d)	i	iv	ii	iii

15. There are many gaps in the organisation and operation of development programmes which are:
(i) Inadequate administrative planning
(ii) Traditional administrative practices
(iii) Procedural deficiencies
(iv) Lack of consciousness of achieving goals

Select the correct answer by using the codes given below:
(a) (i), (ii) and (iii)
(b) (ii), (iii) and (iv)
(c) (i), (iii) and (iv)
(d) (i), (ii), (iii) and (iv)

16. **Assertion (A):** Bureaucracy seems to be an essential ingredient of modern civilization.
Reason (R): Bureaucracies are found in all large and complex organizations.
Codes:
(a) Both (A) and (R) are correct and (R) is the correct explanation of (A).
(b) Both (A) and (R) are correct, but (R) is not the correct explanation of (A).
(c) (A) is true, but (R) is false.
(d) (A) is false, but (R) is true.

17. "Development administration is concerned with maximising innovation for development". Who gave this definition?
(a) John Montgomery
(b) Edward Weidner
(c) F.W. Riggs
(d) Han Been Lee

18. "Improvement in the effectiveness of development administration depends on the quality and training of public servants who man it and on a social and political environment which liberates their energies." Who of the following made this statement?
(a) J.N. Khosla (b) Merle Fainsod
(c) Irving Swerdlow (d) F.W. Riggs

19. **Assertion (A):** The community development programme was launched to secure total development of material and human resources of rural areas.
Reason (R): It was realised while implementing the programme that social change is not possible unless the efforts

are people centred and involvement of people in their development is not ensured.

Codes:

(a) Both (A) and (R) are correct and (R) is the correct explanation of (A).
(b) Both (A) and (R) are correct, but (R) is not the correct explanation of (A).
(c) (A) is true, but (R) is false.
(d) (A) is false, but (R) is true.

20. Which of the following is/are the roles of Gram Sabha in the areas covered under Panchayats Extension to the Scheduled Areas as PESA Act, 1996?
(i) Gram Sabha has the power to prevent alienation of land in the scheduled areas.
(ii) Gram sabha has the ownership of minor forest produce.
(iii) Recommendation of Gram Sabha is required for granting licence or mining lease for any minerals in the scheduled areas.

Select the correct answer by using the codes given below:

Codes:

(a) (i) only (b) (i) and (ii)
(c) (ii) and (iii) (d) (i), (ii) and (iii)

21. According to 2nd ARC, task of delimitation and reservation of constituencies for local governments should be entrusted to
(a) National Election Commission
(b) State Election Commission
(c) Union Parliament
(d) State Legislature

22. The planning departments of the Development Authorities should be merged with District Planning Committee and Metropolitan Planning Committees. This recommendation was made by
(a) Hanumantha Rao Committee
(b) Dantewala Committee
(c) K. Santhanum Committee
(d) 2nd Administrative Reforms Commission

23. The principle of subsidiarity is related to
(a) Assigning more financial powers from centre to states.
(b) Devolution of functions to Panchayats to make them function as an institution of self-government.
(c) Delegation of authority within an organisation
(d) Delegation of authority outside the organisation

24. Which one of the following is not included in the Twelveth Schedule of the Constitution of India?
(a) Planning for economic and social development
(b) Water supply
(c) Technical training and vocational education
(d) Safeguarding the interest of weaker sections

25. **Assertion (A):** Zila Parishad is vested with planning and development functions.
Reason (R): District traditionally has been recognised as the administrative unit required to perform the related functions.

Codes:

(a) Both (A) and (R) are correct and (R) is the correct explanation of (A).
(b) Both (A) and (R) are correct, but (R) is not the correct explanation of (A).
(c) (A) is true, but (R) is false.
(d) (A) is false, but (R) is true.

26. Which of the following statements regarding Budget in India are correct?
(i) The Constitution of India calls Budget as Annual Financial Statement.
(ii) Budget is statement of estimated receipts and expenditure of the Government of India.

(iii) The President of India shall lay it before the House of People.
(iv) The Department of Economic Affairs of Ministry of Finance prepares the Budget of Government of India.

Select correct statements by using codes given below:

Codes:

(a) (i), (ii) and (iii) (b) (i), (ii) and (iv)
(c) (ii), (iii) and (iv) (d) (i), (iii) and (iv)

27. Which one of the following has not been associated with PMO?
(a) Bhuvnesh Chaturvedi
(b) Prithvi Raj Chauhan
(c) Brijesh Mishra
(d) N.R. Pillai

28. 'The Parliament may by law provide for a Legislative Council in each state consisting of members elected by the local Governments'. This recommendation was made by
(a) B.N. Srikrishna Commission
(b) Venkatachelliah Commission
(c) 2nd Administrative Reforms Commission
(d) Justice Punchhi Commission

29. Put the following Chairman of Finance commissions in a sequential order:
(i) K.C. Pant (ii) A.M. Khusro
(iii) N.K.P. Salve (iv) C. Rangrajan

Select the correct answer by using codes given below:

Codes:

(a) (iii) (i) (ii) (iv) (b) (i) (ii) (iii) (iv)
(c) (iv) (iii) (ii) (i) (d) (i) (iii) (ii) (iv)

30. The responsive public administration requires:
(i) Institutional safeguards of technical competence
(ii) Flatter organisation
(iii) High calibre of public personnel
(iv) General standard of efficiency

Select the correct answer from the codes given below:

Codes:

(a) (i), (ii) and (iii) (b) (i), (ii) and (iv)
(c) (i), (iii) and (iv) (d) (iii) and (iv)

31. National Institute of Rural Development was established in 1958. Prior to 1958 it was known as
(a) Central Institute of Planning and Development
(b) Central institute of study and Research in Community Development
(c) Central Institute of Statistical Research
(d) Central Institute of Training and Development

32. Which of the following statements about the functions of NABARD is not correct?
(a) It prepares annual rural credit plans for all the districts in the country.
(b) It undertakes monitoring and evaluation of projects refinanced by it.
(c) It promotes research in the fields of rural banking, agriculture and rural development.
(d) It functions as a regulatory authority in relation to all public sector commercial banks.

33. Which of the following statements regarding All India Services are correct?
(i) New All India services may be created only if Council of States declares to do so by a majority resolution.
(ii) New All India Services may be created if it is necessary or expedient in the national interest.
(iii) All India Services may be created by a law passed by Parliament.
(iv) All India Judicial Service may also be created by Parliament by law.

Select the correct answer by using codes given below:

Codes:
(a) (i), (ii) & (iii)
(b) (ii), (iii) & (iv)
(c) (i), (iii) & (iv)
(d) (i), (ii), (iii) & (iv)

34. Assertion (A): The social responsibility of the judiciary has now been expanded and the principle of locus standi given a liberal interpretation.

Reason (R): In a social awakened ambience, social action groups are encouraged to approach the courts and come up with public interest litigations for redressing injustice.

Codes:
(a) Both (A) and (R) are correct and (R) is the correct explanation of (A).
(b) Both (A) and (R) are correct, but (R) is not the correct explanation of (A).
(c) (A) is true, but (R) is false.
(d) (A) is false, but (R) is true.

35. "There shall be a District Council, constituted in every district, representing all rural and urban areas in the district and exercising powers and functions in accordance with the provisions of Article 243 G and 243 W of the Constitution." Which of the following has recommended this?
(a) National Commission for the review of the working of the Constitution.
(b) Punchhi Commission
(c) 2nd Administrative Reforms Commission
(d) Rural-Urban Relationship Committee

36. Match List I with List II and select the correct answer from the codes given below:

List I (Commissions)
A. 13th Finance Commission
B. 2nd Administrative Reforms Commission
C. Commission on Civil Service Reform
D. Commission on Centre-State Relations

List II (Chair Persons)
i. P.C. Hota
ii. R.S. Sarkaria
iii. Vijay Kelkar
iv. Veerappa Moiley

Codes:	**A**	**B**	**C**	**D**
(a)	iii	iv	i	ii
(b)	iii	iv	ii	i
(c)	ii	iv	i	iii
(d)	i	ii	iii	iv

37. The grants made in advance by the Lok Sabha in respect of estimated expenditure for a part of any financial year is called
(a) Token Grant
(b) Supplementary Grant
(c) Vote on Account
(d) Vote of Credit

38. Which one of the following is not correct regarding the role of District officer as Collector in the district?
(a) Distribution of taccavi loans and their recovery
(b) Assessment of losses to crops because of natural calamities
(c) Sales of excise shops
(d) Administration of Nazu! land

39. The Post of the Deputy Collector (non-covenanted Post) was created in the district under the provision of the following Act:
(a) The Charter Act of 1843
(b) The Regulating Act of 1773
(c) The Charter Act of 1833
(d) Pitts India Act of 1784

40. Arrange the followings in chronological order according to their appointments:
(i) L.M. Singhvi Committee
(ii) Sarkaria Commission
(iii) Hanumantha Rao Committee
(iv) Thungan Committee

Codes:
(a) (i), (ii), (iii), (iv) (b) (i), (iii), (ii), (iv)
(c) (ii), (iv), (iii), (i) (d) (iii), (ii), (i), (iv)

41. According to the Constitution of India the Administrative tribunals cannot be established for
(a) Industrial and Labour disputes
(b) Elections to either House of Parliament
(c) Delimitation of Constituencies
(d) Ceiling on Urban property

42. 'Interview is a process of social interaction'. Who said it?
(a) P.V. Young (b) M.N. Basu
(c) Goode and Hatt (d) V.M. Palmer

43. The various steps in Research process are given below. Place them in the ascending order of the stages.
(i) Sampling
(ii) Data analysis
(iii) Problem formulation
(iv) Report writing
Select the answer by using the codes given below:
Codes:
(a) (i), (ii), (iii), (iv) (b) (iii), (i), (ii), (iv)
(c) (ii), (iii), (iv), (i) (d) (i), (iv), (ii), (iii)

44. Which one of the following does not refer to practical orientation of research?
(a) Basic Research
(b) Action Oriented Research
(c) Practice Oriented Research
(d) All of the above refer to practical uses

45. "N.G.O. is a private enterprise for social progress." This statement is made by
(a) Lord Bryce
(b) Pt. Jawaharlal Nehru
(c) Lord Beveridge
(d) A.P.J. Abdul Kalam

46. Which is not the basis of Public Sector Reform?
(a) Inefficiency
(b) Unprofitability
(c) Lack of Competitiveness
(d) Significance of spill over effects

47. Which of the following are the impact of global economic integration on sovereign states?
(i) Interdependency of Trade
(ii) Interdependency of development policies and programmes and their impact on economy, employment etc.
(iii) Impact of global governance dynamics on the local policies and reform.
(iv) Conductive environment for both the capital and the labour at the local level under the aegis of global economic integration.
Select the answer using the codes given below:
Codes:
(a) (i) (ii) (iii)
(b) (ii) (iii) (iv)
(c) (i) (ii) (iv)
(d) (i) (ii) (iii) (iv)

48. Foreign Exchange Management Act (FEMA) by replacing Foreign Exchange Regulation Act (FERA) was introduced in the year?
(a) 1999 (b) 2000
(c) 2001 (d) 2009

49. Which of the following is/are the most common method of privatisation?
(i) Sale to outside owners
(ii) Restitution
(iii) Spontaneous Privatisation
(iv) Management-employees buyout
Select the correct answer from the codes given below:
Codes:
(a) (i) and (ii)
(b) (i), (ii) and (iii)
(c) (i), (ii), (iii) and (iv)
(d) (iv) only

50. Which of the following is not the function of Competition Commission of India?
(a) To consider and approve all the cases of mergers, acquisition beyond a certain value.
(b) To promote the culture of competition in Indian market.
(c) To conduct in-house market research and sectoral research
(d) To suggest reform in the organisation and functioning of RBI and other banks.

ANSWERS

1. (d)	2. (a)	3. (b)	4. (c)	5. (d)
6. (b)	7. (b)	8. (d)	9. (c)	10. (a)
11. (a)	12. (a)	13. (b)	14. (a)	15. (d)
16. (a)	17. (b)	18. (b)	19. (b)	20. (d)
21. (b)	22. (d)	23. (b)	24. (c)	25. (a)
26. (b)	27. (d)	28. (c)	29. (a)	30. (c)
31. (b)	32. (d)	33. (b)	34. (a)	35. (c)
36. (a)	37. (c)	38. (c)	39. (c)	40. (d)
41. (c)	42. (c)	43. (b)	44. (a)	45. (c)
46. (d)	47. (d)	48. (a)	49. (c)	50. (d)

PAPER–III

Note: This paper contains seventy five (75) objective type questions of two (2) marks each. All questions are compulsory.

1. Which among following is concerned with the definition of Public Administration as socially embedded process of collective relationship, dialogue and action to promote human flourishing for all?
(a) New Public Administration
(b) Third Minnowbrook Conference
(c) New Public Management
(d) New Public Service Theory

2. The scope of Public Administration consists of the study of only three factors namely men, materials and methods. This view is expressed by
(a) P. McQueen
(b) Mooney and Reiley
(c) Louis P. Anderson
(d) None of the above

3. Which of the following is not a matter of difference between public and private administration?
(a) Public Welfare and Public Satisfaction
(b) Public Scrutiny of actions and decisions
(c) Consistency and impartiality in action
(d) POSDCORB activities

4. Match the List I with List II and select the correct answer from the codes given below:

List I (Books)
A. Public Administration in the Time of Turbulence
B. Toward a new public administration: The Minnowbrook perspective
C. New Despotism
D. Politics and Administration

List II (Authors)
i. Lord Hewart
ii. Frank J. Goodnow
iii. Frank Marini
iv. Dwight Waldo

Codes:	A	B	C	D
(a)	iv	iii	i	ii
(b)	iii	iv	ii	i
(c)	i	iii	ii	iv
(d)	ii	iv	i	iii

5. An informal organization is:
(i) Comparatively stable
(ii) Satisfies social needs of its members.

(iii) Helps members in achieving their goals.
(iv) Preserves the cultural values of its members.

Select the correct answer by using codes given below:

Codes:

(a) (i), (ii) & (iii) (b) (i), (ii) & (iv)
(c) (i), (iii) & (iv) (d) (ii), (iii) & (iv)

6. **Assertion (A):** Red-tape has been defined as punctilious exactitude in the observance of regulation.
Reason (R): 'Red tape' is perhaps the best insurance the public has to receive equal treatment at the hand of government.
Codes:
(a) Both (A) and (R) are correct and (R) is the correct explanation of (A).
(b) Both (A) and (R) are correct, but (R) is not the correct explanation of (A).
(c) (A) is true, but (R) is false.
(d) (A) is false, but (R) is true.

7. **Assertion (A):** There is no ideal number of persons a supervisor can supervise.
Reason (R): Span of control varies on the basis of factors like function, time, space and delegation of authority.
Codes:
(a) Both (A) and (R) are correct and (R) is the correct explanation of (A).
(b) Both (A) and (R) are correct, but (R) is not the correct explanation of (A).
(c) (A) is true, but (R) is false.
(d) (A) is false, but (R) is true.

8. Woodrow Wilson was a:
(i) President of U.S.A.
(ii) Governor of New Jersey
(iii) Recipient of Nobel Prize
(iv) President of Princeton University
Select the correct answer by using codes given below:
(a) (i)
(b) (i) and (ii)
(c) (i), (ii) and (iii)
(d) (i), (ii), (iii) and (iv)

9. Which of the following factors influenced the emergence of the theory and practice of Human Relations?
(i) Class antagonisms
(ii) Reaction to Taylorism
(iii) Economic Depression
(iv) Backward material and cultural aspirations of workers.
Select the correct answer by using codes given below:
Codes:
(a) (ii) and (iv)
(b) (i), (ii) and (iii)
(c) (ii), (iii) and (iv)
(d) (i), (ii), (iii) and (iv)

10. **Assertion (A):** Classical writers were concerned with improving the organizational structure as a means of increasing efficiency.
Reason (R): They laid emphasis on the importance of principles for the design of a logical structure of organization.
Codes:
(a) Both (A) and (R) are correct and (R) is the correct explanation of (A).
(b) Both (A) and (R) are correct, but (R) is not the correct explanation of (A).
(c) (A) is true, but (R) is false.
(d) (A) is false, but (R) is true.

11. Match List I with List II and select the correct answer from the codes given below:
List I (Writers)
A. James G. March and Herbert Simon
B. Chester Bernard
C. James D. Mooney and Allan C. Reiley
D. Rensis Likert

List II (Books)
i. The Principles of Organization
ii. The Human Organization
iii. Organisations
iv. Organisation and Management

Codes:	A	B	C	D
(a)	i	iii	iv	ii
(b)	iii	iv	i	ii
(c)	ii	iv	iii	i
(d)	iv	ii	i	iii

12. Which one of the following is not an Independent Regulatory Commission in India?
(a) Telecom Regulatory Authority
(b) National Labour Relations Commission
(c) Monopolies and Restrictive Trade Practices Commission
(d) Securities and Exchange Board

13. Which one among the following books of M.P. Follett was edited by Metcalf and Urwick after the death of M.P. Follett?
(a) Creative Experience
(b) New State
(c) Dynamic Administration
(d) The Speaker of the House of Representative

14. Frederick Herzberg has identified certain determinants of job satisfaction in his two factors theory. Which of the following according to him are not job satisfiers?
(i) Salary
(ii) Achievement
(iii) Working conditions
(iv) Recognition
Select the correct answer by using codes given below:
Codes:
(a) (i) & (ii) (b) (ii) & (iii)
(c) (ii) & (iv) (d) (iii) & (iv)

15. Match the List I with List II and select the correct answer from the codes given below:
List I (Concept)
A. Decision Tree
B. Linking Pin Model
C. Garbage Can Model
D. Sensitivity Training
List II (Thinkers)
i. Cohen, March and Olson
ii. Chris Argyris
iii. Duncan
iv. Rensis Likert

Codes:	A	B	C	D
(a)	i	iv	iii	ii
(b)	iii	iv	ii	i
(c)	i	iv	ii	iii
(d)	iii	iv	i	ii

16. Rensis Likert has suggested which of the following model for removal of hurdles in traditional hierarchies?
(a) Management System I
(b) The Linking Pin Model
(c) Application of System 4
(d) Science based management

17. Who among following has given the concept of 'A New Comparative Public Administration'?
(a) Keith M. Henderson
(b) Ira Sharkansky
(c) Dwight Waldo
(d) Robert P. Biller

18. Who said these words about Comparative Public Administration extended meaning of comparison "is the generalized or global framework of thinking about problems"?
(a) John Montgomery
(b) Jack C. Plano
(c) Fred W. Riggs
(d) Talcott Parsons

19. Robert T. Golembiewski mentions three themes of comparative public administration as:
    (i) Significance of focal concerns
    (ii) Magnitude of resulting effort
    (iii) Motivation for the approach
    (iv) Stress on values
    Select the correct answer by using code given below:
    Codes:
    (a) (i), (ii) and (iii) (b) (ii), (iii) and (iv)
    (c) (i), (ii) and (iv) (d) (i), (iii) and (iv)

20. Which among the following is not a feature of Industrial model as developed by Fred W. Riggs?
    (a) Pre-dominance of ascriptive particularistic and diffuse patterns
    (b) High degree of social mobility
    (c) Prevalence of voluntary associations performing specific functions
    (d) Well-developed occupational systems

21. The salient characteristics of bazaar-canteen economy as described by Riggs is/are
    (i) Price Indeterminacy
    (ii) Agglomeration of values
    (iii) Intrusive access to the elites
    (iv) Pariah entrepreneurship
    Select the correct answer by using codes given below:
    Codes:
    (a) (i)
    (b) (i) and (ii)
    (c) (i), (ii) and (iii)
    (d) (i), (ii), (iii) and (iv)

22. The merit system for recruitment based on competitive examination was introduced first in
    (a) Great Britain
    (b) United States of America
    (c) China
    (d) India

23. Arrange in descending order the following institutions of Local Government of France:
    (i) Canton
    (ii) Department
    (iii) Commune
    (iv) Arrondissement
    Select the correct answer by using codes given below:
    (a) (i), (ii), (iii) and (iv)
    (b) (ii), (i), (iv) and (iii)
    (c) (i), (iii), (ii) and (iv)
    (d) (ii), (iv), (i) and (iii)

24. Which one of the following is top tier of local government in U.K.?
    (a) Metropolitan District
    (b) Metropolitan County
    (c) Parish
    (d) Shire

25. The Hatch Act, 1939 in U.S.A. dealt with
    (a) Right to Strike
    (b) Political activities of Civil Servants
    (c) Right to Association
    (d) Machinery for Negotiation

26. Ferrel Heady identifies major features of national bureaucracy in the developing society. These are
    (i) The basic pattern of administration is Imitative.
    (ii) Widespread discrepancy between Form and Reality.
    (iii) Bureaucracy accepts directions from other legitimate branches of government.
    (iv) The bureaucracies are deficient in skilled Manpower.
    Select the correct answer by using the codes given below.
    Codes:
    (a) (i), (ii) and (iii)
    (b) (i), (ii) and (iv)

(c) (ii), (iii) and (iv)
(d) (i), (ii), (iii) and (iv)

27. "The bureaucratic structure and its orientation to a development role are not necessarily incompatible." This statement in the Indian context was made by
(a) Jawaharlal Nehru
(b) J.N. Khosla
(c) K.M. Munshi
(d) V.A. Pai Panandikar

28. Which one of the following is not correct about the development administration?
(a) Suitable institutions to accomplish the developmental goals are to be established.
(b) It is essential to build up administrative capacity and capability.
(c) Coordination is a basic component of development administration.
(d) Communication is only a desirable component of the development administration.

29. **Assertion (A):** In parliamentary form of government the executive is responsible to legislature.
Reason (R): In the constitution of India the provision is made that the council of Ministers shall be collectively responsible to the Parliament.
Codes:
(a) Both (A) and (R) are correct and (R) is the correct explanation of (A).
(b) Both (A) and (R) are correct, but (R) is not the correct explanation of (A).
(c) (A) is true, but (R) is false.
(d) (A) is false, but (R) is true.

30. Decision Making in development administration is
(i) Flexible (ii) Centralised
(iii) Rigid (iv) Innovative
Select the correct answer by using the codes given below:
Codes:
(a) (i) & (ii) (b) (ii) & (iii)
(c) (iii) & (iv) (d) (i) & (iv)

31. The President of India makes some appointments by warrant under his hand and seal. These are
(i) Judges of Supreme Court
(ii) Comptroller and Auditor General of India
(iii) Attorney-General of India
(iv) Governors of the states
Select correct answer by using codes given below:
(a) (i) and (iv)
(b) (i), (ii) and (iv)
(c) (i), (iii) and (iv)
(d) (i), (ii), (iii) and (iv)

32. Match the List I with List II and select the correct answer from the codes given below:
List I (Reports)
A. Montague-Chemsford Report on constitutional reforms in India
B. State Reorganization Commission
C. Taxation Enquiry Commission
D. Statutory (Simon) Commission
List II (Year)
i. 1955 ii. 1918
iii. 1954 iv. 1927

Codes:	A	B	C	D
(a)	i	ii	iii	iv
(b)	iv	iii	ii	i
(c)	ii	iv	i	iii
(d)	ii	i	iii	iv

33. "Of all the policy making organs in the Government of India, the secretariat stands on an exceptionally high pedestal." This statement is attributed to
(a) K. Subramanyam
(b) Chand Joshi
(c) S.C. Vajpeyi
(d) S.R. Maheshwari

34. Match the List I with List II and select the correct answer from the codes given below:

List I (Parliament's power to make laws)

A. For implementing any international treaty or agreement
B. In the matters enumerated in the State list during Emergency
C. For imposing a tax not mentioned in concurrent list or state list
D. The matters enumerated in Union List

List II (Articles)

i. Article 250 ii. Article 246
iii. Article 253 iv. Article 248

Codes:	**A**	**B**	**C**	**D**
(a)	i	ii	iii	iv
(b)	ii	iii	iv	i
(c)	iii	i	iv	ii
(d)	iv	i	ii	iii

35. Match the List I with List II and select the correct answer from the codes given below:

List I (Reports of the second administrative reforms commission)

A. Crisis Management
B. Local Government
C. Capacity building for conflict resolution
D. Social capital

List II (Title of the Report)

i. Friction to Fusion
ii. From despair to hope
iii. In inspiring journey into future
iv. A Shared Destiny

Codes:	**A**	**B**	**C**	**D**
(a)	i	iii	iv	ii
(b)	ii	iii	i	iv
(c)	iii	ii	iv	i
(d)	iv	i	ii	iii

36. The importance of personnel administration has increased in recent times due to followings:

(i) Recognition of Human aspect of organization
(ii) Long-range needs of manpower
(iii) Large size of the modern organization
(iv) High wage bills necessitating optimum use of manpower.

Select the correct answer by using codes given below:

Codes:

(a) (i) only
(b) (i) and (ii)
(c) (i), (ii) and (iii)
(d) (i), (ii), (iii) and (iv)

37. Match the List I with List II and select the correct answer from the codes given below:

List I (Provisions of Constitution)

a. Article 316(1) b. Article 316(2)
c. Article 317(3) d. Article 319

List II (Contents)

i. Qualification for member of Union Public Service Commission
ii. Ground for removal of member of Public Service Commission
iii. Further employment under Government of India
iv. Resignation of members of Public Service Commission

Codes:	**A**	**B**	**C**	**D**
(a)	i	ii	iii	iv
(b)	i	iii	iv	ii
(c)	i	iv	ii	iii
(d)	i	iii	ii	iv

38. On the recommendations made by Chief Ministers' Conference in 1961, the Parliament resolved to create which of the following three new All India Services?

(i) Indian Service of Engineers (Irrigation, Power, Buildings & Roads)
(ii) Indian Medical and Health Service
(iii) Indian Audit and Accounts Serivce
(iv) Indian Forest Service

Select the correct answer by using codes given below:

Codes:

(a) (i), (ii) and (iii) (b) (i), (ii) and (iv)
(c) (i), (iii) and (iv) (d) (ii), (iii) and (iv)

39. Which of following statements about 'Right to Strike' by Civil Servants in India is correct?
(a) It is prohibited by transaction of business rules.
(b) Right to strike is mentioned in Civil Service Conduct Rules.
(c) It is prohibited by law.
(d) Strike by Civil Servants constitutes breach of discipline.

40. **Assertion (A):** What has been happening in India, in recent times, is Sanskritization of corruption.
Reason (R): People began to adopt corruption not for its inherent utility, but as a means of belonging to the elite class.
Codes:
(a) Both (A) and (R) are correct and (R) is the correct explanation of (A).
(b) Both (A) and (R) are correct, but (R) is not the correct explanation of (A).
(c) (A) is true, but (R) is false.
(d) (A) is false, but (R) is true.

41. Consider the following statements regarding Administrative Tribunals:
(i) Parliament is empowered to make laws for the adjudication or trial by administrative tribunals.
(ii) The disputes and complaints with respect to recruitment and condition of services of persons appointed to public services are adjudicated by the said tribunals.
(iii) The jurisdiction and authority of such tribunals is specified by the law passed by the Parliament.
(iv) The administrative tribunals can also be set up for adjudicating disputes relating to foreign exchange and export and import matters.

Select the correct answer by using codes given below:

Codes:
(a) (i) and (ii)
(b) (i), (ii) and (iii)
(c) (ii), (iii) and (iv)
(d) (i), (ii), (iii) and (iv)

42. Consider the following functions of Standing Committees of Parliament in India:
(i) To consider demand for grants.
(ii) To make a report on demand for grants to the Houses of Parliament.
(iii) To consider annual reports of Ministries and make reports there on.
(iv) To consider national basic short term policy documents presented to the houses.

Select the correct answer using codes given below:

Codes:
(a) (i) and (ii) (b) (i), (ii) and (iii)
(c) (i), (iii) and (iv) (d) (iii) and (iv)

43. 'If the Finance Minister is to be held responsible for filling the reservoir and maintaining certain depth of water in it, he must be in a position to regulate the outflow'. This statement is made by
(a) Hoover Commission
(b) Haldane Committee
(c) Donoughmore Committee
(d) Tenth Finance Commission

44. Which of the following statements are correct?
(i) No tax shall be levied or collected except by authority of law.
(ii) Net proceeds of taxes, duties and other revenues are credited to the consolidated fund of India.
(iii) A law passed by the Parliament has established contingency fund of India

to enable advances to be made by the President for the purpose of meeting unforeseen expenditure.

(iv) Prior authorization under Article 115 or Article 116 is required to make advances out of contingency fund of India.

Select the correct answer by using the codes given below:

Codes:

(a) (i), (ii) and (iii)
(b) (ii), (iii) and (iv)
(c) (i), (iii) and (iv)
(d) (i), (ii), (iii) and (iv)

45. Scientific research intends to:

(i) Generalize Knowledge
(ii) Extend Knowledge
(iii) Correct Knowledge
(iv) Comprehend Knowledge

Select the correct answer by using codes given below:

Codes:

(a) (i) and (ii)
(b) (i), (ii) and (iii)
(c) (i), (iii) and (iv)
(d) (i), (ii), (iii) and (iv)

46. "A set of questions which are asked and filled in by an interviewer in a face-to-face situation with another person" is termed as

(a) Questionnaire (b) Schedule
(c) Interview (d) None of these

47. Which one of the following is not an advantage of the interview as a research tool?

(a) Interview is a highly flexible tool allowing a more permissible atmosphere.
(b) Interview has greater opportunity to appraise the accuracy and validity of replies.
(c) The interviewer may be able to differentiate between fact and fiction supplied by informants.
(d) Interviewer may be able to interject guesses and impressions into respondent's responses.

48. Who of the following described the case study method of research as the social microscope?

(a) Herbert Spencer (b) E. Burgress
(c) Frederic Le Play (d) William Healy

49. What is another name of Measure of Central Tendency?

(a) Index Number (b) Average
(c) Mode (d) Median

50. The Lakhina (Ahmednagar) experiment was related with

(a) District Administration
(b) Rural Development
(c) Tribal Development
(d) Revenue Administration

51. Which one of the following statements regarding research report is not correct?

(a) The communication of findings is an important part of researcher's responsibilities.
(b) The researcher is not under any obligation to consider the audience for whom the given report is intended.
(c) An introduction about the problems investigated is mandatory component of the report.
(d) A discussion of methods/procedures and an elaborate presentation of facts and findings is compulsory.

52. Lord Rippon's Resolution was called as the Magna Carta of Local Government. The resolution includes:

(i) Establishment of a network of local self governing institutions.
(ii) Financial decentralization
(iii) Adoption of election as a means of constituting local bodies.
(iv) Reduction of the number of officials to one third of total membership.

Select the correct answer by using the codes given below:

Codes:

(a) (i) and (ii)
(b) (i) and (iii)
(c) (i), (ii) and (iii)
(d) (i), (ii), (iii) and (iv)

53. Which one of following is the meaning of 'Panchayat' according to the Constitution of India?
(a) Institution of Local Self Government.
(b) Institution of Self Government for Rural areas.
(c) Institution of Rural Local Government.
(d) Institution of Rural Local Administration.

54. **Assertion (A):** The powers and functions of Gram Sabha are prescribed in the Constitution of India.
Reason (R): Gram Sabha is a forum where civic engagement and formation of social capital is possible.
Codes:
(a) Both (A) and (R) are correct and (R) is the correct explanation of (A).
(b) Both (A) and (R) are correct, but (R) is not the correct explanation of (A).
(c) (A) is true, but (R) is false.
(d) (A) is false, but (R) is true.

55. Which of the following committees on Panchayati Raj recommended Zila Parishad as the lynchpin of the PRI structure?
(a) Balwant Rai Mehta Committee
(b) Ashok Mehta Committee
(c) L.M. Singhvi Committee
(d) Paswan Committee

56. **Assertion (A):** Zila Parishad is vested with planning and developmental functions.
Reason (R): The technical manpower is already available at the district level.
Codes:
(a) Both (A) and (R) are correct and (R) is the correct explanation of (A).
(b) Both (A) and (R) are correct, but (R) is not the correct explanation of (A).
(c) (A) is true, but (R) is false.
(d) (A) is false, but (R) is true.

57. Which one of the following recommended mandatory devolution of taxation powers to Panchayati Raj Institutions in India?
(a) Balwantrai Mehta Committee
(b) Ashok Mehta Committee
(c) G.V.K. Rao Committee
(d) M.L. Dantwala Working Group

58. **Assertion (A):** A comprehensive exercise needs to be taken up regarding broadening and deepening of the revenue base of local governments.
Reason (R): The State Government by delegation expand the tax domain of Panchayats.
Codes:
(a) Both (A) and (R) are correct and (R) is the correct explanation of (A).
(b) Both (A) and (R) are correct, but (R) is not the correct explanation of (A).
(c) (A) is true, but (R) is false.
(d) (A) is false, but (R) is true.

59. Which of the following is the form of integrated governing structure at the District level as recommended by the second ARC?
(a) District Assembly
(b) District Council
(c) District Committee
(d) District Board

60. **Assertion (A):** There is need to adopt a common categorisation of urban local bodies across the country to improve clarity in their definition.

Reason (R): There should be three-tier of administration of urban local governments, except in the case of Town Panchayat.

Codes:
(a) Both (A) and (R) are correct and (R) is the correct explanation of (A).
(b) Both (A) and (R) are correct, but (R) is not the correct explanation of (A).
(c) (A) is true, but (R) is false.
(d) (A) is false, but (R) is true.

61. National Policy for persons with disabilities was framed in the year
(a) 2003 (b) 2004
(c) 2005 (d) 2006

62. Which of the following is not one of the objectives of social justice laid down in our Five Year Plans?
(a) Inclusive growth
(b) Bringing balanced regional growth
(c) Removal of unemployment
(d) Promoting economic growth

63. Who recommended for productive planning with constitutional status in India?
(a) B.R. Ambedkar
(b) K.C. Neogi
(c) J.L. Nehru
(d) Manmohan Singh

64. Put the following in an ascending chronological order and select the correct answer by using codes given below:
i. Constitution of National Commission to Review the working of the constitution.
ii. Enactment of SCs and STs (Prevention of Atrocities) Act.
iii. The employment of Manual Scavengers and construction of Dry Latrines (Prohibition) Act.
iv. Amendment of Protection of Civil Rights Act.

Codes:
(a) i ii iii iv (b) ii iii iv i
(c) iii iv ii i (d) iv ii iii i

65. The 12th Five Year Plan document approved by Cabinet aimed at
(i) Rejuvenating India's economy
(ii) Infusing higher government funding in key social sector such as health, education and sanitation.
(iii) Targeted the average economic growth at 8.2%
(iv) Technological advancement
Select the correct answer by using codes given below:
Codes:
(a) (i) and (ii)
(b) (i), (ii) and (iii)
(c) (i), (ii) and (iv)
(d) (i), (ii), (iii) and (iv)

66. Which one of the following has proposed setting up of a Financial Redressal Agency to deal with consumer grievances in a time bound manner?
(a) Economic Commission
(b) 11th Five Year Plan Document
(c) Second Administrative Reforms Commission
(d) The Financial Sector Legislative Reforms Commission

67. Which of the following suggested that there is no need for continuation of the District Rural Development Agency?
(a) Report of the Committee to review the existing administrative arrangement for rural development.
(b) II ARC report on Local Governance
(c) The Chief Ministers Round Table Conference on Panchayati Raj
(d) Evaluation of Panchayati Raj Institutions, 2000 UNNATTI NGO

68. Members of Parliament and state Legislatures should not become members

of Local Bodies. This recommendation was made by
(a) Ashok Mehta Committee
(b) L.M. Singhvi Committee
(c) P.K. Thungon Committee
(d) Veerappan Moiley Committee

69. **Assertion (A):** The Community Development Programme was launched to secure total development of the material and human resources of rural areas.
Reason (R): It was administered in phases at five levels National, State, District, Block and Village level.
Codes:
(a) Both (A) and (R) are correct and (R) is the correct explanation of (A).
(b) Both (A) and (R) are correct, but (R) is not the correct explanation of (A).
(c) (A) is true, but (R) is false.
(d) (A) is false, but (R) is true.

70. Approaches to rural development in India includes:
(i) Area Development Approach
(ii) Target Group Approach
(iii) Social Security Approach
(iv) Self-Employment Approach
Select the correct answer from the codes given below:
Codes:
(a) (i) and (ii)
(b) (i) and (iii)
(c) (ii), (iii) and (iv)
(d) (i), (ii), (iii) and (iv)

71. Which of the following statement/ statements regarding policy analysis is/ are correct?
(i) It gained considerable popularity since 1960's.
(ii) It was first adopted in the United States.
(iii) It aims at improving the quality of a policy.
(iv) It involves a wide range of studies and research activities.
Select the correct answer from the codes given below:
Codes:
(a) (ii) only
(b) (i) and (ii)
(c) (i), (ii) and (iii)
(d) (i), (ii), (iii) and (iv)

72. Project implementation may involve many steps. Arrange those in sequential order by using codes given below:
(i) Initiating the project.
(ii) Clarifying authority, responsibility and relationships.
(iii) Directing and Controlling
(iv) Establishing Control System
(v) Obtaining resources
Codes:
(a) (i), (ii), (iii), (iv), (v)
(b) (i), (ii), (iv), (v), (iii)
(c) (i), (ii), (iv), (iii), (v)
(d) (i), (ii), (v), (iv), (iii)

73. Which one among the following is not a model of Policy formulation and implementation?
(a) Institutional
(b) Garbage Can
(c) Historical
(d) Organized Anarchy

74. Who among the following are not associated with the group model of policy formulation and implementation?
(i) Arthur F. Bentley
(ii) Wayne Parsons
(iii) C. Wright Mills
(iv) Earl Latham
Select the correct answer from the codes given below:

Codes:

(a) (i) and (ii) (b) (ii) and (iii)
(c) (iii) and (iv) (d) (i) and (iv)

75. Which of the following statements about the Rural Electrification Policy of India, 2006 is not correct?
   (a) There has to be a provision of electricity to all Households by 2009.
   (b) A census village is to be taken as village for the purpose of rural electrification.
   (c) The State Governments were supposed to set up District Committees to review and coordinate the extension of electrification at the district level.
   (d) Central government shall endeavour to supply electricity to all areas including villages and hamlets.

ANSWERS

1. (b)	2. (a)	3. (d)	4. (a)	5. (d)
6. (a)	7. (a)	8. (d)	9. (b)	10. (a)
11. (b)	12. (b)	13. (c)	14. (c)	15. (d)
16. (b)	17. (a)	18. (c)	19. (a)	20. (a)
21. (d)	22. (c)	23. (d)	24. (b)	25. (b)
26. (b)	27. (d)	28. (d)	29. (c)	30. (d)
31. (b)	32. (d)	33. (d)	34. (c)	35. (b)
36. (d)	37. (c)	38. (b)	39. (d)	40. (a)
41. (d)	42. (b)	43. (b)	44. (a)	45. (d)
46. (b)	47. (d)	48. (b)	49. (b)	50. (a)
51. (b)	52. (d)	53. (b)	54. (d)	55. (b)
56. (a)	57. (b)	58. (c)	59. (b)	60. (a)
61. (d)	62. (d)	63. (a)	64. (d)	65. (b)
66. (d)	67. (b)	68. (d)	69. (b)	70. (d)
71. (d)	72. (d)	73. (c)	74. (b)	75. (d)

DECEMBER–2012

Note: This paper contains Sixty (60) multiple-choice questions, each question carrying two (2) marks. Candidate is expected to answer any Fifty (50) questions. In case more than Fifty (50) questions are attempted, only the first Fifty (50) questions will be evaluated.

PAPER–I

1. The English word 'Communication' is derived from the words
   (a) Communis and Communicare
   (b) Communist and Commune
   (c) Communism and Communalism
   (d) Communion and Common sense
2. Chinese Cultural Revolution leader Mao Zedong used a type of communication to talk to the masses is known as
   (a) Mass line communication
   (b) Group communication
   (c) Participatory communication
   (d) Dialogue communication
3. Conversing with the spirits and ancestors is termed as
   (a) Transpersonal communication
   (b) Intrapersonal communication
   (c) Interpersonal communication
   (d) Face-to-face communication
4. The largest circulated daily newspaper among the following is
   (a) The Times of India
   (b) The Indian Express
   (c) The Hindu
   (d) The Deccan Herald
5. The pioneer of the silent feature film in India was
   (a) K.A. Abbas
   (b) Satyajit Ray
   (c) B.R. Chopra
   (d) Dada Sahib Phalke
6. Classroom communication of a teacher rests on the principle of
   (a) Infotainment (b) Edutainment
   (c) Entertainment (d) Power equation
7. The missing number in the series: 0, 6, 24, 60, 120, ?, 336, is
   (a) 240 (b) 220
   (c) 280 (d) 210
8. A group of 7 members having a majority of boys is to be formed out of 6 boys and 4 girls. The number of ways the group can be formed is
   (a) 80 (b) 100
   (c) 90 (d) 110
9. The number of observations in a group is 40. The average of the first 10 members is 4.5 and the average of the remaining 30 members is 3.5. The average of the whole group is
   (a) 4 (b) 15/2
   (c) 15/4 (d) 6
10. If MOHAN is represented by the code KMFYL, then COUNT will be represented by
    (a) AMSLR (b) MSLAR
    (c) MASRL (d) SAMLR
11. The sum of the ages of two persons A and B is 50. 5 years ago, the ratio of their

ages was 5/3. The present age of A and B are

(a) 30, 20 (b) 35, 15
(c) 38, 12 (d) 40, 10

12. Let *a* means minus (–), *b* means multiplied by (×), C means divided by (÷) and D means plus (+). The value of 90 D 9 *a* 29 C 10 *b* 2 is

(a) 8 (b) 10
(c) 12 (d) 14

13. Consider the Assertion I and Assertion II and select the right code given below:

Assertion I : Even Bank-lockers are not safe. Thieves can break them and take away your wealth. But thieves cannot go to heaven. So you should keep your wealth in heaven.

Assertion II: The difference of skin- colour of beings is because of the distance from the sun and not because of some permanent traits. Skin-colour is the result of body's reaction to the sun and its rays.

Codes:

(a) Both the assertions I and II are forms of argument.
(b) The assertion I is an argument but the assertion II is not.
(c) The assertion II is an argument but the assertion I is not.
(d) Both the assertions are explanations of facts.

14. By which of the following proposition, the proposition 'some men are not honest' is contradicted?

(a) All men are honest.
(b) Some men are honest.
(c) No men are honest.
(d) All of the above.

15. A stipulative definition is

(a) always true
(b) always false
(c) sometimes true sometimes false
(d) neither true nor false

16. Choose the appropriate alternative given in the codes to replace the question mark.

Examiner – Examinee, Pleader – Client, Preceptor – ?

(a) Customer (b) Path-finder
(c) Perceiver (d) Disciple

17. If the statement 'most of the students are obedient' is taken to be true, which one of the following pair of statements can be claimed to be true?

I. All obedient persons are students.
II. All students are obedient.
III. Some students are obedient.
IV. Some students are not disobedient.

Codes:

(a) I & II (b) II & III
(c) III & IV (d) II & IV

18. Choose the right code:

A deductive argument claims that:

I. The conclusion does not claim something more than that which is contained in the premises.
II. The conclusion is supported by the premise/premises conclusively.
III. If the conclusion is false, then premise/premises may be either true or false.
IV. If premise/combination of premises is true, then conclusion must be true.

Codes:

(a) I and II (b) I and III
(c) II and III (d) All the above

On the basis of the data given in the following table, give answers to questions from 19 to 24:

Government Expenditures on Social Services
(As percent of total expenditure)

Sl.No.	Items	2007-08	2008-09	2009-10	2010-11
	Social Services	11.06	12.94	13.06	14.02
(a)	Education, sports & youth affairs	4.02	4.04	3.96	4.46
(b)	Health & family welfare	2.05	1.91	1.90	2.03
(c)	Water supply, housing, etc.	2.02	2.31	2.20	2.27
(d)	Information & broadcasting	0.22	0.22	0.20	0.22
(e)	Welfare to SC/ST & OBC	0.36	0.35	0.41	0.63
(f)	Labour and employment	0.27	0.27	0.22	0.25
(g)	Social welfare & nutrition	0.82	0.72	0.79	1.06
(h)	North-eastern areas	0.00	1.56	1.50	1.75
(i)	Other social services	1.29	1.55	1.87	1.34
	Total Government expenditure	100.00	100.00	100.00	100.00

19. How many activities in the social services are there where the expenditure has been less than 5 percent of the total expenditures incurred on the social services in 2008-09?
(a) One (b) Three
(c) Five (d) All the above

20. In which year, the expenditures on the social services have increased at the highest rate?
(a) 2007-08 (b) 2008-09
(c) 2009-10 (d) 2010-11

21. Which of the following activities remains almost stagnant in terms of share of expenditures?
(a) North-eastern areas
(b) Welfare to SC/ST & OBC
(c) Information & broadcasting
(d) Social welfare and nutrition

22. Which of the following item's expenditure share is almost equal to the remaining three items in the given years?
(a) Information & broadcasting
(b) Welfare to SC/ST and OBC
(c) Labour and employment
(d) Social welfare & nutrition

23. Which of the following items of social services has registered the highest rate of increase in expenditures during 2007-08 to 2010-11?
(a) Education, sports & youth affairs
(b) Welfare to SC/ST & OBC
(c) Social welfare & nutrition
(d) Overall social services

24. Which of the following items has registered the highest rate of decline in terms of expenditure during 2007-08 to 2009-10?
(a) Labour and employment
(b) Health & family welfare
(c) Social welfare & nutrition
(d) Education, sports & youth affairs

25. ALU stands for
(a) American Logic Unit
(b) Alternate Local Unit
(c) Alternating Logic Unit
(d) Arithmetic Logic Unit

26. A Personal Computer uses a number of chips mounted on a circuit board called
(a) Microprocessor (b) System Board
(c) Daughter Board (d) Mother Board

27. Computer Virus is a
(a) Hardware (b) Bacteria
(c) Software (d) None of these

28. Which one of the following is correct?

(a) $(17)_{10} = (17)_{16}$
(b) $(17)_{10} = (17)_8$
(c) $(17)_{10} = (10111)_2$
(d) $(17)_{10} = (10001)_2$

29. The file extension of MS-Word document in Office 2007 is ________.
(a) .pdf (b) .doc
(c) .docx (d) .txt

30. ______ is a protocol used by e-mail clients to download e-mails to your computer.
(a) TCP (b) FTP
(c) SMTP (d) POP

31. Which of the following is a source of methane?
(a) Wetlands
(b) Foam Industry
(c) Thermal Power Plants
(d) Cement Industry

32. 'Minamata disaster' in Japan was caused by pollution due to
(a) Lead (b) Mercury
(c) Cadmium (d) Zinc

33. Biomagnification means increase in the
(a) concentration of pollutants in living organisms
(b) number of species
(c) size of living organisms
(d) biomass

34. Nagoya Protocol is related to
(a) Climate change
(b) Ozone depletion
(c) Hazardous waste
(d) Biodiversity

35. The second most important source after fossil fuels contributing to India's energy needs is
(a) Solar energy (b) Nuclear energy
(c) Hydropower (d) Wind energy

36. In case of earthquakes, an increase of magnitude 1 on Richter Scale implies
(a) a ten-fold increase in the amplitude of seismic waves.
(b) a ten-fold increase in the energy of the seismic waves.
(c) two-fold increase in the amplitude of seismic waves.
(d) two-fold increase in the energy of seismic waves.

37. Which of the following is not a measure of Human Development Index?
(a) Literacy Rate
(b) Gross Enrolment
(c) Sex Ratio
(d) Life Expectancy

38. India has the highest number of students in colleges after
(a) the U.K. (b) the U.S.A.
(c) Australia (d) Canada

39. Which of the following statement(s) is/are not correct about the Attorney General of India?
1. The President appoints a person, who is qualified to be a Judge of a High Court, to be the Attorney General of India.
2. He has the right of audience in all the Courts of the country.
3. He has the right to take part in the proceedings of the Lok Sabha and the Rajya Sabha.
4. He has a fixed tenure.
Select the correct answer from the codes given below:

Codes:
(a) 1 and 4 (b) 2, 3 and 4
(c) 3 and 4 (d) 3 only

40. Which of the following prefix President Pranab Mukherjee desires to be discontinued while interacting with Indian dignitaries as well as in official notings?
1. His Excellency 2. Mahamahim
3. Hon'ble 4. Shri/Smt.

Select the correct answer from the codes given below:

Codes:

(a) 1 and 3 (b) 2 and 3
(c) 1 and 2 (d) 1, 2 and 3

41. Which of the following can be done under conditions of financial emergency?
 1. State Legislative Assemblies can be abolished.
 2. Central Government can acquire control over the budget and expenditure of States.
 3. Salaries of the Judges of the High Courts and the Supreme Court can be reduced.
 4. Right to Constitutional Remedies can be suspended.

Select the correct answer from the codes given below:

Codes:

(a) 1, 2 and 3 (b) 2, 3 and 4
(c) 1 and 2 (d) 2 and 3

42. Match List I with List II and select the correct answer from the codes given below:

List I

(a) Poverty Reduction Programme
(b) Human Development Scheme
(c) Social Assistance Scheme
(d) Minimum Need Scheme

List II

(i) Mid-day Meals
(ii) Indira Awas Yojana (IAY)
(iii) National Old Age Pension (NOAP)
(iv) MNREGA

Codes:	**A**	**B**	**C**	**D**
(a)	(iv)	(i)	(iii)	(ii)
(b)	(ii)	(iii)	(iv)	(i)
(c)	(iii)	(iv)	(i)	(ii)
(d)	(iv)	(iii)	(ii)	(i)

43. For an efficient and durable learning, learner should have
 (a) ability to learn only
 (b) requisite level of motivation only
 (c) opportunities to learn only
 (d) desired level of ability and motivation

44. Classroom communication must be
 (a) Teacher centric
 (b) Student centric
 (c) General centric
 (d) Textbook centric

45. The best method of teaching is to
 (a) impart information
 (b) ask students to read books
 (c) suggest good reference material
 (d) initiate a discussion and participate in it

46. Interaction inside the classroom should generate
 (a) Argument (b) Information
 (c) Ideas (d) Controversy

47. "Spare the rod and spoil the child", gives the message that
 (a) punishment in the class should be banned.
 (b) corporal punishment is not acceptable.
 (c) undesirable behaviour must be punished.
 (d) children should be beaten with rods.

48. The type of communication that the teacher has in the classroom, is termed as
 (a) Interpersonal
 (b) Mass communication
 (c) Group communication
 (d) Face-to-face communication

49. Which one of the following is an indication of the quality of a research journal?
 (a) Impact factor (b) h-index
 (c) g-index (d) i10-index

50. Good 'research ethics' means
 (a) Not disclosing the holdings of shares/stocks in a company that sponsors your research.

(b) Assigning a particular research problem to one Ph.D./research student only.
(c) Discussing with your colleagues confidential data from a research paper that you are reviewing for an academic journal.
(d) Submitting the same research manuscript for publishing in more than one journal.

51. Which of the following sampling methods is based on probability?
(a) Convenience sampling
(b) Quota sampling
(c) Judgement sampling
(d) Stratified sampling

52. Which one of the following references is written according to American Psychological Association (APA) format?
(a) Sharma, V. (2010). Fundamentals of Computer Science.
New Delhi: Tata McGraw Hill
(b) Sharma, V. 2010. Fundamentals of Computer Science.
New Delhi: Tata McGraw Hill
(c) Sharma.V. 2010. Fundamentals of Computer Science,
New Delhi: Tata McGraw Hill
(d) Sharma, V. (2010), Fundamentals of Computer Science,
New Delhi: Tata McGraw Hill

53. Arrange the following steps of research in correct sequence:
1. Identification of research problem
2. Listing of research objectives
3. Collection of data
4. Methodology
5. Data analysis
6. Results and discussion
(a) 1, 2, 3, 4, 5, 6 (b) 1, 2, 4, 3, 5, 6
(c) 2, 1, 3, 4, 5, 6 (d) 2, 1, 4, 3, 5, 6

54. Identify the incorrect statement:
(a) A hypothesis is made on the basis of limited evidence as a starting point for further investigations.
(b) A hypothesis is a basis for reasoning without any assumption of its truth.
(c) Hypothesis is a proposed explanation for a phenomenon.
(d) Scientific hypothesis is a scientific theory.

Read the following passage carefully and answer the questions (55 to 60):

The popular view of towns and cities in developing countries and of urbanization process is that despite the benefits and comforts it brings, the emergence of such cities connotes environmental degradation, generation of slums and squatters, urban poverty, unemployment, crimes, lawlessness, traffic chaos etc. But what is the reality? Given the unprecedental increase in urban population over the last 50 years from 300 million in 1950 to 2 billion in 2000 in developing countries, the wonder really is how well the world has coped, and not how badly.

In general, the urban quality of life has improved in terms of availability of water and sanitation, power, health and education, communication and transport. By way of illustration, a large number of urban residents have been provided with improved water in urban areas in Asia's largest countries such as China, India, Indonesia and Philippines. Despite that, the access to improved water in terms of percentage of total urban population seems to have declined during the last decade of 20th century, though in absolute numbers, millions of additional urbanites, have been provided improved services. These countries have made significant progress in the provision of sanitation services too, together, providing for an additional population of more than 293 million citizens within a decade (1990-2000). These improvements must be viewed against the backdrop of rapidly increasing urban population, fiscal crunch and strained human resources and efficient and quality-oriented public management.

55. The popular view about the process of urbanization in developing countries is
(a) Positive (b) Negative
(c) Neutral (d) Unspecified

56. The average annual increase in the number of urbanites in developing countries, from 1950 to 2000 A.D. was close to
(a) 30 million (b) 40 million
(c) 50 million (d) 60 million

57. The reality of urbanization is reflected in
(a) How well the situation has been managed.
(b) How badly the situation has gone out of control.
(c) How fast has been the tempo of urbanization.
(d) How fast the environment has degraded.

58. Which one of the following is not considered as an indicator of urban quality of life?
(a) Tempo of urbanization
(b) Provision of basic services
(c) Access to social amenities
(d) All of the above

59. The author in this passage has tried to focus on
(a) Extension of Knowledge
(b) Generation of Environmental Consciousness
(c) Analytical Reasoning
(d) Descriptive Statement

60. In the above passage, the author intends to state
(a) The hazards of the urban life
(b) The sufferings of the urban life
(c) The awareness of human progress
(d) The limits to growth

ANSWERS

1. (a)	2. (d)	3. (a)	4. (a)	5. (d)
6. (b)	7. (d)	8. (b)	9. (c)	10. (a)
11. (a)	12. (d)	13. (a)	14. (a)	15. (d)
16. (c)	17. (c)	18. (d)	19. (d)	20. (d)
21. (c)	22. (d)	23. (d)	24. (b)	25. (d)
26. (d)	27. (c)	28. (d)	29. (b)	30. (d)
31. (a)	32. (b)	33. (a)	34. (d)	35. (c)
36. (a)	37. (c)	38. (b)	39. (d)	40. (c)
41. (c)	42. (a)	43. (d)	44. (b)	45. (d)
46. (c)	47. (c)	48. (c)	49. (a)	50. (a)
51. (d)	52. (a)	53. (b)	54. (d)	55. (b)
56. (a)	57. (a)	58. (a)	59. (d)	60. (d)

PAPER–II

Note: This paper contains fifty (50) objective type questions, each question carrying two (2) marks. All questions are compulsory.

1. The book 'The Intellectual Crisis in American Public Administration' deals with
(a) New Public Administration
(b) Ecological Approach
(c) Developmental Approach
(d) Public Choice Approach

2. Which one of the following is not Taylor's mechanisms of Management?
(a) Using a routing system
(b) Employing a mnemonic system
(c) Employing a modern cost system
(d) Using a gang plank.

3. Which is not true about the Indian Independence Act, 1947?
   (a) Two Dominions were constituted – India and Pakistan.
   (b) The Suzerainty of His Majesty over the Indian States would lapse.
   (c) The Constituent Assembly would function as the Legislative Assembly for the interim period.
   (d) The Governor General would have limited power to assent to any Bill in the name of His Majesty.
4. The Royal Commission on Decentralisation was headed by
   (a) Lord Dalhousie
   (b) Lord HobHouse
   (c) Lord Rippon
   (d) Lord Mayo
5. Who of the following has described authority as the supreme co-ordinating power?
   (a) Karl Marx
   (b) F.W. Riggs
   (c) Max Weber
   (d) Mooney and Reiley
6. Which of the following are correct?
   (i) Theory of Social and Economic Organisation : Max Weber
   (ii) Models of Man : H.A. Simon
   (iii) Organisation and Management : F.W. Taylor
   (iv) Elements of Public Administration : F.M. Marx

   Codes:
   (a) (i), (ii) and (iv) (b) (i), (ii) and (iii)
   (c) (ii), (iii) and (iv) (d) (iv), (i) and (iii)
7. Which one of the following is not correct regarding Downs' categorization of Bureaucrats?
   (a) Climbers (b) Voters
   (c) Advocates (d) Statesmen
8. The phrase 'developmental bureaucracy' was coined by
   (a) La Palambora
   (b) Fred. W. Riggs
   (c) William Siffin
   (d) Edward Weidner
9. Which one of the following terms does not apply to the Vice-President of India?
   (a) He may be removed by Impeachment.
   (b) He may resign by writing to the President.
   (c) He may be removed by a Rajya Sabha Resolution and agreed to by the Lok Sabha.
   (d) He may seek re-election for any number of times.
10. The creation of the post of Policy Adviser in each department of England was suggested by
    (a) Fulton Committee
    (b) Royal Committee
    (c) Priestly Committee
    (d) Appleby Committee
11. Who called the Indian Civil Services as the Steel frame of Indian Constitution?
    (a) Pt. Jawaharlal Nehru
    (b) Sardar Patel
    (c) Dr. B.R. Ambedkar
    (d) Govind Ballabh Pant
12. What is not an advantage of seniority principle of promotion?
    (a) It is more objective and easier in application.
    (b) It eliminates internal strife for advancement.
    (c) It promotes general morale of the personnel.
    (d) It affects the self-improvement efforts of personnel.
13. A public personnel may face disciplinary action on the following basis:
    (i) Inattention to duty
    (ii) Inefficiency
    (iii) Insubordination
    (iv) Integrity

Codes:
(a) (i), (ii), (iii)
(b) (ii), (iii), (iv)
(c) (i), (iii), (iv)
(d) (i), (ii), (iii), (iv)

14. Which of the following motion is not related when the demand for grants are considered and passed by the Lok Sabha?
(a) Policy Cut Motion
(b) Censure Motion
(c) Economy Cut Motion
(d) Token Cut Motion

15. What is not true about a Money Bill?
(a) It can be introduced in any of the House.
(b) The Speaker has the final power to decide its character.
(c) The President or Governor, as the case may be, has limited powers in case of a Money Bill.
(d) It shall not be introduced or moved except on the recommendation of the President or Governor, as the case may be.

16. Which one of the following is not a Constitutional Body?
(a) Union Public Service Commission
(b) Finance Commission
(c) University Grants Commission
(d) Election Commission

17. The Statutory Status was given to the erstwhile Minorities Commission in the year:
(a) 1994 (b) 1978
(c) 1993 (d) 1990

18. Which Independent State merged into Indian Union with the consent of the people?
(a) Jammu & Kashmir
(b) Sikkim
(c) Goa
(d) Hyderabad

19. Who opposed the entry of Political Parties to the Local Bodies Election?
(a) Jawaharlal Nehru
(b) Jaiprakash Narayan
(c) Sardar Vallabhbhai Patel
(d) Abdul Kalam Azad

20. Which one of the following Institutions is responsible for Social Audit?
(a) Gram Sabha
(b) Village Panchayat
(c) Intermediate Panchayat (Panchayat Samiti)
(d) District Panchayat (Zila Parishad)

21. **Assertion (A):** Public Administration is concerned with the management of public programmes.
Reason (R): Public Administration is policy-making.
Codes:
(a) Both (A) and (R) are correct and (R) is the correct explanation of (A).
(b) Both (A) and (R) are correct, but (R) is not the correct explanation of (A).
(c) (A) is true, but (R) is false.
(d) (A) is false, but (R) is true.

22. **Assertion (A):** The Chief Secretary at the State level does not have a fixed tenure.
Reason (R): The First Administrative Reforms Commission did not make a specific recommendation in this regard.
Codes:
(a) Both (A) and (R) are correct and (R) is the correct explanation of (A).
(b) Both (A) and (R) are correct, but (R) is not the correct explanation of (A).
(c) (A) is true, but (R) is false.
(d) (A) is false, but (R) is true.

23. **Assertion (A):** Kautilya's King is the fountain of justice.
Reason (R): The King administers justice in accordance with edicts and evidence.

Codes:

(a) Both (A) and (R) are correct and (R) is the correct explanation of (A).
(b) Both (A) and (R) are correct, but (R) is not the correct explanation of (A).
(c) (A) is true, but (R) is false.
(d) (A) is false, but (R) is true.

24. **Assertion (A):** According to Bernard, authority resides in the relationship between a superior and its acceptance by a subordinate.
Reason (R): To Barnard, authority is the character of an order in an organization by virtue of which it is accepted.
Codes:
(a) Both (A) and (R) are correct and (R) is the correct explanation of (A).
(b) Both (A) and (R) are correct, but (R) is not the correct explanation of (A).
(c) (A) is true, but (R) is false.
(d) (A) is false, but (R) is true.

25. **Assertion (A):** The U.S.A. has no machinery analogous to the Whitley Councils of the U.K.
Reason (R): The U.S.A. is a traditional home of patronage bureaucracy.
Codes:
(a) Both (A) and (R) are correct and (R) is the correct explanation of (A).
(b) Both (A) and (R) are correct, but (R) is not the correct explanation of (A).
(c) (A) is true, but (R) is false.
(d) (A) is false, but (R) is true.

26. **Assertion (A):** Methods of legislative control over administration in a parliamentary system are different from those in a presidential one.
Reason (R): In the presidential system of the United States, powers of administration are vested in the President.
Codes:
(a) Both (A) and (R) are correct and (R) is the correct explanation of (A).
(b) Both (A) and (R) are correct, but (R) is not correct explanation of (A).
(c) (A) is true, but (R) is false.
(d) (A) is false, but (R) is true.

27. **Assertion (A):** Joint Consultative Machinery (JCM) promotes harmony between the employees and employer.
Reason (R): Redressal of employees grievances boosts up their moral.
Codes:
(a) Both (A) and (R) are correct and (R) is the correct explanation of (A).
(b) Both (A) and (R) are correct, but (R) is not the correct explanation of (A).
(c) (A) is true, but (R) is false.
(d) (A) is false, but (R) is true.

28. **Assertion (A):** The relationship of a Minister and a Civil Servant is that of a Master and a Servant.
Reason (R): A Civil Servant is required to render honest advice to the Minister.
Codes:
(a) Both (A) and (R) are correct and (R) is the correct explanation of (A).
(b) Both (A) and (R) are correct, but (R) is not correct explanation of (A).
(c) (A) is true, but (R) is false.
(d) (A) is false, but (R) is true.

29. **Assertion (A):** Transparency in administration is a salient feature of good governance.
Reason (R): The R.T.I. Act, 2005 has contributed in ensuring good governance.
Codes:
(a) Both (A) and (R) are correct and (R) is the correct explanation of (A).
(b) Both (A) and (R) are correct, but (R) is not the correct explanation of (A).
(c) (A) is true, but (R) is false.
(d) (A) is false, but (R) is true.

30. **Assertion (A):** Panchayati Raj Institutions could not become effective even after 73rd Constitutional Amendment.

Reason (R): State Governments have not given adequate powers, finances and personnel to Panchayati Raj Institutions.

Codes:

(a) Both (A) and (R) are correct and (R) is the correct explanation of (A).

(b) Both (A) and (R) are correct, but (R) is not the correct explanation of (A).

(c) (A) is true, but (R) is false.

(d) (A) is false, but (R) is true.

31. What is correct about the formation of new State/s in Indian Union? Use the codes given below for correct answer:

(i) It can be done by separation of territory from any existing State.

(ii) It can be done by uniting two or more States or part of States.

(iii) The creation of new States can be accomplished by an ordinary legislation.

(iv) The Parliament cannot alter the territory of the States without their consent.

Codes:

(a) (i), (ii), (iv) (b) (i), (ii), (iii)

(c) (i), (iii), (iv) (d) (ii), (iii), (iv)

32. Arrange the following in correct sequence of their evolution in the discipline of Public Administration.

Use the codes given below for answer:

(i) Motivation – Hygiene Theory

(ii) Ecological Approach

(iii) Needs Hierarchy Theory

(iv) Scientific Management Approach

Codes:

(a) (i), (ii), (iii), (iv) (b) (iv), (iii), (ii), (i)

(c) (iv), (iii), (i), (ii) (d) (iii), (iv), (i), (ii)

33. Arrange the following works in their chronological order. Use the codes given below for answer:

(i) Papers for the Science of Administration

(ii) The Principles of Scientific Management

(iii) Public Administration in a Time of Turbulence

(iv) Motivation and Personality

Codes:

(a) (i), (ii), (iii), (iv) (b) (ii), (i), (iv), (iii)

(c) (ii), (iii), (iv), (i) (d) (ii), (i), (iii), (iv)

34. Arrange Maslow's Hierarchy of Needs in descending order:

(i) Social Needs

(ii) Self-actualisation Needs

(iii) Physiological Needs

(iv) Ego Needs

(v) Security Needs

Codes:

(a) (iii), (v), (i), (iv) and (ii)

(b) (iii), (v), (i), (ii) and (iv)

(c) (ii), (iv), (i), (iii) and (v)

(d) (ii), (iv), (i), (v) and (iii)

35. Arrange the following experiments conducted by Elton Mayo in the chronological order and select the correct answer from the codes given below:

(i) Mass interviewing programme

(ii) Textile Mill Experiment

(iii) Illumination Experiment

(iv) Bank Wiring Experience

Codes:

(a) (ii), (iii), (i) and (iv)

(b) (iv), (i) and (ii)

(c) (iii), (i), (ii) and (iv)

(d) (ii), (iv) and (iii)

36. What is the correct sequence of Scientific Research? Answer by using the codes given below:

(i) Formulation of Hypothesis

(ii) Selection of Problem

(iii) Generalization

(iv) Collection and Analysis of data

Codes:

(a) (i), (ii), (iii), (iv) (b) (ii), (i), (iv), (iii)

(c) (iv), (ii), (iii), (i) (d) (ii), (iv), (i), (iii)

37. Arrange the following in order of sequence regarding requirements for a rational policy:
    (i) Identification of policy alternatives to attain goals.
    (ii) Analysing cost benefits of policy alternatives.
    (iii) Selecting the most efficient policy alternatives.
    (iv) Identification and ranking of goals.

    Codes:
    (a) (ii), (i), (iii), (iv) (b) (iv), (i), (ii) , (iii)
    (c) (iii), (ii), (iv), (i) (d) (i), (iii), (iv), (ii)

38. Match List I with List II and select the correct answer from the codes given below:

    List I
    A. Chester Barnard
    B. Herbert Simon
    C. M.P. Follett
    D. Douglas McGregor

    List II
    i. Models of Man
    ii. The Human Side of Enterprise
    iii. The Functions of the Executive
    iv. Creative Experience

Codes:	A	B	C	D
(a)	ii	i	iii	iv
(b)	i	ii	iv	iii
(c)	iii	i	iv	ii
(d)	iii	ii	i	iv

39. Match List I with List II and select the correct answer from the codes given below:

    List I
    A. Classical Theory
    B. Behavioural Approach
    C. Systems Approach
    D. Scientific Management

    List II
    i. Interaction between Organisation and Environment
    ii. Shop floor activities of Organisation
    iii. Formulation of Principles of Organisation
    iv. People in the Organisation

Codes:	A	B	C	D
(a)	iv	iii	i	ii
(b)	ii	iv	iii	i
(c)	iii	iv	i	ii
(d)	i	ii	iv	iii

40. Match List I with List II and select the correct answer from the codes given below:

    List I
    A. M.P. Follett B. Hergberg
    C. F.W. Riggs D. A. Maslow

    List II
    i. The Ecology of Public Administration
    ii. Dynamic Administration
    iii. Motivation and Personality
    iv. The Motivation to work

Codes:	A	B	C	D
(a)	ii	iv	i	iii
(b)	i	iv	iii	ii
(c)	iii	ii	i	iv
(d)	iv	iii	ii	i

41. Match List I with List II and select correct answer from the codes given below:

    List I
    A. Autocratic decision making
    B. Democratic decision making
    C. Rational decision making
    D. Consultative decision making

    List II
    i. Making decision with participation
    ii. Making decision with little consultation
    iii. Making decisions on the basis of calculation and choosing the best option
    iv. Making decision by inviting opinions

Codes:	A	B	C	D
(a)	i	ii	iii	iv
(b)	ii	i	iii	iv

(c)	iv	iii	ii	i
(d)	iii	ii	iv	i

42. Match List I with List II. Select the correct answer from the codes given below:

List I
A. Theory – X
B. Theory – Y
C. Job Enrichment
D. Job Enlargement

List II
i. Integration of behaviour is the key process in Management.
ii. Calls for vertical job loading.
iii. Based on the traditional conception of control and command.
iv. To provide more control over one's activities and greater participation in decisions.

Codes:	A	B	C	D
(a)	i	ii	iii	iv
(b)	iii	i	ii	iv
(c)	iii	i	iv	ii
(d)	i	iv	ii	iii

43. Match List I with List II. Select the correct answer from the codes given below:

List I
A. R. Blake and J. Mouton
B. Fred Fiedler
C. Robert House
D. P. Hersey and K. Blanchard

List II
i. Path-goal Theory
ii. Managerial grid
iii. Life Cycle Theory
iv. Theory of Leadership Effectiveness

Codes:	A	B	C	D
(a)	ii	iv	i	iii
(b)	iv	iii	ii	i
(c)	ii	iv	iii	i
(d)	i	ii	iv	iii

44. Match List I with List II. Select the correct answer from the codes given below:

List I
A. Power of the Union or the State to frame recruitment rules for public services
B. Safeguards and protection of civil servants against arbitrary executive orders
C. Public Service Commission for the Union and for the States
D. Creation of All India Services

List II
i. Article 309 ii. Article 310
iii. Article 311 iv. Article 312
v. Article 315

Codes:	A	B	C	D
(a)	i	ii	iii	v
(b)	ii	iii	v	iv
(c)	ii	iii	iv	v
(d)	i	iii	v	iv

45. Match List I with List II. Select the correct answer from the codes given below:

List I
A. Dismissal
B. Removal
C. Suspension
D. Compulsory Retirement

List II
i. Is not a punishment and an employee cannot claim protection against it under Article 311.
ii. Does not make one unfit for reemployment under the Government
iii. Makes one ineligible for reemployment under the Government
iv. Does not attract the safeguard of Article 311(2)

Codes:	A	B	C	D
(a)	i	ii	iii	iv
(b)	ii	iii	i	iv

(c)	iii	ii	i	iv
(d)	iv	i	ii	iii

46. Match List I with List II and select the correct answer by using the codes given below:

List I

A. Public Accounts Committee
B. Estimates Committee
C. Committee on Public Undertakings
D. Joint Parliamentary Committee

List II

i. Suggests alternative policies for bringing efficiency and economy in administration.
ii. Comprises of members from both the Houses.
iii. Scrutinizes the report of CAG in regard to the appropriation accounts of the Government.
iv. An adhoc Committee of the Parliament.

Codes:	**A**	**B**	**C**	**D**
(a)	i	ii	iii	iv
(b)	ii	i	iv	iii
(c)	iii	i	ii	iv
(d)	iii	ii	iv	i

Read the passage below and answer the questions that follow based on your understanding of the passage (47-50):

Kautilya's *Arthashastra* is a treatise concerned with political science and public administration as much as it is with statecraft, economy and diplomacy. It is written with the practical aim of showing how the Government ought to be run. It is also a highly polemical discourse that has astonished scholars, particularly on the themes of violence, conspiracies, espionage, etc. From that point of view, it is highly embarrassing to put forth the *Arthashastra* as the symbol of Indian political thought together with what Greece has to offer by way of Plato's *Republic* and *Laws,* and Aristotle's *Politics*. However, the fact remains that Kautilya recommended such measures only against enemies and traitors in emergencies. His proposition was that politics and ethics do not mix easily. That does not mean that Kautilya disregarded ethics or morality. What he meant was that there is a difference between individual and public morality. Kautilya made no serious attempt at theory building. At best, he described and discussed empirical reality and was normative and prescriptive in his treatment. He was keen on efficiency and rationality aspects of administration. His maxims of administration include characteristics like hierarchy, defined competence of each office, selection by merit, promotion by seniority, compensation, training and discipline. The *Arthashastra* has many insights and lessons to offer even to the present-day students and practitioners of public administration.

47. Explain the main focus of *Arthashastra*.
(a) It is concerned with statecraft, economy and diplomacy.
(b) It is only a concept formation.
(c) It is not a practical guide to administration.
(d) It is not a symbol of Indian Political Thought.

48. Why Kautilya insists the themes of violence, conspiracies and espionage?
(a) It is a practical way to run Government.
(b) It is a diplomatic strategy.
(c) It is a matter of normal administration.
(d) It is concerned with morality.

49. Analyse the relation between politics and ethics as mentioned by Arthashastra.
(a) The phenomena of politics and ethics are separate.
(b) Politics and ethics do not go together easily.
(c) Kautilya disregards ethics.
(d) Kautilya insists morality.

50. Kautilya concentrates more on practical administration but not on
(a) theory building.
(b) efficiency in administration.
(c) maximus of administration.
(d) the rationality of administration.

ANSWERS

1. (d)	2. (d)	3. (d)	4. (b)	5. (d)
6. (a)	7. (b)	8. (a)	9. (a)	10. (a)
11. (b)	12. (d)	13. (a)	14. (b)	15. (a)
16. (c)	17. (a)	18. (b)	19. (b)	20. (a)
21. (b)	22. (c)	23. (a)	24. (a)	25. (b)
26. (b)	27. (a)	28. (d)	29. (a)	30. (a)
31. (b)	32. (c)	33. (b)	34. (d)	35. (a)
36. (b)	37. (b)	38. (c)	39. (c)	40. (a)
41. (b)	42. (b)	43. (a)	44. (d)	45. (c)
46. (c)	47. (a)	48. (a)	49. (b)	50. (a)

PAPER–III

Note: This paper contains seventy five (75) objective type questions of two (2) marks each. All questions are compulsory.

1. "Administration, not the sword, is the key to enduring in the Great Society." Who said it?
   (a) Woodrow Wilson
   (b) Charles A. Bernard
   (c) Adams Brooks
   (d) M.E. Dimock
2. Separation between Politics and Administration had become an 'outworn credo'. Who said this?
   (a) Woodrow Wilson
   (b) Dwight Waldo
   (c) Frank J. Goodnow
   (d) Herbert Simon
3. "In the Science of Administration, whether public or private, the basic good is efficiency." Who among the following made this statement?
   (a) L. Urwick (b) Luther Gullick
   (c) Henry Fayol (d) J.D. Mooney
4. Post-modern Public Administration is based on a trilogy of post-behaviour tenets of Public Administration. Which of the following is the trilogy?
   (a) Critical Theory, New Left Ideology and Constructivism.
   (b) New Public Administration, Critical Theory and New Public Management.
   (c) New Public Administration, Public Choice Theory, and New Public Management.
   (d) Critical Theory, Phenomenology and Structural Theory.
5. Benn and Gaus contend that Publicness and Privateness in society are comprised of three dimensions. Identify the dimensions propounded by them.
   (a) Agency, institution and person
   (b) Agency, interest and access
   (c) Institution, interest and person
   (d) Interest, person and access
6. Public Management is the merger of normative orientation of traditional Public Administration and the instrumental orientation of General Management. Who said it?
   (a) Christopher Hood
   (b) Tullock
   (c) Van ban-Lane
   (d) Perry and Kramer
7. "We are living in the age of organization Man" who among the following had said it?
   (a) W.H. White
   (b) L.D. White
   (c) E.N. Gladden
   (d) Herold E. Dimock
8. **Assertion (A):** Open model theorists dislike the rigidity, inflexibility and anti-humanist view of bureaucracy.

Reason (R): Close-model theorists consider organization as a fluid network structure.

Codes:

(a) Both (A) and (R) are correct and (R) is the correct explanation of (A).
(b) Both (A) and (R) are correct, but (R) is not the correct explanation of (A).
(c) (A) is true, but (R) is false.
(d) (A) is false, but (R) is true.

9. Consider the following factors:
(i) Nature of work
(ii) Age of agency
(iii) Leadership
(iv) Location of the organizational units
Which one of the following principles of organization is determined by above stated factors?
(a) Hierarchy
(b) Unity of command
(c) Span of control
(d) Authority

10. Who among the following has called staff agency as 'it is her alter-ego'?
(a) James D. Mooney
(b) Henry Fayol
(c) Pffifner and Presthus
(d) Dimock, Dimock and Koeing

11. The concept of 'Unity of vision' is a core theme of
(a) Matrix organisations
(b) Missionary agencies
(c) Field based offices
(d) None of the above

12. Match List I with List II. Select the correct answer from the codes given below:

List I (Types of Leaders)
A. Climbers B. Conservers
C. Zealots D. Advocates

List II (Attributes)
1. Motivation and Commitment
2. Maximisation of Roles and Resources
3. Power, Income and Prestige
4. Sense of Public Interest
5. Minimum change

Codes:	A	B	C	D
(a)	3	5	1	2
(b)	2	4	1	2
(c)	3	5	2	1
(d)	1	2	3	4

13. "The process of transfer of administrative authority from lower to higher level of government is called centralization, the converse, decentralization". Who has given the above definition?
(a) Henry Fayol
(b) L.D. White
(c) J.C. Charlesworth
(d) James W. Fester

14. Match List I with List II. Select the correct answer from the codes given follow:

List I (Definitions)
A. An employee should receive orders from one superior only.
B. A man cannot serve two masters.
C. Every member of an organization should report to one and only one leader.
D. Each employee should have only one boss.

List II (Authors)
1. Henry Fayol
2. Pfiffner and Presthus
3. Dimock and Dimock
4. Gullick and Urwick

Codes:	A	B	C	D
(a)	1	4	2	3
(b)	1	3	2	4
(c)	2	3	4	1
(d)	3	2	4	1

15. The term 'Charisma' used by Max Weber in the ideal type is taken from which of the following languages?

(a) German (b) Greek
(c) Italian (d) Roman

16. Which of the following statements are correct in relation to F.W. Taylor's 'Scientific Management'?
(i) Time and methods of study may be used to find out the best way of performing a job.
(ii) Specialists may be employed to perform the tasks.
(iii) Workers must perform the job in whichever way they like.
(iv) Work place and incentives are not linked to output.
Select the correct answer from the codes given below:
Codes:
(a) Only (i) (b) (i), (ii)
(c) (i), (iii) (d) (iii), (iv)

17. Which of the following concepts are related to constructive conflict as suggested by Mary Parker Follet?
(i) Domination (ii) Compromise
(iii) Integration (iv) Delegation
Select the correct answer from the codes given below:
Codes:
(a) (i), (ii) (b) (iii), (iv)
(c) (i), (ii), (iii) (d) (ii), (iii), (iv)

18. **Assertion (A):** The satisfying administrative man is different from the maximising man.
Reason (R): The administrative man does not search for the optimal decision but a satisfactory one.
Codes:
(a) Both (A) and (R) are correct and (R) is the correct explanation of (A).
(b) Both (A) and (R) are correct, but (R) is not the correct explanation of (A).
(c) (A) is true, but (R) is false.
(d) (A) is false, but (R) is true.

19. Match List I with List II. Select the correct answer from the codes given below:
List I (Author)
A. Mooney and Reiley
B. Etzioni
C. Marwick
D. Gowldner
List II (Types of Leadership)
1. Institutionalists, Specialists, Hybrids
2. Titular leaders, Controllers, true organizers
3. Officials, Informal and formal leaders
4. Locals and Cosmopolitans

Codes:	**A**	**B**	**C**	**D**
(a)	1	3	4	2
(b)	2	3	1	4
(c)	2	4	1	3
(d)	4	2	3	1

20. Clayton Alderfer attempted to rework Maslow's need hierarchy to align it more closely with empirical research. His revised need hierarchy is labelled as
(a) Theory of Needs
(b) Self efficiency theory
(c) ERG theory
(d) Equity theory

21. Who is the author of the book titled 'Bureaucrazy'?
(a) Michael Crozier
(b) M.K. Kaw
(c) P.N. Haxer
(d) Veerappa Moily

22. Which of the following is not the assumption of theory X?
(a) Most people must be corrected and controlled.
(b) The average human being prefers to be directed.
(c) Most of the people do not dislike work inherently.
(d) People have relatively little ambitions and wants.

23. Which of the following are the foci areas of research in Comparative Public Administration as identified by Ferrel Heady?
(i) Component approach
(ii) Modified traditional approach
(iii) Development system model
(iv) General system model
(v) Middle range theory
Select the correct answer by using codes given below:
Codes:
(a) (i), (ii), (iii), (iv) (b) (ii), (iii), (iv), (v)
(c) (i), (iii), (iv), (v) (d) (i), (ii), (iii), (v)

24. Which of the following are the features of Diffracted Society according to Fred Riggs"?
(i) Universalilsm (ii) Ascription
(iii) Attainment (iv) Particularism
Select the correct answer from the codes given below:
Codes:
(a) (i), (ii), (iii) (b) (ii), (iii), (iv)
(c) (i), (ii), (iv) (d) (i), (iii), (iv)

25. Which one of the following is the concern of the Hatch Act 1919?
(a) Political activities of Civil Servants
(b) Right to strike
(c) Right to form association
(d) Machinery for Negotiation

26. Who is in-charge of the office of Public Service and Science in Britain?
(a) Lord Chancellor
(b) Chancellor of Exchequer
(c) The Chancellor of the Duchy of Lancaster
(d) Cabinet Secretary

27. In Britain, responsibility for Central Co-ordination and Management of Civil Services is divided between:
(a) Treasury and Home Department
(b) Prime Minister and Home Department
(c) Cabinet Office and Prime Minister's Office
(d) Cabinet Office and Treasury

28. Comparative Public Administration is not concerned with
(i) Search for the theory of administration.
(ii) Practical application of knowledge.
(iii) Observance of Cultural factors.
(iv) Study of ongoing problems of Public Administration.
Select the correct answer from the codes given below:
Codes:
(a) (i), (ii), (iii) (b) (ii), (iii), (iv)
(c) (i), (ii), (iv) (d) (i), (iii), (iv)

29. What type of Budgetary method is used in the context of Development Administration?
(a) Performance Budget
(b) Block vote Budget Allocation System
(c) Zero-base Budget
(d) Line-Item Budget

30. Planning in Development Administration with the objective of optimal location of services like Schools, Hospitals and Banks etc. is known as
(a) Local planning
(b) Spatial planning
(c) Vertical planning
(d) Horizontal planning

31. Catastrophe theory developed by Rene Thom for the study of development administration has been borrowed from
(a) Physics
(b) Applied Mathematics
(c) Applied Economics
(d) Disaster Management

32. Who expressed the view that development administration requires a parallel strengthening of the democratic and representative political process?

(a) F.W. Riggs (b) Lucian Pye
(c) La Palombara (d) George Cant

33. Which of the following features of Development Administration are shared by New Public Administration?
(i) Effective coordination
(ii) Change orientation
(iii) Temporal dimension
(iv) Goal orientation
(v) Ecological perspective
Codes:
(a) (ii) and (iv) (b) (i) and (ii)
(c) (iii) and (v) (d) (iv) and (v)

34. Under which Article of the Indian Constitution, the President is empowered to promulgate an ordinance?
(a) Article 53 (b) Article 54
(c) Article 122 (d) Article 123

35. Consider the following statements regarding the Union Council of Ministers and select the correct answer from the codes given below:
(i) The first Administrative Reforms Commission recommended that the number of Ministers including Prime Minister should be sixteen.
(ii) The Constitution (Ninety-first Amendment) Act, 2003 specify that the total number of Ministers shall not exceed 15 percent of the total number of members of the House of people.
(iii) The Constitution has classified the members of the Council of Ministers into different ranks.
(iv) The National Democratic Alliance Government (headed by Mr. A.B. Vajpai) had all the three types Ministers.
Codes:
(a) (i), (ii) (b) (ii), (iii)
(c) (iii), (iv) (d) (ii), (iv)

36. Which of the following statements is not correct about the National Technical Research Organisation (NTRO)?
(a) It was constituted in 2004 after Kargil War.
(b) If is located in P.M.O. under the supervision of National Defence Adviser.
(c) R.A.W., I.B., and Police Stations of the Country are interlinked with NTRO.
(d) It stocks technical intelligence reports.

37. What is the legal basis for the establishment of Cabinet Committees in India?
(a) Rules for Parliamentary procedure.
(b) Allocation of Business Rules, Government of India.
(c) Resolution of Cabinet.
(d) Decision of Prime Minister.

38. Which of the following has been described as 'the master key to good governance' by the Second Administrative Reforms Commission?
(a) Promoting e-governance
(b) Social Capital—A shared Destiny
(c) Ethics in Governance
(d) Right to information

39. 'The Chief Secretary's job is not a technicians' or even a professionals', he is not a knowledgeable engineer nor even a first class magistrate, he is a part of process of Government and in democratic republic, part of human process'. Who made this statement?
(a) Mohan Mukharjee
(b) Dharmvir
(c) E.N. Mangat Rai
(d) V.D. Murti

40. Which one of the following is the first law on Freedom of information?
(a) Freedom of Information Act (U.K.)
(b) Freedom of Press Act (Sweden)

(c) Freedom of Information Act (USA)
(d) Freedom of Information Act (India)

41. Arrange the following stages in Disciplinary proceedings for major penalty in a correct sequential order and select the answer from the codes given below:
   (i) Compliant followed by Preliminary investigation.
   (ii) Acceptance of charges or rejection of charges.
   (iii) Appointment of Inquiry Officer.
   (iv) Consultation with UPSC.
   (v) Submission of Report by Investigation Officer.
   (vi) Final order.

   Codes:
   (a) (i), (ii), (iii), (iv), (v), (vi)
   (b) (i), (ii), (iii), (iv), (vi), (v)
   (c) (i), (ii), (iii), (v), (iv), (vi)
   (d) (i), (ii), (iii), (v), (vi), (iv)

42. Consider the following statements regarding All India Services established as per the provision of Article 312.
   (i) All India Services are created consequent upon a resolution of Council of States declaring that it is necessary and expedient in the national interest to create an All India Service.
   (ii) The Parliament may provide for the creation of new All India Service by making a law as per the resolution of the council of states.
   (iii) The Supreme Court has also directed the Government of India to take steps for setting up an All India Judicial Service.
   (iv) All the services proposed to be established under the All India Service (Amendment) Act, 1963 have been established.

   Select the correct answer from the codes given below:

   Codes:
   (a) (i), (ii) (b) (i), (ii), (iii)
   (c) (i), (ii), (iv) (d) (i), (ii), (iii), (iv)

43. "The heart of an administrator must be located in his brain"—This statement is given by
   (a) Paul H. Appleby
   (b) S.V.B. Patel
   (c) A.D. Gorwala
   (d) Jawaharlal Nehru

44. Which of the following Committee/ Commisssion recommended the repeal of Article 310 and Article 311 in the Indian Constitution.
   (a) First Administrative Reforms Commission.
   (b) Rajamannar Committee
   (c) P.C. Hota Committee
   (d) Second Administrative Reforms Commission.

45. Under which of the following provision of the Indian Constitution an appropriate legislature may by law regulate the recruitment and conditions of service of Union or State Public Services?
   (a) Article 308 (b) Article 309
   (c) Article 310 (d) Article 311

46. Which one of the following recommended that the name of the Central Police Training College should be changed as the National Police Academy?
   (a) Gore Committee
   (b) National Police Commission
   (c) The Kohli Committee
   (d) First Administrative Reforms Commission

47. Match List I with List II and select the correct answer from the codes given below:

List I (Concepts)
A. Capital expenditure
B. Revenue expenditure
C. Gross Fiscal deficit
D. Monetary deficit
List II (Explanations)
1. Expenditure towards normal running of Government
2. Expenditure for creating concrete assets of a material character.
3. Increase in the net credit by Reserve Bank of India to Central Government
4. Resources gap in terms of excess of total Government expenditure over revenue receipts and grants.

Codes:	A	B	C	D
(a)	1	2	4	3
(b)	2	1	4	3
(c)	2	3	4	1
(d)	3	1	2	4

48. Which of the following statements about Budget are correct?
(i) Budget is an economic horoscope of the country.
(ii) Budget is a political document which provides a glimpse of entire philosophy of Government.
(iii) Budget is formulated by legislature.
(iv) Budget is nut-bolt of public policy.
Select the correct answer from the codes given below:
Codes:
(a) (i), (ii) (b) (i), (ii), (iii)
(c) (i), (iii), (iv) (d) (i), (ii), (iv)

49. Which of the following statements about controller & Auditor General of India are correct?
(i) It is a British Legacy.
(ii) It is independent and autonomous to undertake public audit.
(iii) It does not have the power to determine the nature and extent of the audit.
(iv) It has the inherent right to determine what should be included in the audit report.
Select the correct answer by using the codes given below:
Codes:
(a) (i), (ii), (iii) (b) (i), (ii), (iv)
(c) (ii), (iii), (iv) (d) (i), (ii), (iii), (iv)

50. Which of the following are considered as the criteria for selecting a research topic?
(i) Relevance
(ii) Utility
(iii) Feasibility
(iv) Ethical Acceptability
Select the correct answer using codes given below:
Codes:
(a) (i), (ii), (iii) (b) (i), (iii), (iv)
(c) (ii), (iii), (iv) (d) (i), (ii), (iii), (iv)

51. Which of the following observation about actual engagement behaviour of workers on job with machine is termed as
(a) Simple observation
(b) Systematic observation
(c) Participant observation
(d) Non-participant observation

52. Which of the following is not a type of Attitude Scale?
(a) Summated Rating Scale
(b) Thurston's Equal Appearing Interval Scale
(c) Graphic Scale
(d) Bagardus Social Distance Scale

53. Consider the following statements regarding interview method of data collection and select the incorrect one.
(a) It is the most common method for collecting qualitative information.
(b) It is a method which is usually conducted face to face and involves one interviewer and one interviewee.

(c) It is technique designed to elicit a detailed view point of the informants.
(d) Interviewer's notes may not be considered as research data.

54. Public Methodology affording testing of conclusions is an inherent article of faith of Scientific Method. The reasons are:
(i) It helps in replication of results.
(ii) It explains the context and conditions of Social Science Research.
(iii) It fulfils the scientific obligations for bringing improvements in research tools.
(iv) It helps in exposing inconsistencies in the Social Science Research.
Select the correct answer using codes given below:
Codes:
(a) (i), (ii) (b) (i), (iii)
(c) (i), (ii), (iii) (d) (i), (ii), (iii), (iv)

55. Which report of Second Administrative Reforms Commission is related to 'State and District Administration'?
(a) 12th (b) 13th
(c) 14th (d) 15th

56. Which of the following body remarked that the 'Block Development Office' should be spinal cord of the rural development process?
(a) Balwant Rai Mehta Committee
(b) K. Santhanam Committee
(c) Ashok Mehta Committee
(d) G.V.K. Rao Committee

57. The State Election Commission conducts, controls and supervises municipal elections as per
(a) Article 325 (b) Article 241
(c) Article 243-K (d) Article 245-D

58. K. Shanthanam Committee (1963) was set up to look into
(a) Personnel of Panchayati Raj Institutions
(b) Finances of Panchayati Raj Institutions
(c) Personnel of Urban Local Self Government
(d) Finances of Urban Local Self Government

59. Which of the following are parts of the classification of Urban Poverty Alleviation Programmes made by National Urbanization Commission?
(i) Programmes for employment generation.
(ii) Shelter and Physical environment related programmes.
(iii) Nutrition supplement programmes.
(iv) Development of institutional capacities of service agencies.
Select the correct answer from the codes given below:
Codes:
(a) (i), (ii), (iii) (b) (i), (ii), (iii), (iv)
(c) (ii), (iii), (iv) (d) (i), (iii), (iv)

60. "As the periodicity of constitution of the Central Finance commission is predictable, the State should time the constitution of their State Finance Commissions suitably." It was observed by
(a) 10th Finance Commission
(b) 11th Finance Commission
(c) 12th Finance Commission
(d) 13th Finance Commission

61. "Gram Sabha means a body consisting of persons registered in electoral rolls relating to a village comprised with area of panchayat at the village level." Which of the following has given above description of Gram Sabha?
(a) Balwant Rai Mehta Committee
(b) Ashok Mehta Committee
(c) L.M. Singvi Committee
(d) Constitution of India

62. The term 'Social Justice' is originally based on the teachings of
   (a) St. Thomas Aquinas
   (b) Karl Marx
   (c) John Rawls
   (d) B.R. Ambedkar

63. The Central Social Welfare Board was established by:
   (a) Parliamentary enactment
   (b) Resolution of Cabinet
   (c) Registration under company Act, 1956
   (d) The order of the President

64. The interaction between Government and NGOs in India mostly relates to
   (i) Policies and legislation related to disadvantaged sections.
   (ii) Economic policies
   (iii) Operational collaboration for programmes with or without Government funding.
   (iv) Peaceful protest movement of people in which NGOs are involved.
   Select the correct answer from the codes given below:
   Codes:
   (a) (i), (ii) (b) (i), (ii), (iv)
   (c) (i), (iii), (iv) (d) (iii), (iv)

65. What is the name of the integrated scheme for women empowerment being implemented by the Ministry of Women and Child Development?
   (a) TRYSEM (b) DWACRA
   (c) Swayamsidha (d) Swabhiman

66. Policy monitoring may lead to which of the following actions?
   (i) Strengthening and improving the policy programmes.
   (ii) Replanning of the policy programme.
   (iii) Cancellation of the policy programme.
   Select the correct answer from the codes given below:
   Codes:
   (a) (i) (b) (i), (ii)
   (c) (i), (ii), (iii) (d) (i), (iii)

67. **Assertion (A):** Public Policy is whatever Governments choose to do or not to do.
   Reason (R): Policy making is clearly related to decision making.
   Codes:
   (a) Both (A) and (R) are correct and (R) is the correct explanation of (A).
   (b) Both (A) and (R) are correct, but (R) is not the correct explanation of (A).
   (c) (A) is true, but (R) is false.
   (d) (A) is false, but (R) is true.

68. Arrange the following steps in Policy Analysis in the correct sequence and select the correct answer from the codes given below:
   (i) Problem identification
   (ii) Forecasting and evaluating the alternatives.
   (iii) Determining alternative courses of action.
   (iv) Policy choice
   Codes:
   (a) (i), (ii), (iii), (iv) (b) (i), (iii), (ii), (iv)
   (c) (ii), (iv), (i), (iii) (d) (ii), (iii), (iv), (i)

69. Match List I and List II and select the correct answer from the codes given below:
   List I (Authors)
   A. Thomas R. Dye
   B. B.W. Hogwood and L.A. Gunn
   C. A. Wildavsky
   D. A. Massey
   List II (Books)
   1. Policy Analysis for the Real World
   2. Speaking Truth 'to power the Art and Craft of Policy Analysis
   3. Managing the Public Sector
   4. Understanding Public Policy

Codes:	A	B	C	D
(a)	3	2	1	4
(b)	4	1	2	3
(c)	2	3	4	1
(d)	1	4	3	2

70. Which of the following states does not have 50 percentage seats reserved for women in the local self government institutions/Panchayati Raj Institutions as on March, 2012?
(a) Tripura (b) Tamil Nadu
(c) Odisha (d) Rajasthan

71. Which of the following does not have Panchayati Raj Institutions?
(a) Andaman and Nicobar Islands
(b) Daman and Diu
(c) Delhi
(d) Lakshadweep

72. Which of the following committees recommended the Panchayats (Extension to the Scheduled Areas) Act?
(a) B.D. Sharma Committee
(b) Second Administrative Reforms Commission
(c) M.M. Punchhi Commission
(d) Dileep Singh Bhuria Committee

73. In which part of the Constitution of India, 'Economic and Social Planning' is included?
(a) Union List (b) State List
(c) Concurrent List (d) Eighth Schedule

74. How many Public Sector Undertakings were recognized as 'Maharatnas' in India till the year 2011?
(a) Three (b) Five
(c) Seven (d) Nine

75. Which one of the following is not the correct form and method of Public Private Partnership?
(a) Lease, Concessions, Greenfield Projects and Divestiture.
(b) Management Contract, Lease, Brown field Project and Concessions.
(c) B.O.O., B.O.T., B.O.O.M., and Management Contract
(d) Divestiture, Lease, Greenfield Projects and Public Services.

ANSWERS

1. (b)	2. (b)	3. (b)	4. (d)	5. (b)
6. (d)	7. (a)	8. (c)	9. (c)	10. (c)
11. (a)	12. (a)	13. (b)	14. (a)	15. (b)
16. (b)	17. (c)	18. (a)	19. (b)	20. (c)
21. (b)	22. (c)	23. (b)	24. (d)	25. (a)
26. (c)	27. (d)	28. (c)	29. (a)	30. (b)
31. (b)	32. (b)	33. (a)	34. (d)	35. (a)
36. (c)	37. (b)	38. (d)	39. (c)	40. (b)
41. (c)	42. (b)	43. (b)	44. (d)	45. (b)
46. (c)	47. (b)	48. (d)	49. (b)	50. (d)
51. (b)	52. (c)	53. (d)	54. (c)	55. (d)
56. (d)	57. (c)	58. (b)	59. (b)	60. (c)
61. (d)	62. (a)	63. (c)	64. (c)	65. (c)
66. (c)	67. (a)	68. (b)	69. (b)	70. (b)
71. (c)	72. (d)	73. (c)	74. (b)	75. (d)

JUNE–2012

Note: This paper contains Sixty (60) multiple-choice questions, each question carrying two (2) marks. Candidate is expected to answer any Fifty (50) questions. In case more than Fifty (50) questions are attempted, only the first Fifty (50) questions will be evaluated.

PAPER–I

1. Video-Conferencing can be classified as one of the following types of communication:
   (a) Visual one way
   (b) Audio-Visual one way
   (c) Audio-Visual two way
   (d) Visual two way

2. MC National University of Journalism and Communication is located at
   (a) Lucknow (b) Bhopal
   (c) Chennai (d) Mumbai

3. All India Radio (A.I.R.) for broadcasting was named in the year
   (a) 1926 (b) 1936
   (c) 1946 (d) 1956

4. In India for broadcasting TV programmes which system is followed?
   (a) NTCS (b) PAL
   (c) NTSE (d) SECAM

5. The term 'DAVP' stands for
   (a) Directorate of Advertising & Vocal Publicity
   (b) Division of Audio-Visual Publicity
   (c) Department of Audio-Visual Publicity
   (d) Directorate of Advertising & Visual Publicity

6. The term "TRP" is associated with TV shows stands for
   (a) Total Rating Points
   (b) Time Rating Points
   (c) Thematic Rating Points
   (d) Television Rating Points

7. Which is the number that comes next in the following sequence?
   2, 6, 12, 20, 30, 42, 56, ____
   (a) 60 (b) 64
   (c) 72 (d) 70

8. Find the next letter for the series YVSP ………
   (a) N (b) M
   (c) O (d) L

9. Given that in a code language, '645' means 'day is warm'; '42' means 'warm spring' and '634' means 'spring is sunny'; which digit represents 'sunny'?
   (a) 3 (b) 2
   (c) 4 (d) 5

10. The basis of the following classification is:
    'first President of India' 'author of Godan' 'books in my library', 'blue things' and 'students who work hard'
    (a) Common names
    (b) Proper names
    (c) Descriptive phrases
    (d) Indefinite description

11. In the expression 'Nothing is larger than itself' the relation 'is larger than' is
    (a) antisymmetric (b) asymmetrical
    (c) intransitive (d) irreflexive

12. **Assertion (A):** There are more laws on the books today than ever before, and

more crimes being committed than ever before.

Reason (R): Because to reduce crime we must eliminate the laws.

Choose the correct answer from below:

(a) (A) is true, (R) is doubtful and (R) is not the correct explanation of (A).
(b) (A) is false, (R) is true and (R) is the correct explanation of (A).
(c) (A) is doubtful, (R) is doubtful and (R) is not the correct explanation of (A).
(d) (A) is doubtful, (R) is true and (R) is not the correct explanation of (A).

13. If the proposition "All men are not mortal" is true then which of the following inferences is correct? Choose from the code given below:
   1. "All men are mortal" is true.
   2. "Some men are mortal" is false.
   3. "No men are mortal" is doubtful.
   4. "All men are mortal" is false.

   Codes:
   (a) 1, 2 and 3 (b) 2, 3 and 4
   (c) 1, 3 and 4 (d) 1 and 3

14. Determine the nature of the following definition: "Abortion" means the ruthless murdering of innocent beings.
   (a) Lexical (b) Persuasive
   (c) Stipulative (d) Theoretical

15. Which one of the following is not an argument?
   (a) Devadutt does not eat in the day so he must be eating at night.
   (b) If Devadutt is growing fat and if he does not eat during the day, he will be eating at night.
   (c) Devadutt eats in the night so he does not eat during the day.
   (d) Since Devadutt does not eat in the day, he must be eating in the night.

16. Venn diagram is a kind of diagram to
   (a) represent and assess the validity of elementary inferences of syllogistic form.
   (b) represent but not assess the validity of elementary inferences of syllogistic form.
   (c) represent and assess the truth of elementary inferences of syllogistic form.
   (d) assess but not represent the truth of elementary inferences of syllogistic form.

17. Reasoning by analogy leads to
   (a) certainty
   (b) definite conclusion
   (c) predictive conjecture
   (d) surety

18. Which of the following statements are false? Choose from the code given below:
   1. Inductive arguments always proceed from the particular to the general.
   2. A cogent argument must be inductively strong.
   3. A valid argument may have a false premise and a false conclusion.
   4. An argument may legitimately be spoken of as 'true' or 'false'.

   Codes:
   (a) 2, 3 and 4 (b) 1 and 3
   (c) 2 and 4 (d) 1 and 2

19. Six persons A, B, C, D, E and F are standing in a circle. B is between F and C, A is between E and D, F is to the left of D. Who is between A and F?
   (a) B (b) C
   (c) D (d) E

20. The price of petrol increases by 25%. By what percentage must a customer reduce the consumption so that the earlier bill on the petrol does not alter?

(a) 20% (b) 25%
(c) 30% (d) 33.33%

21. If Ram knows that *y* is an integer greater than 2 and less than 7 and Hari knows that *y* is an integer greater than 5 and less than 10, then they may correctly conclude that
(a) *y* can be exactly determined
(b) *y* may be either of two values
(c) *y* may be any of three values
(d) there is no value of *y* satisfying these conditions

22. Four pipes can fill a reservoir in 15, 20, 30 and 60 hours respectively. The first one was opened at 6 AM, second at 7 AM, third at 8 AM and the fourth at 9 AM. When will the reservoir be filled?
(a) 11 AM (b) 12 Noon
(c) 1 PM (d) 1:30 PM

The total electricity generation in a country is 97 GW. The contribution of various energy sources is indicated in percentage terms in the Pie Chart given below;

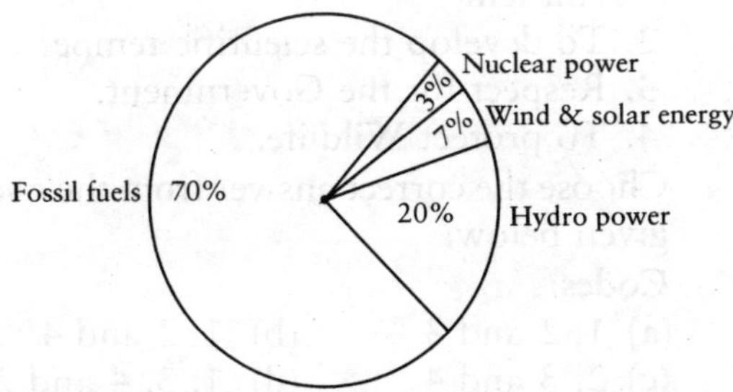

23. What is the contribution of wind and solar power in absolute terms in the electricity generation?
(a) 6.79 GW (b) 19.4 GW
(c) 9.7 GW (d) 29.1 GW

24. What is the contribution of renewable energy sources in absolute terms in the electricity generation?
(a) 29.1 GW (b) 26.19 GW
(c) 67.9 GW (d) 97 GW

25. TCP/IP is necessary if one is to connect to the
(a) Phone lines (b) LAN
(c) Internet (d) a Server

26. Each character on the keyboard of computer has an ASCII value which stands for
(a) American Stock Code for Information Interchange
(b) American Standard Code for Information Interchange
(c) African Standard Code for Information Interchange
(d) Adaptable Standard Code for Information Change

27. Which of the following is not a programming language?
(a) Pascal (b) Microsoft Office
(c) Java (d) C++

28. Minimum number of bits required to store any 3 digit decimal number is equal to
(a) 3 (b) 5
(c) 8 (d) 10

29. Internet explorer is a type of
(a) Operating System
(b) Compiler
(c) Browser
(d) IP address

30. POP3 and IMAP are e-mail accounts in which
(a) One automatically gets one's mail everyday
(b) One has to be connected to the server to read or write one's mail
(c) One only has to be connected to the server to send and receive email
(d) One does not need any telephone lines

31. Irritation in eyes is caused by the pollutant
(a) Sulphur dioxide (b) Ozone
(c) PAN (d) Nitrous oxide

32. Which is the source of chlorofluorocarbons?
(a) Thermal power plants
(b) Automobiles
(c) Refrigeration and Airconditioning
(d) Fertilizers

33. Which of the following is not a renewable natural resource?
(a) Clean air (b) Fertile soil
(c) Fresh water (d) Salt

34. Which of the following parameters is not used as a pollution indicator in water?
(a) Total dissolved solids
(b) Coliform count
(c) Dissolved oxygen
(d) Density

35. S and P waves are associated with
(a) floods (b) wind energy
(c) earthquakes (d) tidal energy

36. Match List I and List II and select the correct answer from the codes given below:

List I
(A) Ozone hole
(B) Greenhouse effect
(C) Natural hazards
(D) Sustainable development

List II
(i) Tsunami (ii) UV radiations
(iii) Methane (iv) Eco-centrism

Codes:	A	B	C	D
(a)	(ii)	(iii)	(i)	(iv)
(b)	(iii)	(ii)	(i)	(iv)
(c)	(iv)	(iii)	(i)	(ii)
(d)	(iv)	(ii)	(iii)	(i)

37. Indian Institute of Advanced Study is located at
(a) Dharmshala (b) Shimla
(c) Solan (d) Chandigarh

38. Indicate the number of Regional Offices of National Council of Teacher Education.
(a) 04 (b) 05
(c) 06 (d) 08

39. Which of the following rights was considered the "Heart and Soul" of the Indian Constitution by Dr. B.R. Ambedkar?
(a) Freedom of Speech
(b) Right to Equality
(c) Right to Freedom of Religion
(d) Right to Constitutional Remedies

40. Who among the following created the office of the District Collector in India?
(a) Lord Cornwallis
(b) Warren Hastings
(c) The Royal Commission on Decentralisation
(d) Sir Charles Metcalfe

41. The Fundamental Duties of a citizen include
1. Respect for the Constitution, the National Flag and the National Anthem
2. To develop the scientific temper.
3. Respect for the Government.
4. To protect Wildlife.

Choose the correct answer from the codes given below:

Codes:
(a) 1, 2 and 3 (b) 1, 2 and 4
(c) 2, 3 and 4 (d) 1, 3, 4 and 2

42. The President of India takes oath
(a) to uphold the sovereignty and integrity of India.
(b) to bear true faith and allegiance to the Constitution of India.
(c) to uphold the Constitution and Laws of the country.
(d) to preserve, protect and defend the Constitution and the law of the country.

43. If you get an opportunity to teach a visually challenged student along with normal students, what type of treatment would you like to give him in the class?
   (a) Not giving extra attention because majority may suffer.
   (b) Take care of him sympathetically in the class-room.
   (c) You will think that blindness is his destiny and hence you cannot do anything.
   (d) Arrange a seat in the front row and try to teach at a pace convenient to him.

44. Which of the following is not a characteristic of a good achievement test?
   (a) Reliability (b) Objectivity
   (c) Ambiguity (d) Validity

45. Which of the following does not belong to a projected aid?
   (a) Overhead projector
   (b) Blackboard
   (c) Epidiascope
   (d) Slide projector

46. For a teacher, which of the following methods would be correct for writing on the blackboard?
   (a) Writing fast and as clearly as possible.
   (b) Writing the matter first and then asking students to read it.
   (c) Asking a question to students and then writing the answer as stated by them.
   (d) Writing the important points as clearly as possible.

47. A teacher can be successful if he/she
   (a) helps students in becoming better citizens
   (b) imparts subject knowledge to students
   (c) prepares students to pass the examination
   (d) presents the subject matter in a well organized manner

48. Dynamic approach to teaching means
   (a) Teaching should be forceful and effective
   (b) Teachers should be energetic and dynamic
   (c) The topics of teaching should not be static, but dynamic
   (d) The students should be required to learn through activities

49. The research that aims at immediate application is
   (a) Action Research
   (b) Empirical Research
   (c) Conceptual Research
   (d) Fundamental Research

50. When two or more successive footnotes refer to the same work which one of the following expressions is used?
   (a) *ibid* (b) *et.al*
   (c) *op.cit* : (d) *loc.cit.*

51. Nine year olds are taller than seven year olds. This is an example of a reference drawn from
   (a) Vertical study
   (b) Cross-sectional study
   (c) Time series study
   (d) Experimental study

52. Conferences are meant for
   (a) Multiple target groups
   (b) Group discussions
   (c) Show-casing new Research
   (d) All of the above

53. Ex Post Facto research means
   (a) The research is carried out after the incident
   (b) The research is carried out prior to the incident
   (c) The research is carried out along with the happening of an incident.
   (d) The research is carried out keeping in mind the possibilities of an incident.

54. Research ethics do not include
(a) Honesty (b) Subjectivity
(c) Integrity (d) Objectivity

Read the following passage carefully and answer the questions 55 to 60:

James Madison said, "A people who mean to be their own governors must arm themselves with power that knowledge gives." In India, the Official Secrets Act, 1923 was a convenient smokescreen to deny members of the public access to information. Public functioning has traditionally been shrouded in secrecy. But in a democracy in which people govern themselves, it is necessary to have more openness. In the maturing of our democracy, right to information is a major step forward; it enables citizens to participate fully in the decision-making process that affects their lives so profoundly. It is in this context that the address of the Prime Minister in the Lok Sabha is significant. He said, "I would only like to see that everyone, particularly our civil servants, should see the Bill in a positive spirit; not as a draconian law for paralyzing Government, but as an instrument for improving Government-Citizen interface resulting in a friendly, caring and effective Government functioning for the good of our People." He further said, "This is an innovative Bill, where there will be scope to review its functioning as we gain experience. Therefore, this is a piece of legislation, whose working will be kept under constant reviews."

The Commission, in its Report, has dealt with the application of the Right to Information in Executive, Legislature and Judiciary. The judiciary could be a pioneer in implementing the Act in letter and spirit because much of the work that the Judiciary does is open to public scrutiny, Government of India has sanctioned an e-governance project in the Judiciary for about ₹700 crores which would bring about systematic classification, standardization and categorization of records. This would help the judiciary to fulfil its mandate under the Act. Similar capacity building would be required in all other public authorities. The transformation from non-transparency to transparency and public accountability is the responsibility of all three organs of State.

55. A person gets power
(a) by acquiring knowledge
(b) from the Official Secrets Act, 1923
(c) through openings
(d) by denying public information

56. Right to Information is a major step forward to
(a) enable citizens to participate fully in the decision making process
(b) to make the people aware of the Act
(c) to gain knowledge of administration
(d) to make the people Government friendly

57. The Prime Minister considered the Bill
(a) to provide power to the civil servants
(b) as an instrument for improving Government-citizen interface resulting in a friendly, caring and effective Government
(c) a draconian law against the officials
(d) to check the harassment of the people

58. The Commission made the Bill effective by
(a) extending power to the executive authorities
(b) combining the executive and legislative power
(c) recognizing Judiciary a pioneer in implementing the act in letter and spirit
(d) educating the people before its implementation

59. The Prime Minister considered the Bill innovative and hoped that

(a) It could be reviewed based on the experience gained on its functioning.
(b) The civil servants would see the Bill in a positive spirit.
(c) It would not be considered as a draconian law for paralyzing Government
(d) All of the above

60. The transparency and public accountability is the responsibility of three organs of the State. These three organs are
(a) Lok Sabha, Rajya Sabha and Judiciary
(b) Lok Sabha, Rajya Sabha and Executive
(c) Judiciary, Legislature and the Commission
(d) Legislature, Executive and Judiciary

ANSWERS

1. (c)	2. (b)	3. (b)	4. (b)	5. (d)
6. (a)	7. (c)	8. (b)	9. (a)	10. (c)
11. (d)	12. (a)	13. (b)	14. (b)	15. (b)
16. (a)	17. (c)	18. (c)	19. (c)	20. (a)
21. (a)	22. (c)	23. (a)	24. (b)	25. (c)
26. (b)	27. (b)	28. (d)	29. (c)	30. (c)
31. (c)	32. (c)	33. (d)	34. (d)	35. (c)
36. (a)	37. (b)	38. (a)	39. (d)	40. (b)
41. (b)	42. (d)	43. (d)	44. (c)	45. (b)
46. (d)	47. (a)	48. (d)	49. (a)	50. (a)
51. (b)	52. (d)	53. (a)	54. (b)	55. (a)
56. (a)	57. (b)	58. (c)	59. (d)	60. (d)

PAPER–II

Note: This paper contains fifty (50) objective type questions, each question carrying two (2) marks. All questions are compulsory.

1. The emergence of New Public Administration is associated with
(a) American Society of Public Administration
(b) Comparative Administration Group
(c) Indian Institute of Public Administration
(d) Minnowbrook Conference

2. Factors responsible for the evolution of the study of Comparative Public Administration is/are
(a) Inadequacy of Traditional Approach
(b) Rise of New Techniques and concepts of Research
(c) Desire to develop Comparative Public Administration as an independent subject
(d) All the above

3. A.V. Dicey has given classical exposition of the Rule of Law in his book
(a) Introduction to the study of the Law of the Constitution
(b) Comparative study of the Constitution
(c) Justice and Administrative Law
(d) Public Administration: A Comparative Perspective

4. Who among the following used the expression 'cow sociologists' for Hawthorne researchers?

(a) Herbert Simon
(b) Peter Drucker
(c) United Auto Workers in the USA
(d) Comparative Administration Group

5. Which one of the following is not correct according to Weber's Charismatic Authority?
(a) It is based on the exceptional qualities of the leader.
(b) Administration under this authority is stable.
(c) There is no hierarchical assignment of tasks under this authority.
(d) On the death of a leader under this authority, the question of succession arises.

6. A prismatic society is characterised by
(a) a high degree of homogeneity
(b) a high degree of heterogeneity
(c) a high degree of flexibility
(d) None of the above

7. Which one of the following reasons is not attributed to the emergence of Development Administration?
(a) Abundance of research funding with the CAG
(b) Financial and technical assistance under the USAID programme
(c) Abundance of knowledge and managerial skills in developing countries
(d) Desire for administrative development in developing countries

8. The USA introduced the performance budgeting after the II World War on the recommendations of
(a) Grace Commission
(b) Hoover Commission
(c) Lee Commission
(d) Islington Commission

9. What is not true about the Constituent Assembly?
(a) It was based on the recommendations of Cabinet Mission.
(b) It was constituted by indirect elections.
(c) At least one seat was given to each Indian State.
(d) Seats in each Province were distributed among the three main communities in proportion to their population.

10. Which of the following is not correctly matched?
(a) Cabinet Secretary – Head of the Union Cabinet
(b) Chief Secretary – Head of State Secretariat
(c) Secretary – Administrative Head of a Ministry
(d) Chief Minister – Head of the State Government

11. Which of the following is not a Constitutional Body?
(a) Inter-State Council
(b) Finance Commission
(c) Union Public Service Commission
(d) National Development Council

12. Which of the following is not correct about the Budget in India?
(a) The President of India has to put it before both the Houses every financial year.
(b) It is a statement of estimated receipts and expenditures of the Government of India.
(c) The Constitution refers to it as annual financial statement.
(d) The Indian Constitution clearly mentioned the word Budget.

13. Which one of the following machineries was created in Britain in 1967 to examine complaints of corruption?
(a) Whitley Council
(b) Ombudsman
(c) Parliamentary Commissioner
(d) Procurator-General

14. The President may remove the Chairman or member of the Public Service Commission without making a reference to the Supreme Court. Which is not true in this context?
(a) The Chairman or Member is adjudged as insolvent.
(b) The Chairman or Member engages in some paid employment outside while in office.
(c) The Chairman or Member is guilty of misbehaviour.
(d) The Chairman or Member is unfit to continue in Office due to infirmity of mind or body.

15. Civil Services preliminary examination (objective type) for the selection of candidates for the Civil Services (Main) was recommended by
(a) Hota Committee
(b) Kothari Committee
(c) Satish Chandra Committee
(d) Gopalaswamy Ayyangar Committee

16. Which one among the following is not the primary source of data collection?
(a) Interview
(b) Observation
(c) Questionnaire
(d) Historical books

17. Smt. Durgabai Deshmukh was the first Chairperson of
(a) Central Social Welfare Board
(b) National Commission for Backward Classes
(c) National Commission for Minorities
(d) National Commission for Women

18. Which of the following Committee was constituted on the recommendations of the Growmore Food Enquiry Committee?
(a) Balwantrai Mehta Committee
(b) Ashok Mehta Committee
(c) L.M. Singhvi Committee
(d) Rural-Urban Enquiry Committee

19. Article 243-B of Indian Constitution provides for
(a) Constitution of Panchayats
(b) Grama Sabha
(c) Election to the Panchayats
(d) Reservation of Seats in Panchayats

20. The Panchayats are described as "Little Republics" by
(a) Metcalfe
(b) Lord Ripon
(c) Lord Hob House
(d) Mahatma Gandhi

21. **Assertion (A):** The tasks of Public Institutions are decided by the Politicians and implemented by Administrators.
Reason (R): Public Institutions perform better when they are decentralized.
Codes:
(a) Both (A) and (R) are correct and (R) is the correct explanation of (A).
(b) Both (A) and (R) are correct, but (R) is not the correct explanation of (A).
(c) (A) is true, but (R) is false.
(d) (A) is false, but (R) is true.

22. **Assertion (A):** The Riggsian model of prismatic society is primarily an explanation of the ecology of Thailand.
Reason (R): Riggs' two-dimensional approach means that the prismatic model would include any society that is differentiated but malintegrated.
Codes:
(a) Both (A) and (R) are correct and (R) is the correct explanation of (A).
(b) Both (A) and (R) are correct, but (R) is not the correct explanation of (A).
(c) (A) is true, but (R) is false.
(d) (A) is false, but (R) is true.

23. **Assertion (A):** The Comptroller and Auditor General is appointed by the Prime Minister in consultation with the Speaker by warrant under his hand and seal.

Reason (R): The duties, powers and conditions of service of the CAG are laid down in the CAG's Act, 1971.

Codes:

(a) Both (A) and (R) are correct and (R) is the correct explanation of (A).
(b) Both (A) and (R) are correct, but (R) is not the correct explanation of (A).
(c) (A) is true, but (R) is false.
(d) (A) is false, but (R) is true.

24. **Assertion (A):** For Simon, administrative man looks for a course of action that is best from those available to him.

Reason (R): For Simon, administrative man is motivated by satisfactory outcome.

Codes:

(a) Both (A) and (R) are correct and (R) is the correct explanation of (A).
(b) Both (A) and (R) are correct, but (R) is not the correct explanation of (A).
(c) (A) is true, but (R) is false.
(d) (A) is false, but (R) is true.

25. **Assertion (A):** To provide avenues of public employment to suitable educated Indians, a separate civil service called the statutory civil service was created in 1879.

Reason (R): All India Services maintain the integrity of the Nation.

Codes:

(a) Both (A) and (R) are correct and (R) is the correct explanation of (A).
(b) Both (A) and (R) are correct, but (R) is not the correct explanation of (A).
(c) (A) is true, but (R) is false.
(d) (A) is false, but (R) is true.

26. **Assertion (A):** The UPSC is the designated recruitment agency for the All India Services.

Reason (R): The All India Services provide a valuable link between the Union and the State Governments.

Codes:

(a) Both (A) and (R) are true and (R) is the correct explanation of (A).
(b) Both (A) and (R) are true, but (R) is not the correct explanation of (A).
(c) (A) is true, but (R) is false.
(d) (A) is false, but (R) is true.

27. **Assertion (A):** Planning, Programming, Budgeting was an attempt to integrate budgeting with overall planning for the Government as a whole.

Reason (R): It combines long range planning with results oriented programmes and evaluation.

Codes:

(a) Both (A) and (R) are correct and (R) is the correct explanation of (A).
(b) Both (A) and (R) are correct, but (R) is not the correct explanation of (A).
(c) (A) is true, but (R) is false.
(d) (A) is false, but (R) is true.

28. **Assertion (A):** The Public Accounts Committee should satisfy itself that the money shown in the accounts as having been disbursed were legally available for and applicable to the service of purpose to which they have been charged.

Reason (R): The Public Accounts Committee suggests alternative policies in order to bring about efficiency and economy in administration.

Codes:

(a) Both (A) and (R) are correct and (R) is the correct explanation of (A).
(b) Both (A) and (R) are correct, but (R) is not the correct explanation of (A).
(c) (A) is true, but (R) is false.
(d) (A) is false, but (R) is true.

29. **Assertion (A):** Judicial Activism is an effective mean of judicial control over Public Administration.

Reason (R): The PILs have enhanced the judicial control over public administration.

Codes:

(a) Both (A) and (R) are correct and (R) is the correct explanation of (A).
(b) Both (A) and (R) are correct, but (R) is not the correct explanation of (A).
(c) (A) is true, but (R) is false.
(d) (A) is false, but (R) is true.

30. **Assertion (A):** The Comptroller and Auditor General (CAG) is the watchdog of public finance.
Reason (R): The CAG is a constitutional body.
Codes:
(a) Both (A) and (R) are correct and (R) is the correct explanation of (A).
(b) Both (A) and (R) are correct, but (R) is not the correct explanation of (A).
(c) (A) is true, but (R) is false.
(d) (A) is false, but (R) is true.

31. What is the correct sequence regarding the evolution of the discipline of Public Administration? Use the codes given below:
(i) Crisis of identity
(ii) The era of Politics – Administration dichotomy
(iii) Principles of Administration
(iv) Focus on inter-disciplinary studies
Codes:
(a) (i), (ii), (iii), (iv) (b) (ii), (iii), (i), (iv)
(c) (iii), (iv), (ii), (i) (d) (ii), (iii), (iv), (i)

32. Arrange the following in chronological order of their origin. Use the codes given below:
(i) 1st Administrative Reforms Commission
(ii) 3rd Minnowbrook Conference
(iii) K. Santhanam Committee
(iv) Sarkaria Commission
Codes:
(a) (i), (ii), (iii), (iv) (b) (ii), (iii), (iv), (i)
(c) (iii), (i), (iv), (ii) (d) (iii) (i), (ii), (iv)

33. Which one of the following is a correct sequence in the ascending order of Maslow's needs' hierarchy?
(i) Esteem needs
(ii) Affiliation needs
(iii) Self-actualization needs
(iv) Physiological needs
(v) Safety needs
Codes:
(a) (i), (ii), (iii), (iv), (v)
(b) (iv), (v), (ii), (i), (iii)
(c) (ii), (v), (i), (iii), (iv)
(d) (iii), (iv), (ii), (i), (v)

34. Which is the correct sequence in descending order of following organization? Give correct answer from codes given below:
(i) Cabinet Secretariat
(ii) Department
(iii) Ministry
(iv) Directorate
Codes:
(a) (i), (ii), (iii), (iv) (b) (i), (iii), (iv), (ii)
(c) (i), (iii), (ii), (iv) (d) (i), (iv), (iii), (ii)

35. Arrange the following in their chronological order. Use the codes given below:
(i) Paul H. Appleby Report
(ii) Gopalaswamy Ayyangar Report
(iii) N.N. Vohra Report
(iv) Raja J. Chelliah Report
Codes:
(a) (i), (ii), (iii), (iv) (b) (ii), (i), (iii), (iv)
(c) (ii), (i), (iv), (iii) (d) (i), (ii), (iv), (iii)

36. What is the correct sequence of execution of Budget? Answer by using the codes given below:
(i) Disbursement of Funds
(ii) Custody of Public Funds
(iii) Assessment and Collection
(iv) Accounting and Audit

Codes:

(a) (i), (ii), (iii), (iv) (b) (i), (iii), (ii), (iv)
(c) (iii), (ii), (i), (iv) (d) (iii), (iv), (i), (ii)

37. Match List I with List II and select the correct answer from the codes given below:

List I

(A) L.D. White
(B) W.F. Willoughby
(C) L. Gulick and L. Urwick
(D) Dwight Waldo

List II

(i) Principles of Public Administration
(ii) Papers on the Science of Administration
(iii) The Study of Public Administration
(iv) Introduction to the Study of Public Administration

Codes:	A	B	C	D
(a)	(i)	(ii)	(iii)	(iv)
(b)	(iv)	(i)	(ii)	(iii)
(c)	(iv)	(iii)	(ii)	(i)
(d)	(iii)	(i)	(ii)	(iv)

38. Match List I with List II and select the correct answer by using the codes given below:

List I

(A) Ecological Approach
(B) Behavioural Approach
(C) Public Choice Approach
(D) Systems Approach

List II

(i) Chris Argyris (ii) W. Niskanen
(iii) F.W. Riggs (iv) David Easton

Codes:	A	B	C	D
(a)	(i)	(iii)	(iv)	(ii)
(b)	(iv)	(ii)	(iii)	(i)
(c)	(iii)	(i)	(ii)	(iv)
(d)	(ii)	(iv)	(i)	(iii)

39. Match List I with List II and select the correct answer from the codes given below:

List I

(A) Aitchison Commission
(B) Federal Public Service Commission
(C) Islington Commission
(D) Lee Commission

List II

(i) 1935 (ii) 1924
(iii) 1886 (iv) 1912

Codes:	A	B	C	D
(a)	(iii)	(i)	(iv)	(ii)
(b)	(i)	(ii)	(iii)	(iv)
(c)	(ii)	(iii)	(iv)	(i)
(d)	(iv)	(i)	(ii)	(iii)

40. Match List I with List II and select the correct answer from the codes given below:

List I

(A) Parliamentary Commissioner
(B) Administrative Courts
(C) Ombudsman
(D) Procurator System

List II

(i) France (ii) Russia
(iii) Britain (iv) USA
(v) Sweden

Codes:	A	B	C	D
(a)	(i)	(ii)	(iii)	(iv)
(b)	(v)	(i)	(iii)	(ii)
(c)	(iii)	(i)	(v)	(ii)
(d)	(ii)	(iv)	(iii)	(v)

41. Match List I with List II. Select the correct answer from the codes given below:

List I

(A) Lal Bahadur Shastri National Academy of Administration
(B) National Police Academy
(C) Indian Audit and Accounts Service School
(D) Indian Institute of Public Administration

List II
(i) Bengaluru (ii) New Delhi
(iii) Shimla (iv) Hyderabad
(v) Mussoorie

Codes:	A	B	C	D
(a)	(v)	(ii)	(iii)	(iv)
(b)	(v)	(iv)	(iii)	(ii)
(c)	(iv)	(iii)	(ii)	(i)
(d)	(ii)	(iii)	(i)	(iv)

42. Match List I with List II and select the correct answer from the codes given below:

List I
(A) Y. Dror (B) A. Etzioni
(C) David Truman (D) V. Ostrom

List II
(i) Mixed Scanning Approach
(ii) Normative Optimum Model
(iii) Governmental Process (Group Theory)
(iv) Public Choice Theory

Codes:	A	B	C	D
(a)	(iv)	(iii)	(ii)	(i)
(b)	(ii)	(i)	(iii)	(iv)
(c)	(iii)	(iv)	(ii)	(i)
(d)	(i)	(ii)	(iii)	(iv)

43. Match List I with List II. Select the correct answer from the codes given below:

List I
(A) Observation (B) Interview
(C) Schedule (D) Questionnaire

List II
(i) Facilitates insight into the respondents.
(ii) Data collected are more reliable.
(iii) The researcher fills up the information collected from respondents himself.
(iv) The respondent has to himself fill the entries.
(v) The time and resources can be saved by selecting a smaller segment of respondents.

Codes:	A	B	C	D
(a)	(i)	(ii)	(iii)	(v)
(b)	(ii)	(i)	(iii)	(iv)
(c)	(v)	(ii)	(iv)	(iii)
(d)	(i)	(ii)	(iii)	(iv)

44. Match List I with List II and select the correct answer by using the codes:

List I
(A) F.W. Riggs (B) Lucian Pye
(C) Gerald Caiden (D) O.P. Dwivedi

List II
(i) Development Administration
(ii) Administrative Reform
(iii) Frontiers of Development Administration
(iv) Aspects of Political Development

Codes:	A	B	C	D
(a)	(ii)	(i)	(iii)	(iv)
(b)	(iv)	(ii)	(i)	(iii)
(c)	(iii)	(iv)	(ii)	(i)
(d)	(i)	(ii)	(iii)	(iv)

45. Match List I with List II and select the correct answer by using the codes:

List I
(A) Mandamus (B) Quo Warranto
(C) Prohibition (D) Certiorari

List II
(i) Writ will not be issued by a High Court to another High Court.
(ii) Writ will not be issued against the Governor of a State for the performance of his official duties.
(iii) Writ enables the court to examine the legality of the claim of a person to a public office.
(iv) Writ cannot be issued against private persons or associations.

Codes:	A	B	C	D
(a)	(ii)	(iv)	(i)	(iii)
(b)	(iii)	(i)	(ii)	(iv)
(c)	(i)	(iv)	(ii)	(iii)
(d)	(ii)	(iii)	(iv)	(i)

46. Match List I with List II and select the correct answer from the codes given below:

List I

(a) B.R.G.F. (b) MNREGA
(c) Bharat Nirman (d) R.M.S.A.

List II

(i) A scheme concerned with infra-structural development in 6 key areas.
(ii) A scheme to bridge the gap of requirements and availability of funds for development in rural areas.
(iii) A scheme for universalisation of elementary education.
(iv) A scheme for assured employment of at least 100 days.

Codes:	A	B	C	D
(a)	(i)	(ii)	(iii)	(iv)
(b)	(ii)	(iii)	(iv)	(i)
(c)	(iii)	(iv)	(ii)	(i)
(d)	(ii)	(iv)	(i)	(iii)

Read the passage below and answer the questions that follow based on your understanding of the passage: (47-50). The main function of civil service is formulation and implementation of public policy.

The civil service engages itself in collection of relevant data and information in order to identify the crux of the problem. The civil service, specially at the secretariat level, is considered as the 'think tank' of the Government and it helps in making sound and effective policies. The civil servants also administer the law of the land. They are to implement and execute the law of the land faithfully and impartially. In finance, the civil servants not only prepare the budget but also influence the taxation and expenditure policy of the government to a great extent. Today they perform quasi-legislative and quasi-judicial functions also. Public relations has become an important part of their official duties. Therefore, they are expected to explain the Government policy to the people and to win their co-operation in its implementation. In a country like India, civil servants are entrusted the responsibility of implementing various programmes of rural development and welfare measures.

Recent decades have seen a shift towards a reduced role for the Government in all countries. Thatcherism in UK and Reaganomics in USA tried to pull out the State from the morass of over-involvement. The decline of Communism in Eastern Europe has furthered the trend towards economic liberalisation and disinvestment in public sector enterprises. India could not have remained unaffected by these global trends.

47. Which one of the following is not the area of Civil Servants?
(a) Collection of Data
(b) Identification of problem
(c) Think-tank of the Government
(d) Enactment of Law

48. Civil Servants are not discharging the following:
(a) Execution of Law of the land
(b) Preparation of the budget
(c) Contacting the people and explaining the programmes of Government
(d) Judicial activities

49. Which one of the following factors has not contributed to the rise of globalization?
(a) Thatcherism in UK
(b) Reaganomics in USA
(c) Decline of Communism in Eastern Europe
(d) Growth of Social Legislation

50. Which one of the following areas is not the concern of the Government Policy in recent trends?
(a) Disinvestment in Public Enterprises
(b) Increasing the efficiency of Civil Servants
(c) Enlarging the role of Government
(d) Deregulation of Monopolies

ANSWERS

1. (d)	2. (d)	3. (a)	4. (c)	5. (b)
6. (b)	7. (c)	8. (b)	9. (c)	10. (a)
11. (d)	12. (d)	13. (c)	14. (c)	15. (b)
16. (d)	17. (a)	18. (a)	19. (a)	20. (a)
21. (b)	22. (b)	23. (d)	24. (d)	25. (b)
26. (b)	27. (a)	28. (c)	29. (a)	30. (b)
31. (b)	32. (c)	33. (b)	34. (c)	35. (c)
36. (c)	37. (b)	38. (c)	39. (a)	40. (c)
41. (b)	42. (b)	43. (b)	44. (c)	45. (d)
46. (d)	47. (d)	48. (d)	49. (d)	50. (c)

PAPER–III

Note: This paper contains seventy five (75) objective type questions of two (2) marks each. All questions are compulsory.

1. "Administration is the most obvious part of Government." Who of the following made this statement?
   (a) Kautilya
   (b) Woodrow Wilson
   (c) L.D. White
   (d) Frank J. Goodnow

2. "The politics—administration dichotomy is a misleading distinction which has become a fetish, a stereotype in the minds of theorists and practitioners alike." Who said this?
   (a) Herbert Simon
   (b) Paul H. Appleby
   (c) Carl J. Friedrich
   (d) Dwight Waldo

3. Which of the following is not the correct source of New Public Management?
   (a) New Public Administration
   (b) Public Choice Theory
   (c) Managerialism
   (d) Chicago School of Economics

4. **Assertion (A):** New Public Administration openly rejected the value neutrality.
   Reason (R): Value neutrality in Public Administration is an impossibility and the discipline should explicitly espouse the cause of the disadvantaged sections of the Society.
   Codes:
   (a) Both (A) and (R) are correct and (R) is the correct explanation of (A).
   (b) Both (A) and (R) are correct, but (R) is not the correct explanation of (A).
   (c) (A) is true but (R) is false.
   (d) (A) is false but (R) is true.

5. Match List I with List II. Select the correct answer from the codes given below:
   List I (Books)
   (A) Administration: The Art and Science of Organisation and Management
   (B) Toward a New Public Administration: Minnow brook Perspective
   (C) Making Democracy Work
   (D) Public Administration and Public Management
   List II (Authors)
   (i) Frank Marini
   (ii) Jan-Erick-Lane
   (iii) Albert Lepawaski
   (iv) Robert D. Putnam

Codes:	**A**	**B**	**C**	**D**
(a)	(i)	(ii)	(iii)	(iv)
(b)	(iii)	(i)	(iv)	(ii)
(c)	(ii)	(iv)	(iii)	(i)
(d)	(iv)	(ii)	(i)	(iii)

6. Match List I with List II. Select the correct answer from the codes given below:
   List I (Type of Organisation)
   (A) Project Organisation
   (B) Matrix Organisation

(C) Horizontal Organisation
(D) Network Organisation

List II (Characteristics)

(i) Existence of horizontal and diagonal relationship
(ii) Facilitates co-operation team work and customer orientation
(iii) Independent unit having link with a web of other units
(iv) Project organisation plus a functional organisation
(v) Flexible to facilitate management change

Codes:	A	B	C	D
(a)	(i)	(ii)	(iv)	(iii)
(b)	(i)	(v)	(ii)	(iii)
(c)	(v)	(ii)	(i)	(iii)
(d)	(ii)	(iv)	(v)	(iii)

7. Which of the following is the basis of influence in an informal organisation?
(a) Organisational position
(b) Person
(c) Authority
(d) Closeness with higher people

8. "Hierarchy is the linchpin that locks the form." Who said it?
(a) Henry Fayol
(b) Urwick and Gullick
(c) Mooney and Reiley
(d) Earl Latham

9. Which one of the following is not a method of co-ordination?
(a) Planning
(b) Standardization of procedures
(c) Centralized house-keeping
(d) Inspection

10. "Bureaucracy is an organization that maximises efficiency in administration or an institutional method of organized social conduct in the interest of administrative efficiency."—Who has made this statement?
(a) Peter M. Blau (b) Max Weber
(c) Thomson (d) Alvin Gouldner

11. Which of the following are the characteristics of communication network, called grapevine in an organisation? Select the correct answer by using the codes given below:
(i) It is not controlled by management.
(ii) It is perceived by most employees as being more believable and reliable.
(iii) It is largely used to serve the organisational interest.
(iv) It is an important source of information.

Codes:
(a) (i) & (ii) (b) (i), (ii) & (iii)
(c) (ii) & (iv) (d) (i), (ii) & (iv)

12. The book 'From Max Weber: Essays in Sociology' was edited by—
(a) H.H. Hearth
(b) C.W. Mills
(c) Talcott Parsons and H.H. Hearth
(d) H.H. Hearth and C.W. Mills

13. Which among the following are major functions of line agency?
(i) Making decisions
(ii) To ensure that Chief Executive is adequately informed
(iii) Maintaining production
(iv) Taking responsibility
Select the correct answer from the codes given below:
(a) (i), (ii), (iii) (b) (i), (iii), (iv)
(c) (ii), (iii), (iv) (d) (i), (ii), (iv)

14. According to Kautilya's 'Arthasastra' a King should avoid—
(i) Lust (ii) Greed
(iii) Confrontation (iv) Vanity
Select the correct answer from the codes given below.

Codes:
(a) (i), (ii) (b) (ii), (iii)
(c) (i), (ii), (iv) (d) (i), (iii), (iv)

15. "Charismatic authority can be routinized so that it continues to exist even after the departure of charismatic leader." Who said it?
(a) Herbert Simon (b) Chester Bernard
(c) Max Weber (d) Peter Blau

16. Match List I with List II. Select the correct answer from the codes given below:
List I (Thinkers)
(A) Herbert Simon
(B) Charles Lindbolm
(C) David Easton
(D) Geoffrey Vickers
List II (Ideas)
(i) Incrementalism
(ii) Black Box Model
(iii) Art of Judgement
(iv) Bounded Rationality
(v) Modified Rationalism

Codes:	**A**	**B**	**C**	**D**
(a)	(iv)	(i)	(ii)	(iii)
(b)	(i)	(iii)	(v)	(iv)
(c)	(ii)	(i)	(iii)	(v)
(d)	(v)	(ii)	(i)	(iii)

17. Who among the following has coined the term 'Representative Bureaucracy'?
(a) Robert Merton
(b) Donald J. Kingsley
(c) F.M. Marx
(d) Herman Finer

18. Which one of the following is not M.P. Follett's Criticism of Classical Theory?
(a) It treats organisation a closed system.
(b) It suffers from one-sidedness.
(c) It is mechanical in approach
(d) It ignores psychological aspects.

19. Match List I with List II. Select the correct answer from the codes given below:
List I (Concepts)
(A) Linking Pin Model
(B) Decision Tree
(C) Garbage Cane Model
(D) ERG Theory
List II (Thinkers)
(i) Rensis Likert
(ii) Duncan
(iii) Alderfer
(iv) Cohen, March and Olson

Codes:	**A**	**B**	**C**	**D**
(a)	(i)	(iii)	(ii)	(iv)
(b)	(ii)	(iii)	(iv)	(i)
(c)	(i)	(ii)	(iv)	(iii)
(d)	(i)	(ii)	(iii)	(iv)

20. Who called the Scientific Management as 'Physiological Organisation Theory'?
(a) Robert Hoxic
(b) Oliver Sheldon
(c) Peter Drucker
(d) Simon and March

21. According to Elton Mayo, a worker's performance is primarily related to
(a) The worker's personality variable
(b) Technological tools
(c) Interaction setting in an organization
(d) Socially acquired attitude of the worker in and outside of the factory.

22. Which of the following statements is/are linked to F.W. Taylor?
(i) Trade Unionism is unacceptable.
(ii) Scientific Management is mechanical.
(iii) Worker is a technical man.
(iv) Piece-rate wage plan is an unhealthy practice.
Select the correct answer from the codes given below:
Codes:
(a) (i) (b) (ii)
(c) (i), (iii) (d) (iii), (iv)

23. **Assertion (A):** Comparative Public Administration is productive and active in nature.
Reason (R): The idea of decline of Comparative Public Administration is

premature, although Comparative Public Administration does not appear to have reached a critical point of development.

Codes:

(a) Both (A) and (R) are correct and (R) is the correct explanation of (A).
(b) Both (A) and (R) are correct, but (R) is not the correct explanation of (A).
(c) (A) is true but (R) is false.
(d) (A) is false but (R) is true.

24. According to Ferrel Heady, which of the following is not a feature of the administrative systems of the developing countries?
(a) Colonial legacy
(b) Lack of technical competence
(c) Formalism
(d) Operational autonomy

25. Which one of the following is not a characteristic of 'Sala Model'?
(a) Institutional corruption
(b) Nepotism
(c) Formalism
(d) Actual behaviour is similar to formal expectations.

26. Which one is the last Independent Regulatory Commission in USA?
(a) Federal Communication Commission
(b) Civil Aeronautic Board
(c) US Maritime Commission
(d) Federal Power Commission

27. The Masterman Committee of Britain dealt with
(a) Political activities of civil servants
(b) Functioning of Whitley Council
(c) Re-organisation of administration
(d) None of the above

28. Which of the following countries has promulgated a new administrative regime in the form of the Enterprise Act, 2002?
(a) USA (b) UK
(c) France (d) India

29. Kofi Annan emphasized on some aspects of sustainable development in 2002 Earth Summit acronymed as WEHAB. This acronym includes—(Select the correct answer by using the codes given below:
(i) Water
(ii) Water and Sanitation
(iii) Energy
(iv) Employment
(v) Health
(vi) Housing
(vii) Agriculture
(viii) Biodiversity and Ecosystem Management
(ix) Biotechnology
(x) Agro-industry

Codes:

(a) (i), (iii), (v), (x) and (viii)
(b) (i), (iv), (vi), (vii) and (ix)
(c) (i), (ii), (v), (x) and (ix)
(d) (ii), (iii), (v), (vii) and (viii)

30. The phenomenon of development administration in India, traced to the inception of the Community Development in October 1952, was started on the recommendations of
(a) Krishnamachari Committee
(b) Project Appraisal Committee
(c) Administrative Reforms Commission
(d) Mahalanobis Model

31. Decision making process under Development Administration is supposed to be—
(i) Flexible (ii) Centralized
(iii) Innovative (iv) Rigid
Select the correct code:

Codes:

(a) (i), (ii) (b) (i), (iii)
(c) (ii), (iii) (d) (ii), (iv)

32. The United Nations Development Programme (UNDP) has prioritized the most significant area under e-governance, which is

(a) Office Automation
(b) Service Delivery
(c) Development Needs
(d) Management Information System

33. Match List I with List II. Select the correct answer from the codes given below:

List I (Traditional Administration)
(A) Regulatory Administration
(B) Oriented towards efficiency and economy
(C) Task orientation
(D) Sharp and elaborate hierarchical structure

List II (Features)
(i) Strict and authoritative climate of mistrust
(ii) Routine operations
(iii) Concern for security and playing safe
(iv) Emphasis on individual performance
(v) Resistance to organization change

Codes:	A	B	C	D
(a)	(i)	(ii)	(iv)	(v)
(b)	(ii)	(iv)	(iii)	(i)
(c)	(i)	(ii)	(iii)	(iv)
(d)	(ii)	(v)	(iv)	(iii)

34. The Cabinet is the integral core of the Council of Ministers and it is—
(i) an extra-constitutional body
(ii) an extra legal creation
(iii) institutionalised by usage
(iv) comprising most important ministers
Select the correct answer from the codes given below:
Codes:
(a) (i), (ii) (b) (i), (ii), (iii)
(c) (ii), (iii), (iv) (d) (i), (ii), (iii), (iv)

35. Which one of the following is the basis for Prime Minister's Office?
(a) A Resolution of Cabinet
(b) Constitution of India
(c) An Act of Parliament
(d) Government of India Allocation of Business Rules, 1961.

36. Consider the following statements regarding the Cabinet Secretariate in India and select the correct answer from the codes given below:
(i) It is a successor of the Secretariate of the Governor General's Executive Council.
(ii) It performs co-ordinating role in the process of policy making at the highest level.
(iii) The office of the Cabinet Secretariate came into existence in 1947.
(iv) The First ARC had recommended that the Cabinet Secretary should ordinarily have a tenure of three years.
Codes:
(a) (i), (ii), (iii) (b) (i), (ii), (iv)
(c) (i), (iii), (iv) (d) (i), (ii), (iii), (iv)

37. While assisting the Minister in formulation of policies, the Secretariate performs which of the following functions?
(i) Making and modifying policies from time to time.
(ii) Drafting bills, rules and regulations.
(iii) Coordinating and interpreting policies.
(iv) To direct the States Government.
Select the correct answer from the codes given below:
Codes:
(a) (i), (ii) (b) (i), (iii)
(c) (i), (ii), (iii) (d) (i), (iii), (iv)

38. The Second Administrative Reforms Commission has identified strengths and weaknesses in the existing structure of Government of India in a report. Identify a weakness cited in the report.

(a) Stability
(b) Commitment to Constitution
(c) Proliferation of Ministries/Department
(d) Proliferation of Administrative Agencies

39. Which one of the following is not created by an Act of Parliament?
(a) National Commission for Backward Classes
(b) University Grants Commission
(c) Atomic Energy Commission
(d) Railway Board

40. Which of the following is not the recommendation of Hota Committee pertaining to the issue of disciplinary procedure for Government Servants in India?
(a) Union Public Service Commission need not be consulted in case of a civil servant facing charges of corrupt practice.
(b) Article 311 of the Constitution may be deleted.
(c) Where minor disciplinary proceedings are sufficient to meet the end of justice, then major penalty proceedings should not be initiated.
(d) An inquiry officer should be relieved from his normal duties.

41. The members of the Union Public Service Commission can be removed on the ground of misbehaviour by
(a) Impeachment by Parliament
(b) The President after an inquiry and verdict of the Supreme Court.
(c) The Chairman of the Union Public Service Commission.
(d) By the President on the recommendation of the Cabinet.

42. Who was of the view that Indian Civil Service was the "steel frame" on which the whole structure of Government and Administration in India rest?
(a) Winston Churchill
(b) Godwin Austin
(c) David Lloyd George
(d) Jawaharlal Nehru

43. Which one of the following is not correct about the 'Civil Service Day' in India?
(a) It is celebrated on 21st April
(b) Prime Minister hands over 'Prime Minister Excellence Award in Public Administration' to the civil servants on this day.
(c) India has started celebrating this day since 2006.
(d) Prime Minister's Office makes arrangements to organise this event every year.

44. The National Training Policy in India
(i) Intends to cultivate democratic values
(ii) Stipulates greater emphasis on the training of higher and supervisory level officials.
(iii) Strives to bring responsiveness to the expectation of citizens
(iv) Earmarks two percent of total salary budget for training which is to be solely used for this purpose

Select the correct answer from the codes given below:

Codes:

(a) (i), (ii) (b) (i), (iii)
(c) (ii), (iii) (d) (i), (iv)

45. The training for IAS is conducted in four stages. Which one of the following is the correct sequence of training stages?
(a) Foundational, Professional, Field and Institutional
(b) Foundational, Institutional, Field and Professional
(c) Foundational, Field, Professional and Institutional
(d) Institutional, Foundational, Field and Professional

46. Match List I with List II and select the correct answer from the codes given below:

List I (Kind of Budget)
(A) Line Item Budget
(B) Performance Budget
(C) Planning Programme Budget
(D) Zero-based Budget

List II (Basic Orientation of Budget)
(i) Control (ii) Decision Making
(iii) Management (iv) Planning

Codes:	A	B	C	D
(a)	(i)	(ii)	(iii)	(iv)
(b)	(i)	(iii)	(iv)	(ii)
(c)	(i)	(ii)	(iv)	(iii)
(d)	(i)	(iv)	(ii)	(iii)

47. Consider the statements regarding Department related Standing Committees in India and select the correct answer from the codes given below:
(i) The maximum number of members in these committees are 31.
(ii) The committees consider the demands for Grants, Annual Reports of Ministries/Departments.
(iii) The reports of these Committees are treated as 'considered advice'.
(iv) The Committees also suggest the Cut Motion.

Codes:
(a) (i), (ii), (iii) (b) (i), (ii), (iv)
(c) (ii), (iii), (iv) (d) (i), (ii), (iii), (iv)

48. When was the All India Services Act passed by the Parliament of India?
(a) 1950 (b) 1951
(c) 1960 (d) 1961

49. The charged expenditure in the Budget is characterized as
(i) charged on the Consolidated Fund of India
(ii) not discussed in the Parliament
(iii) non-votable by the Parliament
(iv) salary and allowances of Comptroller and Auditor General of India is an example of charged expenditure.

Select the correct answer by using the codes given below:

Codes:
(a) (i), (ii), (iii) (b) (i), (ii), (iv)
(c) (i), (iii), (iv) (d) (i), (ii), (iii), (iv)

50. **Assertion (A):** The National Development Council (NDC) is not a product of the Planning Commission's recommendations.
Reason (R): The National Development Council reviews the working of the National Plans and also considers questions of social and economic policy.

Codes:
(a) Both (A) and (R) are correct and (R) is the correct explanation of (A).
(b) Both (A) and (R) are correct, but (R) is not the correct explanation of (A).
(c) (A) is true but (R) is false.
(d) (A) is false but (R) is true.

51. Primarily, a researcher should possess which of the following qualities?
(a) Scientific Attitude
(b) Scientific Thinking
(c) Scientific Behaviour
(d) Scientific Feelings

52. 'Interview is a process of social interaction.' Who said it?
(a) P.V. Young
(b) M.N. Basu
(c) Goode and Hatt
(d) V.M. Palmer

53. Select the correct research design indicated by the following characteristics:
(i) Describes the accurate features of a phenomenon.
(ii) Intends to find out the incidence of relationships between certain variables.
(iii) Makes certain specific predictions.

(a) Exploratory Research Design
(b) Descriptive Research Design
(c) Diagnostic Research Design
(d) Informal Experimental Design

54. According to Dale, a qualitative approach is not necessary in which of the following situations?
(a) When it is possible to study statistically representative samples of beneficiaries.
(b) When changes are the result of complex process.
(c) For the purpose of analysing relevance due to the value of judgements involved.
(d) When studying the organizational issues pertaining to policy implementation.

55. Probability and Non-probability sampling techniques are used to draw a sample of the population under study. Which include
(i) Systematic random sampling
(ii) Stratified random sampling
(iii) Cluster sampling
(iv) Purposive sampling
(v) Quota sampling
Select the correct group of probability sampling techniques by using codes given below:
(a) (i), (ii), (iii) and (iv)
(b) (i), (ii) and (iii)
(c) (i), (ii) and (iv)
(d) (i), (ii) and (v)

56. 'District Administration' means
(i) Collector's Office
(ii) Conglomeration of all the district level administrative departments
(iii) A territory marked off for special administrative purpose
(iv) The total management of public affairs within the territorial unit.
Choose the answer from the codes given below:
(a) (i), (ii) (b) (i), (ii), (iv)
(c) (ii), (iii) (d) (ii), (iv)

57. Which report of Second Administrative Reforms Commission is related to local governance?
(a) 5th (b) 6th
(c) 7th (d) 8th

58. Which Article of the Constitution of India provides for the District Planning Committee?
(a) Article 242 ZD (b) Article 243 ZA
(c) Article 243 ZD (d) Article 244 ZA

59. What was one of the most significant recommendations of L.M. Shinghvi Committee on the Panchayati Raj Institutions?
(a) Involvement of political parties in elections.
(b) Non-involvement of political parties in elections.
(c) Right to Recall
(d) Fixed term for PRIs.

60. What is the title of the United Nations Habitat 2006 Report?
(a) Urban Governance
(b) Urban Development
(c) Urban Millennium
(d) Urban Habitat

61. The Urban Poverty Alleviation Programmes have been clearly classified into some categories by which of the following in India?
(a) Planning Commission
(b) National Development Council
(c) Ministry of Urban Development and Poverty Alleviation
(d) National Commission on Urbanization

62. **Assertion (A):** Jawaharlal Nehru National Urban Renewal Mission (JNNURM) is a

ten years programme beginning from 2005-06

Reason (R): JNNURM's main components are urban infrastructure, urban governance and basic services for the urban poor.

Codes:

(a) Both (A) and (R) are correct and (R) is the correct explanation of (A).
(b) Both (A) and (R) are correct, but (R) is not the correct explanation of (A).
(c) (A) is true but (R) is false.
(d) (A) is false but (R) is true.

63. **Assertion (A):** Social Welfare Administration generates awareness about the challenges of a society in transition where negative use of technologies and practices are impacting on the well being of women and children.

Reason (R): Social Welfare Administration is the summation of social welfare institutions, policies and programmes.

Codes:

(a) Both (A) and (R) are correct and (R) is the correct explanation of (A).
(b) Both (A) and (R) are correct, but (R) is not the correct explanation of (A).
(c) (A) is true but (R) is false.
(d) (A) is false but (R) is true.

64. The most acceptable explanation of Social Justice is
(a) Economic development
(b) Social development
(c) Uplift of specific sections
(d) Uplift of all the sections of society

65. Central Social Welfare Board at present is functioning under the administrative control of—
(a) Ministry of Social Justice and Empowerment
(b) Ministry of Human Resource Development
(c) Ministry of Women and Child Development
(d) Ministry of Tribal Affairs

66. **Assertion (A):** Bio-ethics and Social Justice are interrelated.

Reason (R): Affordable access to health care especially for low income households and families refers to bio-ethics.

Codes:

(a) Both (A) and (R) are correct and (R) is the correct explanation of (A).
(b) Both (A) and (R) are correct, but (R) is not the correct explanation of (A).
(c) (A) is true but (R) is false.
(d) (A) is false but (R) is true.

67. 'Association of Voluntary Agencies for Rural Development' (AVARD) was established in the year:
(a) 1952 (b) 1958
(c) 1962 (d) 1968

68. Which of the following is not the policy implementation model as suggested by R. Elmore?
(a) Systems Management
(b) Conflict and Bargaining
(c) Organizational Development
(d) Policy Action Model

69. According to Poister, which of the following is the basis of Policy Evaluation?
(i) Effectiveness (ii) Adequacy
(iii) Appropriateness
Select the correct answer from the codes given below:

Codes:

(a) (i), (ii), (iii) (b) (i), (ii)
(c) (i), (iii) (d) (ii), (iii)

70. Which of the following is not the approach to policy evaluation?
(a) Evaluability Assessment
(b) Effectiveness Evaluation
(c) Evaluation Synthesis Approach
(d) Experimental method

71. Which of the following States does not have Panchayati Raj Institutions?
(a) Assam
(b) Arunachal Pradesh
(c) Tripura
(d) Nagaland

72. In which Article of the Constitution of India, the provision of 'workers' participation in management of undertakings is given?
(a) Article 42
(b) Article 42 A
(c) Article 43
(d) Article 43 A

73. Which among the following companies was not a 'Maharatna' company as on March, 2012?
(a) Coal India Limited
(b) Indian Oil Corporation Limited
(c) Bharat Petroleum Corporation Limited
(d) Oil and Natural Gas Corporation Limited

74. When did the Government of India first time accord 'Maharatna Status' to the Public Sector Undertakings?
(a) 1997 (b) 2001
(c) 2004 (d) 2009

75. Removal of poverty was stated as the dominant objective in which of the following Five Year Plan in India?
(a) Third Five Year Plan
(b) Fourth Five Year Plan
(c) Fifth Five Year Plan
(d) Sixth Five Year Plan

ANSWERS

1. (b)	2. (c)	3. (a)	4. (b)	5. (b)
6. (b)	7. (b)	8. (d)	9. (d)	10. (a)
11. (d)	12. (c)	13. (b)	14. (c)	15. (c)
16. (a)	17. (b)	18. (a)	19. (c)	20. (d)
21. (c)	22. (c)	23. (b)	24. (d)	25. (d)
26. (b)	27. (a)	28. (b)	29. (d)	30. (a)
31. (b)	32. (c)	33. (b)	34. (d)	35. (d)
36. (a)	37. (c)	38. (c)	39. (a)	40. (b)
41. (b)	42. (c)	43. (d)	44. (b)	45. (a)
46. (b)	47. (a)	48. (b)	49. (c)	50. (d)
51. (a)	52. (c)	53. (b)	54. (a)	55. (b)
56. (d)	57. (b)	58. (c)	59. (b)	60. (c)
61. (d)	62. (b)	63. (b)	64. (d)	65. (c)
66. (a)	67. (b)	68. (d)	69. (a)	70. (d)
71. (d)	72. (d)	73. (c)	74. (d)	75. (c)

DECEMBER–2011

Note: This paper contains Sixty (60) multiple-choice questions, each question carrying two (2) marks. Candidate is expected to answer any Fifty (50) questions. In case more than Fifty (50) questions are attempted, only the first Fifty (50) questions will be evaluated.

PAPER–I

1. Photo bleeding means
   (a) Photo cropping
   (b) Photo placement
   (c) Photo cutting
   (d) Photo colour adjustment

2. While designing communication strategy feed-forward studies are conducted by
   (a) Audience (b) Communicator
   (c) Satellite (d) Media

3. In which language the newspapers have highest circulation?
   (a) English (b) Hindi
   (c) Bengali (d) Tamil

4. Aspect ratio of TV Screen is
   (a) 4 : 3 (b) 3 : 4
   (c) 2 : 3 (d) 2 : 4

5. Communication with oneself is known as
   (a) Organisational Communication
   (b) Grapevine Communication
   (c) Interpersonal Communication
   (d) Intrapersonal Communication

6. The term 'SITE' stands for
   (a) Satellite Indian Television Experiment
   (b) Satellite International Television Experiment
   (c) Satellite Instructional Television Experiment
   (d) Satellite Instructional Teachers Education

7. What is the number that comes next in the sequence?
   2, 5, 9, 19, 37, ___
   (a) 76 (b) 74
   (c) 75 (d) 50

8. Find the next letter for the series MPSV.....
   (a) X (b) Y
   (c) Z (d) A

9. If '367' means 'I am happy'; '748' means 'you are sad' and '469' means 'happy and sad' in a given code, then which of the following represents 'and' in that code?
   (a) 3 (b) 6
   (c) 9 (d) 4

10. The basis of the following classification is 'animal', 'man', 'house', 'book', and 'student':
    (a) Definite descriptions
    (b) Proper names
    (c) Descriptive phrases
    (d) Common names

11. **Assertion (A):** The coin when flipped next time will come up tails.
    Reason (R): Because the coin was flipped five times in a row, and each time it came up heads.
    Choose the correct answer from below:
    (a) Both (A) and (R) are true, and (R) is the correct explanation of (A).
    (b) Both (A) and (R) are false, and (R) is the correct explanation of (A).

(c) (A) is doubtful, (R) is true, and (R) is not the correct explanation of (A).
(d) (A) is doubtful, (R) is false, and (R) is the correct explanation of (A).

12. The relation 'is a sister of' is
(a) non-symmetrical (b) symmetrical
(c) asymmetrical (d) transitive

13. If the proposition "Vegetarians are not meat eaters" is false, then which of the following inferences is correct? Choose from the codes given below:
1. "Some vegetarians are meat eaters" is true.
2. "All vegetarians are meat eaters" is doubtful.
3. "Some vegetarians are not meat eaters" is true.
4. "Some vegetarians are not meat eaters" is doubtful.

Codes:
(a) 1, 2 and 3 (b) 2, 3 and 4
(c) 1, 3 and 4 (d) 1, 2 and 4

14. Determine the nature of the following definition:
'Poor' means having an annual income of ₹ 10,000.
(a) persuasive (b) precising
(c) lexical (d) stipulative

15. Which one of the following is not an argument?
(a) If today is Tuesday, tomorrow will be Wednesday.
(b) Since today is Tuesday, tomorrow will be Wednesday.
(c) Ram insulted me so I punched him in the nose.
(d) Ram is not at home, so he must have gone to town.

16. Venn diagram is a kind of diagram to
(a) represent and assess the truth of elementary inferences with the help of Boolean Algebra of classes.
(b) represent and assess the validity of elementary inferences with the help of Boolean Algebra of classes.
(c) represent but not assess the validity of elementary inferences with the help of Boolean Algebra of classes.
(d) assess but not represent the validity of elementary inferences with the help of Boolean Algebra of classes.

17. Inductive logic studies the way in which a premise may
(a) support and entail a conclusion
(b) not support but entail a conclusion
(c) neither support nor entail a conclusion
(d) support a conclusion without entailing it

18. Which of the following statements are true? Choose from the codes given below.
1. Some arguments, while not completely valid, are almost valid.
2. A sound argument may be invalid.
3. A cogent argument may have a probably false conclusion.
4. A statement may be true or false.

Codes:
(a) 1 and 2 (b) 1, 3 and 4
(c) Only 4 (d) 3 and 4

19. If the side of the square increases by 40%, then the area of the square increases by
(a) 60% (b) 40%
(c) 196% (d) 96%

20. There are 10 lamps in a hall. Each one of them can be switched on independently. The number of ways in which hall can be illuminated is
(a) 10^2 (b) 1023
(c) 2^{10} (d) 10!

21. How many numbers between 100 and 300 begin or end with 2?
(a) 100 (b) 110
(c) 120 (d) 180

22. In a college having 300 students, every student reads 5 newspapers and every newspaper is read by 60 students. The number of newspapers required is
(a) at least 30 (b) at most 20
(c) exactly 25 (d) exactly 5

The total CO_2 emissions from various sectors are 5 mmt. In the Pie Chart given below, the percentage contribution to CO_2 emissions from various sectors is indicated.

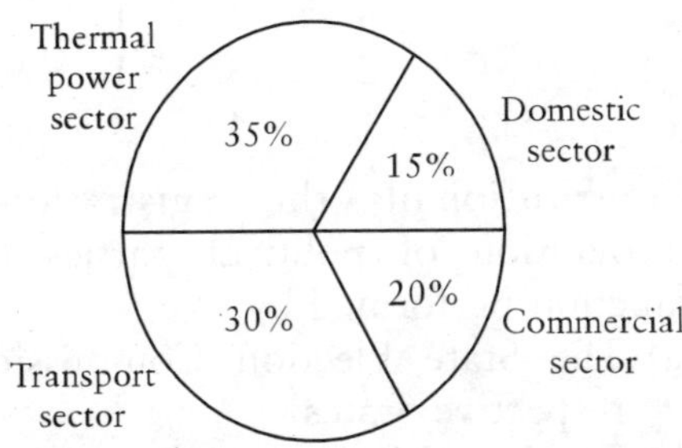

23. What is the absolute CO_2 emission from domestic sector?
(a) 1.5 mmt (b) 2.5 mmt
(c) 1.75 mmt (d) 0.75 mmt

24. What is the absolute CO_2 emission for combined thermal power and transport sectors?
(a) 3.25 mmt (b) 1.5 mmt
(c) 2.5 mmt (d) 4 mmt

25. Which of the following operating system is used on mobile phones?
(a) Windows Vista
(b) Android
(c) Windows XP
(d) All of the above

26. If $(y)_x$ represents a number y in base x, then which of the following numbers is smallest of all?
(a) $(1111)_2$ (b) $(1111)_8$
(c) $(1111)_{10}$ (d) $(1111)_{16}$

27. High level programming language can be converted to machine language using which of the following?
(a) Oracle (b) Compiler
(c) Mat lab (d) Assembler

28. HTML is used to create
(a) machine language program
(b) high level program
(c) web page
(d) web server

29. The term DNS stands for
(a) Domain Name System
(b) Defense Nuclear System
(c) Downloadable New Software
(d) Dependent Name Server

30. IPv4 and IPv6 are addresses used to identify computers on the internet. Find the correct statement out of the following:
(a) Number of bits required for IPv4 address is more than number of bits required for IPv6 address.
(b) Number of bits required for IPv4 address is same as number of bits required for IPv6 address.
(c) Number of bits required for IPv4 address is less than number of bits required for IPv6 address.
(d) Number of bits required for IPv4 address is 64.

31. Which of the following pollutants affects the respiratory tract in humans?
(a) Carbon monoxide
(b) Nitric oxide
(c) Sulphur dioxide
(d) Aerosols

32. Which of the following pollutants is not emitted from the transport sector?
(a) Oxides of nitrogen
(b) Chlorofluorocarbons
(c) Carbon monoxide
(d) Poly aromatic hydrocarbons

33. Which of the following sources of energy has the maximum potential in India?
(a) Solar energy
(b) Wind energy
(c) Ocean thermal energy
(d) Tidal energy

34. Which of the following is not a source of pollution in soil?
(a) Transport sector
(b) Agriculture sector
(c) Thermal power plants
(d) Hydropower plants

35. Which of the following is not a natural hazard?
(a) Earthquake (b) Tsunami
(c) Flash floods (d) Nuclear accident

36. Ecological footprint represents
(a) area of productive land and water to meet the resources requirement
(b) energy consumption
(c) CO_2 emissions per person
(d) forest cover

37. The aim of value education to inculcate in students is
(a) the moral values
(b) the social values
(c) the political values
(d) the economic values

38. Indicate the number of Regional Offices of University Grants Commission of India.
(a) 10 (b) 07
(c) 08 (d) 09

39. One-rupee currency note in India bears the signature of
(a) The President of India
(b) Finance Minister of India
(c) Governor, Reserve Bank of India
(d) Finance Secretary of Government of India

40. Match the List I with the List II and select the correct answer from the codes given below:

List I (Commissions and Committees)
A. First Administrative Reforms Commission
B. Paul H. Appleby Committee I
C. K. Santhanam Committee
D. Second Administrative Reforms Commission

List II (Year)
1. 2005 2. 1962
3. 1966 4. 1953

Codes:	A	B	C	D
(a)	1	3	2	4
(b)	3	4	2	1
(c)	4	2	3	1
(d)	2	1	4	3

41. Constitutionally the registration and recognition of political parties is the function performed by
(a) The State Election Commission of respective States
(b) The Law Ministry of Government of India
(c) The Election Commission of India
(d) Election Department of the State Governments

42. The members of Gram Sabha are
(a) Sarpanch, Upsarpanch and all elected Panchas
(b) Sarpanch, Upsarpanch and Village level worker
(c) Sarpanch, Gram Sevak and elected Panchas
(d) Registered voters of Village Panchayat

43. By which of the following methods the true evaluation of the students is possible?
(a) Evaluation at the end of the course
(b) Evaluation twice in a year
(c) Continuous evaluation
(d) Formative evaluation

44. Suppose a student wants to share his problems with his teacher and he visits the teacher's house for the purpose, the teacher should

(a) contact the student's parents and solve his problem
(b) suggest him that he should never visit his house
(c) suggest him to meet the principal and solve the problem
(d) extend reasonable help and boost his morale

45. When some students are deliberately attempting to disturb the discipline of the class by making mischief, what will be your role as a teacher?
(a) Expelling those students
(b) Isolate those students
(c) Reform the group with your authority
(d) Giving them an opportunity for introspection and improve their behaviour

46. Which of the following belongs to a projected aid?
(a) Blackboard (b) Diorama
(c) Epidiascope (d) Globe

47. A teacher is said to be fluent in asking questions, if he can ask
(a) meaningful questions
(b) as many questions as possible
(c) maximum number of questions in a fixed time
(d) many meaningful questions in a fixed time

48. Which of the following qualities is most essential for a teacher?
(a) He should be a learned person
(b) He should be a well dressed person
(c) He should have patience
(d) He should be an expert in his subject

49. A hypothesis is a
(a) law (b) canon
(c) postulate (d) supposition

50. Suppose you want to investigate the working efficiency of nationalised bank in India, which one of the following would you follow?
(a) Area Sampling
(b) Multi-stage Sampling
(c) Sequential Sampling
(d) Quota Sampling

51. Controlled group condition is applied in
(a) Survey Research
(b) Historical Research
(c) Experimental Research
(d) Descriptive Research

52. Workshops are meant for
(a) giving lectures
(b) multiple target groups
(c) showcase new theories
(d) hands on training/experience

53. Which one of the following is a research tool?
(a) Graph (b) Illustration
(c) Questionnaire (d) Diagram

54. Research is not considered ethical if it
(a) tries to prove a particular point.
(b) does not ensure privacy and anonymity of the respondent.
(c) does not investigate the data scientifically.
(d) is not of a very high standard.

Read the following passage carefully and answer the questions (55 to 60):

The catalytic fact of the twentieth century is uncontrollable development, consumerist society, political materialism, and spiritual devaluation. This inordinate development has led to the transcendental 'second reality' of sacred perception that biologically transcendence is a part of human life. As the century closes, it dawns with imperative vigour that the 'first reality' of enlightened rationalism and the 'second reality' of the Beyond have to be harmonised in a worthy state of man. The *de facto* values describe what we are, they portray the 'is' of our ethic, they are *est* values

(Latin *est* means is). The ideal values tell us what we ought to be, they are *esto* values (Latin *esto* 'ought to be'). Both have to be in the ebb and flow of consciousness. The ever new science and technology and the ever-perennial faith are two modes of one certainty, that is the wholeness of man, his courage to be, his share in Being.

The materialistic foundations of science have crumbled down. Science itself has proved that matter is energy, processes are as valid as facts, and affirmed the non-materiality of the universe. The encounter of the 'two cultures', the scientific and the humane, will restore the normal vision, and will be the bedrock of a 'science of understanding' in the new century. It will give new meaning to the ancient perception that quantity (measure) and quality (value) coexist at the root of nature. Human endeavours cannot afford to be humanistically irresponsible.

55. The problem raised in the passage reflects overall on
    (a) Consumerism
    (b) Materialism
    (c) Spiritual devaluation
    (d) Inordinate development
56. The *de facto* values in the passage means
    (a) What is
    (b) What ought to be
    (c) What can be
    (d) Where it is
57. According to the passage, the 'first reality' constitutes
    (a) Economic prosperity
    (b) Political development
    (c) Sacred perception of life
    (d) Enlightened rationalism
58. Encounter of the 'two cultures', the scientific and the human implies
    (a) Restoration of normal vision
    (b) Universe is both material and non-material
    (c) Man is superior to nature
    (d) Co-existence of quantity and quality in nature
59. The contents of the passage are
    (a) Descriptive (b) Prescriptive
    (c) Axiomatic (d) Optional
60. The passage indicates that science has proved that
    (a) universe is material
    (b) matter is energy
    (c) nature has abundance
    (d) humans are irresponsible

ANSWERS

1. (a)	2. (b)	3. (b)	4. (a)	5. (d)
6. (c)	7. (c)	8. (b)	9. (c)	10. (d)
11. (c)	12. (b)	13. (a)	14. (b)	15. (a)
16. (b)	17. (d)	18. (d)	19. (d)	20. (b)
21. (b)	22. (c)	23. (d)	24. (a)	25. (b)
26. (a)	27. (b)	28. (c)	29. (a)	30. (c)
31. (a)	32. (b)	33. (b)	34. (d)	35. (d)
36. (a)	37. (a)	38. (b)	39. (d)	40. (b)
41. (c)	42. (d)	43. (d)	44. (d)	45. (d)
46. (c)	47. (d)	48. (c)	49. (d)	50. (b)
51. (c)	52. (d)	53. (c)	54. (b)	55. (c)
56. (a)	57. (d)	58. (a)	59. (a)	60. (b)

PAPER–II

Note: This paper contains fifty (50) objective type questions, each question carrying two (2) marks. All questions are compulsory.

1. Who advocated for replacing the 'Law of authority' with 'Law of situation'?
    (a) Chester Barnard
    (b) Max Weber

(c) Mary Parker Follet
(d) Herbert Simon

2. The name of Ivan Major is associated with
(a) Privatization
(b) Bureaucracy
(c) Good Governance
(d) E-Governance

3. Managerialism is the feature of
(a) New Public Administration
(b) Comparative Public Administration
(c) New Public Management
(d) Development Administration

4. 'Daily Routine drives out planning' (James March and Herbert Simon) is called
(a) Parkinson's Law (b) Gresham's Law
(c) Peter Principle (d) Cocroach Effect

5. Chief Minister of a State is a member of
(a) Planning Commission
(b) Programme Evaluation Organisation
(c) State Election Commission
(d) National Development Council

6. 'In hierarchy every employee tends to rise to his level of incompetence.' This statement is given by
(a) Laurence J. Peter (b) Henri Fayol
(c) L. Gulick (d) Fredrickson

7. 'Bureaucracy means specialized hierarchies and long lines of communication.' This statement is given by
(a) Max Weber
(b) Mooney
(c) Herbert Simon
(d) Marshall E. Dimock

8. How many subjects are there in the 11th Schedule of the Indian Constitution?
(a) 18 (b) 28
(c) 29 (d) 19

9. 'Public Administration is administration related to the operation of the Government, whether local or central.' This definition of Public Administration is given by
(a) Woodrow Wilson
(b) Percy Mc Queen
(c) E.W. Russell
(d) David H. Rosenbloom

10. When a researcher or enumerator visits personally to the respondents and filled up the information sheet, the technique is called
(a) Schedule (b) Questionnaire
(c) Interview (d) Observation

11. Which of the following are the grounds of redifferentiation between Public Administration and Private Administration as envisaged by Sir Josiah Stamp?
(i) Principle of Uniformity
(ii) Principle of External Financial Control
(iii) Principle of Ministerial Responsibility
(iv) Principle of Marginal Return
Codes:
(a) (i), (iv)
(b) (ii), (iii)
(c) Only (i)
(d) (i), (ii), (iii) & (iv)

12. Public Administration deals with
(i) Public Finance
(ii) Management of Human Resources
(iii) Administration of Local Bodies
(iv) Aspects of Educational Administration
Codes:
(a) (i), (ii) (b) (ii), (iii), (iv)
(c) (i), (iii) (d) (i), (ii), (iii), (iv)

13. Hawthorne studies of Elton Mayo discovered
(i) The span of control
(ii) Leadership style
(iii) Informal group norms
(iv) Motion study
Codes:
(a) (i), (ii), (iii), (iv) (b) (i), (iv)
(c) (iii) (d) (ii) & (iii)

14. Which of the following are part of British Legacy?
    (i) Secretariat System
    (ii) Tenure System
    (iii) Comptroller and Auditor General of India
    (iv) Railway Board

    Codes:
    (a) (i), (ii) & (iii)
    (b) (i), (ii), (iii) & (iv)
    (c) (i) & (ii)
    (d) (i) & (iv)

15. Which of the following Commissions/ Committees are associated with Civil Service Reforms?
    (i) Aitchison Commission, 1886
    (ii) Islington Commission, 1912
    (iii) Lee Commission, 1923
    (iv) L. Smith Committee, 1919

    Codes:
    (a) (i), (ii), (iii) & (iv)
    (b) (i), (ii) & (iv)
    (c) (i), (ii) & (iii)
    (d) (ii), (iii) & (iv)

16. Which of the following are the advantages of tenure system in the Central Secretariat?
    (i) It provides for a better coordination and understanding between the Centre and States.
    (ii) It establishes a lively link with the grass roots realities.
    (iii) It broadens the vision and outlook of senior civil servants of the States.
    (iv) It facilitates independence of civil servants.

    Codes:
    (a) (i), (ii), (iii) & (iv)
    (b) (i), (ii) & (iii)
    (c) (ii) & (iii)
    (d) (i) & (iv)

17. Mooney and Reiley have supported
    (i) Co-ordinating principle
    (ii) Hierarchical principle
    (iii) Line and Staff Principle
    (iv) Principle of Division of Labour

    Codes:
    (a) (i) & (ii)
    (b) (i) & (iii)
    (c) (i), (ii) & (iii)
    (d) (i), (ii), (iii) & (iv)

18. The top level management of Secretariat includes
    (i) Secretary
    (ii) Additional Secretary
    (iii) Joint Secretary
    (iv) Deputy Secretary

    Codes:
    (a) (i), (ii), (iii) & (iv)
    (b) (i), (ii) & (iii)
    (c) (i) & (ii)
    (d) (i) & (iii)

19. Which of the following factors did not contribute to the size and growth of Comparative Public Administration?
    (i) The rise of the new Public Management approach.
    (ii) Satisfaction with traditional administration which was culture bound.
    (iii) Growth and development of Science and Technology impacting the administrative system.
    (iv) Technical Assistance Programme provided to the countries of the Third World.

    Codes:
    (a) (i), (ii), (iii) & (iv)
    (b) (i), (ii) & (iii)
    (c) (i) & (ii)
    (d) (ii) & (iii)

20. Which of the following are the objectives of training of civil servants?
    (i) Capacity Building
    (ii) Attitudinal Change
    (iii) Broadening of the vision and outlook
    (iv) Strengthening motivation and morale

Codes:
(a) (i), (ii), (iii) & (iv)
(b) (i), (ii) & (iii)
(c) (i) & (ii)
(d) (ii) & (iii)

Note: Instructions to answer Question Nos. 21-30: Given below are two statements, one labelled as Assertion (A) and the other labelled as Reason (R). Examine these two statements carefully and state if the Assertion (A) and the Reason (R) are individually true and if so, whether the Reason is a correct explanation of Assertion.

Select the correct answer from the codes given below the question.

Assertion (A): There are many differences between Public Administration and Private Administration.
Reason (R): These differences are because of working system of the organisations.
Codes:
(a) Both (A) and (R) are correct and (R) is the correct explanation of (A).
(b) Both (A) and (R) are correct, but (R) is not the correct explanation of (A).
(c) (A) is true but (R) is false.
(d) (A) is false but (R) is true.

21. **Assertion (A):** Line of communication should not be interrupted when organization functions.
Reason (R): 'Gang Plank' violates the principle of unity of command.

22. **Assertion (A):** Autonomy is the main feature of Public Corporations.
Reason (R): Public Corporations are established by an Act of Parliament.

23. **Assertion (A):** New Public Administration grew out of the feeling that administration is falling short of the expectations of people.
Reason (R): There were civil strifes, political violence and campus unrest in different countries.

24. **Assertion (A):** There is educative value in supervision.
Reason (R): 'Work that is not supervised is not done.'

25. **Assertion (A):** Traditional Authority is bound on rules.
Reason (R): Rules and regulations help to check arbitrary action.

26. **Assertion (A):** Taylor provided scientific basis to the study of Public Administration.
Reason (R): Taylor has a passion for efficiency.

27. **Assertion (A):** Maintenance of law and order is the responsibility of District Collector.
Reason (R): Law and order is still a major challenge to district administration.

28. **Assertion (A):** Cross-cultural analysis helps study of people from a broader perspective.
Reason (R): Comparison of developing and developed countries come under cross-cultural analysis.

29. **Assertion (A):** The Panchayati Raj Administration is aimed at Empowerment of People.
Reason (R): Empowerment of People is a threat to Federalism.

30. **Assertion (A):** Bureaucracy is the agent of social change.
Reason (R): Bureaucracy thrives under the cloak of ministerial responsibility.

31. Match List I with List II and select the correct answer from the codes given below:
List I
(A) Doresey (B) Y. Dror
(C) Robert Dahl (D) Ordway Tead
List II
1. Comparative Public Administration
2. The Art of Administration

3. Policy Analysis Approach
4. Information Energy Model

Codes:	A	B	C	D
(a)	4	3	1	2
(b)	2	1	4	3
(c)	1	2	3	4
(d)	3	4	2	1

32. Match List I with List II and select the correct answer from the codes given below:

List I
(A) Span of Attention
(B) Supervision
(C) Carl Rogar
(D) Argyris

List II
1. Millet
2. Counselling Therapy
3. V.A. Graicunas
4. Immaturity—Maturity Model

Codes:	A	B	C	D
(a)	1	2	4	3
(b)	3	1	2	4
(c)	2	3	1	4
(d)	4	1	3	2

33. Match List I with List II and select the correct answer from the codes given below:

List I
(A) Theory Z
(B) ERG Theory
(C) Bounded Rationality
(D) Performance—Satisfaction Model

List II
1. Porter Lawler
2. Skinner
3. Alderfer
4. William Ouchi
5. Simon

Codes:	A	B	C	D
(a)	4	2	5	1
(b)	4	1	3	2
(c)	4	3	5	1
(d)	4	2	5	3

34. Match List I with List II and select the correct answer from the codes given below:

List I
(A) National Commission for Review of Working of the Constitution of India
(B) National Commission on Centre-State Relations, 2005
(C) Committee on Administrative Arrangements for Rural Development
(D) Working Groups on District Planning

List II
1. Justice Punchhi
2. G.V.K. Rao
3. C.H. Hanumantha Rao
4. Venkat Challiah

Codes:	A	B	C	D
(a)	2	4	3	1
(b)	1	2	3	4
(c)	4	1	2	3
(d)	3	2	4	1

35. Match List I with List II and select the correct answer from the codes given below:

List I
(A) Epistemological
(B) Catch 22
(C) Peter Principle
(D) Ombudsmanic

List II
1. Grievance handling
2. Rise to level of incompetence
3. F.W. Taylor
4. Critique of Bureaucracy.
5. Disciplines capacity to build theories

Codes:	A	B	C	D
(a)	1	3	5	2
(b)	5	4	2	1
(c)	2	3	5	1
(d)	1	5	3	4

36. Match List I and List II and select the correct answer from the codes given below:

List I

(A) Ecology of Administration
(B) Entrepreneurial Government
(C) New Public Administration
(D) Proverbs of Administration

List II

1. Simon
2. Dwight Waldo
3. Willoughby
4. Osborne and Ted Gaebler
5. F.W. Riggs

Codes:	A	B	C	D
(a)	4	3	3	2
(b)	5	4	1	3
(c)	4	2	1	3
(d)	5	4	2	1

37. Match the List I and List II and select the correct answer from the codes given below:

List I

(A) Robert Jackson (B) F.W. Taylor
(C) Henri Fayol (D) Ferrel Heady

List II

1. Middle Range Theory Formulation
2. Esprit de crops
3. Functional Foremanship
4. Comparative Public Administration
5. Job-Task Pyramid

Codes:	A	B	C	D
(a)	4	2	3	1
(b)	3	1	2	4
(c)	4	3	2	1
(d)	1	2	4	3

38. Match List I and List II and answer from codes given below:

List I

(A) District Planning
(B) Contingency Fund of India
(C) Metropolitan Planning Committee
(D) Union and State Public Service Commission

List II

1. Art. 267 2. Art. 243ZE
3. Art. 243ZD 4. Art. 315
5. Art. 312

Codes:	A	B	C	D
(a)	3	1	2	4
(b)	3	1	5	2
(c)	3	2	4	5
(d)	2	1	3	4

39. Arrange in a correct sequence and select correct answer from the codes given below:

1. Indian Police Act
2. Establishment of Board of Revenue
3. Indian Institute of Public Administration
4. National Commission on Urbanization

Codes:

(a) 1, 2, 3 & 4 (b) 2, 1, 3 & 4
(c) 4, 2, 1 & 3 (d) 3, 2, 1 & 4

40. Arrange in correct chronological order and select answer from the codes given below:

1. Creation of the office of District Collector.
2. Gorewala Committee
3. Dantewala Committee
4. Sarkaria Commission

Codes:

(a) 1, 2, 4 & 3 (b) 4, 2, 1 & 3
(c) 2, 4, 3 & 1 (d) 1, 2, 3 & 4

41. Arrange the following books in chronological order by using the codes given below:

1. The Administrative Behaviour
2. Creative Experience
3. Introduction to the study of Public Administration
4. Reinventing Government

Codes:

(a) 1, 2, 3 & 4 (b) 2, 1, 4 & 3
(c) 3, 2, 1 & 4 (d) 2, 3, 1 & 4

42. Arrange the following steps in the passage of Budget in India in sequential order by using the codes given below:
    1. General Discussion
    2. Presentation of Budget
    3. Passing of Financial Bill
    4. Passing of Appropriation Bill

    Codes:
    (a) 1, 2, 3 & 4 (b) 2, 1, 4 & 3
    (c) 4, 2, 1 & 3 (d) 3, 4, 1 & 2

43. Arrange the following reports in a chronological order and select the correct answer from the codes given below:
    1. Fulton Committee Report
    2. Brownlow Committee Report
    3. First Hoover Commission Report
    4. Assheton Committee Report

    Codes:
    (a) 1, 2, 3 & 4 (b) 2, 4, 3 & 1
    (c) 3, 1, 4 & 2 (d) 4, 1, 2 & 3

44. In Maslow's 'Need Hierarchy' there are five levels of needs. What is the order in which they are placed?
    1. Safety needs
    2. Esteem needs
    3. Social needs
    4. Self Actualization needs
    5. Physical needs

    Codes:
    (a) 1, 2, 3, 4 & 5 (b) 2, 3, 4, 5 & 1
    (c) 5, 1, 3, 2 & 4 (d) 5, 1, 2, 3 & 4

45. Arrange the organizational hierarchy of the Central Secretariat in a descending order and select the correct answer from the codes given below:
    1. Branch 2. Office
    3. Division 4. Wing

    Codes:
    (a) 4, 3, 1 & 2 (b) 3, 4, 2 & 1
    (c) 4, 2, 3 & 1 (d) 1, 2, 3 & 4

Read the following paragraph and answer the Questions from 46-50:

The need for decentralised planning in India has been felt for a long time. But it was strongly articulated during the Fourth Five Year Plan (1969-74). To encourage decentralised planning, a state planning machinery in each State was set up but planning in India continued to remain highly centralised. This was its single most pernicious weakness. But the seventy-third and seventy-fourth constitutional amendments (1992) make it mandatory to decentralise planning in India. Centralised planning has throttled balanced and allround regional development. As a result, people's felt needs have not been reflected in the plans. Particularly, the present mode of planning has not assisted much the weaker sections of the society.

Decentralised planning is bottom-up planning. It is undertaken at the grass-roots level. It involves local people and their organisations. Being closer to the people, it directly meets their needs and aspirations and is thus best suited to enlist people's participation. Being based on citizen participation its implementation would make most effective use of locally available resources. As decentralised planning starts from the lower level it gets integrated with the people and is thus people-oriented.

46. Which of the following statement about decentralised planning is true in present day India?
    (a) It is option of the State to introduce
    (b) It is detrimental to regional development
    (c) It is top down planning
    (d) It is mandatory planning

47. The advantages of decentralised planning is/are (select the correct answer from the codes given below):
    (i) Better use of local resources
    (ii) Effective implementation of the plan

(iii) Ensuring people's participation in planning
(iv) Ensures bureaucratic responsibility to the local people

Codes:
(a) (i), (ii), (iii), (iv) (b) (i), (ii), (iii)
(c) (i), (ii) (d) (i) only

48. Which of the following is the meaning of Decentralised Planning?
(a) It is based on blue-print model
(b) It is directed planning
(c) It is planning from below
(d) It is autonomous of National framework of planning

49. Which one of the following is not the weakness of centralized planning?
(a) Imbalanced Regional Development
(b) Gap between the plan objectives and people felt needs
(c) Integration of national and local resources
(d) Blocking of people's participation in planning

50. The initiative for decentralized planning in India was first taken under
(a) Third Five Year Plan
(b) Fourth Five Year Plan
(c) Fifth Five Year Plan
(d) 73rd Amendment in the Constitution

ANSWERS

1. (c)	2. (a)	3. (a)	4. (b)	5. (d)
6. (a)	7. (a)	8. (c)	9. (b)	10. (a)
11. (c)	12. (a)	13. (c)	14. (b)	15. (c)
16. (b)	17. (c)	18. (b)	19. (c)	20. (c)
21. (b)	22. (a)	23. (b)	24. (c)	25. (b)
26. (a)	27. (b)	28. (d)	29. (b)	30. (a)
31. (a)	32. (b)	33. (c)	34. (c)	35. (*)
36. (b)	37. (a)	38. (a)	39. (d)	40. (a)
41. (c)	42. (b)	43. (b)	44. (c)	45. (c)
46. (a)	47. (b)	48. (c)	49. (c)	50. (b)

JUNE–2011

Note: This paper contains Sixty (60) multiple-choice questions, each question carrying two (2) marks. Candidate is expected to answer any Fifty (50) questions. In case more than Fifty (50) questions are attempted, only the first Fifty (50) questions will be evaluated.

PAPER–I

1. A research paper is a brief report of research work based on
   (a) Primary Data only
   (b) Secondary Data only
   (c) Both Primary and Secondary Data
   (d) None of the above

2. Newton gave three basic laws of motion. This research is categorised as
   (a) Descriptive Research
   (b) Sample Survey
   (c) Fundamental Research
   (d) Applied Research

3. A group of experts in a specific area of knowledge assembled at a place and prepared a syllabus for a new course. The process may be termed as
   (a) Seminar (b) Workshop
   (c) Conference (d) Symposium

4. In the process of conducting research "Formulation of Hypothesis" is followed by
   (a) Statement of Objectives
   (b) Analysis of Data
   (c) Selection of Research Tools
   (d) Collection of Data

Read the following passage carefully and answer questions 5 to 10:

All historians are interpreters of text if they be private letters, Government records or parish birthlists or whatever. For most kinds of historians, these are only the necessary means to understanding something other than the texts themselves, such as a political action or a historical trend, whereas for the intellectual historian, a full understanding of his chosen texts is itself the aim of his enquiries. Of course, the intellectual history is particularly prone to draw on the focus of other disciplines that are habitually interpreting texts for purposes of their own, probing the reasoning that ostensibly connects premises and conclusions. Furthermore, the boundaries with adjacent subdisciplines are shifting and indistinct: the history of art and the history of science both claim a certain autonomy, partly just because they require specialised technical skills, but both can also be seen as part of a wider intellectual history, as is evident when one considers, for example, the common stock of knowledge about cosmological beliefs or moral ideals of a period.

Like all historians, the intellectual historian is a consumer rather than a producer of 'methods'. His distinctiveness lies in which aspect of the past he is trying to illuminate, not in having exclusive possession of either a corpus of evidence or a body of techniques. That being said, it does seem that the label 'intellectual history' attracts a disproportionate share of misunderstanding.

It is alleged that intellectual history is the history of something that never really mattered. The long dominance of the historical profession by political historians bred a kind of philistinism, an unspoken belief that power and its exercise was 'what mattered'. The prejudice was reinforced by the assertion that political action was never really the outcome of principles or ideas that were 'more flapdoodle'. The legacy of this precept is still discernible in the tendency to require ideas to have 'licensed' the political class before they can be deemed worthy of intellectual attention, as if there were some reasons why the history of art or science, of philosophy or literature, were somehow of interest and significance than the history of Parties or Parliaments. Perhaps in recent years the mirror-image of this philistinism has been more common in the claim that ideas of any one is of systematic expression or sophistication do not matter, as if they were only held by a minority.

Answer the following questions:

5. An intellectual historian aims to fully understand
   (a) the chosen texts of his own
   (b) political actions
   (c) historical trends
   (d) his enquiries
6. Intellectual historians do not claim exclusive possession of
   (a) conclusions
   (b) any corpus of evidence
   (c) distinctiveness
   (d) habitual interpretation
7. The misconceptions about intellectual history stem from
   (a) a body of techniques
   (b) the common stock of knowledge
   (c) the dominance of political historians
   (d) cosmological beliefs
8. What is philistinism?
   (a) Reinforcement of prejudice
   (b) Fabrication of reasons
   (c) The hold of land-owning classes
   (d) Belief that power and its exercise matter
9. Knowledge of cosmological beliefs or moral ideas of a period can be drawn as part of
   (a) literary criticism
   (b) history of science
   (c) history of philosophy
   (d) intellectual history
10. The claim that ideas of any one is of systematic expression do not matter, as if they were held by a minority, is
    (a) to have a licensed political class
    (b) a political action
    (c) a philosophy of literature
    (d) the mirror-image of philistinism
11. Public communication tends to occur within a more
    (a) complex structure
    (b) political structure
    (c) convenient structure
    (d) formal structure
12. Transforming thoughts, ideas and messages into verbal and non-verbal signs is referred to as
    (a) channelisation (b) mediation
    (c) encoding (d) decoding
13. Effective communication needs a supportive
    (a) economic environment
    (b) political environment
    (c) social environment
    (d) multi-cultural environment
14. A major barrier in the transmission of cognitive data in the process of communication is an individual's
    (a) personality (b) expectation
    (c) social status (d) coding ability
15. When communicated, institutionalised stereotypes become
    (a) myths (b) reasons
    (c) experiences (d) convictions
16. In mass communication, selective perception is dependent on the receiver's

(a) competence (b) pre-disposition
(c) receptivity (d) ethnicity

17. Determine the relationship between the pair of words NUMERATOR : DENOMINATOR and then select the pair of words from the following which have a similar relationship:
(a) fraction : decimal
(b) divisor : quotient
(c) top : bottom
(d) dividend : divisor

18. Find the wrong number in the sequence
125, 127, 130, 135, 142, 153, 165
(a) 130 (b) 142
(c) 153 (d) 165

19. If HOBBY is coded as IOBY and LOBBY is coded as MOBY; then BOBBY is coded as
(a) BOBY (b) COBY
(c) DOBY (d) OOBY

20. The letters in the first set have certain relationship. On the basis of this relationship, make the right choice for the second set
K/T : 11/20 :: J/R :?
(a) 10/8 (b) 10/18
(c) 11/19 (d) 10/19

21. If A = 5, B = 6, C = 7, D = 8 and so on, what do the following numbers stand for?
17, 19, 20, 9, 8
(a) Plane (b) Moped
(c) Motor (d) Tonga

22. The price of oil is increased by 25%. If the expenditure is not allowed to increase, the ratio between the reduction in consumption and the original consumption is
(a) 1:3 (b) 1:4
(c) 1:5 (d) 1:6

23. How many 8's are there in the following sequence which are preceded by 5 but not immediately followed by 3?
5 8 3 7 5 8 6 3 8 5 4 5 8 4 7 6
5 5 8 3 5 8 7 5 8 2 8 5
(a) 4 (b) 5
(c) 7 (d) 3

24. If a rectangle were called a circle, a circle a point, a point a triangle and a triangle a square, the shape of a wheel is
(a) Rectangle (b) Circle
(c) Point (d) Triangle

25. Which one of the following methods is best suited for mapping the distribution of different crops as provided in the standard classification of crops in India?
(a) Pie diagram
(b) Chorochromatic technique
(c) Isopleth technique
(d) Dot method

26. Which one of the following does not come under the methods of data classification?
(a) Qualitative (b) Normative
(c) Spatial (d) Quantitative

27. Which one of the following is not a source of data?
(a) Administrative records
(b) Population census
(c) GIS
(d) Sample survey

28. If the statement 'some men are cruel' is false, which of the following statements/statement are/is true?
(i) All men are cruel.
(ii) No men are cruel.
(iii) Some men are not cruel.
(a) (i) and (iii) (b) (i) and (ii)
(c) (ii) and (iii) (d) Only (iii)

29. The octal number system consists of the following symbols

(a) 0 – 7 (b) 0 – 9
(c) 0 – 9, A – F (d) None of these

30. The binary equivalent of $(-19)_{10}$ in signed magnitude system is
(a) 11101100 (b) 11101101
(c) 10010011 (d) None of these

31. DNS in internet technology stands for
(a) Dynamic Name System
(b) Domain Name System
(c) Distributed Name System
(d) None of these

32. HTML stands for
(a) Hyper Text Markup Language
(b) Hyper Text Manipulation Language
(c) Hyper Text Managing Links
(d) Hyper Text Manipulating Links

33. Which of the following is type of LAN?
(a) Ethernet (b) Token Ring
(c) FDDI (d) All of the above

34. Which of the following statements is true?
(a) Smart cards do not require an operating system.
(b) Smart cards and PCs use some operating system.
(c) COS is smart card operating system.
(d) The communication between reader and card is in full duplex mode.

35. The Ganga Action Plan was initiated during the year
(a) 1986 (b) 1988
(c) 1990 (d) 1992

36. Identify the correct sequence of energy sources in order of their share in the power sector in India.
(a) Thermal > nuclear > hydro > wind
(b) Thermal > hydro > nuclear > wind
(c) Hydro > nuclear > thermal > wind
(d) Nuclear > hydro > wind > thermal

37. Chromium as a contaminant in drinking water in excess of permissible levels, causes
(a) Skeletal damage
(b) Gastrointestinal problem
(c) Dermal and nervous problems
(d) Liver/Kidney problems

38. The main precursors of winter smog are
(a) N_2O and hydrocarbons
(b) NO_x and hydrocarbons
(c) SO_2 and hydrocarbons
(d) SO_2 and ozone

39. Flash floods are caused when
(a) the atmosphere is convectively unstable and there is considerable vertical wind shear
(b) the atmosphere is stable
(c) the atmosphere is convectively unstable with no vertical windshear
(d) winds are catabatic

40. In mega cities of India, the dominant source of air pollution is
(a) transport sector
(b) thermal power
(c) municipal waste
(d) commercial sector

41. The first Open University in India was set up in the State of
(a) Andhra Pradesh
(b) Delhi
(c) Himachal Pradesh
(d) Tamil Nadu

42. Most of the Universities in India are funded by
(a) the Central Government
(b) the State Governments
(c) the University Grants Commission
(d) Private bodies and Individuals

43. Which of the following organisations looks after the quality of Technical and Management education in India?
(a) NCTE (b) MCI
(c) AICTE (d) CSIR

44. Consider the following statements: Identify the statement which implies natural justice.

(a) The principle of natural justice is followed by the Courts.
(b) Justice delayed is justice denied.
(c) Natural justice is an inalienable right of a citizen.
(d) A reasonable opportunity of being heard must be given.

45. The President of India is
(a) the Head of State
(b) the Head of Government
(c) both Head of the State and the Head of the Government
(d) None of the above

46. Who among the following holds office during the pleasure of the President of India?
(a) Chief Election Commissioner
(b) Comptroller and Auditor General of India
(c) Chairman of the Union Public Service Commission
(d) Governor of a State

Questions 47 to 49 are based upon the following diagram in which there are three interlocking circles A, P and S where A stands for Artists, circle P for Professors and circle S for Sportspersons. Different regions in the figure are lettered from a to f:

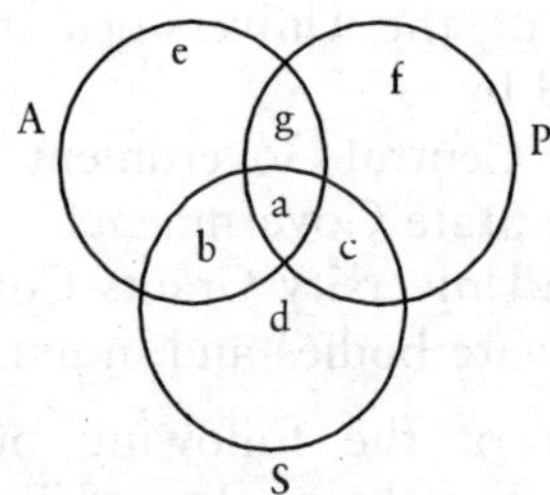

47. The region which represents artists who are neither sportsmen nor professors.
(a) d (b) e
(c) b (d) g

48. The region which represents professors, who are both artists and sportspersons.
(a) a (b) c
(c) d (d) g

49. The region which represents professors, who are also sportspersons, but not artists.
(a) e (b) f
(c) c (d) g

Questions 50 to 52 are based on the following data:

Measurements of some variable X were made at an interval of 1 minute from 10 A.M. to 10:20 A.M. The data, thus, obtained is as follows:

X: 60, 62, 65, 64, 63, 61, 66, 65, 70, 68 63, 62, 64, 69, 65, 64, 66, 67, 66, 64

50. The value of X, which is exceeded 10% of the time in the duration of measurement, is
(a) 69 (b) 68
(c) 67 (d) 66

51. The value of X, which is exceeded 90% of the time in the duration of measurement, is
(a) 63 (b) 62
(c) 61 (d) 60

52. The value of X, which is exceeded 50% of the time in the duration of measurement, is
(a) 66 (b) 65
(c) 64 (d) 63

53. For maintaining an effective discipline in the class, the teacher should
(a) Allow students to do what they like.
(b) Deal with the students strictly.
(c) Give the students some problem to solve.
(d) Deal with them politely and firmly.

54. An effective teaching aid is one which
(a) is colourful and good looking
(b) activates all faculties
(c) is visible to all students
(d) easy to prepare and use

55. Those teachers are popular among students who
(a) develop intimacy with them
(b) help them solve their problems
(c) award good grades
(d) take classes on extra tuition fee

56. The essence of an effective classroom environment is
(a) a variety of teaching aids
(b) lively student-teacher interaction
(c) pin-drop silence
(d) strict discipline

57. On the first day of his class, if a teacher is asked by the students to introduce himself, he should
(a) ask them to meet after the class
(b) tell them about himself in brief
(c) ignore the demand and start teaching
(d) scold the student for this unwanted demand

58. Moral values can be effectively inculcated among the students when the teacher
(a) frequently talks about values
(b) himself practices them
(c) tells stories of great persons
(d) talks of Gods and Goddesses

59. The essential qualities of a researcher are
(a) spirit of free enquiry
(b) reliance on observation and evidence
(c) systematisation or theorising of knowledge
(d) All of the above

60. Research is conducted to
1. Generate new knowledge
2. Not to develop a theory
3. Obtain research degree
4. Reinterpret existing knowledge

Which of the above are correct?
(a) 1, 3 & 2 (b) 3, 2 & 4
(c) 2, 1 & 3 (d) 1, 3 & 4

ANSWERS

1. (c)	2. (c)	3. (b)	4. (c)	5. (a)
6. (b)	7. (c)	8. (d)	9. (d)	10. (d)
11. (d)	12. (c)	13. (d)	14. (c)	15. (d)
16. (b)	17. (d)	18. (d)	19. (b)	20. (b)
21. (b)	22. (c)	23. (a)	24. (c)	25. (a)
26. (b)	27. (a)	28. (b)	29. (a)	30. (d)
31. (b)	32. (a)	33. (d)	34. (c)	35. (a)
36. (b)	37. (d)	38. (c)	39. (a)	40. (a)
41. (a)	42. (c)	43. (c)	44. (d)	45. (b)
46. (d)	47. (b)	48. (a)	49. (c)	50. (c)
51. (b)	52. (d)	53. (d)	54. (b)	55. (b)
56. (b)	57. (b)	58. (b)	59. (d)	60. (d)

PAPER–II

Note: This paper contains fifty (50) objective type questions, each question carrying two (2) marks. All questions are compulsory.

1. Who of the following is not associated with classical theory of organization?
(a) L. Urwick (b) M.P. Follet
(c) Luther Gullick (d) Mooney

2. 'The Government is finance.' This statement was made by
(a) Kautilya
(b) Lloyd George
(c) Hoover Commission
(d) F.M. Marx

3. The transfer of authority from Central Government to State Governments in India implies

(a) Devolution
(b) Decentralization
(c) Delegation
(d) De-concentration

4. In which stage of the evolution of Public Administration, the principles of organization were challenged calling these as 'Proverbs'?
(a) II (b) III
(c) IV (d) V

5. Originally, the 73rd Constitutional Amendment Act has provided reservation to women in PRIs
(a) 33 percent
(b) 29 percent
(c) at least 50 percent
(d) Not less than one-third

6. "We are no longer confronted with several administrative sciences but with one which can be applied equally well to public and private affairs." This statement is given by
(a) Henri Fayol
(b) Luther Gullick
(c) L. Urwick
(d) M.P. Follet

7. In which country 'Performance Budget' was first introduced?
(a) U.K. (b) France
(c) U.S.A. (d) India

8. According to Max Weber, there are three types of Authority. Which one of the following is not in them?
(a) Official Authority
(b) Charismatic Authority
(c) Traditional Authority
(d) Legal-Rational Authority

9. A member of State Public Service Commission, who wants to resign can do so by writing a letter addressed to which of the following?
(a) Chief Minister
(b) Chairman of UPSC
(c) Chairman of concerned P.S.C.
(d) Governor

10. Following Committee was appointed to make recommendations regarding recruitment procedure for Civil Services in India:
(a) Satish Chandra Committee
(b) K. Santhanam Committee
(c) G.V.K. Rao Committee
(d) N.N. Vohra Committee

11. 'Public Administration is concerned with the activities of only the executive branch of Government.' This view point is given by the following scholars:
(i) Simon
(ii) Luther Gullick
(iii) Henri Fayol
(iv) Woodrow Wilson
Codes:
(a) (i), (ii) and (iii) (b) (i), (iii) and (iv)
(c) (ii), (iii) and (iv) (d) (i), (ii) and (iv)

12. Which of the following are correct?
(i) Politics-Administration Dictomy – Frank J. Goodnow
(ii) Principles of Administration – M.P. Follet
(iii) Era of Challenges – Dwight Waldo
(iv) Crisis of Identity – Robert Dahl
Codes:
(a) (i), (ii) and (iv) (b) (ii), (iii) and (iv)
(c) (i), (ii) and (iii) (d) (i), (iii) and (iv)

13. Which of the following are the nonstatutory bodies?
(i) National Human Right Commission
(ii) Planning Commission
(iii) National Development Council
(iv) National Commission for Women
Codes:
(a) (i), (ii), (iii) and (iv)
(b) (i), (ii) and (iii)

(c) (ii) and (iii)
(d) (ii), (iii) and (iv)

14. The CAG cannot audit the accounts of which of the following Corporations?
(i) Reserve Bank of India
(ii) Industrial Finance Corporation
(iii) Life Insurance Corporation of India
(iv) Food Corporation of India

Codes:
(a) (i), (ii), (iii) & (iv)
(b) (i), (ii) & (iv)
(c) (i), (iii) & (iv)
(d) (i), (ii) & (iii)

15. Success of delegation depends upon certain principles. These are
(i) Delegation should always be clear and written.
(ii) Delegation should always be horizontal.
(iii) Delegation should be to immediate subordinate.
(iv) Principle of Unity of Command should be followed.

Codes:
(a) (i), (ii) and (iii)
(b) (i), (ii), (iii) & (iv)
(c) (i) and (ii)
(d) (i), (iii) and (iv)

16. Which of the following statements are correct about the Budget?
(i) It is an instrument of policy.
(ii) Budget estimates should be on a departmental basis.
(iii) It is a tool of people's control over administration.
(iv) Budget should be an integration of revenue and capital aspects.

Codes:
(a) (i) and (ii)
(b) (i), (ii) and (iii)
(c) (i), (ii), (iii) and (iv)
(d) (i), (iii) and (iv)

17. Which of the following are the main features of the Government of India Act, 1935?
(i) Creation of federation.
(ii) Establishment of unicameralism at the provincial level.
(iii) Introduction of responsible system of Government in the provinces.
(iv) Introduction of dyarchy at the centre.

Codes:
(a) (i) and (ii)
(b) (ii) and (iii)
(c) (i), (ii), (iii) and (iv)
(d) (i), (iii) and (iv)

18. In India usually control over public expenditure is exercised through
(i) The Parliament
(ii) The CAG
(iii) The Finance Ministry
(iv) Joint Parliamentary Committee

Codes:
(a) (i), (ii), (iii) & (iv)
(b) (i), (ii) & (iii)
(c) (ii) & (iv)
(d) (i), (iii) & (iv)

19. Which of the following are the advantages of 'split system' as the organizational basis of Secretariat?
(i) Programme execution in the field can be evaluated in an objective manner.
(ii) Secretariat can engage itself effectively in details of administration.
(iii) Proposals from the executive agencies can be examined in a detached manner.
(iv) Delegation and decentralization are encouraged and over centralization is avoided.

Codes:
(a) (i), (ii), (iii) and (iv)
(b) (i), (ii) and (iii)
(c) (i), (iii) and (iv)
(d) (iii) and (iv)

20. Which of the following statements about the role of Cabinet Secretary is correct?
    (i) He is the Chief Advisor to the President.
    (ii) He is the Advisor to the Prime Minister.
    (iii) He is the Administrative Head of the Cabinet Secretariat.
    (iv) He assists the Cabinet Committees.
    Codes:
    (a) (i), (ii), (iii) and (iv)
    (b) (ii), (iii) and (iv)
    (c) (i), (ii) and (iii)
    (d) (iii) and (iv)

21. **Assertion (A):** Neutrality is an important characteristic of Civil Service.
    Reason (R): The concept of neutrality originated in U.S.A.
    Codes:
    (a) Both (A) and (R) are correct and (R) is the correct explanation of (a).
    (b) Both (A) and (R) are correct, but (R) is not the correct explanation of (A).
    (c) (A) is true, but (R) is false.
    (d) (A) is false, but (R) is true.

22. **Assertion (A):** Relationship between superior and subordinate is essential in hierarchy.
    Reason (R): Decentralization is possible in hierarchy.
    Codes:
    (a) Both (A) and (R) are correct and (R) is the correct explanation of (A).
    (b) Both (A) and (R) are correct, but (R) is not the correct explanation of (A).
    (c) (A) is true, but (R) is false.
    (d) (A) is false, but (R) is true.

23. **Assertion (A):** Herbert simon denounced the principles of Administration calling these as proverbs.
    Reason (R): He propounded the theory of decision making.
    Codes:
    (a) Both (A) and (R) are correct and (R) is the correct explanation of (A).
    (b) Both (A) and (R) are correct, but (R) is not the correct explanation of (A).
    (c) (A) is true, but (R) is false.
    (d) (A) is false, but (R) is true.

24. **Assertion (A):** Public Choice Theory came into existence as a critique of traditional public administration.
    Reason (R): It advocates the concept of 'democratic administration.'
    Codes:
    (a) Both (A) and (R) are correct and (R) is the correct explanation of (A).
    (b) Both (A) and (R) are correct, but (R) is not the correct explanation of (A).
    (c) (A) is true, but (R) is false.
    (d) (A) is false, but (R) is true.

25. **Assertion (A):** Appropriation Bill is a Money Bill.
    Reason (R): Token cut motion is meant for censoring the Government.
    Codes:
    (a) Both (A) and (R) are correct and (R) is the correct explanation of (A).
    (b) Both (A) and (R) are correct, but (R) is not the correct explanation of (A).
    (c) (A) is true, but (R) is false.
    (d) (A) is false, but (R) is corect.

26. **Assertion (A):** Planning Commission and National Development Council are complementary.
    Reason (R): National Development Council is an older organisation than the Planning Commission.
    Codes:
    (a) Both (A) and (R) are correct and (R) is correct explanation of (A).
    (b) Both (A) and (R) are correct, but (R) is not correct explanation of (A).

(c) (A) is true, but (R) is false.
(d) (A) is false, but (R) is true.

27. **Assertion (A):** Liberalization is necessary for globalization.
Reason (R): Privatization is a principle of Welfare State.
Codes:
(a) Both (A) and (R) are correct and (R) is correct explanation of (A).
(b) Both (A) and (R) are correct, but (R) is not correct explanation of (A).
(c) (A) is true, but (R) is false.
(d) (A) is false, but (R) is true.

28. **Assertion (A):** 'Morale' is abstract and psychological.
Reason (R): High Morale enhances employees' work output.
Codes:
(a) Both (A) and (R) are correct and (R) is the correct explanation of (A).
(b) Both (A) and (R) are correct, but (R) is not the correct explanation of (A).
(c) (A) is true, but (R) is false.
(d) (A) is false, but (R) is true.

29. **Assertion (A):** Recruitment is appointment.
Reason (R): Recruitment is process of selection of the competent and the efficient.
Codes:
(a) Both (A) and (R) are correct and (R) is correct explanation of (A).
(b) Both (A) and (R) are correct, but (R) is not correct explanation of (A).
(c) (A) is true, but (R) is false.
(d) (A) is false, but (R) is true.

30. **Assertion (A):** State Secretariat is headed by the Chief Minister.
Reason (R): State Secretariat is the steering wheel of State Administration.
Codes:
(a) Both (A) and (R) are correct and (R) is correct explanation of (A).
(b) Both (A) and (R) are correct, but (R) is not correct explanation of (A).
(c) (A) is true, but (R) is false.
(d) (A) is false, but (R) is true.

31. Arrange the following approaches to the study of Public Administration in chronological order of their evolution and select the correct answer from the codes given below:
(i) Policy Approach
(ii) Behavioural Approach
(iii) Classical Approach
(iv) Scientific Management Approach
Codes:
(a) (iii), (iv), (ii), (i) (b) (i), (ii), (iii), (iv)
(c) (iv), (iii), (ii), (i) (d) (ii), (iv), (iii), (i)

32. Arrange the chronological order of following Committees on urban governance and select correct answer from codes:
(i) Rural Urban Relationship Committee.
(ii) Taxation Enquiry Committee.
(iii) Commission on Service Conditions of Municipal Employees.
(iv) National Commission on Urbanization.
Codes:
(a) (ii), (i), (iv), (iii) (b) (iv), (iii), (ii), (i)
(c) (i), (ii), (iii), (iv) (d) (ii), (i), (iii), (iv)

33. Arrange the following experiments of Elton Mayo in a chronological order and select the correct answer from the codes given below:
(i) Human Attitudes and Sentiments
(ii) The First Enquiry
(iii) Social Organization
(iv) The Great Illumination
Codes:
(a) (iv), (iii), (ii), (i) (b) (i), (ii), (iii), (iv)
(c) (ii), (iv), (i), (iii) (d) (ii), (i), (iii), (iv)

34. Arrange in chronological order the establishment of the following training institutions. Select correct answer from codes given below:
   (i) Staff College of India.
   (ii) National Institute of Rural Development.
   (iii) Indian Institute of Public Administration.
   (iv) Institute of Secretariat Training and Management.

   Codes:
   (a) (i), (ii), (iii), (iv) (b) (iii), (iv), (i), (ii)
   (c) (iv), (iii), (ii), (i) (d) (iv), (ii), (i), (iii)

35. Arrange the following steps in policy making in order and select the correct answer from the codes given below:
   (i) Goal setting
   (ii) Agenda setting
   (iii) Implementation of the selected alternatives
   (iv) Alternative selection and development

   Codes:
   (a) (ii), (i), (iv), (iii) (b) (iii), (ii), (i), (iv)
   (c) (i), (iii), (iv), (ii) (d) (iv), (i), (iii), (ii)

36. Arrange the following in a chronological order and select the correct answer from the codes given below:
   (i) Introduction of Performance Budgeting in India.
   (ii) Introduction of the Scheme of Delegation of Financial Powers.
   (iii) Introduction of the Public Accounts Committee.
   (iv) Separation of Audit from Accounts.

   Codes:
   (a) (i), (ii), (iii), (iv) (b) (iii), (ii), (i), (iv)
   (c) (ii), (iii), (iv), (i) (d) (iv), (i), (iii), (ii)

37. Arrange the evolution of Public Administration in a correct sequence and select the answer from the codes given below:
   (i) Principles of Administration
   (ii) Crisis of Identity
   (iii) Public Policy Perspective
   (iv) Era of Challenges and Criticism

   Codes:
   (a) (i), (iv), (ii), (iii) (b) (i), (ii), (iii), (iv)
   (c) (iv), (iii), (ii), (i) (d) (ii), (iii), (iv), (i)

38. Match List I with List II and select the correct answer by using the codes given below:

   List I
   (A) E.N. Gladden
   (B) F.M. Marx
   (C) Pfiffner and Presthus
   (D) W.F. Willoughby

   List II
   1. Principles of Public Administration
   2. Elements of Public Administration
   3. Public Administration
   4. An Introduction to Public Administration

Codes:	A	B	C	D
(a)	2	3	4	1
(b)	4	2	3	1
(c)	3	1	2	4
(d)	1	2	3	4

39. Match List I with List II and select the correct answer by using the codes given below:

   List I
   (A) Scientific Management Theory
   (B) Decision Making Theory
   (C) Human Relation Theory
   (D) Motivation Theory

   List II
   1. Elton Mayo 2. F.W. Taylor
   3. Abraham Maslow 4. Herbert Simon

Codes:	A	B	C	D
(a)	1	2	3	4
(b)	2	4	1	3
(c)	4	3	2	1
(d)	1	3	4	2

40. Match List I with List II and select the correct answer by using the codes given below:

List I
(A) Satisficing
(B) Zone of Indifference
(C) Job Enrichment
(D) Functional Foremanship

List II
1. F.W. Riggs 2. Herbert Simon
3. F.W. Taylor 4. C.I. Barnard
5. Herzberg

Codes:	A	B	C	D
(a)	2	4	5	3
(b)	2	1	4	3
(c)	1	2	3	4
(d)	5	2	1	3

41. Match List I with List II and select the correct answer from the given below codes:

List I
(A) Suggests the economy in public expenditure
(B) Enquires the regularity of public transactions
(C) Works after the expenditure is made by the public authorities
(D) Responsible for preparing the Budget of Union Government

List II
1. Public Accounts Committee
2. Comptroller and Auditor General
3. Estimate Committee
4. Finance Ministry

Codes:	A	B	C	D
(a)	1	2	3	4
(b)	3	2	1	4
(c)	4	2	1	3
(d)	3	1	4	2

42. Match List I with List II and give the correct answer by using the codes given below:

List I
(A) Cabinet Secretary
(B) Chief Secretary
(C) Secretary
(D) Director

List II
1. Head of State Administration
2. Administrative Head of the Department
3. Head of Union Administration
4. Executive Head of the Department

Codes:	A	B	C	D
(a)	1	3	4	2
(b)	3	2	1	4
(c)	3	1	2	4
(d)	1	3	2	4

43. Match List I with List II and select the correct answer by using the codes given below:

List I
(A) Sardar Patel
(B) P.V. Rajamannar
(C) S.P.P. Thorat
(D) Satish Chandra

List II
1. Abolition of All India Services
2. Adoption of alternative method of recruitment to All India Services
3. Advocated for strengthening of All India Services
4. Reforms in recruitment of All India Services

Codes:	A	B	C	D
(a)	3	2	1	4
(b)	1	2	3	4
(c)	4	1	3	2
(d)	3	1	2	4

44. Match List I with List II and choose the correct answer by using the codes given below:

List I
(A) Bureaucratic Theory
(B) Scientific Management Theory
(C) System Approach
(D) Classical Theory

List II

1. Interaction between organisation and environment
2. Formulation of principles of organisation
3. Shop floor activities of organisation
4. Put emphasis on legal-rational authority

Codes:	A	B	C	D
(a)	4	2	1	3
(b)	3	2	1	4
(c)	1	2	3	4
(d)	4	3	1	2

45. Match List I with List II and supply the correct answer by using the codes given below:

List I

(A) Chris Argyris
(B) Rensis Likert
(C) Douglas McGregor
(D) Abraham Maslow

List II

1. Persônality and Organisation
2. New Pattern of Management
3. The Human Side of Enterprises
4. Motivation and Personality

Codes:	A	B	C	D
(a)	2	4	1	3
(b)	3	2	4	1
(c)	4	1	3	2
(d)	1	3	2	4

Read the passage given below and answer the questions that follow based on your understanding of the passage: (46-50)

Civil Society

The term 'civil society' has a fairly long history but finds no mention in early political science studies, having originated later. Aristotle, the father of political science, is absolutely silent about the use of the term, apparently believing that civil society was coterminous with the State and that the Civil Society and the State were inter-changeable terms. The term first originated in Europe at the end of the eighteenth century and enjoyed a remarkable career. But it fell into obscurity in the later part of the nineteenth century.

Happily, it has attracted widespread attention since the later part of the twentieth century. The concept of civil society was first used by George Wilhelm Freidrich Hegel (1770-1831) in his book *Philosophy of Right* published in 1821 in which he discusses civil society, law, the bureaucracy, the King, War, etc., his objective being the restoration of harmony and overcoming of the contradiction immanent within a liberal State. According to him civil society refers to organised bodies that are intermediate between the State and the family. He described it as a stage in the dialectical development from the family to the State. He made a distinction between the State and Civil Society. Civil society is separate from the State, which, as we know, has its own organs of governance. The State is equipped with military, police, legal and administrative organs. The civil society is different and comprises non-state institutions which are market-regulated and voluntarily organised. A civil society is autonomous although clearly subject to the State and its Governmental Authority.

46. Aristotle was silent about the use of the term 'Civil Society' because:
    (i) his apparent belief that Civil Society and State are Coterminus.
    (ii) Civil Society and State are mutually antagonistic.
    (iii) Civil Society and State are interchangeable.
    (iv) his focus was only on State.

    Codes:
    (a) (i) only
    (b) (iii) only
    (c) (i) & (iii)
    (d) (i), (ii), (iii) and (iv)

47. The main characteristics of civil society are
(i) Autonomy
(ii) Neutrality
(iii) Voluntary Organization
(iv) Intermediatory between family and State

Codes:
(a) (i), (ii)
(b) (i), (iii) & (iv)
(c) (i), (ii), (iii) & (iv)
(d) (ii), (iii) & (iv)

48. Which of the following is not one of the difference between the State and Civil Society?
(a) State has its own law and order machinery.
(b) State has legislative and executive organs.
(c) State is a sovereign entity.
(d) State is a voluntary institution.

49. The objective/s of Hegal's book 'Philosophy of Right' was/were
(i) Analysis of Civil Society, Law and Harmony
(ii) To establish harmony
(iii) Discussion of issues pertaining to King and War
(iv) Removing the contradictions of a liberal State

Codes:
(a) (i) and (ii)
(b) (ii) and (iii)
(c) (iii) and (iv)
(d) (ii) and (iv)

50. The concept of Civil Society was reviewed at which of the following stage of its evolution?
(a) End of the 18th Century
(b) End of the 19th Century
(c) End of the 20th Century
(d) Beginning of the 21st Century

ANSWERS

1. (d)	2. (c)	3. (a)	4. (b)	5. (d)
6. (a)	7. (c)	8. (a)	9. (d)	10. (a)
11. (a)	12. (c)	13. (c)	14. (b)	15. (d)
16. (c)	17. (d)	18. (b)	19. (c)	20. (b)
21. (c)	22. (b)	23. (b)	24. (a)	25. (b)
26. (c)	27. (c)	28. (a)	29. (a)	30. (d)
31. (c)	32. (d)	33. (c)	34. (c)	35. (a)
36. (d)	37. (a)	38. (b)	39. (b)	40. (a)
41. (b)	42. (c)	43. (d)	44. (d)	45. (d)
46. (c)	47. (b)	48. (d)	49. (d)	50. (c)

DECEMBER–2010

Note: This paper contains Sixty (60) multiple-choice questions, each question carrying two (2) marks. Candidate is expected to answer any Fifty (50) questions. In case more than Fifty (50) questions are attempted, only the first Fifty (50) questions will be evaluated.

PAPER–I

1. Which of the following variables cannot be expressed in quantitative terms?
   (a) Socio-economic Status
   (b) Marital Status
   (c) Numerical Aptitude
   (d) Professional Attitude

2. A doctor studies the relative effectiveness of two drugs of dengue fever. His research would be classified as
   (a) Descriptive Survey
   (b) Experimental Research
   (c) Case Study
   (d) Ethnography

3. The term 'phenomenology' is associated with the process of
   (a) Qualitative Research
   (b) Analysis of Variance
   (c) Correlational Study
   (d) Probability Sampling

4. The 'Sociogram' technique is used to study
   (a) Vocational Interest
   (b) Professional Competence
   (c) Human Relations
   (d) Achievement Motivation

Read the following passage carefully and answer questions from 5 to 10.

It should be remembered that the nationalist movement in India, like all nationalist movements, was essentially a bourgeois movement. It represented the natural historical stage of development, and to consider it or to criticise it as a working-class movement is wrong. Gandhi represented that movement and the Indian masses in relation to that movement to a supreme degree, and he became the voice of Indian people to that extent. The main contribution of Gandhi to India and the Indian masses has been through the powerful movements which he launched through the National Congress. Through nation-wide action he sought to mould the millions, and largely succeeded in doing so, and changing them from a demoralised, timid and hopeless mass, bullied and crushed by every dominant interest, and incapable of resistance, into a people with self-respect and self-reliance, resisting tyranny, and capable of united action and sacrifice for a larger cause.

Gandhi made people think of political and economic issues and every village and every bazaar hummed with argument and debate on the new ideas and hopes that filled the people. That was an amazing psychological change. The time was ripe for it, of course, and circumstances and world conditions worked for this change. But a great leader is necessary to take advantage of circumstances and conditions. Gandhi was that leader, and he released many of the bonds that imprisoned and disabled our minds, and none of us who experienced it can ever forget that great feeling of release and exhilaration that came over the Indian people.

Gandhi has played a revolutionary role in India of the greatest importance because he knew how to make the most of the objective conditions and could reach the heart of the masses, while groups with a more advanced ideology functioned largely in the air because they did not fit in with those conditions and could therefore not evoke any substantial response from the masses.

It is perfectly true that Gandhi, functioning in the nationalist plane, does not think in terms of the conflict of classes, and tries to compose their differences. But the action he has indulged and taught the people has inevitably raised mass consciousness tremendously and made social issues vital. Gandhi and the Congress must be judged by the policies they pursue and the action they indulge in. But behind this, personality counts and colours those policies and activities. In the case of very exceptional person like Gandhi the question of personality becomes especially important in order to understand and appraise him. To us he has represented the spirit and honour of India, the yearning of her sorrowing millions to be rid of their innumerable burdens, and an insult to him by the British Government or others has been an insult to India and her people.

5. Which one of the following is true of the given passage?
   (a) The passage is a critique of Gandhi's role in Indian movement for independence
   (b) The passage hails the role of Gandhi in India's freedom movement
   (c) The author is neutral on Gandhi's role in India's freedom movement
   (d) It is an account of Indian National Congress's support to the working-class movement
6. The change that the Gandhian movement brought among the Indian masses was
   (a) Physical (b) Cultural
   (c) Technological (d) Psychological
7. To consider the nationalist movement or to criticise it as a working-class movement was wrong because it was a
   (a) historical movement
   (b) voice of the Indian people
   (c) bourgeois movement
   (d) movement represented by Gandhi
8. Gandhi played a revolutionary role in India because he could
   (a) preach morality
   (b) reach the heart of Indians
   (c) see the conflict of classes
   (d) lead the Indian National Congress
9. Groups with advanced ideology functioned in the air as they did not fit in with
   (a) objective conditions of masses
   (b) the Gandhian ideology
   (c) the class consciousness of the people
   (d) the differences among masses
10. The author concludes the passage by
    (a) criticising the Indian masses
    (b) the Gandhian movement
    (c) pointing out the importance of the personality of Gandhi
    (d) identifying the sorrows of millions of Indians
11. Media that exist in an interconnected series of communication—points are referred to as
    (a) Networked media
    (b) Connective media
    (c) Nodal media
    (d) Multimedia
12. The information function of mass communication is described as
    (a) diffusion (b) publicity
    (c) surveillance (d) diversion
13. An example of asynchronous medium is

(a) Radio (b) Television
(c) Film (d) Newspaper

14. In communication, connotative words are
(a) explicit (c) abstract
(b) simple (d) cultural

15. A message beneath a message is labelled as
(a) embedded text (b) internal text
(c) inter-text (d) sub-text

16. In analogue mass communication, stories are
(a) static (b) dynamic
(c) interactive (d) exploratory

17. Determine the relationship between the pair of words ALWAYS : NEVER and then select from the following pair of words which have a similar relationship
(a) often : rarely
(b) frequently : occasionally
(c) constantly : frequently
(d) intermittently : casually

18. Find the wrong number in the sequence 52, 51, 48, 43, 34, 27, 16
(a) 27 (b) 34
(c) 43 (d) 48

19. In a certain code, PAN is written as 31 and PAR as 35, then PAT is written in the same code as
(a) 30 (b) 37
(c) 39 (d) 41

20. The letters in the first set have certain relationship. On the basis of this relationship, make the right choice for the second set:
AF : IK : : LQ :?
(a) MO (b) NP
(c) OR (d) TV

21. If 5472 = 9, 6342 = 6, 7584 = 6, what is 9236?
(a) 2 (b) 3
(c) 4 (d) 5

22. In an examination, 35% of the total students failed in Hindi, 45% failed in English and 20% in both. The percentage of those who passed in both subjects is
(a) 10 (b) 20
(c) 30 (d) 40

23. Two statements I and II given below are followed by two conclusions (a) and (b). Supposing the statements are true, which of the following conclusions can logically follow?
Statements:
i. Some flowers are red.
ii. Some flowers are blue.
Conclusions:
(a) Some flowers are neither red nor blue.
(b) Some flowers are both red and blue.
(a) Only (i) follows
(b) Only (ii) follows
(c) Both (i) and (ii) follows
(d) Neither (i) nor (ii) follows

24. If the statement 'all students are intelligent' is true, which of the following statements are false?
(i) No students are intelligent.
(ii) Some students are intelligent.
(iii) Some students are not intelligent.
(a) (i) and (ii) (b) (i) and (iii)
(c) (ii) and (iii) (d) Only (i)

25. A reasoning where we start with certain particular statements and conclude with a universal statement is called
(a) Deductive Reasoning
(b) Inductive Reasoning
(c) Abnormal Reasoning
(d) Transcendental Reasoning

26. What is the smallest number of ducks that could swim in this formation—two ducks in front of a duck, two ducks behind a duck and a duck between two ducks?

(a) 5 (b) 7
(c) 4 (d) 3

27. Mr. A, Miss B, Mr. C and Miss D are sitting around a table and discussing their trades.
(i) Mr. A sits opposite to the cook.
(ii) Miss B sits right to the barber.
(iii) The washerman sits right to the barber.
(iv) Miss D sits opposite to Mr. C.
What are the trades of A and B?
(a) Tailor and barber
(b) Barber and cook
(c) Tailor and cook
(d) Tailor and washerman

28. Which one of the following methods serve to measure correlation between two variables?
(a) Scatter Diagram
(b) Frequency Distribution
(c) Two-way table
(d) Coefficient of Rank Correlation

29. Which one of the following is not an Internet Service Provider (ISP)?
(a) MTNL
(b) BSNL
(c) ERNET India
(d) Infotech India Ltd.

30. The hexadecimal number system consists of the symbols
(a) 0 - 7 (b) 0 - 9, A - F
(c) 0 - 7, A - F (d) None of these

31. The binary equivalent of $(-15)_{10}$ is (2's complement system is used)
(a) 11110001 (b) 11110000
(c) 10001111 (d) None of these

32. 1 GB is equal to
(a) 2^{30} bits (b) 2^{30} bytes
(c) 2^{20} bits (d) 2^{20} bytes

33. The set of computer programs that manage the hardware/software of a computer is called
(a) Compiler system
(b) Operation system
(c) Operating system
(d) None of these

34. SMIME in Internet technology stands for
(a) Secure Multipurpose Internet Mail Extension
(b) Secure Multimedia Internet Mail Extension
(c) Simple Multipurpose Internet Mail Extension
(d) Simple Multimedia Internet Mail Extension

35. Which of the following is not covered in 8 missions under the Climate Action Plan of Government of India?
(a) Solar power
(b) Waste to energy conversion
(c) Afforestation
(d) Nuclear energy

36. The concentration of Total Dissolved Solids (TDS) in drinking water should not exceed
(a) 500 mg/L (b) 400 mg/L
(c) 300 mg/L (d) 200 mg/L

37. 'Chipko' movement was first started by
(a) Arundhati Roy
(b) Medha Patkar
(c) Ila Bhatt
(d) Sunderlal Bahuguna

38. The constituents of photochemical smog responsible for eye irritation are
(a) SO_2 and O_3
(b) SO_2 and NO_2
(c) HCHO and PAN
(d) SO_2 and SPM

39. **Assertion (A):** Some carbonaceous aerosols may be carcinogenic.
Reason (R): They may contain polycyclic aromatic hydrocarbons (PAHs).
(a) Both (A) and (R) are correct and (R) is the correct explanation of (A).

(b) Both (A) and (R) are correct but (R) is not the correct explanation of (A).
(c) (A) is correct, but (R) is false.
(d) (A) is false, but (R) is correct.

40. Volcanic eruptions affect
(a) atmosphere and hydrosphere
(b) hydrosphere and biosphere
(c) lithosphere, biosphere and atmosphere
(d) lithosphere, hydrosphere and atmosphere

41. India's first Defence University is in the State of
(a) Haryana
(b) Andhra Pradesh
(c) Uttar Pradesh
(d) Punjab

42. Most of the Universities in India
(a) conduct teaching and research only
(b) affiliate colleges and conduct examinations
(c) conduct teaching/research and examinations
(d) promote research only

43. Which one of the following is not a Constitutional Body?
(a) Election Commission
(b) Finance Commission
(c) Union Public Service Commission
(d) Planning Commission

44. Which one of the following statements is not correct?
(a) Indian Parliament is supreme.
(b) The Supreme Court of India has the power of judicial review.
(c) There is a division of powers between the Centre and the States.
(d) There is a Council of Ministers to aid and advise the President.

45. Which one of the following statements reflects the republic character of Indian democracy?
(a) Written constitution
(b) No State religion
(c) Devolution of power to local Government institutions
(d) Elected President and directly or indirectly elected Parliament

46. Who among the following appointed by the Governor can be removed by only the President of India?
(a) Chief Minister of a State
(b) A member of the State Public Service Commission
(c) Advocate-General
(d) Vice-Chancellor of a State University

47. If two small circles represent the class of the 'men' and the class of the 'plants' and the big circle represents 'mortality', which one of the following figures represent the proposition 'All men are mortal?.'

The following table presents the production of electronic items (TVs and LCDs) in a factory during the period from 2006 to 2010. Study the table carefully and answer the questions from 48 to 52:

Year	2006	2007	2008	2009	2010
TVs	6000	9000	13000	11000	8000
LCDs	7000	9400	9000	10000	12000

48. In which year, the total production of electronic items is maximum?
(a) 2006 (b) 2007
(c) 2008 (d) 2010

49. What is the difference between averages of production of LCDs and TVs from 2006 to 2008?

(a) 3000 (b) 2867
(c) 3015 (d) None of these

50. What is the year in which production of TVs is half the production of LCDs in the year 2010?
(a) 2007 (b) 2006
(c) 2009 (d) 2008

51. What is the ratio of production of LCDs in the years 2008 and 2010?
(a) 4:3 (b) 3:4
(c) 1:3 (d) 2:3

52. What is the ratio of production of TVs in the years 2006 and 2007?
(a) 6:7 (b) 7:6
(c) 2:3 (d) 3:2

53. Some students in a class exhibit great curiosity for learning. It may be because such children
(a) Are gifted
(b) Come from rich families
(c) Show artificial behaviour
(d) Create indiscipline in the class

54. The most important quality of a good teacher is
(a) Sound knowledge of subject matter
(b) Good communication skills
(c) Concern for students' welfare
(d) Effective leadership qualities

55. Which one of the following is appropriate in respect of teacher-student relationship?
(a) Very informal and intimate
(b) Limited to classroom only
(c) Cordial and respectful
(d) Indifferent

56. The academic performance of students can be improved if parents are encouraged to
(a) supervise the work of their wards
(b) arrange for extra tuition
(c) remain unconcerned about it
(d) interact with teachers frequently

57. In a lively classroom situation, there is likely to be
(a) occasional roars of laughter
(b) complete silence
(c) frequent teacher-student dialogue
(d) loud discussion among students

58. If a parent approaches the teacher to do some favour to his/her ward in the examination, the teacher should
(a) try to help him
(b) ask him not to talk in those terms
(c) refuse politely and firmly
(d) ask him rudely to go away

59. Which of the following phrases is not relevant to describe the meaning of research as a process?
(a) Systematic Activity
(b) Objective Observation
(c) Trial and Error
(d) Problem Solving

60. Which of the following is not an example of a continuous variable?
(a) Family size (b) Intelligence
(c) Height (d) Attitude

ANSWERS

1. (d)	2. (b)	3. (a)	4. (c)	5. (b)
6. (d)	7. (c)	8. (b)	9. (a)	10. (c)
11. (a)	12. (c)	13. (d)	14. (d)	15. (d)
16. (a)	17. (a)	18. (b)	19. (b)	20. (d)
21. (a)	22. (b)	23. (c)	24. (d)	25. (b)
26. (a)	27. (c)	28. (d)	29. (d)	30. (b)
31. (d)	32. (b)	33. (c)	34. (a)	35. (d)
36. (a)	37. (d)	38. (b)	39. (a)	40. (d)
41. (a)	42. (c)	43. (d)	44. (b)	45. (d)
46. (b)	47. (c)	48. (c)	49. (d)	50. (b)
51. (b)	52. (c)	53. (a)	54. (b)	55. (c)
56. (d)	57. (c)	58. (c)	59. (c)	60. (c)

PAPER–II

Note: This paper contains fifty (50) objective type questions, each question carrying two (2) marks. All questions are compulsory.

1. "Administration has to do with getting things done; with the accomplishment of defined objectives." The above statement reflects the
   (a) Narrower view of public administration
   (b) Integral view of public administration
   (c) Wider view of public administration
   (d) Managerial view of public administration

2. The public choice school sets a concept of
   (a) Democratic administration
   (b) Comparative administration
   (c) Rural and local administration
   (d) International administration

3. Who suggested the concept of "Gang Plank"?
   (a) Frederic W. Taylor
   (b) Henry Fayol
   (c) Max Weber
   (d) Luther Gulick

4. According to Herbert A. Simon 'satisficing' refers to satisfaction which is
   (a) subjective (b) good enough
   (c) client-oriented (d) objective

5. 'Heuristics' in the context of decision making implies
   (a) Judgemental shortcuts in decision making.
   (b) Judgement based on indepth analysis.
   (c) Reviewing training methods for employees.
   (d) Reviewing recruitment methods for employees.

6. The statement regarding authority as "The right to give orders and the power to exact obedience" is attributed to
   (a) Henry Fayol (b) J.D. Millet
   (c) C.I. Barnard (d) Max Weber

7. The main functions of Cabinet Secretariat are
   (i) to prepare and finalise rules of business of Government.
   (ii) to function as chief coordinating agency in Central Government.
   (iii) organisation and reorganisation of Ministries.
   (iv) maintain liaison with President, Governors and Foreign representatives in the country.

   Select the correct answer from the codes given below:

   Codes:
   (a) (i) (ii) (iv) (b) (ii) (iii) (i)
   (c) (i) (ii) (iii) (d) (i) (iii) (iv)

8. National Development Council is concerned with the work of
   (i) assessment of resources for the National Plan.
   (ii) formation of National Plan.
   (iii) consideration of the National Plan.
   (iv) review of the National Plan.

   Choose the correct answer from the following answer code:

   Codes:
   (a) (i) (iii) (iv) (b) (i) (ii) (iii)
   (c) (ii) (iii) (iv) (d) (i) (ii) (iv)

9. Prime Minister's Office has the following characteristics:
   (i) It is a staff agency.
   (ii) It enjoys status of a Ministry.
   (iii) It has replaced Prime Minister's Secretariat.
   (iv) It is an extra-constitutional body.

   Select the answer from the codes given below:

Codes:
(a) (i) (ii) (iii) (iv) (b) (ii) (iii) (iv)
(c) (i) (iii) (iv) (d) (i) (ii) (iii)

10. In the USA, the 'Spoils System' was discarded in favour of the 'Merit Principle' by the
(a) Civil Services Reforms Act, 1978.
(b) Pendleton Act, 1939.
(c) Hatch Act, 1939.
(d) Civil Service Act of 1853.

11. In ancient history, the necessity of sound recruitment policy for the public services was first recognised by
(a) China (b) Egypt
(c) Greece (d) Prussia

12. The principle of political neutrality of the Civil Servants does not postulate that
(a) Civil Servants must advise without any fear.
(b) Civil Servants must place at the disposal of the Minister all their expertise and knowledge.
(c) Civil Servants must help the Ministers at the time of political crisis in the country.
(d) Civil Servants must accept and implement the decisions of the Minister with full loyalty and zeal.

13. A member of State Public Service Commission is eligible to become
(a) Chairman of State Public Service Commission
(b) Chairman of any other State Public Service Commission.
(c) Chairman of U.P.S.C.
(d) All the above

14. The electoral college for election of President of India consists of
(a) Elected Members of State Legislative Assemblies.
(b) Elected Members of Parliament.
(c) Members of State Legislative Assemblies, Lok Sabha and Rajya Sabha
(d) Elected M.L.A.s, M.P.s and members from some Union Territories

15. Which of the following is not a feature of "Sala" prismatic administration of the Riggsian Model?
(a) Nepotism
(b) Administrative rationality and efficiency
(c) Unofficial income (corruption)
(d) Political policies are not clearly designed

16. 'No tax shall be levied or collected except by an authority of law." Which Article of the Constitution of India provides this?
(a) Article 209 (b) Article 215
(c) Article 256 (d) Article 265

17. A 'questionnaire' has the following characteristics:
(i) Well structured
(ii) Administered personally
(iii) Simple and concise
(iv) Administered to sampled respondents
Select the correct answer from the codes given below:
Codes:
(a) (i) (ii) (iii) (b) (ii) (iii) (iv)
(c) (i) (iii) (iv) (d) (i) (ii) (iv)

18. The Finance Commission constituted under Article 243 Y is required to make recommendations to the Governor on
(i) Distribution between the State and Municipalities of the net proceeds of duties, tolls and fees levied by the State.
(ii) Grants-in-aid to Municipalities from Consolidated Fund of India.
(iii) The measures needed to improve financial position of Municipalities.

(iv) Determination of duties, tolls and fees which may be assigned to the Municipalities.

Choose the correct answer from the following codes:

Codes:

(a) (i) (ii) (iii) (b) (i) (iii) (iv)
(c) (i) (ii) (iii) (iv) (d) (ii) (iii) (iv)

19. A "Nagar Panchayat" under Art. 243 Q refers to
 (a) a smaller urban area
 (b) a transition from a rural to urban area
 (c) a larger urban area
 (d) None of above

Given below are two statements, one labelled as Assertion (A) and the other labelled as Reason (R). Examine these two statements carefully and state if the Assertion (A) and the Reason (R) are individually true and if so, whether the Reason is a correct explanation of Assertion:

Select the correct answer from the codes given below the question.

20. **Assertion (A):** Minnowbrook Conference has concentrated more on client orientation and social equity.

Reason (R): The technologies of E-Governance serve to provide delivery of Government services to citizens and improved reaction with business and industry.

Codes:

(a) Both (A) and (R) are correct and (R) is the correct explanation of (A).
(b) Both (A) and (R) are correct, but (R) is not the correct explanation of (A).
(c) (A) is true, but (R) is false.
(d) (A) is false, but (R) is true.

21. **Assertion (A):** According to Weber, all power and all authority is legitimate.

Reason (R): According to Weber, authority is always based on a popular belief structure.

Codes:

(a) Both (A) and (R) are correct and (R) is the correct explanation of (A).
(b) Both (A) and (R) are correct, but (R) is not the correct explanation of (A).
(c) (A) is true, but (R) is false.
(d) (A) is false, but (R) is true.

22. **Assertion (A):** Each individual has a set of needs.

Reason (R): Interests are usually a product of a fusion of several needs.

Codes:

(a) Both (A) and (R) are true.
(b) Both (A) and (R) are true, but (R) is not the correct explanation.
(c) (A) is true, but (R) is false.
(d) (A) is false, but (R) is true.

23. **Assertion (A):** Decentralization, devolution and deconcentration signify transfer of authority.

Reason (R): Delegation is a means of distributing authority in the organisation.

Codes:

(a) Both (A) and (R) are correct and (R) is the correct explanation of (A).
(b) Both (A) and (R) are correct, but (R) is not the correct explanation of (A).
(c) (A) is true, but (R) is false.
(d) (A) is false, but (R) is true.

24. **Assertion (A):** Comparative Public Administration is an effort to study administrative systems in their ecological context.

Reason (R): Social and economic factors influence administration.

Codes:

(a) Both (A) and (R) are correct and (R) is the correct explanation of (A).
(b) Both (A) and (R) are correct, but (R) is not the correct explanation of (A).

(c) (A) is true, but (R) is false.
(d) (A) is false, but (R) is true.

25. **Assertion (A):** There is a lack of public participation in development activities in India.
Reason (R): Indian bureaucracy is not properly trained for development activities.
Codes:
(a) Both (A) and (R) are correct and (R) is the correct explanation of (A).
(b) Both (A) and (R) are correct, but (R) is not the correct explanation of (A).
(c) (A) is true, but (R) is false.
(d) (A) is false, but (R) is true.

26. **Assertion (A):** All India Services have made a dent on the principle of federalism and autonomy of the States.
Reason (R): Officers of All India Services are under the rules and regulations of Central Government and the States cannot keep proper control over them.
Codes:
(a) Both (A) and (R) are correct and (R) is the correct explanation of (A).
(b) Both (A) and (R) are correct, but (R) is not the correct explanation of (A).
(c) (A) is true, but (R) is false.
(d) (A) is false, but (R) is true.

27. **Assertion (A):** Planning Commission is neither a statutory body nor a constitutional body.
Reason (R): It has been established by an Executive Order.
Codes:
(a) Both (A) and (R) are correct and (R) is the correct explanation of (A).
(b) Both (A) and (R) are correct, but (R) is not the correct explanation of (A).
(c) (A) is true, but (R) is false.
(d) (A) is false, but (R) is true.

28. **Assertion (A):** Company form of Public Enterprise is described as a fraud on the Constitution.
Reason (R): It evades constitutional responsibility.
Codes:
(a) Both (A) and (R) are correct and (R) is the correct explanation of (A).
(b) Both (A) and (R) are correct, but (R) is not the correct explanation of (A).
(c) (A) is true, but (R) is false.
(d) (A) is false, but (R) is true.

29. **Assertion (A):** The Sarvodaya Philosophy has totally opposed the Political Parties entry to contest village panchayat elections.
Reason (R): Dr. Ambedkar has described the village as "the hub of parochialism, narrow minded, oppressed and caste oriented one".
Codes:
(a) Both (A) and (R) are true
(b) Both (A) and (R) are true, but (R) is not the correct explanation (A).
(c) (A) is true, but (R) is false.
(d) (A) is false, but (R) is true.

30. Arrange the following thinkers in chronological order. Select the right answer from the codes given below:
(i) Herbert A. Simon
(ii) F.W. Taylor
(iii) Elton Mayo
(iv) Yehezkel Dror
Codes:
(a) (i) (ii) (iii) (iv)
(b) (ii) (iii) (iv) (i)
(c) (ii) (iii) (i) (iv)
(d) (i) (iii) (ii) (iv)

31. Arrange the following theories of motivation in a chronological order. Select the correct answer from the codes given below:
(i) Maturity – Immaturity Theory
(ii) ERG Theory

(iii) Expectancy Theory
(iv) Equity Theory
(v) Theory X and Theory Y

Codes:
(a) (i) (v) (iii) (iv) (ii)
(b) (v) (i) (ii) (iv) (iii)
(c) (i) (v) (iv) (ii) (iii)
(d) (i) (v) (iv) (iii) (ii)

32. Arrange the following in their chronological order. Select the right answer from the codes given below:
(i) Sala Model
(ii) Mental Revolution
(iii) Disjointed Incrementalism
(iv) Hygiene Factor

Codes:
(a) (i) (iii) (iv) (ii) (b) (ii) (iv) (i) (iii)
(c) (i) (ii) (iii) (iv) (d) (ii) (iii) (iv) (i)

33. Arrange the following in their chronological order. Select the right answer from the codes given below:
(i) National Commission to Review the Working of the Constitution – M.N. Venkatachaliah.
(ii) Committee on Civil Service Reforms – P.C. Hota
(iii) Finance Commission – C. Rangarajan
(iv) Commission on Centre-State Relations – R.S. Sarkaria

Codes:
(a) (iv) (ii) (i) (iii) (b) (ii) (i) (iii) (iv)
(c) (i) (ii) (iii) (iv) (d) (iv) (i) (ii) (iii)

34. Which of the following is the correct sequence for budget preparation? Select the correct answer from the given code:
(i) Scrutiny by Controlling Officers.
(ii) Scrutiny by Finance Ministry.
(iii) Scrutiny by Estimates Committee.
(iv) Scrutiny by Administrative Ministry.

Codes:
(a) (i) (ii) (iii) (iv) (b) (i) (iv) (ii) (iii)
(c) (iv) (i) (iii) (ii) (d) (i) (iii) (ii) (iv)

35. Arrange the Project Planning exercise in a sequential manner. Select the correct answer from the given code:
(i) Plan (ii) Programme
(iii) Policy (iv) Project
(v) Activity

Codes:
(a) (i) (ii) (iii) (iv) (v)
(b) (iii) (i) (ii) (iv) (v)
(c) (ii) (iii) (iv) (v) (i)
(d) (iv) (ii) (i) (iii) (v)

36. The sequence in which the classification of accounting structure in India is followed. Choose the correct answer from the given code:
(i) Major Head (ii) Sub Head
(iii) Minor Head (iv) Detailed Head
(v) Sectoral Head

Codes:
(a) (v) (i) (iii) (ii) (iv)
(b) (i) (v) (ii) (iv) (iii)
(c) (iv) (i) (v) (ii) (iii)
(d) (ii) (iii) (iv) (i) (v)

37. Arrange the following units of local Government in France in descending order. Choose the correct answer from the given code:
(i) Arrondisement (ii) Commune
(iii) Department (iv) Canton

Codes:
(a) (iii) (iv) (ii) (i) (b) (iii) (i) (iv) (ii)
(c) (iii) (i) (ii) (iv) (d) (iii) (iv) (i) (ii)

38. Match the nature of the management systems of 1 – 4 of Renesis Likert.

List I
(A) Management System-2
(B) Management System-1
(C) Management System-4
(D) Management System-3

List II
(i) Consultative (ii) Benevolent
(iii) Exploitative (iv) Participative
(v) Authoritative

Codes:	A	B	C	D
(a)	(v)	(iii)	(iv)	(ii)
(b)	(iii)	(iv)	(v)	(ii)
(c)	(ii)	(iii)	(iv)	(i)
(d)	(iv)	(ii)	(iii)	(i)

39. Match the models conceived by the authors.

List I

(A) The Linking PIN Model
(B) Need Hierarchy Model
(C) T Group Model
(D) Decision Making Model

List II

(i) Herbert A. Simon
(ii) Renesis Likert
(iii) Abraham Maslow
(iv) Chris Argyris
(v) Max Weber

Codes:	A	B	C	D
(a)	(ii)	(v)	(iii)	(i)
(b)	(ii)	(iii)	(iv)	(i)
(c)	(i)	(iii)	(ii)	(iv)
(d)	(i)	(iv)	(iii)	(v)

40. Match List I with List II, select the correct answer from the codes given below:

List I

(A) Security of Civil Servants
(B) Union Public Service Commission
(C) Recruitment and conditions of service of persons serving the Union or a State
(D) Administrative Tribunal

List II

(i) Article 309 (ii) Article 323 A
(iii) Article 315 (iv) Article 311
(v) Article 312

Codes:	A	B	C	D
(a)	(i)	(ii)	(v)	(iv)
(b)	(iv)	(ii)	(i)	(iii)
(c)	(iv)	(iii)	(i)	(ii)
(d)	(iii)	(ii)	(v)	(i)

41. Match List I with List II, select the correct answer from the codes given below:

List I

(A) CBI Academy
(B) National Institute for SMART Government
(C) Indira Gandhi Institute of Development Research
(D) National Judicial Academy

List II

(i) Bhopal (ii) Ghaziabad
(iii) Hyderabad (iv) Mumbai
(v) New Delhi

Codes:	A	B	C	D
(a)	(ii)	(iii)	(iv)	(i)
(b)	(i)	(ii)	(iii)	(iv)
(c)	(iii)	(v)	(ii)	(iv)
(d)	(iv)	(iii)	(ii)	(i)

42. Match List I with List II and select the correct answer by using codes given below the lists:

List I

(A) First Finance Commission, 1951
(B) Fifth Finance Commission, 1968
(C) Ninth Finance Commission, 1987
(D) Thirteenth Finance Commission, 2007

List II

(i) Dr. C. Rangarajan
(ii) Dr. Vijay Kelkar
(iii) N.K.P. Salve
(iv) Mahavir Tyagi
(v) K.C. Neogy

Codes:	A	B	C	D
(a)	(v)	(iv)	(iii)	(ii)
(b)	(i)	(iv)	(iii)	(ii)
(c)	(ii)	(iv)	(v)	(i)
(d)	(v)	(iii)	(i)	(ii)

43. Match List I with List II, select the correct answer from the codes given below:

List I

(A) PPBS
(B) Top-down Budgeting

(C) Zero-based Budgeting
(D) Performance Budget

List II

(i) Truman (ii) Carter
(iii) Johnson (iv) Nicholas Henry
(v) Herbert Simon

Codes:	A	B	C	D
(a)	(iii)	(iv)	(i)	(v)
(b)	(iv)	(iii)	(ii)	(i)
(c)	(ii)	(v)	(iii)	(iv)
(d)	(iii)	(iv)	(ii)	(i)

44. Match List I with List II, select the correct answer from the codes given below:

List I

(A) Economy cut (B) Policy cut
(C) Token cut

List II

(i) The amount of demand reduced by Rs. 100/-
(ii) The amount of demand be reduced by a specific amount
(iii) The amount of demand be reduced by a sum of Re. 1/-
(iv) That the whole demand be rejected.

Codes:	A	B	C
(a)	(ii)	(iii)	(i)
(b)	(iv)	(iii)	(ii)
(c)	(i)	(ii)	(iv)
(d)	(iii)	(i)	(ii)

45. Match List I with List II and select the correct answer using the codes given below the lists:

List I

(A) Comparative Administration
(B) New Public Administration
(C) Administrative Development
(D) Development Administration

List II

(i) Robert Dahl (ii) Dwight Waldo
(iii) Edward Weidner (iv) F.W. Riggs
(v) John M. Gaus

Codes:	A	B	C	D
(a)	(i)	(ii)	(iv)	(iii)
(b)	(ii)	(v)	(iii)	(i)
(c)	(iii)	(ii)	(iv)	(v)
(d)	(iv)	(i)	(ii)	(iii)

46. Match List I with List II, select the correct answer from the codes given below:

List I

(A) Rural Works Programme (RWP)
(B) Command Area Development (CAD)
(C) National Rural Employment Programme (NREP)
(D) Rural Landless Employment Guarantee Programme (RLEGP)

List II

(i) It was replaced by the Bonded Labour Rehabilitation Scheme in 1989
(ii) It took inspiration partially from Maharashtra Employment Generation Scheme (EGS) and is also known as Million wells
(iii) It was replaced by the Draught Prone Area Programme (DPAP) in 1973.
(iv) It ensures allround development of the major irrigation projects
(v) It was restructured form of the food for work programme

Codes:	A	B	C	D
(a)	(iii)	(iv)	(v)	(ii)
(b)	(v)	(iv)	(ii)	(i)
(c)	(ii)	(i)	(iv)	(iii)
(d)	(i)	(v)	(iii)	(iv)

Read the passage below, and answer the questions that follow based on your understanding of the passage:

Citizen's charter is the latest device to structure citizen administration relationship. Citizens' charter is aimed at demanding from the Government and the service organizations the fundamentals of accountability, transparency, quality and choice of services supplied to people. The concept of citizens' charter was initiated by 'Common Cause' in 1994. In UK, where the charter has been widely in use, a committee was constituted under John Major, the then Prime Minister. The Prime Minister's office was continuously monitoring the progress of citizens' charter in different departments and service organizations. It has now become customary for the Prime Minister to submit a report to Parliament about the progress of the Charter formulated by different ministries. The Prime Minister's report contains comparative estimate of performance over time and explains whether efficiency has been up to some standards. If the performance has excelled, it is shown with a 'right' mark and if deteriorated, with a cross (×) mark.

The charter marks are awarded to the personnel in specific ministries and agencies. The nominations are sent by citizens who avail the services. As a mark of honour for the excellent services rendered, the photographs of recipients of charter mark awards are exhibited in the offices. If the standards of performance are not maintained or for any delay or shortfall in performance, the concerned department has to pay compensation.

The charter is no doubt an innovative device; but its formulation and enforcement are no easy tasks. Fairly precise standards of performance have to be set. There has to be some body or authority to monitor performance and watch violations and maintenance. The citizens have to play an active role in giving timely and necessary feedback about services rendered by the Government agencies. Within the organizations, the employees must be psychologically and infrastructurally well prepared to serve the public as per the agreed-upon standards.

In India the Prime Minister inaugurated a Conference of the Chief Secretaries in November 1996 on "an agenda for an effective and responsive administration" in order to restore the faith of the people in the fairness and capacity of the administration at different levels. It was admitted that the public agencies had been inward looking and were alienated from the people.... As explained by the Government, the charter places the citizen at the centre of administration, instead of treating him as a passive recipient of services rendered without regard for quality, cost or timeliness.

47. Citizens' Charter aims at
   (a) Accountability
   (b) Transparency
   (c) Quality and choice of services
   (d) All the above

48. P.M.'s Office does not do the following:
   (a) Monitoring the progress of citizen's charter.
   (b) Estimating the performance of different ministries.
   (c) Paying compensation for low performance.
   (d) Submitting the report to Parliament about the progress of the charters formulated by different ministries.

49. Successful implementation of citizens' charter requires
   (a) setting up of precise standards of performance.
   (b) having an authority to monitor performance.
   (c) having feedback by the citizens about the services rendered.
   (d) All the above

50. The Government of India does not want
   (a) to treat citizens as passive recipients of services
   (b) to treat citizens at the centre of administration.
   (c) to restore faith of the people in the fairness of administration
   (d) All the above

ANSWERS

1. (d)	2. (a)	3. (b)	4. (b)	5. (a)
6. (a)	7. (a)	8. (a)	9. (a)	10. (b)
11. (a)	12. (d)	13. (d)	14. (d)	15. (b)
16. (d)	17. (a)	18. (b)	19. (b)	20. (b)
21. (c)	22. (b)	23. (a)	24. (b)	25. (a)
26. (b)	27. (a)	28. (a)	29. (a)	30. (c)
31. (a)	32. (b)	33. (d)	34. (c)	35. (d)
36. (a)	37. (b)	38. (c)	39. (b)	40. (c)
41. (a)	42. (a)	43. (d)	44. (a)	45. (d)
46. (a)	47. (d)	48. (c)	49. (d)	50. (d)

JUNE–2010

Note: This paper contains Sixty (60) multiple-choice questions, each question carrying two (2) marks. Candidate is expected to answer any Fifty (50) questions. In case more than Fifty (50) questions are attempted, only the first Fifty (50) questions will be evaluated.

PAPER–I

1. Which one of the following is the most important quality of a good teacher?
   (a) Punctuality and sincerity
   (b) Content mastery
   (c) Content mastery and reactive
   (d) Content mastery and sociable
2. The primary responsibility for the teacher's adjustment lies with
   (a) The children
   (b) The principal
   (c) The teacher himself
   (d) The community
3. As per the NCTE norms, what should be the staff strength for a unit of 100 students at B.Ed. level?
   (a) 1 + 7 (b) 1 + 9
   (c) 1 + 10 (d) 1 + 5
4. Research has shown that the most frequent symptom of nervous instability among teachers is
   (a) Digestive upsets
   (b) Explosive behaviour
   (c) Fatigue
   (d) Worry
5. Which one of the following statements is correct?
   (a) Syllabus is an annexure to the curriculum.
   (b) Curriculum is the same in all educational institutions.
   (c) Curriculum includes both formal and informal education.
   (d) Curriculum does not include methods of evaluation.
6. A successful teacher is one who is
   (a) Compassionate and disciplinarian
   (b) Quite and reactive
   (c) Tolerant and dominating
   (d) Passive and active

Read the following passage carefully and answer the questions 7 to 12.

The phrase "What is it like?" stands for a fundamental thought process. How does one go about observing and reporting on things and events that occupy segments of earth space? Of all the infinite variety of phenomena on the face of the earth, how does one decide what phenomena to observe? There is no such thing as a complete description of the earth or any part of it, for every microscopic point on the earth's surface differs from every other such point. Experience shows that the things observed are already familiar, because they are like phenomena that occur at home or because they resemble the abstract images and models developed in the human mind.

How are abstract images formed? Humans alone among the animals possess language; their words symbolise not only specific things but also mental images of classes of things. People can remember what they have seen or experienced because they attach a word symbol to them.

During the long record of our efforts to gain more and more knowledge about the face of the earth as the human habitat, there has been a continuing interplay between things and events. The direct observation through the senses is described as a percept; the mental image is described as a concept. Percepts are what some people describe as reality, in contrast to mental images, which are theoretical, implying that they are not real.

The relation of Percept to Concept is not as simple as the definition implies. It is now quite clear that people of different cultures or even individuals in the same culture develop different mental images of reality and what they perceive is a reflection of these preconceptions. The direct observation of things and events on the face of the earth is so clearly a function of the mental images of the mind of the observer that the whole idea of reality must be reconsidered.

Concepts determine what the observer perceives, yet concepts are derived from the generalisations of previous percepts. What happens is that the educated observer is taught to accept a set of concepts and then sharpens or changes these concepts during a professional career. In any one field of scholarship, professional opinion at one time determines what concepts and procedures are acceptable, and these form a kind of model of scholarly behaviour.

7. The problem raised in the passage reflects on
   (a) thought process
   (b) human behaviour
   (c) cultural perceptions
   (d) professional opinion
8. According to the passage, human beings have mostly in mind
   (a) Observation of things
   (b) Preparation of mental images
   (c) Expression through language
   (d) To gain knowledge
9. Concept means
   (a) A mental image
   (b) A reality
   (c) An idea expressed in language form
   (d) All the above
10. The relation of Percept to Concept is
    (a) Positive (b) Negative
    (c) Reflective (d) Absolute
11. In the passage, the earth is taken as
    (a) The Globe
    (b) The Human Habitat
    (c) A Celestial Body
    (d) A Planet
12. Percept means
    (a) Direct observation through the senses
    (b) A conceived idea
    (c) Ends of a spectrum
    (d) An abstract image
13. Action research means
    (a) A longitudinal research
    (b) An applied research
    (c) A research initiated to solve an immediate problem
    (d) A research with socio-economic objective
14. Research is
    (a) Searching again and again
    (b) Finding solution to any problem
    (c) Working in a scientific way to search for truth of any problem
    (d) None of the above
15. A common test in research demands much priority on
    (a) Reliability (b) Usability
    (c) Objectivity (d) All of the above
16. Which of the following is the first step in starting the research process?
    (a) Searching sources of information to locate problem
    (b) Survey of related literature
    (c) Identification of problem
    (d) Searching for solutions to the problem
17. If a researcher conducts a research on finding out which administrative style

contributes more to institutional effectiveness? This will be an example of
(a) Basic Research
(b) Action Research
(c) Applied Research
(d) None of the above

18. Normal Probability Curve should be
(a) Positively skewed
(b) Negatively skewed
(c) Leptokurtic skewed
(d) Zero skewed

19. In communication, a major barrier to reception of messages is
(a) audience attitude
(b) audience knowledge
(c) audience education
(d) audience income

20. Post-modernism is associated with
(a) Newspapers (b) Magazines
(c) Radio (d) Television

21. Didactic communication is
(a) intra-porsonal (b) inter-personal
(c) organisational (d) relational

22. In communication, the language is
(a) the non-verbal code
(b) the verbal code
(c) the symbolic code
(d) the iconic code

23. Identify the correct sequence of the following:
(a) Source, channel, message, receiver
(b) Source, receiver, channel, message
(c) Source, message, receiver, channel
(d) Source, message, channel, receiver

24. **Assertion (A):** Mass media promote a culture of violence in the society.
Reason (R): Because violence sells in the market as people themselves are violent in character.
(a) Both (A) and (R) are true and (R) is the correct explanation of (A).
(b) Both (A) and (R) are true, but (R) is not the correct explanation of (A).
(c) (A) is true, but (R) is false.
(d) Both (A) and (R) are false.

25. When an error of 1% is made in the length of a square, the percentage error in the area of a square will be
(a) 0 (b) 1/2
(c) 1 (d) 2

26. On January 12, 1980, it was a Saturday. The day of the week on January 12, 1979 was
(a) Thursday (b) Friday
(c) Saturday (d) Sunday

27. If water is called food, food is called tree, tree is called earth, earth is called world, which of the following grows a fruit?
(a) Water (b) Tree
(c) World (d) Earth

28. E is the son of A, D is the son of B, E is married to C, C is the daughter of E. How is D related to E?
(a) Brother (b) Uncle
(c) Father-in-law (d) Brother-in-law

29. If INSURANCE is coded as ECNARUSNI, how HINDRANCE will be coded?
(a) CADNIHWCE (b) HANODEINR
(c) AENIRHDCN (d) ECNARDNIH

30. Find the next number in the following series: 2, 5, 10, 17, 26, 37, 50, ?
(a) 63 (b) 65
(c) 67 (d) 69

31. Which of the following is an example of circular argument?
(a) God created man in his image and man created God in his own image.
(b) God is the source of a scripture and the scripture is the source of our knowledge of God.
(c) Some of the Indians are great because India is great.
(d) Rama is great because he is Rama.

32. Lakshmana is a morally good person because
    (a) he is religious (b) he is educated
    (c) he is rich (d) he is rational

33. Two statements I and II given below are followed by two conclusions (A) and (B). Supposing the statements are true, which of the following conclusions can logically follow?

    Statements:

    I. Some religious people are morally good.
    II. Some religious people are rational.

    Conclusion:

    (A) Rationally religious people are good morally.
    (B) Non-rational religious persons are not morally good.

    (a) Only (A) follows
    (b) Only (B) follows
    (c) Both (A) and (B) follow
    (d) Neither (A) nor (B) follows

34. Certainty is
    (a) an objective fact
    (b) emotionally satisfying
    (c) logical
    (d) ontological

Questions from 35 to 36 are based on the following diagram in which there are three intersecting circles I, S and P where circle I stands for Indians, circle S stands for Scientists and circle P for Politicians. Different regions of the figure are lettered from a to g.

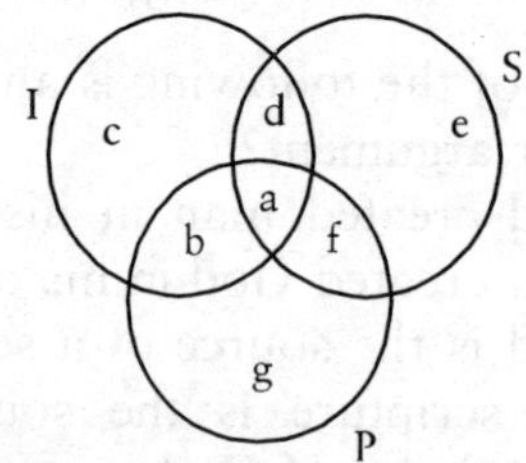

35. The region which represents non Indian-scientists who are politicians.
    (a) f (b) d
    (c) a (d) c

36. The region which represents politicians who are Indians as well as scientists.
    (a) b (b) c
    (c) a (d) d

37. The population of a city is plotted as a function of time (years) in graphic form below:

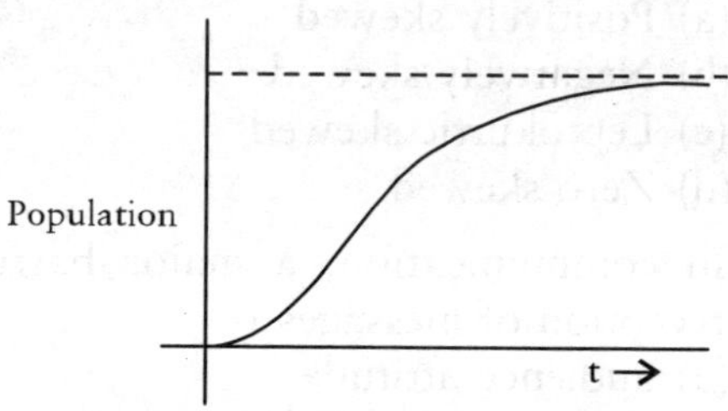

Which of the following inference can be drawn from above plot?

(a) The population increases exponentially.
(b) The population increases in parabolic fashion.
(c) The population initially increases in a linear fashion and then stabilises.
(d) The population initially increases exponentially and then stabilises.

In the following chart, the price of logs is shown in per cubic metre and that of Plywood and Saw Timber in per tonnes. Study the chart and answer the following questions 38, 39 and 40.

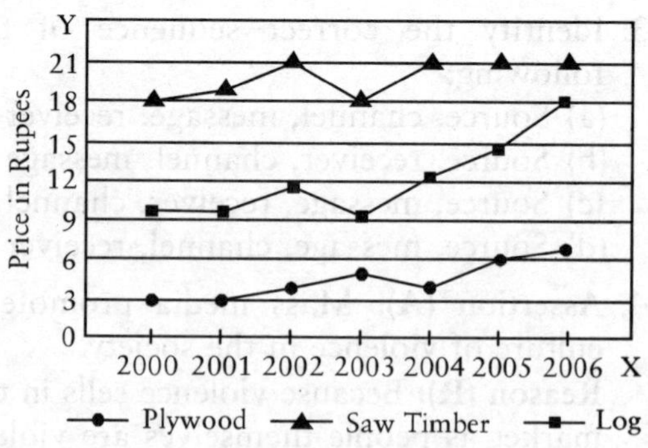

38. Which product shows the maximum percentage increase in price over the period?

(a) Saw timber (b) Plywood
(c) Log (d) None of these

39. What is the maximum percentage increase in price per cubic metre of log?
(a) 6 (b) 12
(c) 18 (d) None of these

40. In which year the prices of two products decreased and that of the third increased?
(a) 2000 (b) 2002
(c) 2003 (d) 2006

41. Which one of the following is the oldest Archival source of data in India?
(a) National Sample Surveys
(b) Agricultural Statistics
(c) Census
(d) Vital Statistics

42. In a large random data set following normal distribution, the ratio (%) of number of data points which are in the range of (mean ± standard deviation) to the total number of data points, is
(a) ~ 50% (b) ~ 67%
(c) ~ 97% (d) ~ 47%

43. Which number system is usually followed in a typical 32-bit computer?
(a) 2 (b) 8
(c) 10 (d) 16

44. Which one of the following is an example of Operating System?
(a) Microsoft Word
(b) Microsoft Excel
(c) Microsoft Access
(d) Microsoft Windows

45. Which one of the following represent the binary equivalent of the decimal number 23?
(a) 01011 (b) 10111
(c) 10011 (d) None of these

46. Which one of the following is different from other members?
(a) Google (b) Windows
(c) Linux (d) Mac

47. Where does a computer add and compare its data?
(a) CPU (b) Memory
(c) Hard disk (d) Floppy disk

48. Computers on an internet are identified by
(a) e-mail address
(b) street address
(c) IP address
(d) None of the above

49. The Right to Information Act, 2005 makes the provision of
(a) Dissemination of all types of information by all Public authorities to any person
(b) Establishment of Central, State and District Level Information Commissions as an appellate body
(c) Transparency and accountability in Public authorities
(d) All of the above

50. Which type of natural hazards cause maximum damage to property and lives?
(a) Hydrological
(b) Hydro-meteorological
(c) Geological
(d) Geo-chemical

51. Dioxins are produced from
(a) Wastelands
(b) Power plants
(c) Sugar factories
(d) Combustion of plastics

52. The slogan "A tree for each child" was coined for
(a) Social forestry program
(b) Clean Air program
(c) Soil conservation program
(d) Environmental protection program

53. The main constituents of biogas are

(a) Methane and Carbon dioxide
(b) Methane and Nitric oxide
(c) Methane, Hydrogen and Nitric oxide
(d) Methane and Sulphur dioxide

54. **Assertion (A):** In the world as a whole, the environment has degraded during past several decades.
Reason (R): The population of the world has been growing significantly.
(a) (A) is correct, (R) is correct and (R) is the correct explanation of (A).
(b) (A) is correct, (R) is correct and (R) is not the correct explanation of (A).
(c) (A) is correct, but (R) is false.
(d) (A) is false, but (R) is correct.

55. Climate change has implications for
1. soil moisture 2. forest fires
3. biodiversity 4. groundwater
Identify the correct combination according to the code:
Codes:
(a) 1 and 3 (b) 1, 2 and 3
(c) 1, 3 and 4 (d) 1, 2, 3 and 4

56. The accreditation process by National Assessment and Accreditation Council (NAAC) differs from that of National Board of Accreditation (NBA) in terms of
(a) Disciplines covered by both being the same, there is duplication of efforts.
(b) One has institutional grading approach and the other has program grading approach.
(c) Once get accredited by NBA or NAAC, the institution is free from renewal of grading, which is not a progressive decision.
(d) This accreditation amounts to approval of minimum standards in the quality of education in the institution concerned.

57. Which option is not correct?
(a) Most of the educational institutions of National repute in scientific and technical sphere fall under 64th entry of Union list.
(b) Education, in general, is the subject of concurrent list since 42nd Constitutional Amendment Act 1976.
(c) Central Advisory Board on Education (CABE) was first established in 1920.
(d) India had implemented the right to Free and Compulsory Primary Education in 2002 through 86th Constitutional Amendment.

58. Which statement is not correct about the "National Education Day" of India?
(a) It is celebrated on 5th September every year.
(b) It is celebrated on 11th November every year.
(c) It is celebrated in the memory of India's first Union Minister of Education, Dr. Abul Kalam Azad.
(d) It is being celebrated since 2008.

59. Match List I with List II and select the correct answer from the codes given below:
List I (Articles of the Constitution)
A. Article 280 B. Article 324
C. Article 323 D. Article 315
List II (Institutions)
1. Administrative Tribunals
2. Election Commission of India
3. Finance Commission at Union level
4. Union Public Service Commission

Codes:	**A**	**B**	**C**	**D**
(a)	1	2	3	4
(b)	3	2	1	4
(c)	2	3	4	1
(d)	2	4	3	1

60. Deemed Universities declared by UGC under Section 3 of the UGC Act 1956, are not permitted to

(a) offer programs in higher education and issue degrees
(b) give affiliation to any institute of higher education
(c) open off-campus and off-shore campus anywhere in the country and overseas respectively without the permission of the UGC
(d) offer distance education programs without the approval of the Distance Education Council

ANSWERS

1. (b)	2. (c)	3. (c)	4. (b)	5. (c)
6. (a)	7. (c)	8. (a)	9. (a)	10. (c)
11. (b)	12. (a)	13. (c)	14. (c)	15. (d)
16. (c)	17. (c)	18. (d)	19. (c)	20. (d)
21. (b)	22. (b)	23. (d)	24. (d)	25. (d)
26. (b)	27. (c)	28. (d)	29. (d)	30. (b)
31. (b)	32. (a)	33. (d)	34. (c)	35. (a)
36. (c)	37. (d)	38. (c)	39. (d)	40. (b)
41. (c)	42. (b)	43. (a)	44. (d)	45. (b)
46. (b)	47. (a)	48. (c)	49. (d)	50. (c)
51. (d)	52. (d)	53. (a)	54. (b)	55. (d)
56. (c)	57. (a)	58. (a)	59. (b)	60. (b)

PAPER–II

Note: This paper contains fifty (50) objective type questions, each question carrying two (2) marks. All questions are compulsory.

1. 'Politics and Administration' by F. Goodnow
(a) further advances Wilsonian Theme
(b) contradicted the Wilsonian dichotomy
(c) supplemented Wilson's arguments
(d) although agreeing with Wilson's thesis offered new arguments.

2. 'Administration is politics since it must be responsive to the public interest.' The above statement is attributed to
(a) L. Urwick (b) J.M. Pfiffner
(c) P.H. Appleby (d) L. Gullick

3. Which of the following is described as anti-theoretic, anti-positivist and anti-hierarchical?
(a) Comparative Public Administration
(b) Development Administration
(c) New Public Administration
(d) Traditional Public Administration

4. Integration is considered as the best method of resolving conflicts according to
(a) Elton Mayo
(b) Urwick
(c) Mary Parker Follett
(d) Chris Argyris

5. The significance of secretariat can be high-lighted as
(a) it serves as a nucleus for a ministry
(b) indispensable for proper functioning of Govt.
(c) it facilitates inter-ministry coordination
(d) All the above

6. Which constitutional provision deals with adjudication of disputes relating to waters of inter-state or rivervalleys?
(a) Article 261 (b) Article 262
(c) Article 263 (d) Article 253

7. The National Development Council consists of
(a) The Prime Minister, the Chief Ministers of all the States and the members of the Planning Commission.
(b) The Prime Minister, the Chief Ministers of all the States, the Central Cabinet Ministers and the members of the Planning Commission.

(c) The Prime Minister, the Chief Ministers of all the States, selected Central Cabinet Ministers, Administrators of Union Territories and the members of the Planning Commission.
(d) The Prime Minister, all Union Cabinet Ministers, Chief Ministers of all the States, Administrators of Union Territories and the Members of the Planning Commission.

8. Which one of the following American President was assassinated due to the 'Spoils System' of Civil Service?
(a) Abraham Lincoln
(b) Garefield
(c) Robert Kennedy
(d) George Washington

9. Which of the following is not applicable in Position-Classification?
(a) An individual employee having a clear understanding of his responsibilities and powers.
(b) Better management and efficiency.
(c) Equal pay for equal work.
(d) Easy mobility of personnel from one position to another.

10. Which is not true about a No Confidence Motion?
(a) It is moved against the entire Council of Ministers.
(b) It has to state the reasons for its adoption in Lok Sabha.
(c) If passed by Lok Sabha, the Government has to resign.
(d) It is moved for ascertaining confidence of Lok Sabha in Council of Ministers.

11. The Parliamentary Commissioner of U.K. is responsible
(a) To study in depth all the bills placed before the Parliament.
(b) To carry out the directions of the Speaker.
(c) To look into grievances submitted by MPs
(d) To maintain liaison with MPs.

12. Which is not the eligibility criteria to become a member of the Finance Commission?
(a) Wide public experience.
(b) Specialised knowledge of finance.
(c) Specialised knowledge of economics.
(d) Experience as a judge of High Court.

13. Disinvestment policy of New Economic policy aims
(i) to raise revenue from public sector units.
(ii) to relieve the burden from public sector units.
(iii) to encourage private sector.
(iv) to avoid the criticisms of low profile of public sector undertakings.
(a) (i) (ii) and (iii) are correct.
(b) (i) and (iv) are correct.
(c) (ii) and (iii) are correct.
(d) (ii) and (iv) are correct.

14. The Chairman of the National Commission on Urbanisation is
(a) C.M. Correa (b) Sam Pitroda
(c) G.V.K. Rao (d) Yash Pal

15. Which was the first country to introduce the 'Right to Information'?
(a) Canada (b) Japan
(c) Sweden (d) U.S.A.

16. Under which of the following Articles of the Constitution of India, do the State Legislatives delegate powers and functions to the Panchayats?
(a) 243 and 243 A
(b) 243 A and 243 B
(c) 243 G and 243 H
(d) 243 D and 243 F

17. Which one is not the function of Union Finance Commission?
(a) Distribution of Plan Grants
(b) Distribution of net proceeds of taxes

(c) Distribution of Non-Plan Grants
(d) Measures to augment resources of Municipalities.

18. Which is not true about C & AG of India?
(a) Appointed by President by warrant under his hand
(b) Takes an oath according to form set out for the purpose in the fourth (IVth) schedule.
(c) Not eligible for further office after he has ceased to hold office.
(d) The administrative expenses for his office are charged upon Consolidated Fund of India.

19. Which of the following is not the essential feature of 'Writs' issued by the Courts?
(a) Writ jurisdiction of High Courts is wider than that of Supreme Court.
(b) Parliament under Article 32 cannot empower any other court (other than Supreme Court and High Court) to issue writs.
(c) Supreme Court can issue writs for enforcement of Fundamental Rights.
(d) High Court can issue writs for enforcement of Fundamental Rights.

20. Which one in the following is not the component of New Public Management?
(a) Delivery of high quality services.
(b) Rigorous performance measures of individuals.
(c) Managerial support services to facilitate achievement.
(d) To formulate welfare policies of the Government.

Given below are two statements, one labelled as Assertion (A) and the other labelled as Reason (R). Examine these two statements carefully and state if the Assertion (A) and the Reason (R) are individually true and if so, whether the Reason is a correct explanation of Assertion:

Select the correct answer from the codes given below the question.

21. **Assertion (A):** There are many differences between public administration and private administration.
Reason (R): These differences are because of working system of the organisations.
Codes:
(a) Both (A) and (R) are correct and (R) is the correct explanation of (A).
(b) Both (A) and (R) are correct, but (R) is not the correct explanation of (A).
(c) (A) is true but (R) is false.
(d) (A) is false but (R) is true.

22. **Assertion (A):** Relationship between the superior and subordinate is not essential in hierarchy.
Reason (R): Delegation of authority is possible in hierarchy.
Codes:
(a) Both (A) and (R) are correct and (R) is the correct explanation of (A).
(b) Both (A) and (R) are correct, but (R) is not the correct explanation of (A).
(c) (A) is true but (R) is false.
(d) (A) is false but (R) is true.

23. **Assertion (A):** Restrictions on political activities of Public employees are in their own interests.
Reason (R): Neutrality of civil servants ensures that all of them are treated alike.
Codes:
(a) Both (A) and (R) are correct and (R) is the correct explanation of (A).
(b) Both (A) and (R) are correct, but (R) is not the correct explanation of (A).
(c) (A) is true but (R) is false.
(d) (A) is false but (R) is true.

24. **Assertion (A):** Civil servants in the developing countries need to be trained in the art and science of Public Administration.

Reason (R): Training in the art and science of Public Administration is involving huge expenditure in the developing countries.

Codes:

(a) Both (A) and (R) are correct and (R) is the correct explanation of (A).
(b) Both (A) and (R) are correct, but (R) is not the correct explanation of (A).
(c) (A) is true but (R) is false.
(d) (A) is false but (R) is true.

25. **Assertion (A):** A Public Corporation is essentially accountable to the Legislature.

Reason (R): Legislature is the custodian of public finances.

Codes:

(a) Both (A) and (R) are correct and (R) is the correct explanation of (A).
(b) Both (A) and (R) are correct, but (R) is not the correct explanation of (A).
(c) (A) is true but (R) is false.
(d) (A) is false but (R) is true.

26. **Assertion (A):** Indian Public Administration is an excellent example of efficiency and sensitivity.

Reason (R): Government has many a time made efforts for administrative reforms and rejuvenation.

Codes:

(a) Both (A) and (R) are correct and (R) is the correct explanation of (A).
(b) Both (A) and (R) are correct, but (R) is not the correct explanation of (A).
(c) (A) is true but (R) is false.
(d) (A) is false but (R) is true.

27. **Assertion (A):** The Government raises funds by public borrowings, leving fresh taxes and duties for economic and social growth.

Reason (R): Dis-investment in public enterprises since 1991 has not generated sufficient funds.

Codes:

(a) Both (A) and (R) are correct and (R) is the correct explanation of (A).
(b) Both (A) and (R) are correct, but (R) is not the correct explanation of (A).
(c) (A) is true but (R) is false.
(d) (A) is false but (R) is true.

28. **Assertion (A):** People want to know what is being done, why it is being done and how it is being done in their district.

Reason (R): The district administration holds a different view about transparency and accountability.

Codes:

(a) Both (A) and (R) are correct and (R) is the correct explanation of (A).
(b) Both (A) and (R) are correct, but (R) is not the correct explanation of (A).
(c) (A) is true but (R) is false.
(d) (A) is false but (R) is true.

29. **Assertion (A):** New Public Management is nothing but debureaucratization.

Reason (R): The public services and market economy are closely linked to one another.

Codes:

(a) Both (A) and (R) are true.
(b) Both (A) and (R) are true but (R) is not the correct explanation.
(c) (A) is true but (R) is false.
(d) (A) is false but (R) is true.

30. Arrange the following in their chronological order. Use the following code:

(i) National Extension Service.
(ii) Community Development Programme.
(iii) Integrated Rural Development Programme.
(iv) Antyodaya.

Codes:

(a) (i), (ii), (iii), (iv) (b) (ii), (iii), (i), (iv)
(c) (ii), (i), (iv), (iii) (d) (ii), (i), (iii), (iv)

31. Match List I with List II. Select the correct answer from the codes given below:

List I
(A) Lyndall Urwick
(B) P.H. Appleby
(C) Herbert Simon
(D) Henry Fayol

List II
(i) General Principles of Administration
(ii) The Golden Book of Administration
(iii) Big Democracy
(iv) New Science of Management
(v) Work and Nature of Man

Codes:	**A**	**B**	**C**	**D**
(a)	(ii)	(iii)	(iv)	(i)
(b)	(iii)	(ii)	(v)	(i)
(c)	(iv)	(i)	(iii)	(ii)
(d)	(v)	(iv)	(ii)	(iii)

32. Arrange the following in their chronological order. Use the code given below:
(i) Committee on Administrative arrangement for Rural Development and Poverty Alleviation Programmes (GVK Rao).
(ii) Committee on Revitalisation of Panchayati Raj institutions for Democracy and Development (LM Singhvi)
(iii) Committee on Block-Level Planning (Dantwala)
(iv) Committee on District Planning (Hanumantha Rao)

Codes:
(a) (i), (ii), (iv), (iii) (b) (iii), (iv), (i), (ii)
(c) (iii), (i), (ii), (iv) (d) (iii), (ii), (i), (iv)

33. Arrange the following stages in the evolution of Public Administration as a discipline in chronological order.
Select the correct answer from the code given below:
(i) Administrative Behaviour
(ii) Principles approach
(iii) Public Policy approach
(iv) Politics-administration dichotomy
(v) Ecological approach

Codes:
(a) (iv), (i), (ii), (v), (iii)
(b) (iv), (ii), (i), (v), (iii)
(c) (iv), (ii), (i), (iii), (v)
(d) (iv), (i), (ii), (iii), (v)

34. Arrange the following in their chronological order. Select the right answer from the code given below:
(i) Shop Management
(ii) Human side of Enterprise
(iii) Ecology of Public Administration
(iv) Administrative Behaviour

Codes:
(a) (i), (ii), (iii), (iv) (b) (ii), (iii), (i), (iv)
(c) (iii), (i), (ii), (iv) (d) (i), (iv), (ii), (iii)

35. Arrange the following steps in decision-making process in chronological order: Select the correct answer from the code given below:
(i) Stating the best course of action.
(ii) Evaluating tentative decisions.
(iii) Acquiring different viewpoints.
(iv) Investigating tentative decisions.
(v) Instituting follow-up action

Codes:
(a) (iv), (i), (iii), (v), (ii)
(b) (i), (iii), (iv), (ii), (v)
(c) (iii), (i), (iv), (ii), (v)
(d) (iii), (iv), (i), (ii), (v)

36. Arrange the following in a chronological sequence using the codes given below:
(i) Administrative Reforms Commission.
(ii) Gorwala Committee Report.
(iii) Gopalaswamy Aiyangar Committee Report
(iv) Paul H. Appleby Report

Codes:
(a) (ii), (iv), (i), (iii) (b) (iii), (ii), (iv), (i)
(c) (i), (ii), (iv), (iii) (d) (iv), (ii), (iii), (i)

37. The classification of accounting structure in India is adopted in the following sequence:
Select the correct answer from the code given below:
1. Major Head 2. Sub Head
3. Minor Head 4. Detailed Head
5. Sectoral Head

Codes:
(a) 5, 1, 3, 2, 4 (b) 1, 5, 2, 4, 3
(c) 4, 1, 5, 2, 3 (d) 2, 3, 4, 1, 5

38. Which one is the correct sequence for Budget preparations? Select the answer from the codes given below:
(i) Scrutiny by Controlling Officers.
(ii) Scrutiny by Ministry of Finance.
(iii) Scrutiny by Estimates Committee.
(iv) Scrutiny by Administrative Ministry.

Codes:
(a) (i), (ii), (iii), (iv) (b) (i), (iv), (ii), (iii)
(c) (iv), (i), (ii), (iii) (d) (i), (iii), (ii), (iv)

39. Match List I with List II. Select the correct answer from the codes given below:
List I (Experiments)
(A) Illumination experiments
(B) Relay Assembly Test Room experiments
(C) Bank wiring Observation Room experiments
(D) Interviewing programmes
List II (Focus)
(i) Fatigue
(ii) Physical working
(iii) Human Relations
(iv) Employee relations with supervisor and management

Codes:	**A**	**B**	**C**	**D**
(a)	(ii)	(i)	(iv)	(iii)
(b)	(ii)	(iii)	(iv)	(i)
(c)	(iv)	(i)	(ii)	(iii)
(d)	(iv)	(iii)	(ii)	(i)

40. Match List I with List II. Select the correct answer from the codes given below:
List I
(A) Zone of acceptance
(B) Differential piece rate plan
(C) Zone of indifference
(D) Y. Theory
List II
(i) Herzberg (ii) Bernard
(iii) Taylor (iv) Herbert Simon
(v) Abraham Maslow

Codes:	**A**	**B**	**C**	**D**
(a)	(v)	(ii)	(iii)	(iv)
(b)	(ii)	(iii)	(iv)	(v)
(c)	(iii)	(i)	(iv)	(ii)
(d)	(iv)	(iii)	(ii)	(i)

41. Match List I with List II. Select the correct answer from the codes given below:
List I (Commissions/Position of The Union of India)
(A) Finance Commission
(B) Union Public Service Commission
(C) Election Commission
(D) Comptroller and Auditor General of India
List II (Article under the Constitution of India)
(i) 148 (ii) 280
(iii) 315 (iv) 324
(v) 156

Codes:	**A**	**B**	**C**	**D**
(a)	(iv)	(v)	(ii)	(iii)
(b)	(ii)	(iii)	(iv)	(i)
(c)	(iv)	(iii)	(ii)	(i)
(d)	(ii)	(v)	(iv)	(iii)

42. Match List I with List II. Select the correct answer from the codes given below:
List I
(A) Santhanam Committee
(B) Sarkaria Committee
(C) Satish Chandra Committee
(D) Yashpal Committee
List II
(i) Centre-State Relations
(ii) Higher Education Reforms

(iii) To prevent corruption
(iv) Civil Service reforms
(v) Health Reform

Codes:	A	B	C	D
(a)	(v)	(iv)	(ii)	(iii)
(b)	(iii)	(i)	(iv)	(ii)
(c)	(iv)	(ii)	(iii)	(i)
(d)	(ii)	(iii)	(i)	(iv)

43. Match List I with List II and select the correct answer from the given codes:

List I (Positions)
(A) Constitutional position of the Governor
(B) Constitutional position of Chairman of Rajya Sabha
(C) Constitutional position of Vice President
(D) Constitutional position of President

List II (Article)
(i) Article 52 (ii) Article 153
(iii) Article 63 (iv) Article 93
(v) Article 89

Codes:	A	B	C	D
(a)	(i)	(ii)	(iv)	(v)
(b)	(ii)	(v)	(iv)	(iii)
(c)	(v)	(i)	(ii)	(iv)
(d)	(ii)	(v)	(iii)	(i)

44. Match List I with List II. Select the correct answer from the codes given below:

List I
(A) Tenure of office of persons serving in the Union or a State.
(B) Public Service Commission for the Union and for the States.
(C) Recruitment and conditions of service of persons serving in the Union or a State.
(D) Dismissal, removal or reduction in the rank of persons employed in civil capacity under the Union or a State.

List II
(i) Article 315 (ii) Article 310
(iii) Article 312 (iv) Article 309
(v) Article 311

Codes:	A	B	C	D
(a)	(ii)	(v)	(iv)	(i)
(b)	(iv)	(i)	(iii)	(v)
(c)	(ii)	(i)	(iv)	(v)
(d)	(iv)	(v)	(iii)	(i)

45. Match List I with List II. Select the correct answer from the codes given below:

List I
(A) Ashok Mehta
(B) G.V.K. Rao
(C) L.M. Singhvi
(D) Balvant Rai Mehta

List II
(i) Zila Parishad to play pivotal role
(ii) Two tier system
(iii) Panchayat Samiti to be the executive body
(iv) Setting up of Nyay Panchayats
(v) Constitutionalization of Panchayati Raj

Codes:	A	B	C	D
(a)	(ii)	(i)	(iv)	(iii)
(b)	(i)	(ii)	(v)	(iii)
(c)	(v)	(i)	(iv)	(iii)
(d)	(iii)	(iv)	(ii)	(v)

46. Match List I with List II. Select the correct answer from the codes given below:

List I
(A) Bhoodan Movement
(B) Drought-Prone Area Programme
(C) Integrated Rural Development Programme
(D) Indira Aawaas Yojna

List II
(i) 1986 (ii) 1978
(iii) 1970 (iv) 1951
(v) 1981

Codes:	A	B	C	D
(a)	(v)	(iii)	(i)	(iv)
(b)	(ii)	(i)	(iv)	(v)
(c)	(iv)	(iii)	(ii)	(i)
(d)	(iii)	(ii)	(iv)	(i)

Read the passage below and answer the questions that follow based on your understanding of the passage: (47-50)

The Indian Constitution makes the provision for the appointment of the Chairman and members of the UPSC. It states that the Chairman and members will be appointed by the President of India. As the President is only the nominal head of the government, these appointments are, in reality, made by the Prime Minister and his cabinet. The exact strength of the Commission is not specified in the Constitution. The President determines its strength. Over the years, the Commission's membership has increased, depending on the workload.

The Constitution provides that, as nearly as may be, one-half of the members must be persons who have held office for at least ten years under the Government of India. The expression 'as nearly as may be, one-half' in Article 316 indicates only approximation and cannot be read as equivalent to not more than half.

The Administrative Reforms Commission, in its report on Personnel Administration, had recommended that the Chairman of UPSC should be consulted while making appointments of members of the Commission, and besides, he should be consulted by the Government even with regard to the appointment of his successor. Stressing the value of the 'experience factor', the ARC had suggested that not less than two-thirds of the members of UPSC should be drawn from among the Chairmen and members of State Public Service Commissions.

The Constitution explains the grounds on which the members of the Commission can be removed or suspended by the President. When a member is to be removed on grounds of misbehaviour, the President has to refer the matter to the Supreme Court for enquiry.

The Supreme Court sends its verdict to the President and the latter is bound by this advice. If the Court advises removal, the President can remove the Chairman or a member. While the enquiry is going on, the President can remove the Chairman or a member on these grounds too: (i) if he is adjudged insolvent, (ii) if he engages in paid employment outside the duties of his office during his tenure, and (iii) if he is unfit by reason of infirmity of body and mind.

Besides, if the Chairman or a member becomes concerned or interested in any contract or agreement made by or on behalf of the Government of India and participates in any way in the profit, benefit or emoluments therefrom, otherwise than as a member, he shall be deemed guilty of misbehaviour. In cases of misbehaviour alone, the matter is referred to the Supreme Court so that the Commission is immune from political pressures. However, the Constitution does not elaborate the categories of acts falling under 'misbehaviour.' So far, no Chairman or member of the Commission has been removed on this ground.

47. Under which Article of the Constitution, the Chairman of UPSC is appointed?
   (a) 311 (b) 315
   (c) 316 (d) 309
48. Point-out the option which prescribes the eligibility of appointment for the members of UPSC.
   (a) 50% of the members having held the office for at least 10 years under the Government of India.
   (b) 50% members having held the office for at least 15 years under the Government of India.
   (c) As nearly as may be ½ having served for at least 10 years under the Government of India.

(d) As nearly as may be ½ having served for at least 15 years under the Government of India.

49. The procedure for initiating an enquiry against the members of the Commission has been prescribed in the Constitution under Article:

(a) 143 (b) 144
(c) 145 (d) 146

50. On what ground, President of India can remove a member of the Commission?

(a) Engaged in paid employment elsewhere
(b) Infirmity of body and mind
(c) Adjudged as insolvent
(d) All the above

ANSWERS

1. (a)	2. (c)	3. (c)	4. (c)	5. (d)
6. (b)	7. (d)	8. (b)	9. (d)	10. (d)
11. (c)	12. (a)	13. (d)	14. (a)	15. (c)
16. (c)	17. (d)	18. (b)	19. (b)	20. (b)
21. (a)	22. (d)	23. (a)	24. (b)	25. (a)
26. (a)	27. (b)	28. (a)	29. (c)	30. (d)
31. (a)	32. (b)	33. (b)	34. (d)	35. (b)
36. (d)	37. (a)	38. (d)	39. (b)	40. (b)
41. (b)	42. (b)	43. (d)	44. (c)	45. (a)
46. (c)	47. (c)	48. (a)	49. (c)	50. (d)

DECEMBER–2009

Note: This paper contains Sixty (60) multiple-choice questions, each question carrying two (2) marks. Candidate is expected to answer any Fifty (50) questions. In case more than Fifty (50) questions are attempted, only the first Fifty (50) questions will be evaluated.

PAPER–I

1. The University which telecasts interaction educational programs through its own channel is
   (a) Osmania University
   (b) University of Pune
   (c) Annamalai University
   (d) Indira Gandhi National University (IGNOU)

2. Which of the following skills are needed for present day teacher to adjust effectively with the classroom teaching?
   1. Knowledge of technology
   2. Use of technology in teaching learning
   3. Knowledge of students' needs
   4. Content mastery

   (a) 1 and 3 (b) 2 and 3
   (c) 2, 3 and 4 (d) 2 and 4

3. Who has signed as MoU for Accreditation of Teacher Education Institutions in India?
   (a) NAAC and UGC
   (b) NCTE and NAAC
   (c) UGC and NCTE
   (d) NCTE and IGNOU

4. The primary duty of the teacher is to
   (a) raise the intellectual standard of the students
   (b) improve the physical standard of the students
   (c) help all-round development of the students
   (d) imbibe value system in the students

5. Micro teaching is more effective
   (a) during the preparation for teaching-practice
   (b) during the teaching-practice
   (c) after the teaching-practice
   (d) always

6. What quality the students like the most in a teacher?
   (a) Idealist philosophy
   (b) Compassion
   (c) Discipline
   (d) Entertaining

7. A null hypothesis is
   (a) when there is no difference between the variables
   (b) the same as research hypothesis
   (c) subjective in nature
   (d) when there is difference between the variables

8. The research which is exploring new facts through the study of the past is called
   (a) Philosophical research
   (b) Historical research
   (c) Mythological research
   (d) Content analysis

9. Action research is
   (a) An applied research
   (b) A research carried out to solve immediate problems
   (c) A longitudinal research
   (d) Simulative research

10. The process not needed in Experimental Researches is
(a) Observation (b) Manipulation
(c) Controlling (d) Content Analysis

11. Manipulation is always a part of
(a) Historical research
(b) Fundamental research
(c) Descriptive research
(d) Experimental research

12. Which correlation co-efficient best explains the relationship between creativity and intelligence?
(a) 1.00 (b) 0.6
(c) 0.5 (d) 0.3

Read the following passage and answer the Question Nos. 13 to 18:

The decisive shift in British Policy really came about under mass pressure in the autumn and winter of 1945 to 46—the months which Penderel Moon while editing Wavell's Journal has perceptively described as 'The Edge of a Volcano'. Very foolishly, the British initially decided to hold public trials of several hundreds of the 20,000 I.N.A. prisoners (as well as dismissing from service and detaining without trial no less than 7,000). They compounded the folly by holding the first trial in the Red Fort, Delhi in November 1945, and putting on the dock together a Hindu, a Muslim and a Sikh (P.K. Sehgal, Shah Nawaz, Gurbaksh Singh Dhillon). Bhulabhai Desai, Tejbahadur Sapru and Nehru appeared for the defence (the latter putting on his barrister's gown after 25 years), and the Muslim League also joined the countrywide protest. On 20 November, an Intelligence Bureau note admitted that "there has seldom been a matter which has attracted so much Indian public interest and, it is safe to say, sympathy...this particular brand of sympathy cuts across communal barriers". A journalist (B. Shiva Rao) visiting the Red Fort prisoners on the same day reported that 'There is not the slightest feeling among them of Hindu and Muslim.... A majority of the men now awaiting trial in the Red Fort is Muslim. Some of these men are bitter that Mr. Jinnah is keeping alive a controversy about Pakistan.' The British became extremely nervous about the I.N.A. spirit spreading to the Indian Army, and in January the Punjab Governor reported that a Lahore reception for released I.N.A. prisoners had been attended by Indian soldiers in uniform.

13. Which heading is more appropriate to assign to the above passage?
(a) Wavell's Journal
(b) Role of Muslim League
(c) I.N.A. Trials
(d) Red Fort Prisoners

14. The trial of P.K. Sehgal, Shah Nawaz and Gurbaksh Singh Dhillon symbolises
(a) communal harmony
(b) threat to all religious persons
(c) threat to persons fighting for the freedom
(d) British reaction against the natives

15. I.N.A. stands for
(a) Indian National Assembly
(b) Indian National Association
(c) Inter-national Association
(d) Indian National Army

16. 'There has seldom been a matter which has attracted so much Indian Public Interest and, it is safe to say, sympathy... this particular brand of sympathy cuts across communal barriers.' Who sympathises to whom and against whom?
(a) Muslims sympathised with Shah Nawaz against the British
(b) Hindus sympathised with P.K. Sehgal against the British
(c) Sikhs sympathised with Gurbaksh Singh Dhillon against the British
(d) Indians sympathised with the persons who were to be trialled

17. The majority of people waiting for trial outside the Red Fort and criticising Jinnah were the
 (a) Hindus
 (b) Muslims
 (c) Sikhs
 (d) Hindus and Muslims both

18. The sympathy of Indian soldiers in uniform with the released I.N.A. prisoners at Lahore indicates
 (a) Feeling of Nationalism and Fraternity
 (b) Rebellion nature of Indian soldiers
 (c) Simply to participate in the reception party
 (d) None of the above

19. The country which has the distinction of having the two largest circulated newspapers in the world is
 (a) Great Britain
 (b) The United States
 (c) Japan
 (d) China

20. The chronological order of non-verbal communication is
 (a) Signs, symbols, codes, colours
 (b) Symbols, codes, signs, colours
 (c) Colours, signs, codes, symbols
 (d) Codes, colours, symbols, signs

21. Which of the following statements is not connected with communication?
 (a) Medium is the message.
 (b) The world is an electronic cocoon.
 (c) Information is power.
 (d) Telepathy is technological.

22. Communication becomes circular when
 (a) the decoder becomes an encoder
 (b) the feedback is absent
 (c) the source is credible
 (d) the channel is clear

23. The site that played a major role during the terrorist attack on Mumbai (26/11) in 2008 was
 (a) Orkut (b) Facebook
 (c) Amazon.com (d) Twitter

24. **Assertion (A):** For an effective classroom communication at times it is desirable to use the projection technology.
 Reason (R): Using the projection technology facilitates extensive coverage of course contents.
 (a) Both (A) and (R) are true, and (R) is the correct explanation.
 (b) Both (A) and (R) are true, but (R) is not the correct explanation.
 (c) (A) is true, but (R) is false.
 (d) (A) is false, but (R) is true.

25. January 1, 1995 was a Sunday. What day of the week lies on January 1, 1996?
 (a) Sunday (b) Monday
 (c) Wednesday (d) Saturday

26. When an error of 1% is made in the length and breadth of a rectangle, the percentage error (%) in the area of a rectangle will be
 (a) 0 (b) 1
 (c) 2 (d) 4

27. The next number in the series 2, 5, 9, 19, 37, ? will be
 (a) 74 (b) 75
 (c) 76 (d) None of these

28. There are 10 true-false questions in an examination. Then these questions can be answered in
 (a) 20 ways (b) 100 ways
 (c) 240 ways (d) 1024 ways

29. What will be the next term in the following?
 DCXW, FEVU, HGTS, ?
 (a) AKPO (b) ABYZ
 (c) JIRQ (d) LMRS

30. Three individuals X, Y, Z hired a car on a sharing basis and paid ₹ 1,040. They used it for 7, 8, 11 hours, respectively.

What are the charges paid by Y?
(a) ₹ 290 (b) ₹ 320
(c) ₹ 360 (d) ₹ 440

31. Deductive argument involves
(a) sufficient evidence
(b) critical thinking
(c) seeing logical relations
(d) repeated observation

32. Inductive reasoning is based on or presupposes
(a) uniformity of nature
(b) God created the world
(c) unity of nature
(d) laws of nature

33. To be critical, thinking must be
(a) practical
(b) socially relevant
(c) individually satisfying
(d) analytical

34. Which of the following is an analogous statement?
(a) Man is like God
(b) God is great
(c) Gandhiji is the Father of the Nation
(d) Man is a rational being

Questions from 35-36 are based on the following diagram in which there are three intersecting circles. H representing The Hindu, I representing Indian Express and T representing The Times of India. A total of 50 persons were surveyed and the number in the Venn diagram indicates the number of persons reading the newspapers.

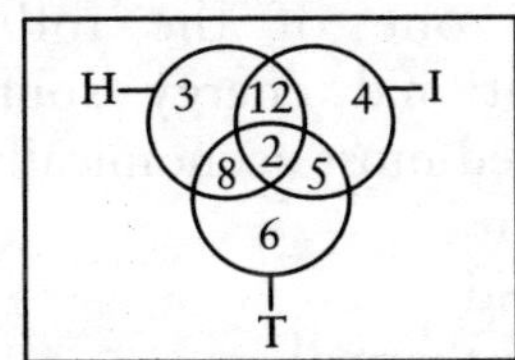

35. How many persons would be reading at least two newspapers?
(a) 23 (b) 25
(c) 27 (d) 29

36. How many persons would be reading almost two newspapers?
(a) 23 (b) 25
(c) 27 (d) 48

37. Which of the following graphs does not represent regular (periodic) behaviour of the variable f(t)?

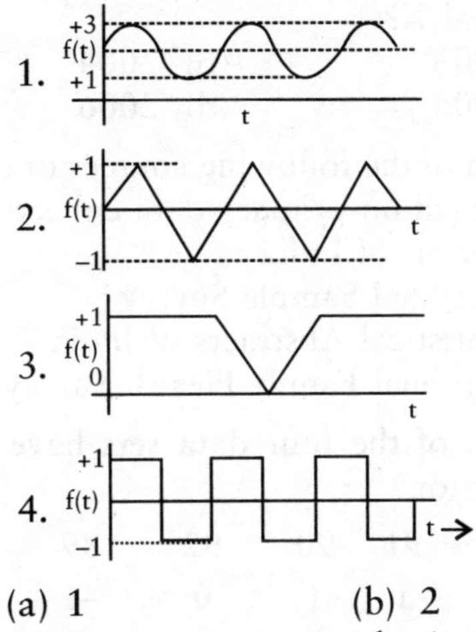

(a) 1 (b) 2
(c) 3 (d) 4

Study the following graph and answer the questions 38 to 40.

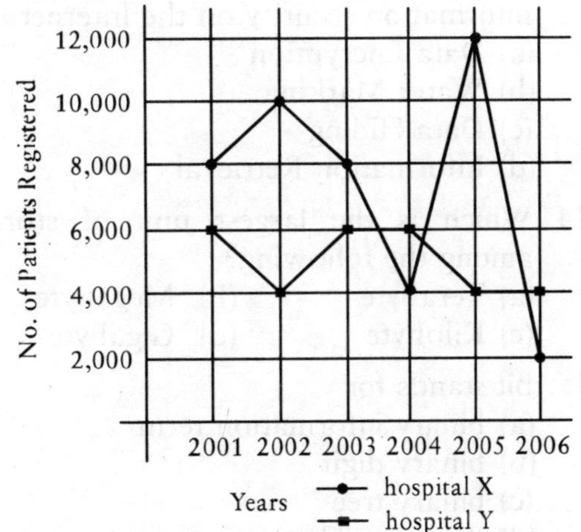

38. In which year total number of patients registered in hospital X and hospital Y was the maximum?

(a) 2003 (b) 2004
(c) 2005 (d) 2006

39. What is the maximum dispersion in the registration of patients in the two hospitals in a year?
(a) 8000 (b) 6000
(c) 4000 (d) 2000

40. In which year there was maximum decrease in registration of patients in hospital X?
(a) 2003 (b) 2004
(c) 2005 (d) 2006

41. Which of the following sources of data is not based on primary data collection?
(a) Census of India
(b) National Sample Survey
(c) Statistical Abstracts of India
(d) National Family Health Survey

42. Which of the four data sets have more dispersion?

(a)	88	91	90	92	89	91
(b)	0	1	1	0	–1	–2
(c)	3	5	2	4	1	5
(d)	0	5	8	10	–2	–8

43. Which of the following is not related to information security on the Internet?
(a) Data Encryption
(b) Water Marking
(c) Data Hiding
(d) Information Retrieval

44. Which is the largest unit of storage among the following?
(a) Terabyte (b) Megabyte
(c) Kilobyte (d) Gigabyte

45. bit stands for
(a) binary information term
(b) binary digit
(c) binary tree
(d) Bivariate Theory

46. Which one of the following is not a linear data structure?
(a) Array (b) Binary Tree
(c) Queue (d) Stack

47. Which one of the following is not a network device?
(a) Router (b) Switch
(c) Hub (d) CPU

48. A compiler is used to convert the following to object code which can be executed
(a) High-level language
(b) Low-level language
(c) Assembly language
(d) Natural language

49. The great Indian Bustard bird is found in
(a) Thar Desert of Rajasthan
(b) Malabar Coast
(c) Coastal regions of India
(d) Delta regions

50. The Sagarmanthan National Park has been established to preserve the eco-system of which mountain peak?
(a) Kanchenjunga (b) Mount Everest
(c) Annapurna (d) Dhaulavira

51. Maximum soot is released from
(a) Petrol vehicles
(b) CNG vehicles
(c) Diesel vehicles
(d) Thermal Power Plants

52. Surface Ozone is produced from
(a) Transport sector
(b) Cement plants
(c) Textile industry
(d) Chemical industry

53. Which one of the following non-conventional energy sources can be exploited most economically?
(a) Solar
(b) Wind
(c) Geo-thermal
(d) Ocean Thermal Energy Conversion (OTEC)

54. The most recurring natural hazard in India is
(a) Earthquakes (b) Floods
(c) Landslides (d) Volcanoes

55. The recommendation of National Knowledge Commission for the establishment of 1500 Universities is to
(a) create more teaching jobs
(b) ensure increase in student enrolment in higher education
(c) replace or substitute the privately managed higher education institutions by public institutions
(d) enable increased movement of students from rural areas to urban areas

56. According to Article 120 of the Constitution of India, the business in Parliament shall be transacted in
(a) Only English
(b) Only Hindi
(c) Both English and Hindi
(d) All the languages included in Eighth Schedule of the Constitution

57. Which of the following is more interactive and student centric?
(a) Seminar
(b) Workshop
(c) Lecture
(d) Group Discussion

58. The Parliament in India is composed of
(a) Lok Sabha and Rajya Sabha
(b) Lok Sabha, Rajya Sabha and Vice President
(c) Lok Sabha, Rajya Sabha and President
(d) Lok Sabha, Rajya Sabha with their Secretariats

59. The enrolment in higher education in India is contributed both by Formal System of Education and by System of Distance Education. Distance education contributes
(a) 50% of formal system
(b) 25% of formal system
(c) 10% of the formal system
(d) Distance education system's contribution is not taken into account while considering the figures of enrolment in higher education

60. **Assertion (A):** The UGC Academic Staff Colleges came into existence to improve the quality of teachers.
Reason (R): University and college teachers have to undergo both orientation and refresher courses.
(a) Both (A) and (R) are true and (R) is the correct explanation.
(b) Both (A) and (R) are correct but (R) is not the correct explanation of (A).
(c) (A) is correct and (R) is false.
(d) (A) is false and (R) is correct.

ANSWERS

1. (d)	2. (c)	3. (b)	4. (c)	5. (b)
6. (c)	7. (a)	8. (b)	9. (b)	10. (b)
11. (c)	12. (b)	13. (c)	14. (a)	15. (d)
16. (d)	17. (b)	18. (a)	19. (c)	20. (a)
21. (d)	22. (a)	23. (a)	24. (a)	25. (b)
26. (c)	27. (b)	28. (d)	29. (c)	30. (b)
31. (c)	32. (a)	33. (b)	34. (a)	35. (c)
36. (d)	37. (c)	38. (c)	39. (a)	40. (d)
41. (c)	42. (d)	43. (d)	44. (a)	45. (b)
46. (b)	47. (d)	48. (a)	49. (a)	50. (b)
51. (d)	52. (a)	53. (a)	54. (b)	55. (b)
56. (c)	57. (d)	58. (c)	59. (b)	60. (a)

PAPER–II

Note: This paper contains fifty (50) objective type questions, each question carrying two (2) marks. All questions are compulsory.

1. Public Administration is similar to Private Administration in
   (a) Scope
   (b) Techniques
   (c) Accountability
   (d) Financial Control
2. Theory Y
   (a) Neglects social needs of individual
   (b) Believes in coercion
   (c) Values human dignity
   (d) Supports unvelenting supervision at work
3. Job-centered leadership believes in
   (a) Open relations with employers
   (b) Close control
   (c) Little interaction
   (d) Group involvement
4. Coordination is hampered by
   (a) Two way communication channels
   (b) Multi-layered hierarchy
   (c) Incompetent leadership
   (d) Division of labour
5. The Civil Service in UK is managed by
   (a) Treasury
   (b) Treasury and Office of the Minister for Civil Service
   (c) Treasury and Civil Service Commission
   (d) Management and Personnel Office
6. Which of the following is not a feature of US personnel system?
   (a) Competitive service
   (b) Lateral entry
   (c) Post entry training
   (d) Rule of three
7. Unstructured interviews are
   (a) Planned (b) Focused
   (c) Informal (d) Guided
8. Public Administration first of all as a discipline emerged in
   (a) Great Britain
   (b) United States of America
   (c) West Germany
   (d) Scandinavian Countries
9. Who was the first Chief Justice of India?
   (a) Justice M.P. Sastri
   (b) Justice J. Kania
   (c) Justice M.C. Mahajan
   (d) Justice B.K. Mukherjee
10. The principles of supervision is inherent in the principle of
    (a) Span of control
    (b) Co-ordination
    (c) Hierarchy
    (d) Unity of Command
11. Vote on account is
    (a) $\frac{1}{4}$ of estimated budget
    (b) $\frac{1}{3}$ of estimated budget
    (c) $\frac{1}{6}$ of estimated budget
    (d) $\frac{1}{10}$ of estimated budget
12. Who is called the Father of 'Spoils System' in U.S.A.?
    (a) George Washington
    (b) Andrew Jackson
    (c) Lyndon Johnson
    (d) George Bush
13. The need for constitutional sanction to Village Panchayats was first felt by
    (a) B.R. Mehta Committee
    (b) Ashok Mehta Committee
    (c) G.V.K. Rao Committee
    (d) L.M. Singhvi Committee

14. The basic operating principle under liberation is
    (a) Regulated economy
    (b) Market economy
    (c) Mixed economy
    (d) Totally deregulated economy
15. Who said that "if our civilization fails it will be mainly because of a breakdown of administration"?
    (a) Donham (b) Ordway Tead
    (c) L.D. White (d) John A. Vieg
16. The hall mark of leadership is
    (a) Achievement of goals of the organization
    (b) Settlement of disputes
    (c) Capacity to influence followers
    (d) Maintain values of organization
17. The first State to create the institution of Lokayukta in India was
    (a) Andhra Pradesh (b) Uttar Pradesh
    (c) Orissa (d) Maharashtra
18. National Academy of Administration was established in
    (a) 1959 (b) 1948
    (c) 1960 (d) 1978
19. The performance budget was introduced in India on the recommendation of
    (a) 53rd Estimates Committee Report
    (b) Administrative Reforms Commission
    (c) Comptroller & Auditor General of India
    (d) Santhanam Committee
20. Office of the District Collector in India has a parallel in
    (a) France (b) U.S.A.
    (c) U.K. (d) Germany
21. **Assertion (A):** Power and authority are synonymous.
    Reason (R): Both seek to influence the behaviour of others.
    Choose the correct answer from the following answer code:
    Codes:
    (a) Both (A) and (R) are correct and (R) is the correct explanation of (A).
    (b) Both (A) and (R) are correct, but (R) is not the correct explanation of (A).
    (c) (A) is true, but (R) is false.
    (d) (A) is false, but (R) is true.
22. **Assertion (A):** All Parliamentary Committees submit their reports to the President annually.
    Reason (R): The President is the Chief Executive of the Government.
    Choose the correct answer from the following answer code:
    Codes:
    (a) Both (A) and (R) are correct and (R) is the correct explanation of (A).
    (b) Both (A) and (R) are correct, but (R) is not the correct explanation of (A).
    (c) (A) is true, but (R) is false.
    (d) (A) is false, but (R) is true.
23. **Assertion (A):** Finance Ministry exercises financial control over Administrative Ministries.
    Reason (R): It is responsible for the formulation and execution of the budget.
    Choose the correct answer from the following answer code:
    Codes:
    (a) Both (A) and (R) are correct and (R) is the correct explanation of (A).
    (b) Both (A) and (R) are correct, but (R) is not the correct explanation of (A).
    (c) (A) is true, but (R) is false.
    (d) (A) is false, but (R) is true.
24. **Assertion (A):** Bureaucracy in a developing country is likely to play a predominant role.
    Reason (R): In many of the developing countries political institutions are comparatively weak.
    Choose the correct answer from the followings code:

Codes:
(a) Both (A) and (R) are correct and (R) is the correct explanation of (A).
(b) Both (A) and (R) are correct, but (R) is not the correct explanation of (A).
(c) (A) is true, but (R) is false.
(d) (A) is false, but (R) is true.

25. **Assertion (A):** Cabinet Secretary acts as a liaison between the Ministries and Civil Servants.
Reason (R): Cabinet Secretary is the head of the Civil Service.
Choose the correct answer from the following answer code:
Codes:
(a) Both (A) and (R) are correct and (R) is the correct explanation of (A).
(b) Both (A) and (R) are correct, but (R) is not the correct explanation of (A).
(c) (A) is true, but (R) is false.
(d) (A) is false, but (R) is true.

26. **Assertion (A):** Legislature has the right to increase the amount of demands made by the Executive.
Reason (R): Legislature can pass the public expenditure of the Executive.
Choose the correct answer from the following answer code:
Codes:
(a) Both (A) and (R) are correct and (R) is the correct explanation of (A).
(b) Both (A) and (R) are correct, but (R) is not the correct explanation of (A).
(c) (A) is true, but (R) is false.
(d) (A) is false, but (R) is true.

27. **Assertion (A):** Increasing use of computers increase organizational rationality.
Reason (R): With the use of computers and simulation models more decisions can be made.
Choose the correct answer from the following answer code:
Codes:
(a) Both (A) and (R) are correct and (R) is the correct explanation of (A).
(b) Both (A) and (R) are correct, but (R) is not the correct explanation of (A).
(c) (A) is true, but (R) is false.
(d) (A) is false, but (R) is true.

28. **Assertion (A):** A group has more information than an individual.
Reason (R): A group often works more slowly than individuals.
Choose the correct answer from the following answer code:
Codes:
(a) Both (A) and (R) are correct and (R) is the correct explanation of (A).
(b) Both (A) and (R) are correct, but (R) is not the correct explanation of (A).
(c) (A) is true, but (R) is false.
(d) (A) is false, but (R) is true.

29. **Assertion (A):** Planning process should not involve hurried decisions.
Reason (R): Planning process should have rational consideration of cost-benefits and alternatives.
Choose the correct answer from the following answer code:
Codes:
(a) Both (A) and (R) are correct and (R) is the correct explanation of (A).
(b) Both (A) and (R) are correct, but (R) is not the correct explanation of (A).
(c) (A) is true, but (R) is false.
(d) (A) is false, but (R) is true.

30. **Assertion (A):** Administration particularly at the higher levels has ceased to be merely regulatory.
Reason (R): Science and technology in the nuclear age have projected new tasks for administration.
Choose the correct answer from the following answer code:

Codes:

(a) Both (A) and (R) are correct and (R) is the correct explanation of (A).

(b) Both (A) and (R) are correct, but (R) is not the correct explanation of (A).

(c) (A) is true, but (R) is false.

(d) (A) is false, but (R) is true.

31. Match List I with List II. Select the correct answer from the codes given below:

List I

(A) Fred Fiedler

(B) Hersy & Blancard

(C) Robert Horse

(D) Brake & Mouton

List II

(i) Contingency Theory

(ii) Managerial Grid Theory

(iii) Situational Leadership Theory

(iv) Pathgoal Models of Leadership

Codes:	**A**	**B**	**C**	**D**
(a)	(i)	(iii)	(iv)	(ii)
(b)	(iii)	(iv)	(ii)	(i)
(c)	(iv)	(ii)	(i)	(iii)
(d)	(ii)	(i)	(iii)	(iv)

32. Match List I with List II. Select the correct answer from the codes given below:

List I

(A) A critique on US administration development

(B) Authority legitimacy and social development

(C) Importance of work groups social relations in organizations.

(D) Organization as a human enterprise seeking internal and external equilibrium.

List II

(i) Hawthrone Experiments – Elton Mayo

(ii) The Making of Scientific Management – Urwick

(iii) Administrative behaviour – Simon.

(iv) Wirtschaft and Gesellschaft. (Economy & Society) – Max Weber

Codes:	**A**	**B**	**C**	**D**
(a)	(iv)	(i)	(iii)	(ii)
(b)	(ii)	(iv)	(i)	(iii)
(c)	(iii)	(i)	(ii)	(iv)
(d)	(i)	(iv)	(ii)	(iii)

33. Match List I with List II. Select the correct answer from the codes given below:

List I

(A) Models of Man

(B) Organizations

(C) Administrative Behaviour

(D) New Science of Management Decision

List II

(i) 1965 (ii) 1957

(iii) 1960 (iv) 1947

(v) 1958

Codes:	**A**	**B**	**C**	**D**
(a)	(i)	(iii)	(ii)	(iv)
(b)	(v)	(ii)	(iii)	(iv)
(c)	(i)	(v)	(iv)	(iii)
(d)	(ii)	(iii)	(i)	(iv)

34. Match List I with List II. Select the correct answer from the codes given below:

List I

(A) Public Accounts Committee

(B) Zonal Council

(C) Centre State Administrative Relations

(D) Inter State Council

List II

(i) Art. 263

(ii) Art. 256-263

(iii) 1921

(iv) State Reorganization Act, 1956

Codes:	**A**	**B**	**C**	**D**
(a)	(iii)	(iv)	(ii)	(i)
(b)	(i)	(ii)	(iii)	(iv)
(c)	(i)	(iv)	(iii)	(ii)
(d)	(ii)	(iii)	(iv)	(i)

35. Match List I with List II. Select the correct answer from the codes given below:

List I	List II
(A) Vote on credit	(i) Emergency
(B) Vote on A/c	(ii) Contingency fund
(C) Special grant	(iii) Vote without debate
(D) Guillotine	(iv) Advanced grants sanction

Codes:	A	B	C	D
(a)	(i)	(iv)	(ii)	(iii)
(b)	(ii)	(iii)	(iv)	(i)
(c)	(ii)	(i)	(iii)	(iv)
(d)	(i)	(ii)	(iii)	(iv)

36. Match List I with List II. Select the correct answer from the codes given below:

List I

(A) First Municipal Corporation
(B) System of Budget
(C) Decentralization of Financial Administration
(D) Reserve Bank of India

List II

(i) 1867 (ii) 1860
(iii) 1870 (iv) 1935

Codes:	A	B	C	D
(a)	(iii)	(ii)	(iv)	(i)
(b)	(ii)	(iii)	(i)	(iv)
(c)	(i)	(ii)	(iii)	(iv)
(d)	(iii)	(i)	(ii)	(iv)

37. Match List I with List II. Select the correct answer from the codes given below:

List I	List II
(A) Cybernetics	(i) Grapevine
(B) Language	(ii) Entropy
(C) Informal Communication	(iii) Barrier
(D) System	(iv) Feedback

Codes:	A	B	C	D
(a)	(i)	(iii)	(ii)	(iv)
(b)	(iv)	(i)	(ii)	(iii)
(c)	(iv)	(iii)	(i)	(ii)
(d)	(i)	(iv)	(ii)	(iii)

38. Match List I with List II. Select the correct answer from the codes given below:

List I

(A) Bureaucracy
(B) Closed system
(C) Normative control structure
(D) Scalar chain

List II

(i) Generation of moral involvement
(ii) Vertical differentiation
(iii) Facts and values
(iv) Entropy and disorganization
(v) Administration by appointed officials

Codes:	A	B	C	D
(a)	(v)	(iv)	(i)	(ii)
(b)	(i)	(ii)	(iii)	(iv)
(c)	(iv)	(i)	(iii)	(ii)
(d)	(iii)	(ii)	(i)	(v)

39. Match List I with List II. Select the correct answer from the codes given below:

List I

(A) Zone of acceptance
(B) Span of supervision
(C) Zone of indifference
(D) Span of control

List II

(i) Chester Barnard (ii) Herbert Simon
(iii) Gracuinas (iv) Luther Gullick

Codes:	A	B	C	D
(a)	(i)	(iii)	(iv)	(ii)
(b)	(ii)	(iii)	(iv)	(i)
(c)	(ii)	(iii)	(i)	(iv)
(d)	(i)	(iv)	(iii)	(ii)

40. Match List I with List II. Select the correct answer from the codes given below:

List I

(A) President (B) Prime Minister
(C) Governor (D) Speaker

List II

(i) Restoring order in Lok Sabha.
(ii) Summoning, provoguing and dissolving the Lok Sabha.

(iii) Reserving the State Bill for President's consideration.
(iv) Fixing the Council of Ministers.

Codes:	A	B	C	D
(a)	(i)	(ii)	(iii)	(iv)
(b)	(ii)	(iv)	(iii)	(i)
(c)	(i)	(iv)	(ii)	(iii)
(d)	(iv)	(iii)	(i)	(ii)

41. Indicate the ascending order of the following committees on Panchayati Raj affairs.
(I) Balwant Rai Mehta
(II) Ashok Mehta
(III) G.V.K. Rao
(IV) L.M. Singhvi
Codes:
(a) (I) (II) (IV) (III) (b) (II) (III) (IV) (I)
(c) (I) (II) (III) (IV) (d) (III) (I) (II) (IV)

42. Arrange the hierarchy of the department in ascending order.
(I) Wing (II) Branch
(III) Section (IV) Division
Codes:
(a) (I) (IV) (III) (II) (b) (II) (III) (IV) (I)
(c) (III) (I) (II) (IV) (d) (IV) (III) (II) (I)

43. Arrange the following gradation of post in ascending order:
(I) Deputy Secretary
(II) Additional Secretary
(III) Joint Secretary
(IV) Secretary
Codes:
(a) (I) (III) (IV) (II) (b) (II) (III) (IV) (I)
(c) (I) (III) (II) (IV) (d) (IV) (II) (III) (I)

44. Arrange following stages of report writing in ascending order:
(I) Final outline (II) Draft
(III) Final Report (IV) Analysis
Codes:
(a) (I) (III) (II) (IV) (b) (III) (I) (IV) (II)
(c) (II) (III) (I) (IV) (d) (IV) (III) (II) (I)

45. Arrange following Prime Ministers of India in decending order.
(I) I.K. Gujaral
(II) Lal Bahadur Sastri
(III) P.V. Narasimha Rao
(IV) A.B. Vajpayee
Codes:
(a) (IV) (III) (I) (II) (b) (III) (II) (I) (IV)
(c) (IV) (I) (II) (III) (d) (IV) (I) (III) (II)

Read the passage below and answer the questions that follow based on your understanding of the passage.

The Human Relations approach assumed that the most satisfying organisation would be the most efficient. It suggested that the workers would not be happy in the cold, formal, "rational" organisation that satisfied only their economic needs. The Human Relations School did not believe that management would be able to establish an organisation that would keep the workers satisfied by simply allocating labour and authority in the most efficient way as determined by the intrinsic nature of the task. But, like Scientific Management, it did not view the problem of worker satisfaction and productivity as inherently unsolvable. True, management had to be enlightened and certain steps had to be taken, such as encouraging the development of social groups on the job and providing them with democratic participating, and communicative leadership, but once the real nature of the workers' needs and their informal group life and organisations are understood, nothing prevents management from making the organisational life a happy one.

Moreover, the Human Relations School taught that it is necessary to relate work and the organisational structure to the social needs of the employees, for in this way, by making the employee happy, the organisation would obtain their full cooperation and effort and thus increase its efficiency. Thus the way to make the organisation fully rational was to increase by deliberate efforts the happiness of the workers. There are many almost lyric pages in Human Relations writing which depict the worker as anxious not to miss a day at the factory or to come too late lest he miss spending some time with his friends, and even as anxious not to disappoint his foreman who is like a warm and understanding father to him. The work team itself is often referred to as a family. The Human Relations approach maintained that "employees should have a feeling that the company's goal is worth their effort; they should feel themselves part of the company and take pride in their contribution to its goal. This means that the company's objectives must be such as to inspire confidence in the intentions of management and belief that each will get rewards and satisfactions by working for these objectives."

46. Like Scientific Management, Human Relations School do not believe in
   (a) Efficiency with economy
   (b) Fulfilling the social needs of workers
   (c) Appeasement of Employees
   (d) None of the above
47. The Human Relations Approach suggests that
   (a) The workers would be happy in a formal organisation
   (b) The workers would be happy in a cold-rational organisation
   (c) The workers would be unhappy in a formal, cold organisation
   (d) None of the above
48. Development of Informal Social groups in an organisation is an invention of
   (a) Scientific Management School
   (b) Human Relations School
   (c) Structural Functional School
   (d) All the above
49. The Human Relations School depicts that
   (a) Work and organisational structure are two separate entities.
   (b) Social needs are subservient to the organisational needs.
   (c) Employees feel happy in taking leave from the work place (factory).
   (d) None of the above.
50. Who supported the concept that "Employees should have a feeling to work as a family in the organisation'?
   (a) Classical Thinkers
   (b) Scientific – Management Thinkers
   (c) Human Relations Thinkers
   (d) Systems Theory Scholars

ANSWERS

1. (b)	2. (c)	3. (b)	4. (c)	5. (b)
6. (b)	7. (c)	8. (b)	9. (b)	10. (a)
11. (b)	12. (b)	13. (d)	14. (b)	15. (a)
16. (c)	17. (c)	18. (a)	19. (a)	20. (a)
21. (a)	22. (d)	23. (d)	24. (a)	25. (a)
26. (d)	27. (a)	28. (a)	29. (a)	30. (a)
31. (a)	32. (b)	33. (c)	34. (a)	35. (a)
36. (c)	37. (c)	38. (a)	39. (c)	40. (b)
41. (c)	42. (b)	43. (d)	44. (d)	45. (a)
46. (a)	47. (d)	48. (b)	49. (b)	50. (c)

JUNE–2009

Note: This paper contains fifty (50) multiple-choice questions, each question carrying two (2) marks. Attempt all of them.

PAPER–I

1. Good evaluation of written material should not be based on
   (a) Linguistic expression
   (b) Logical presentation
   (c) Ability to reproduce whatever is read
   (d) Comprehension of subject

2. Why do teachers use teaching aid?
   (a) To make teaching fun-filled
   (b) To teach within understanding level of students
   (c) For students' attention
   (d) To make students attentive

3. Attitudes, concepts, skills and knowledge are products of
   (a) Learning (b) Research
   (c) Heredity (d) Explanation

4. Which among the following gives more freedom to the learner to interact?
   (a) Use of film
   (b) Small group discussion
   (c) Lectures by experts
   (d) Viewing country-wide classroom program on TV

5. Which of the following is not a product of learning?
   (a) Attitudes (b) Concepts
   (c) Knowledge (d) Maturation

6. How can the objectivity of the research be enhanced?
   (a) Through its impartiality
   (b) Through its reliability
   (c) Through its validity
   (d) All of these

7. Action-research is
   (a) An applied research
   (b) A research carried out to solve immediate problems
   (c) A longitudinal research
   (d) All the above

8. The basis on which assumptions are formulated
   (a) Cultural background of the country
   (b) Universities
   (c) Specific characteristics of the castes
   (d) All of these

9. Which of the following is classified in the category of the developmental research?
   (a) Philosophical research
   (b) Action research
   (c) Descriptive research
   (d) All the above

10. We use Factorial Analysis
    (a) To know the relationship between two variables
    (b) To test the Hypothesis
    (c) To know the difference between two variables
    (d) To know the difference among the many variables

Read the following passage and answer the questions 11 to 15:

While the British rule in India was detrimental to the economic development of the country, it did help in starting of the process of modernising Indian society and formed several progressive institutions during that process. One of the most beneficial institutions, which were initiated by the British, was democracy. Nobody can dispute that despite its many shortcomings, democracy was and is far better alternative to the arbitrary rule of the rajas and nawabs, which prevailed in India in the pre-British days.

However, one of the harmful traditions of British democracy inherited by India was that of conflict instead of cooperation between elected members. This was its essential feature. The party, which got the support of the majority of elected members, formed the Government while the others constituted a standing opposition. The existence of the opposition to those in power was and is regarded as a hallmark of democracy.

In principle, democracy consists of rule by the people; but where direct rule is not possible, it's rule by persons elected by the people. It is natural that there would be some differences of opinion among the elected members as in the rest of the society.

Normally, members of any organisations have differences of opinion between themselves on different issues but they manage to work on the basis of a consensus and they do not normally form a division between some who are in majority and are placed in power, while treating the others as in opposition.

The members of an organisation usually work on consensus. Consensus simply means that after an adequate discussion, members agree that the majority opinion may prevail for the time being. Thus persons who form a majority on one issue and whose opinion is allowed to prevail may not be on the same side if there is a difference on some other issue.

It was largely by accident that instead of this normal procedure, a two-party system came to prevail in Britain and that is now being generally taken as the best method of democratic rule.

Many democratically inclined persons in India regret that such a two-party system was not brought about in the country. It appears that to have two parties in India—of more or less equal strength—is a virtual impossibility. Those who regret the absence of a two-party system should take the reasons into consideration.

When the two-party system got established in Britain, there were two groups among the rulers (consisting of a limited electorate) who had the same economic interests among themselves and who therefore formed two groups within the selected members of Parliament.

There were members of the British aristocracy (which landed interests and consisting of lord, barons, etc.) and members of the new commercial class consisting of merchants and artisans. These groups were more or less of equal strength and they were able to establish their separate rule at different times.

Answer the following questions:

11. In pre-British period, when India was ruled by the independent rulers
    (a) Peace and prosperity prevailed in the society
    (b) People were isolated from political affairs
    (c) Public opinion was inevitable for policy making
    (d) Law was equal for one and all
12. What is the distinguishing feature of the democracy practiced in Britain?
    (a) End to the rule of might is right.
    (b) Rule of the people, by the people and for the people.
    (c) It has stood the test of time.
    (d) Cooperation between elected members.

13. Democracy is practised where
  (a) Elected members form a uniform opinion regarding policy matter.
  (b) Opposition is more powerful than the ruling combine.
  (c) Representatives of masses.
  (d) None of these.

14. Which of the following is true about the British rule in India?
  (a) It was behind the modernisation of the Indian society.
  (b) India gained economically during that period.
  (c) Various establishments were formed for the purpose of progress.
  (d) None of these.

15. Who became the members of the new commercial class during that time?
  (a) British Aristocrats
  (b) Lords and Barons
  (c) Political Persons
  (d) Merchants and Artisans

16. Which one of the following Telephonic Conferencing with a radio link is very popular throughout the world?
  (a) TPS (b) Telepresence
  (c) Video conference (d) Video teletext

17. Which is not 24 hours news channel?
  (a) NDTV 24×7
  (b) ZEE News
  (c) Aajtak
  (d) Lok Sabha Channel

18. The main objective of FM station in radio is
  (a) Information, Entertainment and Tourism
  (b) Entertainment, Information and Interaction
  (c) Tourism, Interaction and Entertainment
  (d) Entertainment only

19. In communication chatting on internet is
  (a) Verbal communication
  (b) Non-verbal communication
  (c) Parallel communication
  (d) Grapevine communication

20. Match List I with List II and select the correct answer using the codes given below:

List I (Artists)
A. Pandit Jasraj B. Kishan Maharaj
C. Ravi Shankar D. Udai Shankar

List II (Art)
1. Hindustani vocalist
2. Sitar
3. Tabla
4. Dance

Codes:	A	B	C	D
(a)	1	2	3	4
(b)	1	3	4	2
(c)	1	3	2	4
(d)	3	2	1	4

21. Insert the missing number in the following.
3, 8, 18, 23, 33, ?, 48
  (a) 37 (b) 40
  (c) 38 (d) 45

22. In a certain code, CLOCK is written as KCOLC. How would STEPS be written in that code?
  (a) SPEST (b) SPSET
  (c) SPETS (d) SEPTS

23. The letters in the first set have a certain relationship. On the basis of this relationship mark the right choice for the second set
BDFH : OMKI :: GHIK : ?
  (a) FHJL (b) RPNL
  (c) LNPR (d) LJHF

24. What was the day of the week on 1st January 2001?
  (a) Friday (b) Monday
  (c) Sunday (d) Wednesday

25. Find out the wrong number in the sequence.
52, 51, 48, 43, 34, 27, 16
(a) 27 (b) 34
(c) 43 (d) 48

26. In a deductive argument conclusion is
(a) Summing up of the premises
(b) Not necessarily based on premises
(c) Entailed by the premises
(d) Additional to the premises

27. 'No man are mortal' is contradictory of
(a) Some man are mortal
(b) Some man are not mortal
(c) All men are mortal
(d) No mortal is man

28. A deductive argument is valid if
(a) premises are false and conclusion is true
(b) premises are false and conclusion is also false
(c) premises are true and conclusion is false
(d) premises are true and conclusion is true

29. Structure of logical argument is based on
(a) Formal validity
(b) Material truth
(c) Linguistic expression
(d) Aptness of examples

30. Two ladies and two men are playing bridge and seated at North, East, South and West of a table. No lady is facing East. Persons sitting opposite to each other are not of the same sex. One man is facing South. Which direction are the ladies facing to?
(a) East and West
(b) North and West
(c) South and East
(d) None of these

Questions 31 and 32 are based on the following Venn diagram in which there are three intersecting circles representing Hindi knowing persons, English knowing persons and persons who are working as teachers. Different regions so obtained in the figure are marked as a, b, c, d, e, f and g.

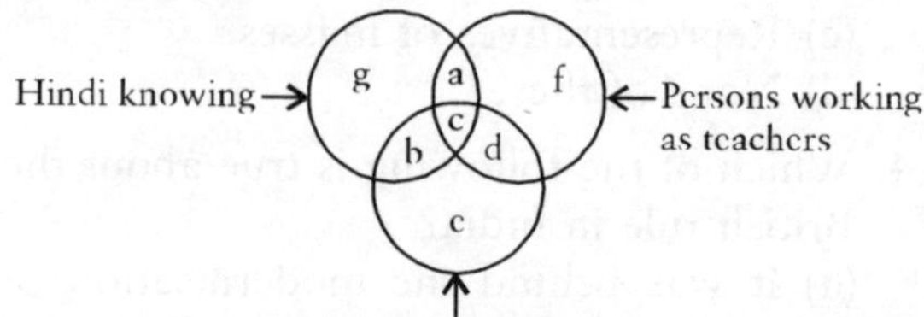

31. If you want to select Hindi and English knowing teachers, which of the following is to be selected?
(a) g (b) b
(c) c (d) e

32. If you want to select persons, who do not know English and are not teachers, which of the region is to be selected?
(a) e (b) g
(c) b (d) a

Study the following graph carefully and answer questions 33 to 35.

Export of Engineering Goods

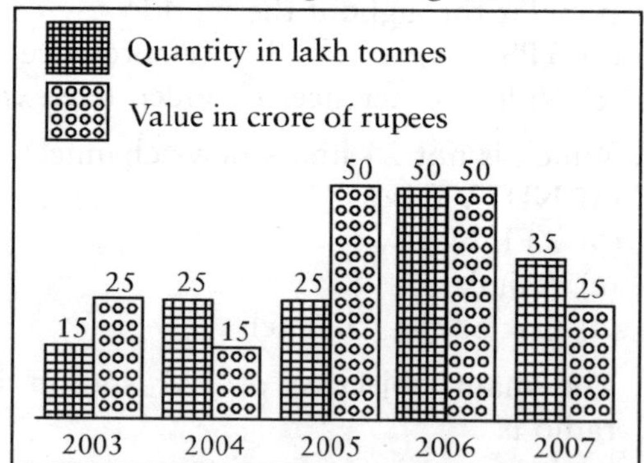

33. In which year the quantity of engineering goods' exports was maximum?
(a) 2005 (b) 2006
(c) 2004 (d) 2007

34. In which year the value of engineering goods decreased by 50 percent compared to the previous year?

(a) 2004 (b) 2007
(c) 2005 (d) 2006

35. In which year the quantity of exports was 100 percent higher than the quantity of previous year?
(a) 2004 (b) 2005
(c) 2006 (d) 2007

36. What do you need to put your web pages on the www?
(a) a connection to internet
(b) a web browser
(c) a web server
(d) All of the above

37. Which was the first company to launch mobile phone services in India?
(a) Essar (b) BPL
(c) Hutchison (d) Airtel

38. Chandrayan I was launched on 22nd October, 2008 in India from
(a) Bangalore (b) Sri Harikota
(c) Chennai (d) Ahmedabad

39. What is blog?
(a) Online music
(b) Intranet
(c) A personal or corporate website in the form of an online journal
(d) A personal or corporate Google search

40. Which is not online Indian Matrimonial website?
(a) www.jeevansathi.com
(b) www.bharatmatrimony.com
(c) www.shaadi.com
(d) www.u.k.singlemuslim.com

41. Environmental impact assessment is an objective analysis of the probable changes in
(a) physical characteristics of the environment
(b) biophysical characteristics of the environment
(c) socio-economic characteristics of the environment
(d) All of the above

42. Bog is a wetland that receives water from
(a) nearby water bodies
(b) melting
(c) Only rainfall
(d) Only sea

43. Which of the following region is in the very high risk zone of earthquakes?
(a) Central Indian Highland
(b) Coastal region
(c) Himalayan region
(d) Indian desert

44. Match List I with List II and select the correct answer using the codes given below.

List I (Institutes)
A. Central Arid Zone Institute
B. Space Application Centre
C. Indian Institute of Public Administration
D. Headquarters of Indian Science Congress

List II (Cities)
1. Kolkata 2. New Delhi
3. Ahmedabad 4. Jodhpur

Codes:	A	B	C	D
(a)	4	3	2	1
(b)	4	2	1	3
(c)	3	1	2	4
(d)	1	2	4	3

45. Indian coastal areas experienced Tsunami disaster in the year
(a) 2005 (b) 2004
(c) 2006 (d) 2007

46. The Kothari Commission's report was entitled on
(a) Education and National Development
(b) Learning to be adventure
(c) Diversification of Education
(d) Education and socialisation in democracy

47. Which of the following is not a Dual mode University?
(a) Delhi University
(b) Bangalore University

(c) Madras University
(d) Indira Gandhi National Open University

48. Which part of the Constitution of India is known as "Code of Administrators"?
(a) Part I (b) Part II
(c) Part III (d) Part IV

49. Which article of the constitution provides safeguards to Naga Customary and their social practices against any act of Parliament?
(a) Article 371 A (b) Article 371 B
(c) Article 371 C (d) Article 263

50. Which one of the following is not the tool of good governance?
(a) Right to Information
(b) Citizens' Charter
(c) Social Auditing
(d) Judicial Activism

ANSWERS

1. (a)	2. (a)	3. (a)	4. (b)	5. (d)
6. (d)	7. (b)	8. (a)	9. (d)	10. (d)
11. (b)	12. (d)	13. (a)	14. (c)	15. (a)
16. (b)	17. (d)	18. (b)	19. (b)	20. (c)
21. (c)	22. (c)	23. (b)	24. (b)	25. (b)
26. (c)	27. (c)	28. (d)	29. (b)	30. (b)
31. (c)	32. (b)	33. (b)	34. (b)	35. (c)
36. (d)	37. (d)	38. (b)	39. (c)	40. (d)
41. (d)	42. (a)	43. (b)	44. (a)	45. (b)
46. (a)	47. (d)	48. (d)	49. (a)	50. (d)

PAPER–II

1. Kautilya's dandniti primarily relates to:
(a) Science of administration
(b) Art of administration
(c) Policy of the State
(d) Power to punish

2. Barnard and Simon believed that authority:
(a) Implies right to command
(b) Rests on the consent of the Subordinates
(c) Issues orders that must be obyed
(d) Relates to the superior and not to the subordinates

3. Public Administration is not different from Private Administration in:
(a) Equality of treatment
(b) Legal authority
(c) Public welfare
(d) Managerial techniques

4. Who said that distinction between Management and Administration is misleading and False?
(a) Gulick (b) Taylor
(c) Fayol (d) Barnard

5. Which of the following theories does not relate to leadership and its style?
(a) Contingency theory
(b) Path goal theory
(c) Incremental theory
(d) Great Man theory

6. Comparative Public Administration ultimately leads to:
(a) Detailed Knowledge of administrative structures.
(b) Detailed knowledge of administrative patterns.
(c) Theory building
(d) Administrative development

7. The tool employed by Riggs in explaining the typology of development was:
(a) Analytical approach
(b) Structural-functional approach
(c) Ideal model building
(d) Ecological approach

8. Hawthrone experiments were carried out in:

(a) USA (b) UK
(c) Japan (d) France

9. The Word "Administration" has originated from which language?
(a) Greek (b) French
(c) English (d) Latin

10. Which is the oldest approach to the study of Public Administration
(a) Historical Approach
(b) Legal Approach
(c) Philosophical Approach
(d) The Case Method Approach

11. The constitution provides for supplimentary budget in Article:
(a) 110 (b) 114
(c) 120 (d) 314

12. Establishment of merit system and open competetive examination in U.S. is associated with:
(a) Civil Service Act 1883
(b) Rampspeck Act 1940
(c) Civil Service Reform Act 1978
(d) Hoover Commission 1949

13. The primary source of finances of Local Government in US is:
(a) Income Tax (b) Property Tax
(c) Sales Tax (d) Utility revenues

14. Who has defined mixed economy as dual economy?
(a) Adam Smith (b) Keynes
(c) J.L. Nehru (d) A. H. Henson

15. The term "Development Administration" was coined by:
(a) Edward Weidner (b) F.W. Riggs
(c) Montegomery (d) Goswami

16. The office of the District collector is based on the principle of:
(a) Decentralization
(b) Deconcentration
(c) Delegation
(d) Devolution

17. The Santhanam committee on prevention of corruption was appointed in this year:
(a) 1961 (b) 1962
(c) 1963 (d) 1964

18. The Zero base budget was created by:
(a) Peter A. Phyrr
(b) Jimmy carter
(c) Hoover Commission
(d) Guy peters

19. Which of the following correctly explains the token cut motion?
(a) The amount of the demand be reduced to Re. 1.
(b) The amount of the demand be reduced to Rs. 100.
(c) The amount of the demand be reduced by Rs. 100.
(d) The amount of the demand be reduced by a specific amount.

20. The election to the office of the president is conducted by:
(a) Speaker of the Lok Sabha
(b) Ministry of Parliamentary affairs
(c) Chief Justice of India
(d) The Election Commission of India

21. **Assertion (A):** The Science of Public Administration is based on observation not on experimentation.
Reason (R): Public Administration is a social Science.
Choose the correct answers from the following answer code:
Codes:
(a) Both (A) and (R) are correct and (R) is the correct explanation of (A)
(b) Both (A) and (R) are correct but (R) is not the correct explanation of (A)
(c) (A) is true but (R) is false
(d) (A) is false but (R) is true

22. **Assertion (A):** France is a unitary country and it is more unitary than Britain.

Reason (R): In Britain local governments enjoy a certain degree of autonomy.

Choose the correct answer from the following answer code:

Codes:

(a) Both (A) and (R) are correct and (R) is the correct explanation of (A)
(b) Both (A) and (R) are correct but (R) is not the correct explanation of (A)
(c) (A) is true but (R) is false
(d) (A) is false but (R) is true

23. **Assertion (A):** Neutrality has been an important virtue of civil service

Reason (R): It is a tradition of Britain.

Choose the correct answer from the following answer code:

Codes:

(a) Both (A) and (R) are correct and (R) is the correct explanation of (A)
(b) Both (A) and (R) are correct but (R) is not the correct explanation of (A)
(c) (A) is true but (R) is false
(d) (A) is false but (R) is true

24. **Assertion (A):** Ministry of Finance prepares the budget

Reason (R) : Ministry of Finance is the central financial agency of the Government of India

Choose the correct answer from the following answer code:

Codes:

(a) Both (A) and (R) are correct and (R) is the correct explanation of (A)
(b) Both (A) and (R) are correct but (R) is not the correct explanation of (A)
(c) (A) is true but (R) is false
(d) (A) is false but (R) is true

25. **Assertion (A):** Lord Ripon's Resolution is the Magna Carta of Local Government in India.

Reason (R): Lord Ripon is regarded as the father of local-self government in India.

Choose the correct answer from the following answer code:

Codes:

(a) Both (A) and (R) are correct and (R) is the correct explanation of (A)
(b) Both (A) and (R) are correct but (R) is not the correct explanation of (A)
(c) (A) is true but (R) is false
(d) (A) is false but (R) is true

26. **Assertion (A):** Simon viewed an orgainsation as a structure of decision makers.

Reason (R): Decision making pervades the entire organisation.

Choose the correct answer from the following answer code:

Codes:

(a) Both (A) and (R) are correct and (R) is the correct explanation of (A)
(b) Both (A) and (R) are correct but (R) is not the correct explanation of (A)
(c) (A) is true but (R) is false
(d) (A) is false but (R) is true

27. **Assertion (A):** Administrative decisions are not always based on rationality

Reason (R): Values and attitudes influence decisions.

Choose the correct answer from the following answer code:

Codes:

(a) Both (A) and (R) are correct and (R) is the correct explanation of (A)
(b) Both (A) and (R) are correct but (R) is not the correct explanation of (A)
(c) (A) is true but (R) is false
(d) (A) is false but (R) is true

28. **Assertion (A):** Prices tend to increase with the increase in money supply.

Reason (R): Inflation is regressive in terms of economic development.

Choose the correct answer from the following answer code:

Codes:
(a) Both (A) and (R) are correct and (R) is the correct explanation of (A)
(b) Both (A) and (R) are correct but (R) is not the correct explanation of (A)
(c) (A) is true but (R) is false
(d) (A) is false but (R) is true

29. **Assertion (A):** Finance is the life-blood of administration
Reason (R): Financial administration is a systematised knowledge of financial transaction of the government
Choose the correct answer from the following answer code:
Codes:
(a) Both (A) and (R) are correct and (R) is the correct explanation of (A)
(b) Both (A) and (R) are correct but (R) is not the correct explanation of (A)
(c) (A) is true but (R) is false
(d) (A) is false but (R) is true

30. **Assertion (A):** The auxiliary function is undertaken to enable the line agency to perform its primary functions.
Reason (R): The function of the auxiliary agency is not a secondary function.
Choose the correct answer from the following answer code:
Codes:
(a) Both (A) and (R) are correct and (R) is the correct explanation of (A)
(b) Both (A) and (R) are correct but (R) is not the correct explanation of (A)
(c) (A) is true but (R) is false
(d) (A) is false but (R) is true

31. Match List I with List II. Select the correct answer from the codes given below:
List I
(A) The Saint of Organizational Humanism
(B) Francis Bacon of Management Literature
(C) Founder of Modern Sociological of Bureaucracy
(D) Father of Public Administration
List II
(i) Max Weber
(ii) Woodrow Wilson
(iii) Abraham Maslow
(iv) Henri Fayol

Codes:	**A**	**B**	**C**	**D**
(a)	(ii)	(i)	(iv)	(iii)
(b)	(iii)	(iv)	(i)	(ii)
(c)	(i)	(iv)	(iii)	(ii)
(d)	(iv)	(ii)	(i)	(iii)

32. Match List I with List II. Select the correct answer from the codes given below:
List I
(A) Monte carlo (B) Risk averter
(C) Gambler (D) Synesis
List II
(i) Generation of alternative solutions
(ii) Narrow form of Simulation
(iii) To avert risk
(iv) To take greater risk

Codes:	**A**	**B**	**C**	**D**
(a)	(iv)	(iii)	(ii)	(i)
(b)	(iii)	(i)	(ii)	(iv)
(c)	(i)	(iv)	(iii)	(ii)
(d)	(ii)	(iii)	(iv)	(i)

33. Match List I with List II. Select the correct answer from the codes given below:
List I
(A) Leadership (B) Supervision
(C) Coordination (D) Delegation
List II
(i) Monitoring Subordinates
(ii) Cooperation
(iii) It implies pursuit of common goals
(iv) Different from Cooperation
(v) Authority is revokable by the boss

Codes:	**A**	**B**	**C**	**D**
(a)	(i)	(ii)	(iv)	(iii)
(b)	(i)	(v)	(ii)	(iii)

(c)	(iii)	(i)	(iv)	(v)
(d)	(ii)	(iii)	(v)	(iv)

34. Match List I with List II. Select the correct answer from the codes given below:

List I

(A) Informal communication
(B) Formal communication
(C) Rate buster
(D) Squealor

List II

(i) Responsibility is fixed
(ii) Person who does too much work
(iii) Grapevine
(iv) Person doing little work
(v) Persons passing negative news about co-workers.

Codes:	A	B	C	D
(a)	(i)	(ii)	(v)	(iii)
(b)	(ii)	(iii)	(iv)	(v)
(c)	(iii)	(iv)	(ii)	(v)
(d)	(iii)	(i)	(ii)	(v)

35. Match List I with List II. Select the correct answer from the codes given below:

List I	List II
(A) Poly functionalism	(i) Development
(B) Ascription	(ii) Diffracted Society
(C) Universalism	(iii) Prismatic Society
(D) Integration	(iv) Fused Society

Codes:	A	B	C	D
(a)	(iii)	(ii)	(i)	(iv)
(b)	(i)	(iii)	(ii)	(iv)
(c)	(iii)	(iv)	(ii)	(i)
(d)	(ii)	(iv)	(i)	(iii)

36. Match List I with List II. Select the correct answer from the codes given below:

List I	List II
(A) Portfolio System	(i) Lord Canning
(B) Tenure System	(ii) Lord Curzon
(C) District collector	(iii) Warren Hasting
(D) Divisional Commissioner	(iv) Lord Bentinck

Codes:	A	B	C	D
(a)	(i)	(ii)	(iii)	(iv)
(b)	(iii)	(i)	(ii)	(iv)
(c)	(i)	(iii)	(ii)	(iv)
(d)	(iv)	(i)	(iii)	(ii)

37. Match List I with List II. Select the correct answer from the codes given below:

List I (Book)

(A) Bureaucratic Phenomenon
(B) Management and worker
(C) Element di sienza politica
(D) Shop Management

List II (Year)

(i) 1939 (ii) 1903
(iii) 1895 (iv) 1901

Codes:	A	B	C	D
(a)	(iv)	(ii)	(iii)	(i)
(b)	(i)	(ii)	(iv)	(iii)
(c)	(i)	(iii)	(ii)	(iv)
(d)	(iv)	(i)	(iii)	(ii)

38. Match List I with List II. Select the correct answer from the codes given below:

List I

(A) Laissez-Faire-Leader
(B) Country-Club-Leader
(C) Task Management Leader
(D) Team Management Leader

List II

(i) Deserter (ii) Compromiser
(iii) Missionary (iv) Executive

Codes:	A	B	C	D
(a)	(i)	(ii)	(iii)	(iv)
(b)	(ii)	(i)	(iii)	(iv)
(c)	(iv)	(i)	(ii)	(iii)
(d)	(ii)	(i)	(iv)	(iii)

39. Match List I with List II. Select the correct answer from the codes given below:

List I

(A) The Institutional Model
(B) Elite Mass Model
(C) Incremental Model
(D) Strategic Planning Model

List II
(i) Austin Raney (ii) Etzioni
(iii) Carl Frederich (iv) Lindblom

Codes:	A	B	C	D
(a)	(i)	(iii)	(iv)	(ii)
(b)	(iv)	(iii)	(i)	(ii)
(c)	(iii)	(i)	(iv)	(ii)
(d)	(i)	(ii)	(iv)	(iii)

40. Match List I with List II. Select the correct answer from the codes given below:
List I
(A) Mayor Council Plan
(B) City Manager Plan
(C) Commission Plan
(D) Special districts
List II
(i) Professional Administrator
(ii) Quasi Municipal Organization
(iii) Concentration of Executive and Legislative authority
(iv) Weak Mayor

Codes:	A	B	C	D
(a)	(i)	(ii)	(iv)	(iii)
(b)	(iv)	(i)	(iii)	(ii)
(c)	(ii)	(i)	(iv)	(iii)
(d)	(iii)	(ii)	(i)	(iv)

41. Arrange the Elton Mayo's Experiments in a chronological (ascending) order:
(i) Illumination Experiments
(ii) Reley assembly test rooms experiments
(iii) Bank wiring observation study
(iv) Mass interview programmes
Codes:
(a) (i), (ii), (iii), (iv) (b) (i), (iii), (ii), (iv)
(c) (i), (ii), (iv), (iii) (d) (ii), (i), (iii), (iv)

42. Arrange correct sequence of the following Presidents of India in descending order:
(i) Shri V.V. Giri
(ii) Shri R. Venkataraman
(iii) Dr. Zakir Hussain
(iv) Shri N. Sanjeeva Reddy
Codes:
(a) (i), (iii), (ii), (iv) (b) (ii), (iv), (iii), (i)
(c) (iii), (i), (iv), (ii) (d) (iv), (ii), (i), (iii)

43. Arrange the following stages in the evolution of Public Administration in the ascending order of their development.
(i) Principles approach
(ii) Ecological approach
(iii) Administrative behavioural approach
(iv) Public Policy approach
Codes:
(a) (iv), (iii), (ii), (i) (b) (iii), (ii), (i), (iv)
(c) (i), (iii), (ii), (iv) (d) (ii), (iv), (iii), (i)

44. Arrange the following chairman of Finance Commission in decending order:
(i) P.B. Rajamannar (ii) A.K. Chandra
(iii) K.C. Neogi (iv) K. Santhanam
Codes:
(a) (i), (ii), (iv), (iii) (b) (iv), (iii), (i), (ii)
(c) (iii), (iv), (ii), (i) (d) (ii), (iv), (iii), (i)

45. Arrange the stages of report writing in decending order:
(i) Collection of Data
(ii) Formulation of Concepts
(iii) Preparation of an Outline
(iv) Comparison and Interpretation
Codes:
(a) (ii), (iii), (i), (iv) (b) (iii), (ii), (iv), (i)
(c) (i), (iii), (ii), (iv) (d) (ii), (iv), (iii), (i)

Read the passage below, and answer the questions that follow based on your understanding of the passage:

Bureaucracy includes certain negative behavioural traits also. Subsequent Sociologists have taken Weber's concept as a starting point but have not been content to be limited by his definition. In particular one school of thought emphasises that Weber's Ideal type of bureaucracy itself entails the features responsible for the inefficiency so often associated with the term (bureaucracy). These features are dysfunctional and pathological and even frustrate the attainment of organisational goals. Robert Merton has made a classic statement of this point of view. He is concerned with the fact that "The very elements which are conduce toward efficiency in general produce inefficiency in specific instances" and, "also lead to an over concern with strict adherence to regulations which induces timidity, conservatism and technicism". Stress on "depersonalisation of relationships" leads to conflict in relations with bureaucratic clientele. Specific behavioural orientations often mentioned are passing the buck, red tape, rigidity and inflexibility, excessive impersonality over-secretiveness, unwillingness to delegate', and reluctance to' exercise discretion. Behaviour of this sort is typical of the "trained in capacity" of the bureaucracy the implication is that behaviour most typically bureaucratic is behaviour emerging from over emphasis on the rationality of bureaucratic organisation and dys-functional in its effects. This problem persists to this day.

Morstein Marx refers to such traits as "ailment of organisation" explained by the fact that "the bureaucratic type of organisation gives rise to certain tendencies that prevent its purpose. Some of its strength—and in extreme cases all of it-is drained off constantly by vices that paradoxically spring from virtues". Michel Crozier described his valuable study 'The Bureaucratic Phenomenon', as scientific attempt to understand better this "malady of bureaucracy". He explains that the subject to which he refers in speaking of the bureaucratic phenomenon is that of the Maladaptation, the inadequecies, or to use Merton's expression, the "dysfunctions" which necessarily develop with in an organisation.

46. Bureaucracy includes negative behavioural traits:
   (a) Inefficiency (b) Over concern
   (c) Conservatism (d) All the above

47. Depersonalisation of relationships leads to:
   (a) Red tape
   (b) Flexibility
   (c) Informal relations
   (d) Open ness

48. Specific Behavioural Orientation results in:
   (a) Trained in capacity of the Bureaucrats
   (b) Improved Capacity of the Bureaucrat
   (c) Exercising discretion
   (d) Functional effectiveness

49. Morstein Marx refers to such traits as:
   (a) Harm only
   (b) Ailments of organisation
   (c) Co-ordination
   (d) Purposive ness

50. Malady of bureaucracy is:
   (a) Maladaptation
   (b) Dysfunctionalism
   (c) Both of the above
   (d) None of the above

ANSWERS

1. (a)	2. (b)	3. (c)	4. (c)	5. (c)
6. (c)	7. (d)	8. (a)	9. (d)	10. (b)
11. (b)	12. (a)	13. (b)	14. (b)	15. (a)
16. (b)	17. (c)	18. (a)	19. (c)	20. (d)
21. (a)	22. (a)	23. (c)	24. (a)	25. (a)
26. (a)	27. (a)	28. (c)	29. (a)	30. (c)
31. (b)	32. (d)	33. (c)	34. (d)	35. (c)
36. (a)	37. (d)	38. (c)	39. (b)	40. (b)
41. (c)	42. (c)	43. (c)	44. (a)	45. (a)
46. (c)	47. (c)	48. (a)	49. (b)	50. (c)

DECEMBER–2008

Note: This paper contains fifty (50) objective type questions, each question carrying two (2) marks. All questions are compulsory.

PAPER–I

1. According to Swami Vivekananda, teacher's success depends on
   (a) His renunciation of personal gain and service to others
   (b) His professional training and creativity
   (c) His concentration on his work and duties with a spirit of obedience to God
   (d) His mastery on the subject and capacity in controlling the students
2. Which of the following teacher will be liked most?
   (a) A teacher of high idealistic attitude
   (b) A loving teacher
   (c) A teacher who is disciplined
   (d) A teacher who often amuses his students
3. A teacher's most important challenge is
   (a) To make students do their home work
   (b) To make teaching-learning process enjoyable
   (c) To maintain discipline in the class-room
   (d) To prepare the question paper
4. Value-education stands for
   (a) making a student healthy
   (b) making a student to get a job
   (c) inculcation of virtues
   (d) all-round development of personality
5. When a normal student behaves in an erratic manner in the class, you would
   (a) pull up the student then and there
   (b) talk to the student after the class
   (c) ask the student to leave the class
   (d) ignore the student
6. The research is always
   (a) verifying the old knowledge
   (b) exploring new knowledge
   (c) filling the gap between knowledge
   (d) All of these
7. The research that applies the laws at the time of field study to draw more and more clear ideas about the problem is
   (a) Applied research
   (b) Action research
   (c) Experimental research
   (d) None of these
8. When a research problem is related to heterogeneous population, the most suitable sampling method is
   (a) Cluster Sampling
   (b) Stratified Sampling
   (c) Convenient Sampling
   (d) Lottery Method
9. The process not needed in experimental research is:
   (a) Observation
   (b) Manipulation and replication
   (c) Controlling
   (d) Reference collection
10. A research problem is not feasible only when

(a) it is researchable
(b) it is new and adds something to knowledge
(c) it consists of independent and dependent variables
(d) it has utility and relevance

Read the following passage carefully and answer the questions 11 to 15:

Radically changing monsoon patterns, reduction in the winter rice harvest and a quantum increase in respiratory diseases all part of the environmental doomsday scenario which is reportedly playing out in South Asia. According to a United Nations Environment Program report, a deadly three-kilometer deep blanket of pollution comprising a fearsome, cocktail of ash, acids, aerosols and other particles has enveloped in this region. For India, already struggling to cope with a drought, the implication of this are devastating and further crop failure will amount to a life and death question for many Indians. The increase in premature deaths will have adverse social and economic consequences and a rise in morbidities will place an unbearable burden on our crumbling health system. And there is no one to blame but ourselves. Both official and corporate India has always been allergic to any mention of clean technology. Most mechanical two wheelers roll of the assembly line without proper pollution control system. Little effort is made for R&D on simple technologies, which could make a vital difference to people's lives and the environment.

However, while there is no denying that South Asia must clean up its act, skeptics might question the timing of the haze report. The Kyoto meet on climate change is just two weeks away and the stage is set for the usual battle between the developing world and the West, particularly the Unites States of America. President Mr. Bush has adamantly refused to sign any protocol, which would mean a change in American consumption level. U.N. environment report will likely find a place in the U.S. arsenal as it plants an accusing finger towards controls like India and China. Yet the U.S.A. can hardly deny its own dubious role in the matter of erasing trading quotas.

Richer countries can simply buy up excess credits from poorer countries and continue to pollute. Rather than try to get the better of developing countries, who undoubtedly have taken up environmental shortcuts in their bid to catch up with the West, the USA should take a look at the environmental profigacy, which is going on within. From opening up virgin territories for oil exploration to relaxing the standards for drinking water, Mr. Bush's policies are not exactly beneficial, not even to America's interests. We realise that we are all in this together and that pollution anywhere should be a global concern otherwise there will only be more tunnels at the end of the tunnel.

11. Both official and corporate India is allergic to
(a) Failure of Monsoon
(b) Poverty and Inequality
(c) Slowdown in Industrial Production
(d) Mention of Clean Technology

12. If the rate of premature death increases it will
(a) Exert added burden on the crumbling economy
(b) Have adverse social and economic consequences
(c) Make positive effect on our effort to control population
(d) Have less job aspirants in the society

13. According to the passage, the two-wheeler industry is not adequately concerned about
(a) Passenger safety on the roads
(b) Life cover insurance of the vehicle owner

(c) Pollution control system in the vehicle
(d) Rising cost of the two wheelers

14. What could be the reason behind timing of the haze report just before the Kyoto meet?
(a) United Nations is working hand-in-glove with U.S.A.
(b) Organisers of the forthcoming meet to teach a lesson to the U.S.A.
(c) Drawing attention of the world towards devastating effects of environment degradation.
(d) U.S.A. wants to use it as a handle against the developing countries in the forthcoming meet.

15. Which of the following is the indication of environmental degradation in South Asia?
(a) Social and economic inequality
(b) Crumbling health care system
(c) Inadequate pollution control system
(d) Radically changing monsoon pattern

16. Community Radio is a type of radio service that caters to the interest of
(a) Local audience (b) Education
(c) Entertainment (d) News

17. Orkut is a part of
(a) Intrapersonal Communication
(b) Mass Communication
(c) Group Communication
(d) Interpersonal Communication

18. Match List I with List II and select the correct answer using the codes given below.

List I (Artists)
A. Amrita Shergill
B. T. Swaminathan Pillai
C. Bhimsen Joshi
D. Padma Subramaniyam

List II (Art)
1. Flute 2. Classical Song
3. Painting 4. Bharat Natyam

Codes:	A	B	C	D
(a)	3	1	2	4
(b)	2	3	1	4
(c)	4	2	3	1
(d)	1	4	2	3

19. Which is not correct in latest communication award?
(a) Salman Rushdie - Booker's Prize—July 20, 2008
(b) Dilip Sanghavi - Business Standard CEO Award, July 22, 2008
(c) Tapan Sinha - Dada Saheb Falke Award, July 21, 2008
(d) Gautam Ghosh - Osians Lifetime Achievement Award, July 11, 2008

20. Firewalls are used to protect a communication network system against
(a) Unauthorised attacks
(b) Virus attacks
(c) Data-driven attacks
(d) Fire-attacks

21. Insert the missing number in the following

$\frac{2}{7}, \frac{4}{7}, ?, \frac{11}{21}, \frac{16}{31},$

(a) $\frac{10}{8}$ (b) $\frac{6}{10}$
(c) $\frac{5}{10}$ (d) $\frac{7}{13}$

22. In a certain code, GAMESMAN is written as AGMEMSAN. How would DISCLOSE be written in that code?
(a) IDSCOLSE (b) IDCSOLES
(c) IDSCOLES (d) IDSCLOSE

23. The letters in the first set have a certain relationship. On the basis of this

relationship mark the right choice for the second set : AST : BRU :: NQV: ?
(a) ORW (b) MPU
(c) MRW (d) OPW

24. On what dates of April, 1994 did Sunday fall?
(a) 2, 9, 16, 23, 30
(b) 3, 10, 17, 24
(c) 4, 11, 18, 25
(d) 1, 8, 15, 22, 29

25. Find out the wrong number in the sequence
125, 127, 130, 135, 142, 153, 165
(a) 130 (b) 142
(c) 153 (d) 165

26. There are five books A, B, C, D and E. The book C lies above D, the book E is below A and B is below E. Which is at the bottom?
(a) E (b) B
(c) A (d) C

27. Logical reasoning is based on
(a) Truth of involved propositions
(b) Valid relation among the involved propositions
(c) Employment of symbolic language
(d) Employment of ordinary language

28. Two propositions with the same subject and predicate terms but different in quality are
(a) Contradictory (b) Contrary
(c) Subaltern (d) Identical

29. The premises of a valid deductive argument
(a) Provide some evidence for its conclusion
(b) Provide no evidence for its conclusion
(c) Are irrelevant for its conclusion
(d) Provide conclusive evidence for its conclusion

30. Syllogistic reasoning is
(a) Deductive (b) Inductive
(c) Experimental (d) Hypothetical

Study the following Venn diagram and answer questions nos. 31 to 33.

Three circles representing GRADUATES, CLERKS and GOVERNMENT EMPLOYEES are intersecting. The intersections are marked A, B, C, e, f, g and h. Which part best represents the statements in questions 31 to 33?

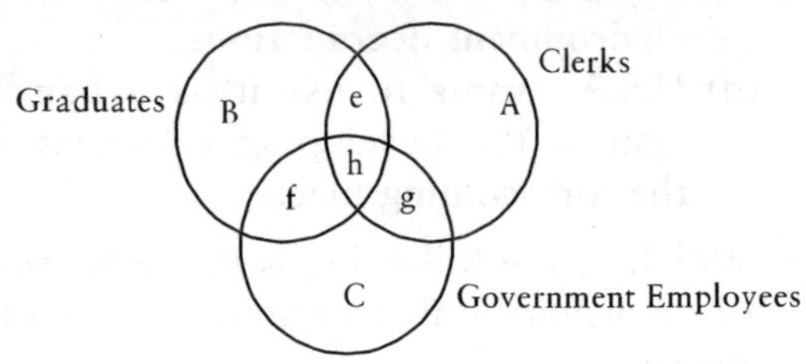

31. Some Graduates are Government employees but not as Clerks.
(a) h (b) g
(c) f (d) e

32. Clerks who are graduates as well as government employees.
(a) e (b) f
(c) g (d) h

33. Some graduates are Clerks but not Government employees.
(a) f (b) g
(c) h (d) e

Study the following graph and answer questions numbers from 34 to 35

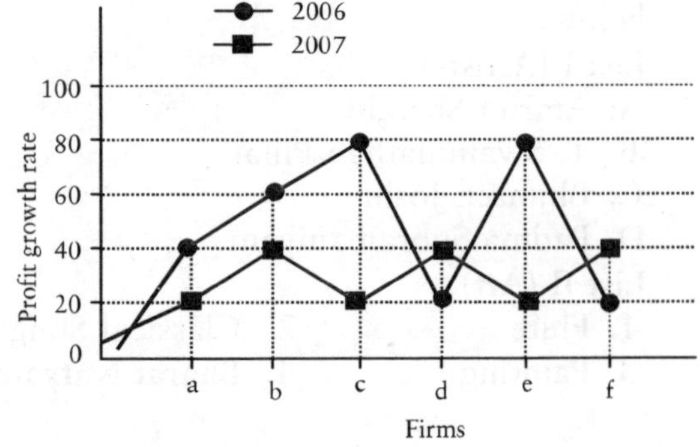

34. Which of the firms got maximum profit growth rate in the year 2006.
(a) ab (b) ce
(c) cd (d) ef

35. Which of the firms got maximum profit growth rate in the year 2007.
(a) bdf (b) acf
(c) bed (d) ace

36. The accounting software 'Tally' was developed by
(a) HCL (b) TCS
(c) Infosys (d) Wipro

37. Errors in computer programs are called
(a) Follies (b) Mistakes
(c) Bugs (d) Spam

38. HTML is basically used to design
(a) Webpage
(b) Website
(c) Graphics
(d) Tables and Frames

39. 'Micro Processing' is made for
(a) Computer
(b) Digital System
(c) Calculator
(d) Electronic Goods

40. Information, a combination of graphics, text, sound, video and animation is called
(a) Multiprogram (b) Multifacet
(c) Multimedia (d) Multiprocess

41. Which of the following pairs regarding typical composition of hospital wastes is incorrect?
(a) Plastic - 9-12%
(b) Metals - 1-2%
(c) Ceramic - 8-10%
(d) Biodegradable - 35-40%

42. Freshwater achieves its greatest density at
(a) –4°C (b) 0°C
(c) 4°C (d) –2.5°C

43. Which one of the following is not associated with earthquakes?
(a) Focus (b) Epicenter
(c) Seismograph (d) Swells

44. The tallest trees in the world are found in the region
(a) Equatorial region
(b) Temperate region
(c) Monsoon region
(d) Mediterranean region

45. Match List I with List II and select the correct answer from the codes given below.

List I (National Parks)
A. Periyar
B. Nandan Kanan
C. Corbett National Park
D. Sariska Tiger Reserve

List II (States)
1. Orissa
2. Kerala
3. Rajasthan
4. Uttarakhand

Codes:	**A**	**B**	**C**	**D**
(a)	2	1	4	3
(b)	1	2	4	3
(c)	3	2	1	4
(d)	1	2	3	4

46. According to Radhakrishnan Commission, the aim of Higher Education is
(a) To develop the democratic values, peace and harmony
(b) To develop great personalities who can give their contributions in politics, administration, industry and commerce
(c) Both (a) and (b)
(d) None of these

47. The National Museum at New Delhi is attached to

(a) Delhi University
(b) a Deemed University
(c) a Subordinate Office of the JNU
(d) Part of Ministry of Tourism and Culture

48. Match List I with List II and select the correct answer from the code given below.

List I (Institutions)
A. National Law Institute
B. Indian Institute of Advanced Studies
C. National Judicial Academy
D. National Savings Institute

List II (Locations)
1. Shimla 2. Bhopal
3. Hyderabad 4. Nagpur

Codes:	A	B	C	D
(a)	3	2	4	1
(b)	1	2	3	4
(c)	4	3	1	2
(d)	3	1	2	4

49. Election of Rural and Urban local bodies are conducted and ultimately supervised by
(a) Election Commission of India
(b) State Election Commission
(c) District Collector and District Magistrate
(d) Concerned Returning Officer

50. Which opinion is not correct?
(a) Education is a subject of concurrent list of VII schedule of Constitution of India
(b) University Grants Commission is a statutory body
(c) Patent, inventions, design, copyright and trade marks are the subject of concurrent list
(d) Indian Council of Social Science Research is a statutory body related to research in social sciences

ANSWERS

1. (d)	2. (c)	3. (b)	4. (c)	5. (b)
6. (d)	7. (a)	8. (b)	9. (d)	10. (b)
11. (d)	12. (b)	13. (c)	14. (c)	15. (d)
16. (a)	17. (d)	18. (a)	19. (b)	20. (a)
21. (d)	22. (a)	23. (d)	24. (b)	25. (d)
26. (b)	27. (b)	28. (a)	29. (d)	30. (a)
31. (c)	32. (d)	33. (d)	34. (b)	35. (a)
36. (b)	37. (c)	38. (a)	39. (a)	40. (c)
41. (d)	42. (c)	43. (d)	44. (b)	45. (a)
46. (c)	47. (d)	48. (d)	49. (b)	50. (c)

PAPER–II

Note: This paper contains fifty (50) objective type questions, each question carrying two (2) marks. All questions are compulsory.

1. "We are no longer confronted with several administrative sciences but with one which can be applied equally well to public and private affairs". The above statement is by:
(a) Henry Fayol (b) Luther Gullick
(c) L. Urwick (d) M.P. Follet

2. The following is generally not associated with the Classical Theory:
(a) J.D. Mooney (b) M.P. Follet
(c) A.C. Reiley (d) R. Shelton

3. A diagrammatic presentation about the structure of an organisation is known as:
(a) Organography (b) Matrix
(c) Organogram (d) Lay-out

4. Who amongst the following type of leaders were considered to be more effective by Likert?
   (a) People oriented
   (b) Task oriented
   (c) Production oriented
   (d) Goal oriented
5. The decision in which detailed procedures are worked out to deal with the recurrent and repetitive situations is known as:
   (a) Programmed decision
   (b) Non-Programmed decision
   (c) Structural decision
   (d) Objective decision
6. In USA, the budget is presented before:
   (a) The Senate
   (b) House of Representatives
   (c) Joint Session of both the Houses
   (d) Financial Committee of the Congress
7. The behaviour characteristic of a SALA official is:
   (a) Efficiency
   (b) Self-aggrandizement
   (c) Social welfare
   (d) Interest towards clients
8. The list of various posts proposed by the American Congress for appointments by the newly elected President of America is known as:
   (a) Plum Book (b) Yellow Book
   (c) Blue Book (d) Gerry wandering
9. Which of the following statement is not applicable to India with reference to the general characteristics of administration of developing countries?
   (a) A wide discrepancy between form and reality
   (b) A weak administrative structure
   (c) Excessive rule bound bureaucratic structure
   (d) Participatory public administration
10. To initiate and to sustain concerted effort to improve administrative efficiency in all branches of government is the main aim of:
   (a) Public Administration
   (b) Ombudsman
   (c) Administrative Reforms Commission
   (d) O and M
11. In which country was 'Performance Budget' first introduced in:
   (a) UK (b) France
   (c) USA (d) India
12. According to which Article of the Constitution the President of India cannot return a money bill for reconsideration to the House?
   (a) Article 110 (b) Article 111
   (c) Article 112 (d) Article 115
13. The civil list of IAS officers is maintained and updated by:
   (a) Ministry of Home Affairs
   (b) Cabinet Secretariat
   (c) Union Public Service Commission
   (d) Ministry of Personnel, Public Grievances and Pensions
14. In the field of Parliamentary practice, the 'Zero Hour' emerged in India in:
   (a) 1982 (b) 1972
   (c) 1962 (d) 1952
15. A member of a State Public Service Commission, who wants to resign can do by writing a letter addressed to which of the following?
   (a) Chief Minister
   (b) Chairman of UPSC
   (c) Chairman of concerned PSC
   (d) Governor
16. The Department of Jammu and Kashmir Affairs was created in 1994 and was then attached to the:
   (a) Ministry of Defence
   (b) PMO

(c) Ministry of External Affairs
(d) Ministry of Home Affairs

17. The important means of executive control over administration are:
(i) Civil Service Code
(ii) Budget
(iii) Rule Making Power
(iv) Power to appoint and remove
The correct code is:
(a) (i) and (ii)
(b) (i), (ii) and (iv)
(c) (i), (ii) and (iii)
(d) (i), (ii), (iii) and (iv)

18. Which of the following sampling techniques would be appropriate if sample is drawn from a heterogeneous population?
(a) Random
(b) Purposive
(c) Multi-Stage Sampling
(d) Stratified

19. Which of the following committees recommended open participation of political parties in Panchayati Raj elections?
(a) L.M. Singhvi Committee
(b) Balwant Rai Mehta Committee
(c) G.V.K. Rao Committee
(d) Ashok Mehta Committee

20. The most popular form of city Government in USA is:
(a) The Mayor-Administrator Plan
(b) The Mayor-Council Plan
(c) The City-Manager Plan
(d) The Commission Plan

Given below are two statements, one labelled as Assertion (A) and the other labelled as Reason (R). In the context of the two statements write the correct answer from the codes given below:

21. **Assertion (A):** Public Administration provides stability in the society.
Reason (R): Public Administration is responsible for bringing socio-economic change in the society.
Codes:
(a) Both (A) and (R) are true and (R) is the correct explanation of (A)
(b) Both (A) and (R) are true but (R) is not the correct explanation of (A)
(c) (A) is true but, (R) is false
(d) (A) is false but, (R) is true

22. **Assertion (A):** Power and authority are synonymous.
Reason (R): Behaviour of the people is influenced by power and authority.
Codes:
(a) Both (A) and (R) are true and (R) is the correct explanation of (A)
(b) Both (A) and (R) are true but, (R) is not the correct explanation of (A)
(c) (A) is true but, (R) is false
(d) (A) is false but, (R) is true

23. **Assertion (A):** 'Decisions' have either ethical or factual content.
Reason (R): 'Decisions' are choices among different alternatives.
Codes:
(a) Both (A) and (R) are true and (R) is the correct explanation of (A)
(b) Both (A) and (R) are true but, (R) is not the correct explanation of (A)
(c) (A) is true but, (R) is false
(d) (A) is false but, (R) is true

24. **Assertion (A):** Pre-auditing is meant for preventing illegal and excess expenditure.
Reason (R): The legality of proposed expenditure and budgetary provisions are examined in pre-audit.
Codes:
(a) Both (A) and (R) are true and (R) is the correct explanation of (A)
(b) Both (A) and (R) are true but, (R) is not the correct explanation of (A)

(c) (A) is true but, (R) is false
(d) (A) is false but, (R) is true

25. **Assertion (A):** Proper Public Administrative System is indispensable for the functioning of a democratic country.
Reason (R): An impartial, honest and efficient administration helps in attaining the ideals of democracy.
Codes:
(a) Both (A) and (R) are true and (R) is the correct explanation of (A)
(b) Both (A) and (R) are true but, (R) is not the correct explanation of (A)
(c) (A) is true but, (R) is false
(d) (A) is false but, (R) is true

26. **Assertion (A):** In a federal set up, sovereignty is divided between the Union and the State Governments.
Reason (R): The powers of the government are divided in a federal set-up.
Codes:
(a) Both (A) and (R) are true and (R) is the correct explanation of (A)
(b) Both (A) and (R) are true but, (R) is not the correct explanation of (A)
(c) (A) is true but (R) is false
(d) (A) is false but (R) is true

27. **Assertion (A):** The President of India occupies almost the same position as the king or Queen of England.
Reason (R): The President is ultimately bound to act in accordance with the advice given by the Council of Ministers.
Choose the correct answer from the following using the code:
(a) Both (A) and (R) are correct and (R) is the correct explanation of (A)
(b) Both (A) and (R) are correct but, (R) is not the correct explanation of (A)
(c) (A) is true but (R) is false
(d) (A) is false but (R) is true

28. **Assertion (A):** Though six decades have passed since Independence yet number of people below the poverty line has increased.
Reason (R): Successive plans have failed to achieve the targeted growth rate.
Choose the correct answer from the following using the code:
(a) Both (A) and (R) are true and (R) is the correct explanation of (A)
(b) Both (A) and (R) are true but, (R) is not the correct explanation of (A)
(c) (A) is true but (R) is false
(d) (A) is false but (R) is true

29. What is the correct sequence of Maslow's Hierarchy of needs (lower to higher order)?
(i) Physiological needs
(ii) Esteem needs
(iii) Social needs
(iv) Self-Actualization needs
(a) (i) (iii) (iv) (ii) (b) (i) (iii) (ii) (iv)
(c) (i) (iv) (iii) (ii) (d) (i) (ii) (iii) (iv)

30. Arrange the following experiments conducted by Elton Mayo in a chronological order:
(i) Illumination experiments
(ii) Relay Assembly Test Room experiments
(iii) Bank Wiring Observation Study
(iv) Mass Interview Programme
(a) (i) (ii) (iii) (iv) (b) (i) (iii) (ii) (iv)
(c) (i) (ii) (iv) (iii) (d) (i) (iv) (iii) (ii)

31. In the execution of the Budget the following machinery is devised. Arrange them in sequence:
(i) A system of controlling officers
(ii) A system of authority for issuing sanctions
(iii) A system of payment and accounts
(iv) A system of Drawing and Disbursing officers
(a) (i) (ii) (iii) (iv) (b) (iv) (iii) (ii) (i)
(c) (iv) (ii) (iii) (i) (d) (i) (ii) (iv) (iii)

32. Arrange the following in correct sequence with regard to recruitment:
   (i) Advertisement
   (ii) Job Requisition
   (iii) Requisitioning and scrutiny of the application forms
   (iv) Selection
   (a) (ii) (i) (iii) (iv) (b) (i) (ii) (iii) (iv)
   (c) (iv) (iii) (ii) (i) (d) (ii) (iii) (iv) (i)
33. Arrange the following reports in chronological order (with regard to reforms in Indian administration):
   (i) Gopalaswamy Aiyyangar Report
   (ii) Appleby Report
   (iii) Gorwala Report
   (iv) Administrative Reforms Commission-I
   (a) (i) (ii) (iii) (iv) (b) (i) (iii) (ii) (iv)
   (c) (iv) (iii) (ii) (i) (d) (i) (iv) (iii) (ii)
34. What is the proper sequence of the steps of budget enactment in India?
   (i) Finance Bill, Appropriation Bill, Voting on Demands, General discussion
   (ii) General discussion, Appropriation Bill, Voting on Demands, Finance Bill
   (iii) General discussion, Voting on Demands, Appropriation Bill, Finance Bill
   (iv) Finance Bill, Voting on Demands, General discussion, Appropriation Bill
   (a) (ii) (b) (iv)
   (c) (iii) (d) (i)
35. Give the chronological order of the following:
   (i) Balwant Rai Mehta
   (ii) Lord Mayo
   (iii) Lord Ripon
   (iv) Ashok Mehta
   (a) (ii) (iii) (i) (iv) (b) (i) (ii) (iii) (iv)
   (c) (iii) (ii) (iv) (i) (d) (iv) (i) (iii) (ii)
36. The following programmes were launched for the improvement of the socio-economic conditions of rural population. Put them in chronological order:
   (i) Bhoodan Movement
   (ii) Gramdan Movement
   (iii) Applied Nutrition Programme
   (iv) Community Development
   (a) (i) (ii) (iv) (iii) (b) (i) (iii) (iv) (ii)
   (c) (i) (ii) (iii) (iv) (d) (iv) (iii) (ii) (i)
37. Match List I and List II and select the correct answer from the codes given below:

   List I
   (A) Principles of Organisation
   (B) Industrial and General Management
   (C) Organisations
   (D) The function of the Executive

   List II
   (i) Chester Barnard
   (ii) Henry Fayol
   (iii) Mooney and Reiley
   (iv) March and Simon

Codes:	**A**	**B**	**C**	**D**
(a)	(iii)	(ii)	(iv)	(i)
(b)	(ii)	(iv)	(iii)	(i)
(c)	(iv)	(iii)	(ii)	(i)
(d)	(iii)	(iv)	(i)	(ii)

38. Match List I with List II and select the correct answer from the codes given below:

   List I (Agencies)
   (A) Line Agencies
   (B) Staff Agencies
   (C) Auxillary Agencies
   (D) Technical Staff Agencies

   List II (Functions)
   (i) Committed to accomplishment of fundamental objectives
   (ii) Collects resources for achievement of objectives
   (iii) Suggest measures for improving the system
   (iv) Facilitates the task

Codes:	**A**	**B**	**C**	**D**
(a)	(ii)	(iv)	(i)	(iii)
(b)	(i)	(iii)	(ii)	(iv)
(c)	(i)	(iv)	(ii)	(iii)
(d)	(ii)	(iii)	(i)	(iv)

39. Match List I with List II and select the correct answer from the codes given below:

List I

(A) Scientific Management Theory
(B) Decision Making Theory
(C) Human Relations Theory
(D) Motivation Theory

List II

(i) Elton Mayo (ii) F.W. Taylor
(iii) Maslow (iv) Herbert Simon

Codes:	**A**	**B**	**C**	**D**
(a)	(i)	(ii)	(iii)	(iv)
(b)	(ii)	(iv)	(i)	(iii)
(c)	(iv)	(iii)	(ii)	(i)
(d)	(i)	(iii)	(iv)	(ii)

40. Match List I with List II and select the correct answer from the codes given below:

List I

(A) Hawthorne experiments
(B) The Functions of the Executive
(C) Group Dynamics in Administration
(D) Administrative Behaviour

List II

(i) Herbert Simon
(ii) M.P. Follett
(iii) Chester I. Bernard
(iv) Elton Mayo

Codes:	**A**	**B**	**C**	**D**
(a)	(i)	(ii)	(iii)	(iv)
(b)	(iv)	(iii)	(ii)	(i)
(c)	(ii)	(i)	(iv)	(iii)
(d)	(i)	(iii)	(ii)	(iv)

41. Match List I with List II and select the correct answer from the codes given below:

List I

(A) Peter Self (B) Woodrow Wilson
(C) Chester Bernard (D) Chris Argyris

List II

(i) Functions of the Executive
(ii) Personality and Organisation
(iii) The study of Public Administration
(iv) Administrative theories and Politics

Codes:	**A**	**B**	**C**	**D**
(a)	(iv)	(iii)	(i)	(ii)
(b)	(i)	(iii)	(iv)	(ii)
(c)	(i)	(iv)	(iii)	(ii)
(d)	(iv)	(iii)	(ii)	(i)

42. Match List I with List II and select the correct answer from the codes given below:

List I

(A) Fused Society (B) Diffracted Society
(C) Overlapping (D) Heterogeneity

List II

(i) different kinds of systems, practices and view points
(ii) poly communalism
(iii) particularism and ascription
(iv) functionally specific

Codes:	**A**	**B**	**C**	**D**
(a)	(iii)	(iv)	(ii)	(i)
(b)	(i)	(ii)	(iii)	(iv)
(c)	(iv)	(iii)	(i)	(ii)
(d)	(iii)	(iv)	(i)	(ii)

43. Match List I with List II and select the correct answer from the codes given below:

List I

(A) Finance Ministry
(B) Government of India
(C) Planning Commission
(D) The Comptroller and Auditor General of India

List II

(i) Plan Grants
(ii) Certification of 'net proceeds'
(iii) Terms of reference of Finance Commission
(iv) Allocation of income-tax proceeds
(v) Corporate taxes to be shared

Codes:	**A**	**B**	**C**	**D**
(a)	(v)	(i)	(iv)	(iii)
(b)	(iv)	(iii)	(i)	(ii)
(c)	(iii)	(iv)	(ii)	(i)
(d)	(ii)	(i)	(iii)	(iv)

44. Match List I with List II and select the correct answer from the codes given below:

List I

(A) Emergency powers of the President
(B) Vice-President of India
(C) Appointment of Prime Minister of India
(D) Collective responsibility of the Cabinet

List II

(i) Article 75(3) (ii) Article 74(i)
(iii) Article 63 (iv) Article 360

Codes:	A	B	C	D
(a)	(i)	(ii)	(iii)	(iv)
(b)	(iv)	(iii)	(ii)	(i)
(c)	(i)	(iii)	(ii)	(iv)
(d)	(iii)	(i)	(ii)	(iv)

45. Match List I with List II and select the correct answer from the codes given below:

List I

(A) Habeas Corpus (B) Mandamus
(C) Quo Warranto (D) Injunction

List II

(i) Show legal authority
(ii) Restraining an official from doing something
(iii) Must do your duty under the law
(iv) Produce the person illegally held

Codes:	A	B	C	D
(a)	(i)	(ii)	(iv)	(iii)
(b)	(iv)	(i)	(iii)	(ii)
(c)	(ii)	(iii)	(i)	(iv)
(d)	(iv)	(iii)	(i)	(ii)

Read the following passage and answer the questions that follow on the basis of your understanding of the passage:

Public human resource management has served many masters. In the late nineteenth and early twentieth centuries, it was used to make government more honest and more accountable to the public instead of to the political parties. In the 1960s and 1970s, public human resource management was used to pry open public jobs for women, people of color, and older and disabled Americans. Beginning in the late 1970s and continuing into our own time, it is being used to improve the management of government.

The irony of today's phase of public human resource management is that policy makers believe public personnel administration can best improve the management of Government by getting out of the way—or even by getting out of government altogether.

Increasingly, policy makers are of the opinion that the traditional functions of human resource management in the public sector are obsolete. Job classification and analysis a basic tenet of public personnel administration is an example. Agency administrators typically must bargain with human resource managers about how high or low a position should be ranked in the agency hierarchy, and what kinds of qualifications prospective applications should have. Often agency heads, who are interested in strategic and effective management and personnel administrators, who want uniformity and fairness in the classification system, find themselves at odds.

46. The dominant feature of human resource management during the period 60s and 70s was pry open jobs for:

(a) Women (b) Colored people
(c) Disabled (d) All the above

47. Match List I with List II and select the correct answer from the codes given below the lists:

List I

(A) Making Government more accountable to the public
(B) To pry open public jobs for women
(C) To improve the management of Government
(D) Public personnel administration can be used to improve the management of Government by getting out of the way

List II
(i) during 1970s
(ii) present times
(iii) during 1960s and 1970s
(iv) 19th Century

Codes:	**A**	**B**	**C**	**D**
(a)	(iii)	(iv)	(i)	(ii)
(b)	(i)	(ii)	(iii)	(iv)
(c)	(iv)	(iii)	(i)	(ii)
(d)	(iv)	(iii)	(ii)	(i)

48. The policy makers believe that the personnel administration can best be used in the improvement of management of Government by:
(a) getting out of the way
(b) getting out of Government altogether
(c) Both (a) and (b)
(d) None of the above

49. The basic tenet of public personnel administration is:
(a) Job classification and Analysis
(b) Uniformity and fairness
(c) Both (a) and (b)
(d) None of the above

50. The points of difference between Agency administrators and Personnel administrators include:
(a) Rank classification
(b) Kinds of qualifications of the applicants
(c) Uniformity and fairness
(d) All of the above

ANSWERS

1. (a)	2. (d)	3. (c)	4. (a)	5. (a)
6. (b)	7. (b)	8. (a)	9. (d)	10. (c)
11. (c)	12. (a)	13. (a)	14. (c)	15. (d)
16. (d)	17. (d)	18. (d)	19. (d)	20. (c)
21. (a)	22. (b)	23. (d)	24. (b)	25. (a)
26. (a)	27. (a)	28. (d)	29. (b)	30. (c)
31. (c)	32. (b)	33. (b)	34. (c)	35. (a)
36. (a)	37. (a)	38. (c)	39. (b)	40. (b)
41. (a)	42. (d)	43. (b)	44. (b)	45. (d)
46. (d)	47. (d)	48. (c)	49. (c)	50. (d)

JUNE–2008

Note: This paper contains fifty (50) objective type questions, each question carrying two (2) marks. All questions are compulsory.

PAPER–I

1. The teacher has been glorified by the phrase "Friend, philosopher and guide" because
   (a) He has to play all vital roles in the context of society
   (b) He transmits the high value of humanity to students
   (c) He is the great reformer of the society
   (d) He is a great patriot
2. The most important cause of failure for teacher lies in the area of
   (a) interpersonal relationship
   (b) lack of command over the knowledge of the subject
   (c) verbal ability
   (d) strict handling of the students
3. A teacher can establish rapport with his students by
   (a) becoming a figure of authority
   (b) impressing students with knowledge and skill
   (c) playing the role of a guide
   (d) becoming a friend to the students
4. Education is a powerful instrument of
   (a) Social transformation
   (b) Personal transformation
   (c) Cultural transformation
   (d) All of the above
5. A teacher's major contribution towards the maximum self-realisation of the student is affected through
   (a) Constant fulfilment of the students' needs
   (b) Strict control of classroom activities
   (c) Sensitivity to students' needs, goals and purposes
   (d) Strict reinforcement of academic standards
6. Research problem is selected from the stand point of
   (a) Researcher's interest
   (b) Financial support
   (c) Social relevance
   (d) Availability of relevant literature
7. Which one is called non-probability sampling?
   (a) Cluster sampling
   (b) Quota sampling
   (c) Systematic sampling
   (d) Stratified random sampling
8. Formulation of hypothesis may not be required in
   (a) Survey method
   (b) Historical studies
   (c) Experimental studies
   (d) Normative studies
9. Field-work based research is classified as
   (a) Empirical (b) Historical
   (c) Experimental (d) Biographical
10. Which of the following sampling method is appropriate to study the prevalence of AIDS amongst male and female in India in 1976, 1986, 1996 and 2006?

(a) Cluster sampling
(b) Systematic sampling
(c) Quota sampling
(d) Stratified random sampling

Read the following passage and answer the questions 11 to 15:

The fundamental principle is that Article 14 forbids class legislation but permits reasonable classification for the purpose of legislation which classification must satisfy the twin tests of classification being founded on an intelligible differentia which distinguishes persons or things that are grouped together from those that are left out of the group and that differentia must have a rational nexus to the object sought to be achieved by the Statute in question. The thrust of Article 14 is that the citizen is entitled to equality before law and equal protection of laws. In the very nature of things the society being composed of unequals a welfare State will have to strive by both executive and legislative action to help the less fortunate in society to ameliorate their condition so that the social and economic inequality in the society may be bridged. This would necessitate a legislative application to a group of citizens otherwise unequal and amelioration of whose lot is the object of state affirmative action. In the absence of the doctrine of classification such legislation is likely to flounder on the bedrock of equality enshrined in Article 14. The Court realistically appraising the social and economic inequality and keeping in view the guidelines on which the State action must move as constitutionally laid down in Part IV of the Constitution evolved the doctrine of classification. The doctrine was evolved to sustain a legislation or State action designed to help weaker sections of the society or some such segments of the society in need of succour. Legislative and executive action may accordingly be sustained if it satisfies the twin tests of reasonable classification and the rational principle correlated to the object sought to be achieved.

The concept of equality before the law does not involve the idea of absolute equality among human beings which is a physical impossibility. All that Article 14 guarantees is a similarity of treatment contra-distinguished from identical treatment. Equality before law means that among equals the law should be equal and should be equally administered and that the likes should be treated alike. Equality before the law does not mean that things which are different shall be as though they are the same. It of course means denial of any special privilege by reason of birth, creed or the like. The legislation as well as the executive government, while dealing with diverse problems arising out of an infinite variety of human relations must of necessity have the power of making special laws, to attain any particular object and to achieve that object it must have the power of selection or classification of persons and things upon which such laws are to operate.

11. Right to equality, one of the fundamental rights, is enunciated in the Constitution under Part III, Article
(a) 12 (b) 13
(c) 14 (d) 15

12. The main thrust of Right to equality is that it permits
(a) class legislation
(b) equality before law and equal protection under the law
(c) absolute equality
(d) special privilege by reason of birth

13. The social and economic inequality in the society can be bridged by
(a) executive and legislative action
(b) universal suffrage
(c) identical treatment
(d) None of the above

14. The doctrine of classification is evolved to
   (a) Help weaker sections of the society
   (b) Provide absolute equality
   (c) Provide identical treatment
   (d) None of the above

15. While dealing with diverse problems arising out of an infinite variety of human relations, the government
   (a) must have the power of making special laws
   (b) must not have any power to make special laws
   (c) must have power to withdraw equal rights
   (d) None of the above

16. Communication with oneself is known as
   (a) Group communication
   (b) Grapevine communication
   (c) Interpersonal communication
   (d) Intrapersonal communication

17. Which broadcasting system for TV is followed in India?
   (a) NTSE (b) PAL
   (c) SECAM (d) NTCS

18. All India Radio before 1936 was known as
   (a) Indian Radio Broadcasting
   (b) Broadcasting Service of India
   (c) Indian State Broadcasting Service
   (d) All India Broadcasting Service

19. The biggest news agency of India is
   (a) PTI
   (b) UNI
   (c) NANAP
   (d) Samachar Bharati

20. Prasar Bharati was launched in the year
   (a) 1995 (b) 1997
   (c) 1999 (d) 2001

21. A statistical measure based upon the entire population is called parameter while measure based upon a sample is known as
   (a) Sample parameter
   (b) Inference
   (c) Statistics
   (d) None of these

22. The importance of the correlation co-efficient lies in the fact that
   (a) There is a linear relationship between the correlated variables
   (b) It is one of the most valid measure of statistics
   (c) It allows one to determine the degree or strength of the association between two variables
   (d) It is a non-parametric method of statistical analysis

23. The F-test
   (a) is essentially a two tailed test
   (b) is essentially a one tailed test
   (c) can be one tailed as well as two tailed depending on the hypothesis
   (d) can never be a one tailed test

24. What will be the next letter in the following series
   DCXW, FEVU, HGTS, ______
   (a) AKPO (b) JBYZ
   (c) JIRQ (d) LMRS

25. The following question is based on the diagram given below. If the two small circles represent formal classroom education and distance education and the big circle stands for university system of education, which figure represents the university systems.

   (a)  (b) 

   (c) 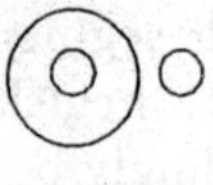 (d) 

26. The statement, 'To be non-violent is good' is a

(a) Moral judgement
(b) Factual judgement
(c) Religious judgement
(d) Value judgement

27. **Assertion (A):** Man is a rational being.
Reason (R): Man is a social being.
(a) Both (A) and (R) are true and (R) is the correct explanation of (A)
(b) Both (A) and (R) are true but (R) is not the correct explanation of (A)
(c) (A) is true but (R) is false
(d) (A) is false but (R) is true

28. Value Judgements are
(a) Factual Judgements
(b) Ordinary Judgements
(c) Normative Judgements
(d) Expression of public opinion

29. Deductive reasoning proceeds from
(a) general to particular
(b) particular to general
(c) one general conclusion to another general conclusion
(d) one particular conclusion to another particular conclusion

30. AGARTALA is written in code as 14168171, the code for AGRA is
(a) 1641 (b) 1416
(c) 1441 (d) 1461

31. Which one of the following is the most comprehensive source of population data?
(a) National Family Health Surveys
(b) National Sample Surveys
(c) Census
(d) Demographic Health Surveys

32. Which one of the following principles is not applicable to sampling?
(a) Sample units must be clearly defined
(b) Sample units must be dependent on each other
(c) Same units of sample should be used throughout the study
(d) Sample units must be chosen in a systematic and objective manner

33. If January 1st, 2007 is Monday, what was the day on 1st January 1995?
(a) Sunday (b) Monday
(c) Friday (d) Saturday

34. Insert the missing number in the following series
4 16 8 64 ? 256
(a) 16 (b) 24
(c) 32 (d) 20

35. If an article is sold for ₹ 178 at a loss of 11%; what would be its selling price in order to earn a profit of 11%?
(a) ₹ 222.50 (b) ₹ 267
(c) ₹ 222 (d) ₹ 220

36. WYSIWYG—describes the display of a document on screen as it will actually print
(a) What you state is what you get
(b) What you see is what you get
(c) What you save is what you get
(d) What you suggest is what you get

37. Which of the following is not a Computer language?
(a) PASCAL (b) UNIX
(c) FORTRAN (d) COBOL

38. A keyboard has at least
(a) 91 keys (b) 101 keys
(c) 111 keys (d) 121 keys

39. An E-mail address is composed of
(a) two parts (b) three parts
(c) four parts (d) five parts

40. Corel Draw is a popular
(a) Illustration program
(b) Programming language
(c) Text program
(d) None of the above

41. Human ear is most sensitive to noise in which of the following ranges
(a) 1-2 KHz (b) 100-500 Hz
(c) 10-12 KHz (d) 13-16 KHz

42. Which one of the following units is used to measure intensity of noise?
(a) decible (b) Hz
(c) Phon (d) Watts/m^2

43. If the population growth follows a logistic curve, the maximum sustainable yield
(a) is equal to half the carrying capacity
(b) is equal to the carrying capacity
(c) depends on growth rates
(d) depends on the initial population

44. Chemical weathering of rocks is largely dependent upon
(a) high temperature
(b) strong wind action
(c) heavy rainfall
(d) glaciation

45. Structure of earth's system consists of the following: Match List I with List II and give the correct answer.
List I (Zone)
A. Atmosphere B. Biosphere
C. Hydrosphere D. Lithosphere
List II (Chemical Character)
1. Inert gases
2. Salt, freshwater, snow and ice
3. Organic substances, skeleton matter
4. Light silicates

Codes:	A	B	C	D
(a)	2	3	1	4
(b)	1	3	2	4
(c)	2	1	3	4
(d)	3	1	2	4

46. NAAC is an autonomous institution under the aegis of
(a) ICSSR (b) CSIR
(c) AICTE (d) UGC

47. National Council for Women's Education was established in
(a) 1958 (b) 1976
(c) 1989 (d) 2000

48. Which one of the following is not situated in New Delhi?
(a) Indian Council of Cultural Relations
(b) Indian Council of Scientific Research
(c) National Council of Educational Research and Training
(d) Indian Institute of Advanced Studies

49. Autonomy in higher education implies freedom in
(a) Administration
(b) Policy-making
(c) Finance
(d) Curriculum development

50. Match List I with List II and select the correct answer from the code given below
List I (Institutions)
A. Dr. Hari Singh Gour University
B. S.N.D.T. University
C. M.S. University
D. J.N. Vyas University
List II (Locations)
1. Mumbai 2. Baroda
3. Jodhpur 4. Sagar

Codes:	A	B	C	D
(a)	4	1	2	3
(b)	1	2	3	4
(c)	3	1	2	4
(d)	2	4	1	3

ANSWERS

1. (b)	2. (b)	3. (b)	4. (d)	5. (c)
6. (c)	7. (b)	8. (b)	9. (a)	10. (d)
11. (c)	12. (b)	13. (a)	14. (a)	15. (a)
16. (d)	17. (b)	18. (c)	19. (a)	20. (b)
21. (a)	22. (c)	23. (c)	24. (c)	25. (b)
26. (a)	27. (b)	28. (c)	29. (a)	30. (d)
31. (c)	32. (b)	33. (d)	34. (a)	35. (c)
36. (b)	37. (b)	38. (b)	39. (a)	40. (a)
41. (b)	42. (a)	43. (a)	44. (c)	45. (b)
46. (d)	47. (a)	48. (d)	49. (c)	50. (a)

PAPER–II

Note: This paper contains fifty (50) objective type questions, each question carrying two (2) marks. All questions are compulsory.

1. The word 'administration' has been defined as "the organisation and direction of human and material resources to achieve desired ends" by:
   (a) John M. Pfiffner and R. Vance Presthus
   (b) John A. Vieg
   (c) L.D. White
   (d) Woodrow Wilson
2. Which of the following statements is true according to Wilson:
   (a) Politics is concerned with values and administration with facts.
   (b) Politics is value free and administration is value laden
   (c) Politics and administration are value free
   (d) Politics and administration are value laden
3. The administrative theories viewed organisation as:
   (a) a rational instrument
   (b) an ethical instrument
   (c) a social instrument
   (d) an economical instrument
4. Behavioural approach recognizes three main factors in the decision—making process:
   (a) Assumptions, facts and policies
   (b) Purpose, location and people
   (c) Objectives, policies and commands
   (d) Rationale, assumptions and effect
5. The term 'Representative Bureaucracy' has been coined by:
   (a) Martin Albraw (b) Max Weber
   (c) Karl Marx (d) Donald Kingsley
6. 'Administration in Developing Countries: The Theory of Prismatic Society' has been authored by:
   (a) Weidner (b) Riggs
   (c) Mayo (d) Wilson
7. Programme Evaluation Organisation is an integral part of:
   (a) National Development Council
   (b) Central Secretariat
   (c) Department of Public Undertaking
   (d) Planning Commission
8. Which of the following formulates and co-ordinates the Federal Fiscal Policy in USA:
   (a) Department of Finance
   (b) State Department
   (c) Budget and Management Board
   (d) Federal Reserve Board
9. CPWD is an example of:
   (a) Line Agency
   (b) Staff Agency
   (c) Both Line and Staff Agencies
   (d) Neither Line nor Staff Agencies
10. The 'Classification of Services' in India is governed by the Civil Services Rules of:
    (a) 1930 (b) 1950
    (c) 1960 (d) 1987
11. "Recruitment is the cornerstone of the entire public personnel structure" was stated by:
    (a) Stahl (b) E.N. Gladden
    (c) Nigro (d) Karl Marx
12. Permission by the Parliament for the estimated expenditure for a partial period of the ensuing financial year before the approval of the regular budget is called:
    (a) Vote on Account
    (b) Appropriation Bill
    (c) Cut Motion
    (d) Finance Bill
13. In India, the term deficit financing was first defined by:

(a) Finance Commission
(b) First Five year plan
(c) Public Accounts Committee
(d) Estimates Committee

14. The Contingency Fund of India was created in:
(a) 1954 (b) 1955
(c) 1958 (d) 1950

15. Which of the following is a correct point of difference between Accounting and Auditing:
(a) Auditing guides accounting
(b) Auditing begins where Accounting ends
(c) Audit is the function of the legislature while Accounting is an executive function
(d) All of the above

16. The office of the Advocate General in the State Government is constitutionally provided for through Article:
(a) Art. 160 (b) Art. 161
(c) Art. 164 (d) Art. 165

17. Performance Budgeting means:
(a) an appraisal of accomplishments
(b) detecting extravagance and waste
(c) detecting fraud and technical errors
(d) appraisal of correct state of affairs

18. If the following which type of research is related to the examination of cause and effect?
(a) Pure (b) Investigative
(c) Descriptive (d) Behavioural

19. In actual practice, the initiative with regard to policy-making has shifted to:
(a) The Executive (b) The legislature
(c) The Judiciary (d) Pressure groups

20. How many functions have been assigned to municipal bodies in India under the 74th Constitution Amendment Act?
(a) 33 (b) 18
(c) 29 (d) 12

21. **Assertion (A):** The exercise of authority is always based on rules.
Reason (R): Rules and regulations help to check arbitrary action.
Codes:
(a) Both (A) and (R) are true and (R) is the correct explanation of (A)
(b) Both (A) and (R) are true but (R) is not the correct explanation of (A)
(c) (A) is true but (R) is false
(d) (A) is false but (R) is true

22. **Assertion (A):** The discipline of Public Administration has been facing a crisis of identity.
Reason (R): As an academic discipline, Public Administration has passed through many phases in its evolution.
Codes:
(a) Both (A) and (R) are true and (R) is the correct explanation of (A)
(b) Both (A) and (R) are true but (R) is not the correct explanation of (A)
(c) (A) is true but (R) is false
(d) (A) is false but (R) is true

23. **Assertion (A):** The 'man' in the organization is broadly dealt with in both the Behavioural and Human Relations approaches.
Reason (R): The relationships of the people in the organization are dealt with in both the approaches.
Codes:
(a) Both (A) and (R) are true and (R) is the correct explanation of (A)
(b) Both (A) and (R) are true but (R) is not the correct explanation of (A)
(c) (A) is true but (R) is false
(d) (A) is false but (R) is true

24. **Assertion (A):** Neutrality is an important characteristic of Civil Services in India.
Reason (R): The concept of neutrality has its roots in British System.

Codes:
(a) Both (A) and (R) are true and (R) is the correct explanation of (A)
(b) Both (A) and (R) are true but (R) is not the correct explanation of (A)
(c) (A) is true but (R) is false
(d) (A) is false but (R) is true

25. **Assertion (A):** Audit in India is governed by Indian Audit and Accounts order.
Reason (R): Audit of the State Accounts is the part of union list.
Codes:
(a) Both (A) and (R) are true and (R) is the correct explanation of (A)
(b) Both (A) and (R) are true but (R) is not the correct explanation of (A)
(c) (A) is true but (R) is false
(d) (A) is false but (R) is true

26. **Assertion (A):** Public opinion plays vital role in a democratic society.
Reason (R): In a democratic society there is freedom of press.
Codes:
(a) Both (A) and (R) are true and (R) is the correct explanation of (A)
(b) Both (A) and (R) are true but (R) is not the correct explanation of (A)
(c) (A) is true but (R) is false
(d) (A) is false but (R) is true

27. **Assertion (A):** Right to Information Act has been accepted by all the States of India.
Reason (R): India follows the 'Rule of Law'.
Codes:
(a) Both (A) and (R) are true and (R) is the correct explanation of (A)
(b) Both (A) and (R) are true but (R) is not the correct explanation of (A)
(c) (A) is true but (R) is false
(d) (A) is false but (R) is true

28. **Assertion (A):** Local Self-Government is the basis of a democratic system.
Reason (R): Democracy at the top may not be successful unless it is built on the foundation of Local Self-Government.
Codes:
(a) Both (A) and (R) are true and (R) is the correct explanation of (A)
(b) Both (A) and (R) are true but (R) is not the correct explanation of (A)
(c) (A) is true but (R) is false
(d) (A) is false but (R) is true

29. Arrange the following theories of Public Administration in a sequential order:
(i) Bureaucratic theory
(ii) Behavioural theory
(iii) The Classical theory
(iv) The Scientific Management theory
Codes:
(a) (i), (ii), (iii) and (iv)
(b) (iv), (iii), (ii) and (i)
(c) (iv), (iii), (i) and (ii)
(d) (iii), (iv), (i) and (ii)

30. Arrange the following stages in the evolution of Public Administration in sequencial order:
(i) Golden era of principles
(ii) Period of challenges and criticisms
(iii) Period of dichotomy
(iv) Period of crisis of identity
Codes:
(a) (iii), (i), (ii), (iv) (b) (iv), (iii), (ii), (i)
(c) (iii), (ii), (i), (iv) (d) (iii), (ii), (iv), (i)

31. Arrange in sequential order the following supporters of Politics—Administration dichotomy theory:
(i) Woodrow Wilson
(ii) F.J. Goodnow
(iii) F.W. Taylor
(iv) Henry Fayol
Codes:
(a) (iii), (ii), (i), (iv) (b) (iv), (iii), (ii), (i)
(c) (i), (ii), (iii), (iv) (d) (ii), (iii), (iv), (i)

32. Identify the correct order of the reports given below:

(i) P.H. Appleby Report I
(ii) A.D. Gorwala Report
(iii) Santhanam Committee Report
(iv) Administrative Reforms Commission Report

Codes:
(a) (ii), (i), (iv), (iii) (b) (ii), (i), (iii), (iv)
(c) (i), (ii), (iii), (iv) (d) (i), (ii), (iv), (iii)

33. Following Committees have been appointed from time to time to bring reforms in the Panchayati Raj System in India. Their correct chronological order is:
(i) L.M. Singhvi Committee
(ii) Ashok Mehta Committee
(iii) P.K. Thungan Committee
(iv) G.V.K. Rao Committee

Codes:
(a) (ii), (iv), (i), (iii) (b) (i), (ii), (iii), (iv)
(c) (iv), (iii), (ii), (i) (d) (i), (iii), (ii), (iv)

34. Arrange the following stages of India's Central level planning in a chronological order:
(i) perspective targeting
(ii) preparation of the approach paper
(iii) formulation of guidelines
(iv) publication of the draft plan

Codes:
(a) (iv), (iii), (i), (ii) (b) (ii), (i), (iii), (iv)
(c) (i), (iii), (ii), (iv) (d) (i), (ii), (iii), (iv)

35. Following programmes were launched for the improvement of the socio-economic conditions of the rural population. Put them in chronological order:
(i) Rural Landless Employment Guarantee Programme
(ii) TRYSEM
(iii) IRDP
(iv) DPAP

Codes:
(a) (i), (ii), (iii), (iv) (b) (ii), (iii), (iv), (i)
(c) (iii), (iv), (i), (ii) (d) (iv), (iii), (ii), (i)

36. Match List I with List II and select the correct answer from the codes given below:

List II
(A) Upward Communication
(B) Downward Communication
(C) Horizontal Communication
(D) Grapevine

List II
(i) Reports of grievances
(ii) Discussion
(iii) Gossip
(iv) Instruction Circulars

Codes:	**A**	**B**	**C**	**D**
(a)	(iv)	(i)	(ii)	(iii)
(b)	(iv)	(ii)	(iii)	(i)
(c)	(iii)	(ii)	(i)	(iv)
(d)	(ii)	(iii)	(iv)	(i)

37. Match List I with List II and select the correct answer from the codes given below:

List I
(A) Bounded Rationality
(B) Maturity and Immaturity theory
(C) Hierarchy of Needs
(D) Systems of Management

List II
(i) Rensis Likert
(ii) Abraham Moslow
(iii) Argyris
(iv) Simon

Codes:	**A**	**B**	**C**	**D**
(a)	(i)	(ii)	(iii)	(iv)
(b)	(iv)	(iii)	(ii)	(i)
(c)	(iii)	(iv)	(ii)	(i)
(d)	(ii)	(iii)	(iv)	(i)

38. Match List I with List II and select the correct answer by using the codes given below:

List I
(A) E.N. Gladden
(B) F.M. Marx
(C) Pfiffner and Presthus
(D) W.F. Willoughby

List II

(i) Principles of Public Administration
(ii) Elements of Public Administration
(iii) Public Administration
(iv) An Introduction to Public Administration

Codes:	A	B	C	D
(a)	(ii)	(iii)	(iv)	(i)
(b)	(iv)	(ii)	(iii)	(i)
(c)	(iii)	(i)	(ii)	(iv)
(d)	(i)	(ii)	(iii)	(iv)

39. Match List I with List II and select the correct answer from the codes given below:

List I

(A) Unity of Command
(B) Unity of Direction
(C) Human Relationists
(D) Traditionalists

List II

(i) One head one plan
(ii) One subordinate, one superior
(iii) Focus on physical environment
(iv) Focus on social environment

Codes:	A	B	C	D
(a)	(ii)	(i)	(iv)	(iii)
(b)	(i)	(ii)	(iii)	(iv)
(c)	(iv)	(iii)	(i)	(ii)
(d)	(iii)	(iv)	(ii)	(i)

40. Match List I with List II and select the correct answer from the codes given below:

List I

(A) Abandonment of the political development concept
(B) Development as an Ideal type
(C) Political authority and competition for politically allocated values
(D) Political culture and development

List II

(i) F.W. Riggs (ii) Hans. S. Park
(iv) Almond (iii) Harry Eckstein

Codes:	A	B	C	D
(a)	(ii)	(i)	(iv)	(iii)
(b)	(i)	(ii)	(iii)	(iv)
(c)	(iv)	(iii)	(ii)	(i)
(d)	(iii)	(i)	(iv)	(ii)

41. Match List I with List II and select the correct answer from the codes given below:

List I	List II
(A) USA	(i) Disintegrated system
(B) UK	(ii) Colonical Legacy
(C) India	(iii) Result of evolution
(D) France	(iv) Separation of powers

Codes:	A	B	C	D
(a)	(i)	(ii)	(iii)	(iv)
(b)	(ii)	(iii)	(i)	(iv)
(c)	(iv)	(iii)	(ii)	(i)
(d)	(iii)	(i)	(iv)	(ii)

42. Match List I with List II and select the correct answer from the codes given below:

List I

(A) Annual financial statement
(B) Money bill
(C) Vote on account
(D) Supplementary grants

List II

(i) Article 115 (ii) Article 110
(iii) Article 112 (iv) Article 116

Codes:	A	B	C	D
(a)	(i)	(ii)	(iii)	(iv)
(b)	(iv)	(iii)	(ii)	(i)
(c)	(iii)	(ii)	(iv)	(i)
(d)	(i)	(iv)	(ii)	(iii)

43. Match List I with List II and select the correct answer from the codes given below:

List I

(A) Public Accounts Committee
(B) Estimates Committee
(C) Committee on Public Undertakings
(D) Separation of Accounting from Audit

List II

(i) 1950 (ii) 1921
(iii) 1976 (iv) 1964

Codes:	A	B	C	D
(a)	(i)	(iv)	(ii)	(iii)
(b)	(iv)	(i)	(ii)	(iii)

(c)	(i)	(ii)	(iv)	(iii)
(d)	(ii)	(i)	(iv)	(iii)

44. Match List I with List II and select the correct answer from the codes given below:

List I

(A) Kothari Commission
(B) First Pay Commission
(C) Emergence of Formal Bureaucracy in India
(D) Central Public Service Commission

List II

(i) 1975-1976 (ii) 1947
(iii) 1854 (iv) 1226

Codes:	**A**	**B**	**C**	**D**
(a)	(i)	(ii)	(iii)	(iv)
(b)	(iv)	(iii)	(ii)	(i)
(c)	(i)	(ii)	(iv)	(iii)
(d)	(ii)	(i)	(iii)	(iv)

45. Match List I with List II and select the correct answer from the codes given below:

List I

(A) Motilal Nehru Committee
(B) Government of India Act, 1935
(C) Aitchison Committee
(D) Lee Commission

List II

(i) Establishment of Public Service Commission in India
(ii) Recommended for imperial, provincial and sub-ordinate services
(iii) Recommended for separate Civil Services for the centre
(iv) Recommend for Federal Public Service Commission

Codes:	**A**	**B**	**C**	**D**
(a)	(iii)	(iv)	(ii)	(i)
(b)	(i)	(ii)	(iii)	(iv)
(c)	(ii)	(i)	(iv)	(iii)
(d)	(ii)	(iii)	(iv)	(i)

Read the following passage and answer the questions that follow on the basis of your understanding of the passage:

Public Administration as an aspect of governmental activity has existed as long as political systems have been functioning and trying to achieve program objectives set by the political decision-makers. Public Administration as a field of systematic study is much more recent. Advisors to rulers and commentators on the workings of government have recorded their observations from time to time in sources as varied as Kautilya's 'Arthasastra' in ancient India, the 'Bible', Aristotle's 'Politics', and Machiavelli's 'The Prince', but it was not until the eighteenth century that cameralism, concerned with the systematic management of governmental affairs, became a speciality of German scholars in Western Europe. In the United States, such a development did not take place until the latter part of the nineteenth century with the publication in 1887 of Woodrow Wilson's famous essay, "The study of Administration", generally considered the starting point. Since that time, public administration has become a well-recognized area of specialized interest, either as a subfield of political science or as an academic discipline in its own right.

46. In Public Administration the word "Public" denotes:
(a) Masses (b) Democracy
(c) Bureaucracy (d) Governmental

47. Which statement regarding Public Administration is incorrect?
(a) After publication of Woodrow Wilson's Article, Public Administration was considered a separate discipline
(b) Public Administration as an activity has been prevalent in our society since long
(c) Public Administration deals with the study of only organisations
(d) Public Administration is concerned with achieving programme objectives

48. Which of the following pair have been the advisers to the rulers. Select the correct answer from the codes given below:
(a) Kautilya and Aristotle
(b) Machiavelli and Aristotle
(c) Machiavelli and Kautilya
(d) Woodrow Wilson and Aristotle

49. Arrange the following in chronological order in the evolution of Public Administration.
(i) Machiavelli
(ii) Woodrow Wilson
(iii) Aristotle
(iv) German Scholars
(a) (iii), (i), (iv), (ii) (b) (ii), (i), (iii), (iv)
(c) (iv), (ii), (iii), (i) (d) (i), (ii), (iii), (iv)

50. Public Administration has become an academic discipline in its own right after the writings of:
(a) Woodrow Wilson
(b) Machiavelli
(c) Aristotle
(d) Kautilya

ANSWERS

1. (a)	2. (d)	3. (a)	4. (a)	5. (d)
6. (b)	7. (a)	8. (c)	9. (d)	10. (a)
11. (a)	12. (a)	13. (b)	14. (d)	15. (d)
16. (d)	17. (a)	18. (d)	19. (d)	20. (b)
21. (a)	22. (d)	23. (a)	24. (c)	25. (b)
26. (a)	27. (d)	28. (a)	29. (c)	30. (a)
31. (c)	32. (b)	33. (a)	34. (d)	35. (d)
36. (a)	37. (b)	38. (b)	39. (a)	40. (b)
41. (a)	42. (c)	43. (d)	44. (a)	45. (a)
46. (d)	47. (a)	48. (d)	49. (a)	50. (a)

DECEMBER–2007

Note: This paper contains fifty (50) objective type questions, each question carrying two (2) marks. All questions are compulsory.

PAPER–I

1. Verbal guidance is least effective in the learning of
   (a) Aptitudes (b) Skills
   (c) Attitudes (d) Relationship

2. Which is the most important aspect of the teacher's role in learning?
   (a) The development of insight into what consititutes an adequate performance
   (b) The development of insight into what consititutes the pitfalls and dangers to be avoided
   (c) The provision of encouragement and moral support
   (d) The provision of continuous diagnostic and remedial help

3. The most appropriate purpose of learning is
   (a) personal adjustment
   (b) modification of behaviour
   (c) social and political awarness
   (d) preparing oneself for employment

4. The students who keep on asking questions in the class should be
   (a) encouraged to find answer independently
   (b) advised to meet the teacher after the class
   (c) encouraged to continue questioning
   (d) advised not to disturb during the lecture

5. Maximum participation of students is possible in teaching through
   (a) discussion method
   (b) lecture method
   (c) audio-visual aids
   (d) textbook method

6. Generalised conclusion on the basis of a sample is technically known as
   (a) Data analysis and interpretation
   (b) Parameter inference
   (c) Statistical inference
   (d) All of the above

7. The experimental study is based on
   (a) The manipulation of variables
   (b) Conceptual parameters
   (c) Replication of research
   (d) Survey of literature

8. The main characteristic of scientific research is
   (a) empirical (b) theoretical
   (c) experimental (d) All of the above

9. Authenticity of a research finding is its
   (a) Originality (b) Validity
   (c) Objectivity (d) All of the above

10. Which technique is generally followed when the population is finite?
    (a) Area Sampling Technique
    (b) Purposive Sampling Technique
    (c) Systematic Sampling Technique
    (d) None of the above

Read the following passage and answer the questions 11 to 15:

Gandhi's overall social and environmental philosophy is based on what human beings need rather than what they want. His early introduction to the teachings of Jains, Theosophists, Christian sermons, Ruskin and Tolstoy, and most significantly the *Bhagavad Gita*, were to have profound impact on the development of Gandhi's holistic thinking on humanity, nature and their ecological interrelation. His deep concern for the disadvantaged, the poor and rural population created an ambience for an alternative social thinking that was at once far-sighted, local and immediate. For Gandhi was acutely aware that the demands generated by the need to feed and sustain human life, compounded by the growing industrialisation of India, far outstripped the finite resources of nature. This might nowadays appear naive or commonplace, but such pronouncements were as rare as they were heretical a century ago. Gandhi was also concerned about the destruction, under colonial and modernist designs, of the existing infrastructures which had more potential for keeping a community flourishing within ecologically-sensitive traditional patterns of subsistence, especially in the rural areas, than did the incoming Western alternatives based on nature-blind technology and the enslavement of human spirit and energies.

Perhaps the moral principle for which Gandhi is best known is that of active non-violence, derived from the traditional moral restraint of not injuring another being. The most refined expression of this value is in the great epic of the *Mahabharata*, (c. 100 BCE to 200 CE), where moral development proceeds through placing constraints on the liberties, desires and acquisitiveness endemic to human life. One's action is judged in terms of consequences and the impact it is likely to have on another. Jainas had generalised this principle to include all sentient creatures and biocommunities alike. Advanced Jaina monks and nuns will sweep their path to avoid harming insects and even bacteria. Non-injury is a non-negotiable universal prescription.

11. Which one of the following have a profound impact on the development of Gandhi's holistic thinking on humanity, nature and their ecological interrelations?
    (a) Jain teachings
    (b) Christian sermons
    (c) *Bhagavad Gita*
    (d) Ruskin and Tolstoy

12. Gandhi's overall social and environmental philosophy is based on human beings'
    (a) need (b) desire
    (c) wealth (d) welfare

13. Gandhiji's deep concern for the disadvantaged, the poor and rural population created an ambience for an alternative
    (a) rural policy
    (b) social thinking
    (c) urban policy
    (d) economic thinking

14. Colonial policy and modernisation led to the destruction of
    (a) major industrial infrastructure
    (b) irrigation infrastructure
    (c) urban infrastructure
    (d) rural infrastructure

15. Gandhi's active non-violence is derived from
    (a) Moral restraint of not injuring another being
    (b) Having liberties, desires and acquisitiveness
    (c) Freedom of action
    (d) Nature-blind technology and enslavement of human spirit and energies

16. DTH service was started in the year
    (a) 2000 (b) 2002
    (c) 2004 (d) 2006

17. National Press day is celebrated on
    (a) 16th November (b) 19th November
    (c) 21st November (d) 30th November

18. The total number of members in the Press Council of India are
(a) 28 (b) 14
(c) 17 (d) 20

19. The right to impart and receive information is guaranteed in the Constitution of India by Article
(a) 19(2)(a) (b) 19(16)
(c) 19(2) (d) 19(1)(a)

20. Use of radio for higher education is based on the presumption of
(a) Enriching curriculum based instruction
(b) Replacing teacher in the long run
(c) Everybody having access to a radio set
(d) Other means of instruction getting outdated

21. Find out the number which should come at the place of question mark which will complete the following series.
5, 4, 9, 17, 35, ? = 139
(a) 149 (b) 79
(c) 49 (d) 69

Questions 22 to 24 are based on the following diagram in which there are three interlocking circles I, S and P, where circle I stands for Indians, circle S for Scientists and circle P for Politicians. Different regions in the figure are lettered from a to f.

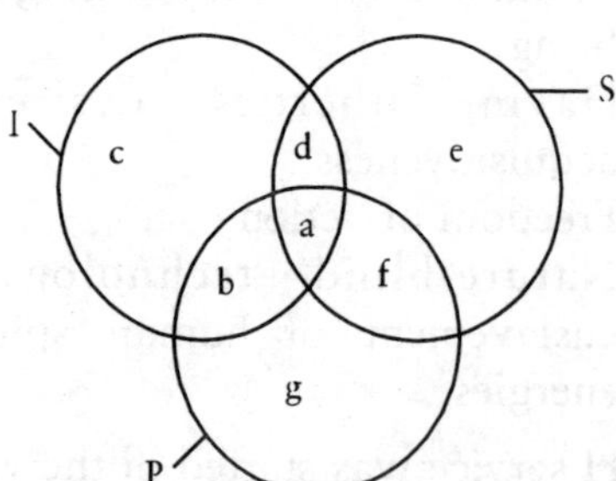

22. The region which represents Non-Indian Scientists who are Politicians.
(a) f (b) d
(c) a (d) c

23. The region which represents Indians who are neither Scientists nor Politicians.
(a) g (b) c
(c) f (d) a

24. The region which represents Politicians who are Indians as well as Scientists.
(a) b (b) c
(c) a (d) d

25. Which number is missing in the following series?
2, 5, 10, 17, 26, 37, 50, ?
(a) 63 (b) 65
(c) 67 (d) 69

26. The function of measurement includes.
(a) Prognosis (b) Diagnosis
(c) Prediction (d) All of the above

27. Logical arguments are based on.
(a) Scientific reasoning
(b) Customary reasoning
(c) Mathematical reasoning
(d) Syllogistic reasoning

28. Insert the missing number 4 : 17 : : 7 : ?
(a) 48 (b) 49
(c) 50 (d) 51

29. Choose the odd word.
(a) Nun (b) Knight
(c) Monk (d) Priest

30. Choose the number which is different from others in the group.
(a) 49 (b) 63
(c) 77 (d) 81

31. Probability sampling implies.
(a) Stratified Random Sampling
(b) Systematic Random Sampling
(c) Simple Random Sampling
(d) All of the above

32. Insert the missing number.
$\frac{36}{62}, \frac{39}{63}, \frac{43}{61}, \frac{48}{64}, ?$

(a) $\frac{51}{65}$ (b) $\frac{56}{60}$
(c) $\frac{54}{65}$ (d) $\frac{33}{60}$

33. At what time between 3 and 4 O'clock will the hands of a watch point in opposite directions?
(a) 40 minutes past three
(b) 45 minutes past three
(c) 50 minutes past three
(d) 55 minutes past three

34. Mary has three children. What is the probability that none of the three children is a boy?
(a) $\frac{1}{2}$ (b) $\frac{1}{3}$
(c) $\frac{3}{4}$ (d) 1

35. If the radius of a circle is increased by 50 percent. Its area is increased by
(a) 125 percent (b) 100 percent
(c) 75 percent (d) 50 percent

36. CD ROM stands for
(a) Computer Disk Read Only Memory
(b) Compact Disk Read Over Memory
(c) Compact Disk Read Only Memory
(d) Computer Disk Read Over Memory

37. The 'brain' of a computer which keeps peripherals under its control is called
(a) Common Power Unit
(b) Common Processing Unit
(c) Central Power Unit
(d) Central Processing Unit

38. Data can be saved on backing storage medium known as
(a) Compact Disk Recordable
(b) Computer Disk Rewritable
(c) Compact Disk Rewritable
(d) Computer Data Rewritable

39. RAM means
(a) Random Access Memory
(b) Rigid Access Memory
(c) Rapid Access Memory
(d) Revolving Access Memory

40. www represents
(a) who what and where
(b) weird wide web
(c) word wide web
(d) world wide web

41. Deforestation during the recent decades has led to
(a) Soil erosion
(b) Landslides
(c) Loss of bio-diversity
(d) All of the above

42. Which one of the following natural hazards is responsible for causing highest human disaster?
(a) Earthquakes
(b) Volcanic eruptions
(c) Snowstorms
(d) Tsunami

43. Which one of the following is appropriate for natural hazard mitigation?
(a) International AID
(b) Timely Warning System
(c) Rehabilitation
(d) Community Participation

44. Slums in metro city are the result of
(a) Rural to urban migration
(b) Poverty of the city-scape
(c) Lack of urban infrastructure
(d) Urban-governance

45. The great Indian Bustard bird is found in
(a) Thar Desert of India
(b) Coastal regions of India
(c) Temperate Forests in the Himalaya
(d) Tarai zones of the Himalayan Foot

46. The first Indian Satellite for serving the educational sector is known as
(a) SATEDU (b) INSAT-B
(c) EDUSAT (d) INSAT-C

47. Exclusive educational channel of IGNOU is known as
    (a) Gyan Darshan (b) Gyan Vani
    (c) Door Darshan (d) Prasar Bharati
48. The headquarter of Mahatma Gandhi Antarrashtriya Hindi Vishwavidyalaya is situated in
    (a) Sevagram (b) New Delhi
    (c) Wardha (d) Ahmedabad
49. Match List I with List II and select the correct answer using the codes given below.

    List I (Institutes)
    A. Central Institute of English and Foreign Languages
    B. Gramodaya Vishwavidyalaya
    C. Central Institute of Higher Tibetan Studies
    D. IGNOU

    List II (Locations)
    1. Chitrakoot 2. Hyderabad
    3. New Delhi 4. Dharmasala

Codes:	A	B	C	D
(a)	2	1	4	3
(b)	4	3	2	1
(c)	3	4	1	2
(d)	1	2	4	3

50. The aim of vocationalisation of education is
    (a) preparing students for a vocation along with knowledge
    (b) converting liberal education into vocational education
    (c) giving more importance to vocational than general education
    (d) making liberal education job-oriented

ANSWERS

1. (b)	2. (a)	3. (b)	4. (a)	5. (a)
6. (c)	7. (c)	8. (c)	9. (d)	10. (c)
11. (c)	12. (a)	13. (b)	14. (c)	15. (a)
16. (d)	17. (a)	18. (a)	19. (d)	20. (b)
21. (d)	22. (a)	23. (b)	24. (d)	25. (b)
26. (d)	27. (d)	28. (c)	29. (b)	30. (c)
31. (d)	32. (c)	33. (c)	34. (d)	35. (a)
36. (c)	37. (d)	38. (c)	39. (a)	40. (d)
41. (d)	42. (a)	43. (b)	44. (a)	45. (a)
46. (c)	47. (a)	48. (c)	49. (a)	50. (d)

PAPER–II

Note: This paper contains fifty (50) objective type questions, each question carrying two (2) marks. All questions are compulsory.

1. Impact of WTO on Administration is:
   (a) Draped with unparalleled powers
   (b) Shrinking in scope and functions
   (c) Draped with nominal powers
   (d) None of the above
2. Who wrote these words: "Public Administration is a detailed and systematic application of Law":
   (a) L.D. White
   (b) Woodrow Wilson
   (c) Ptiffner
   (d) Herbert Simon
3. Who among the following said: "Leadership and authority are plural because of involvement of many people"?
   (a) Mary Parker Follett
   (b) Ordway Tead
   (c) Chester Barnard
   (d) Marshall Dimmock
4. Herbert Simon's Model of decision-making is known as:

(a) Behaviour alternative
(b) Policy science
(c) Mixed scanning
(d) Disjointed incrementalism

5. Which one of the following is incorrect?
(a) Informal organizations are spontaneous and sentimental
(b) Informal organizations are customary and social
(c) Informal organizations are legal and rational
(d) Informal organizations are personal and emotional

6. Which of the following is not related to the Personnel Administration in USA?
(a) The Hatch Act
(b) The Ramspact Act
(c) Civil Service Reforms Act
(d) Fulton Committee Report

7. What is the common principle between the Constitution of India and Britain?
(a) Fundamental Rights
(b) Federalism
(c) Directive Principles of State Policy
(d) Rule of Law

8. Who among the following introduced the Indianisation of Civil Services in the Country?
(a) Lord Lytton (b) Warren Hastings
(c) Lord Cornwallis (d) Lord Clive

9. Who among the following said, "Financial administration is at the core of Modern Government."?
(a) Movstain Marx
(b) Llyod George
(c) Hoover Commission
(d) Willoughby

10. Under the Indian federation, which institution can rightly be called the "Balance Wheel"?
(a) Parliament
(b) President
(c) Inter-State Council
(d) Judiciary

11. The most important Parliamentary Committee that exercises control on public administration is:
(a) Committee on Public undertakings
(b) Public accounts committee
(c) Committee on Assurances
(d) Committee on Subordinate legislation

12. The Comptroller and Auditor General exercises Control over State finances through his power to:
(a) Make suggestions for affecting economies in expenditure of the State
(b) Make suggestions for re-allocation of revenues between the States
(c) Prescribe the forms or norms in which accounts of the States have to be maintained
(d) None of the above

13. The Expenses of UPSC are:
(a) Made from its own fund
(b) Charged upon consolidated fund of India
(c) Drawn from contingency fund
(d) Made from the public account of India

14. Generalist character of the Civil service in India was designed by:
(a) Northcote Trevelyan Report
(b) Fulton Committee Report
(c) Haldane Committee Report
(d) Sarkaria Committee Report

15. Desk-officer system is in operation in the Central Government since:
(a) 1953 (b) 1963
(c) 1973 (d) 1983

16. The Comptroller and Auditor General's (Duties, Powers and Conditions of Service) Act was passed in:
(a) 1961 (b) 1971
(c) 1981 (d) 1991

17. Who are not the members of the National Development Council?
    (a) Prime Minister
    (b) Chief Ministers of the States
    (c) All the Central Ministers
    (d) Members of the Planning Commission
18. Research hypothesis is concerned with the:
    (a) Prediction
    (b) Analysis
    (c) Relationship with some variables
    (d) Report writing
19. 73rd Amendment is related to:
    (a) Urban Local Government
    (b) Rural Local Government
    (c) Both
    (d) None
20. Open participation of political parties in Panchayati Raj affairs was a major recommendation of which of the following committees?
    (a) Balwant Rai Mehta
    (b) Ashok Mehta
    (c) G.V.K. Rao
    (d) L.M. Singhvi

Given below are two statements, one labelled as Assertion (A) and the other labelled as Reason (R). In the context of the two statements write the correct answer from the codes given below:

21. **Assertion (A):** Transparency and free flow of information are the main conditions for achieving good governance.
    Reason (R): For good governance democratic government is not just to be elected by the people but should also have credibility and accountability.
    Choose the correct answer from the following answer code:
    Codes:
    (a) Both (A) and (R) are correct and (R) is the correct explanation of (A)
    (b) Both (A) and (R) are correct but (R) is not the correct explanation of (A)
    (c) (A) is true but (R) is false
    (d) (A) is false but (R) is true
22. **Assertion (A):** The human relationship approach gave much importance to the formal aspects of the organisation.
    Reason (R): The human relations approach sought to increase production by humanizing the organisation.
    Choose the correct answer from the following answer code:
    Codes:
    (a) Both (A) and (R) are correct and (R) is the correct explanation of (A)
    (b) Both (A) and (R) are correct but (R) is not the correct explanation of (A)
    (c) (A) is true but (R) is false
    (d) (A) is false but (R) is true
23. **Assertion (A):** The main function of the Estimates committee is to examine the reports of the CAG to ascertain whether the money is well laid out within the limits of the policy implied in the estimates.
    Reason (R): Examining the estimates would enable the estimates committee to suggest alternative policies in order to bring about economy in administration.
    Choose the correct answer from the following answer code:
    Codes:
    (a) Both (A) and (R) are correct and (R) is the correct explanation of (A)
    (b) Both (A) and (R) are correct but (R) is not the correct explanation of (A)
    (c) (A) is true but (R) is false
    (d) (A) is false but (R) is true
24. **Assertion (A):** Given the framework, the local governments still have a limited functional and fiscal jurisdiction of their own.

Reason (R): Consequent upon the 73rd and 74th constitution Amendment Act, decentralization had made much headway beyond the level of the federating states.
Choose the correct answer from the following answer code:
Codes:
(a) Both (A) and (R) are correct and (R) is the correct explanation of (A)
(b) Both (A) and (R) are correct but (R) is not the correct explanation of (A)
(c) (A) is true but (R) is false
(d) (A) is false but (R) is true

25. **Assertion (A):** The senior administrators have the responsibility of advising on the financial and administrative implications of different policy alternatives.
Reason (R): By virtue of their formal education, training and administrative experience, senior administrators exercise much more power than their formal authority suggests.
Choose the correct answer from the following answer code:
Codes:
(a) Both (A) and (R) are correct and (R) is the correct explanation of (A)
(b) Both (A) and (R) are correct but (R) is not the correct explanation of (A)
(c) (A) is true but (R) is false
(d) (A) is false but (R) is true

26. **Assertion (A):** In Independent India the authority of the Deputy Commissioner/District collector has declined substantially.
Reason (R): The 73rd and 74th Constitution Amendment Acts have ushered in democratic decentralization.
Choose the correct answer from the following answer code:
Codes:
(a) Both (A) and (R) are correct and (R) is the correct explanation of (A)
(b) Both (A) and (R) are correct but (R) is not the correct explanation of (A)
(c) (A) is true but (R) is false
(d) (A) is false but (R) is true

27. **Assertion (A):** Justice under traditional authority is more or less a personal discretion.
Reason (R): Traditional authority rests on the belief in the sanctity of immemorial traditions.
Choose the correct answer from the following answer code:
Codes:
(a) Both (A) and (R) are correct and (R) is the correct explanation of (A)
(b) Both (A) and (R) are correct but (R) is not the correct explanation of (A)
(c) (A) is true but (R) is false
(d) (A) is false but (R) is true

28. **Assertion (A):** State governments look upon the All-India services as alien and encroaches upon their autonomy.
Reason (R): The members of the services are governed by the All-India Services Act and the rules framed by the central government.
Choose the correct answer from the following answer code:
Codes:
(a) Both (A) and (R) are correct and (R) is the correct explanation of (A)
(b) Both (A) and (R) are correct but (R) is not the correct explanation of (A)
(c) (A) is true but (R) is false
(d) (A) is false but (R) is true

29. **Assertion (A):** The classical stage of organisation emphasized the rational aspects of human behaviour.
Reason (R): The classical approach ignored the irrational and informal aspects of organisation.
Choose the correct answer from the following answer code:

Codes:
(a) Both (A) and (R) are correct and (R) is the correct explanation of (A)
(b) Both (A) and (R) are correct but (R) is not the correct explanation of (A)
(c) (A) is true but (R) is false
(d) (A) is false but (R) is true

30. **Assertion (A):** The judiciary in U.K. has the power to declare a parliamentary law unconstitutional.
Reason (R): The highest court in U.K. has the appellate and advisory jurisdictions.
Choose the correct answer from the following answer code:
Codes:
(a) Both (A) and (R) are correct and (R) is the correct explanation of (A)
(b) Both (A) and (R) are correct but (R) is not the correct explanation of (A)
(c) (A) is true but (R) is false
(d) (A) is false but (R) is true

31. Arrange the following in the correct descending order:
(i) Wing (ii) Branch
(iii) Department (iv) Section
(v) Division
Codes:
(a) (i), (ii), (iii), (iv), (v)
(b) (i), (iii), (v), (ii), (iv)
(c) (iii), (ii), (v), (i), (iv)
(d) (iii), (i), (v), (ii), (iv)

32. Arrange the following theories of motivation in the ascending order of their development.
(i) Douglas McGregor's Theory X and Y
(ii) Theory Z
(iii) McClelland's Needs Theory
(iv) A.H. Maslow's Hierarchy of Needs Theory
Codes:
(a) (i) (ii) (iii) (iv) (b) (i) (iv) (iii) (ii)
(c) (iv) (i) (ii) (iii) (d) (i) (iii) (iv) (ii)

33. Indicate the ascending order of the following programmes:
(i) Community Development Programme
(ii) Twenty Point Programme
(iii) Integrated Rural Development Programme
(iv) National Rural Employment Programme
(v) Antyoda Programme
Codes:
(a) (i) (ii) (iii) (iv) (v)
(b) (ii) (iii) (i) (iv) (v)
(c) (i) (iii) (v) (ii) (iv)
(d) (i) (ii) (v) (iii) (iv)

34. Arrange the following in order of their precedence:
(i) F. Goodnow, Politics and Administration
(ii) L.D. White, Introduction to the Study of Public Administration
(iii) Paul H. Appleby, Policy and Administration
(iv) Herbert Simon, Administrative Behaviour
(v) Woodrow Wilson, A Study of Public Administration
Codes:
(a) (i) (ii) (iii) (iv) (v)
(b) (v) (ii) (iii) (iv) (i)
(c) (ii) (v) (iv) (iii) (i)
(d) (v) (i) (ii) (iv) (iii)

35. Which is the correct sequence in budgeting:
(i) Preparation of Estimates
(ii) Vote on Account
(iii) Cut Motion
(iv) Passing of Finance Bill
(v) Passing of Appropriation Bill
Codes:
(a) (i) (ii) (iii) (iv) (v)
(b) (ii) (iii) (i) (iv) (v)
(c) (i) (iii) (ii) (v) (iv)
(d) (i) (iv) (v) (ii) (iii)

36. Match List I and List II and select correct answer from codes given below:

List I
(A) Trait theory
(B) Situational theory
(C) Theory 'Y'
(D) Managerial Leadership System

List II
(i) Participation and involvement of individuals in the managerial process
(ii) Leadership is participative and teamwork
(iii) Personal qualities which a leader possesses
(iv) Situation in which a leader works

Codes:	**A**	**B**	**C**	**D**
(a)	(iii)	(iv)	(ii)	(i)
(b)	(iii)	(ii)	(iv)	(i)
(c)	(iv)	(iii)	(ii)	(i)
(d)	(i)	(iii)	(iv)	(ii)

37. Match List I and List II and select correct answer from the code given below:

List I
(A) Payment in accordance with output
(B) Most rational and efficient form of the organization
(C) Primacy on Open model
(D) Application of economics to Political Science

List II
(i) Bureaucratic Theory
(ii) Human Behaviour Model
(iii) Public Choice Approach
(iv) Scientific Management Theory

Codes:	**A**	**B**	**C**	**D**
(a)	(iv)	(i)	(ii)	(iii)
(b)	(iv)	(iii)	(i)	(ii)
(c)	(ii)	(iv)	(iii)	(i)
(d)	(ii)	(iv)	(i)	(iii)

38. Match List I and List II and select correct answer from the codes given below:

List I
(A) Appointment of Judges of the State High Courts
(B) Principle governing the grants-in-aid to the municipalities
(C) Assisting the Minister in the process of policy making
(D) Auditing and reporting on all transactions of the Union and of the States

List II
(i) Central Secretariat
(ii) Comptroller and Auditor General of India
(iii) President of India
(iv) State Finance Commission

Codes:	**A**	**B**	**C**	**D**
(a)	(iii)	(ii)	(iv)	(i)
(b)	(iii)	(iv)	(ii)	(i)
(c)	(iii)	(iv)	(i)	(ii)
(d)	(iv)	(iii)	(i)	(ii)

39. Match List I and List II and select correct answer from codes given below:

List I
(A) Job satisfaction and Job dissatisfaction
(B) Hierarchy of needs
(C) Democratic participative management
(D) Contribution satisfaction equilibrium

List II
(i) A. Maslow (ii) F. Herzberg
(iii) C. Barnard (iv) Rensis Likert

Codes:	**A**	**B**	**C**	**D**
(a)	(i)	(iii)	(iv)	(ii)
(b)	(ii)	(i)	(iv)	(iii)
(c)	(iii)	(ii)	(i)	(iv)
(d)	(ii)	(i)	(iii)	(iv)

40. Match List I and List II and select correct answer from the codes given below:

List I
(A) Satish Chandra Committee
(B) Kothari Committee
(C) Aitchison Commission
(D) Northcote Trevelyan Report

List II
(i) Recruitment Policy and selection methods

(ii) System of Examination to the Higher Civil Servants
(iii) Organization of permanent civil service
(iv) Division of the civil services into 3 categories

Codes:	A	B	C	D
(a)	(ii)	(iv)	(iii)	(i)
(b)	(iii)	(ii)	(i)	(iv)
(c)	(ii)	(i)	(iv)	(iii)
(d)	(ii)	(iv)	(i)	(iii)

41. Match List I and List II and select correct answer from codes given below:

List I
(A) L.D. White (B) Paul Appleby
(C) Herbert Simon (D) F. Goodnow

List II
(i) Administrative Behaviour
(ii) Politics and Administration
(iii) Introduction to the Study of Public Administration
(iv) Big Democracy

Codes:	A	B	C	D
(a)	(iii)	(ii)	(i)	(iv)
(b)	(iii)	(iv)	(i)	(ii)
(c)	(ii)	(iii)	(i)	(iv)
(d)	(iv)	(iii)	(i)	(ii)

42. Match List I and List II and select correct answer from codes given below:

List I
(A) Public Choice Theory
(B) Scientific Management Theory
(C) Classical Theory
(D) Human Relations Theory

List II
(i) Use of Scientific research methods
(ii) Machine model of the organization
(iii) Application of economic logic to problems of public distribution
(iv) Recognition of the importance of the informal organization

Codes:	A	B	C	D
(a)	(iii)	(i)	(iv)	(ii)
(b)	(iv)	(iii)	(i)	(ii)
(c)	(ii)	(iv)	(iii)	(i)
(d)	(iii)	(i)	(ii)	(iv)

43. Match List I and List II and select correct answer from the code given below:

List I (Author)
(A) Herbert Simon
(B) Charles Lindblom
(C) David Easton
(D) D. Mueller

List II (Decision Making Process)
(i) Systems approach
(ii) Bounded rationality
(iii) Incrementalism approach
(iv) Public choice

Codes:	A	B	C	D
(a)	(ii)	(iii)	(i)	(iv)
(b)	(ii)	(i)	(iv)	(iii)
(c)	(iii)	(i)	(iv)	(ii)
(d)	(iv)	(iii)	(i)	(ii)

44. Match List I and List II and select correct answer from codes given below:

List I
(A) Public Accounts Committee
(B) Estimates Committee
(C) Committee on Public undertakings
(D) Standing Committee of the Parliament

List II
(i) To see that the expenditure conforms to the authority which governs it.
(ii) To examine the reports of the CAG on the public undertakings
(iii) To ensure efficient use of government
(iv) To examine whether the money is well laid out within the policy

Codes:	A	B	C	D
(a)	(iii)	(iv)	(i)	(ii)
(b)	(i)	(iv)	(iii)	(ii)
(c)	(i)	(iv)	(ii)	(iii)
(d)	(iii)	(ii)	(i)	(iv)

45. Match List I and List II and select correct answer from the codes given below:

List I

(A) Approaches to Public Administration
(B) Modern Public Administration
(C) Big Democracy
(D) Public Administration: a Comparative Approach

List II

(i) Paul H. Appleby (ii) E.N. Gladden
(iii) Nigro (iv) Ferrel Heady

Codes:	**A**	**B**	**C**	**D**
(a)	(i)	(ii)	(iii)	(iv)
(b)	(ii)	(i)	(iii)	(iv)
(c)	(ii)	(iii)	(i)	(iv)
(d)	(iii)	(i)	(iv)	(ii)

Read the passage below, and answer the questions that follow based on your understanding of the passage.

Corporation can take place as a means to achieve greater efficiency, cost-savings or service quality improvements, in which case it is accompanied by the setting of performance targets along the lines of executive agencies in the UK or State owned enterprises in New Zealand. This is the kind we have just reviewed. But it can also take place simply for convenience, a way of freeing a particular public function from the constraints of Civil Service red tape. The first is a clear example of the new public management in action; the second, much less so.

There are no data to indicate with any certainty which of these two varieties of corporatization is predominant. There is no doubt, however, that the second variety is very important in its own right in many developing countries. Civil Service departments in all kinds of fields are being converted to authorities, institutes, corporations, companies and other free-standing public bodies, even in countries which have no systematic programme of corporatization along British or New Zealand lines.

There are two reasons behind this trend. First, developing countries have been converting government departments to parastatal bodies for decades. There is little new above this, save that the trend may have accelerated in recent years. And second, the management constraints which newly corporatized bodies are being set up to escape can be very severe. In many African and Latin American countries such constraints go beyond the procedural red tape which those familiar with government in industrialized countries would expect to find. They can extend to, among other things, public-private pay gaps that are so wide after years of restraint compounded by galloping inflation that it becomes impossible to recruit and retain qualified staff.

46. Corporatization aims at the following:
(a) Efficiency
(b) Economy
(c) Quality improvement
(d) All of the above

47. Which one is not a clear example of the new public management in action?
(a) Setting of performance Targets
(b) Red Tapism
(c) Both
(d) None

48. Civil service departments are being converted into the following:
(a) Authorities (b) Institutes
(c) Corporations (d) All the above

49. What are the trends in the government departments in developing countries?
(a) Corporatization
(b) Conversion to parastatal bodies
(c) Both
(d) None

50. Management constraints in many African and Latin American countries are:

(a) Public-Private Pay Gaps
(b) Galloping inflation
(c) Recruitment
(d) All of the above

ANSWERS

1. (b)	2. (b)	3. (a)	4. (a)	5. (c)
6. (d)	7. (d)	8. (a)	9. (c)	10. (d)
11. (b)	12. (c)	13. (b)	14. (a)	15. (c)
16. (b)	17. (c)	18. (a)	19. (b)	20. (b)
21. (a)	22. (d)	23. (a)	24. (b)	25. (a)
26. (a)	27. (a)	28. (a)	29. (a)	30. (d)
31. (d)	32. (c)	33. (a)	34. (d)	35. (c)
36. (a)	37. (a)	38. (c)	39. (b)	40. (c)
41. (b)	42. (d)	43. (a)	44. (c)	45. (c)
46. (d)	47. (b)	48. (b)	49. (c)	50. (d)

JUNE–2007

Note: This paper contains fifty (50) objective type questions, each question carrying two (2) marks. All questions are compulsory.

PAPER–I

1. Teacher uses visual-aids to make learning
   (a) simple
   (b) more knowledgeable
   (c) quicker
   (d) interesting
2. The teacher's role at the higher educational level is to
   (a) provide information to students
   (b) promote self-learning in students
   (c) encourage healthy competition among students
   (d) help students to solve their personal problems
3. Which one of the following teachers would you like the most?
   (a) Punctual
   (b) Having research aptitude
   (c) Loving and having high idealistic philosophy
   (d) Who often amuses his students
4. Micro teaching is most effective for the student-teacher
   (a) during the practice-teaching
   (b) after the practice-teaching
   (c) before the practice-teaching
   (d) None of the above
5. Which is the least important factor in teaching?
   (a) Punishing the students
   (b) Maintaining discipline in the class
   (c) Lecturing in impressive way
   (d) Drawing sketches and diagrams on the blackboard
6. To test null hypothesis, a researcher uses
   (a) t test (b) ANOVA
   (c) χ^2 (d) factorial analysis
7. A research problem is feasible only when
   (a) it has utility and relevance
   (b) it is researchable
   (c) it is new and adds something to knowledge
   (d) All of the above
8. Bibliography given in a research report
   (a) shows vast knowledge of the researcher
   (b) helps those interested in further research
   (c) has no relevance to research
   (d) All of the above
9. Fundamental research reflects the ability to
   (a) Synthesise new ideals
   (b) Expound new principles
   (c) Evaluate the existing material concerning research
   (d) Study the existing literature regarding various topics
10. The study in which the investigators attempt to trace an effect is known as
    (a) Survey Research
    (b) *Ex-post Facto* Research

(c) Historical Research
(d) Summative Research

Read the following passage and answer the questions 11 to 15:

All political systems need to mediate the relationship between private wealth and public power. Those that fail risk a dysfunctional government captured by wealthy interests. Corruption is one symptom of such failure with private willingness-to-pay trumping public goals. Private individuals and business firms pay to get routine services and to get to the head of the bureaucratic queue. They pay to limit their taxes, avoid costly regulations, obtain contracts at inflated prices and get concessions and privatised firms at low prices. If corruption is endemic, public officials—both bureaucrats and elected officials—may redesign programs and propose public projects with few public benefits and many opportunities for private profit. Of course, corruption, in the sense of bribes, pay-offs and kickbacks, is only one type of government failure. Efforts to promote "good governance' must be broader than anti-corruption campaigns. Governments may be honest but inefficient because no one has an incentive to work productively, and narrow elites may capture the state and exert excess influence on policy. Bribery may induce the lazy to work hard and permit those not in the inner circle of cronies to obtain benefits. However, even in such cases, corruption cannot be confined to 'functional' areas. It will be a temptation whenever private benefits are positive. It may be a reasonable response to a harsh reality but, over time, it can facilitate a spiral into an even worse situation.

11. The governments which fail to focus on the relationship between private wealth and public power are likely to become
(a) Functional
(b) Dysfunctional
(c) Normal functioning
(d) Good governance

12. One important symptom of bad governance is
(a) Corruption
(b) High taxes
(c) Complicated rules and regulations
(d) High prices

13. When corruption is rampant, public officials always aim at many opportunities for:
(a) Public benefits (b) Public profit
(c) Private profit (d) Corporate gains

14. Productivity linked incentives to public/private officials is one of the indicatives for
(a) Efficient government
(b) Bad governance
(c) Inefficient government
(d) Corruption

15. The spiralling corruption can only be contained by promoting
(a) Private profit
(b) Anti-corruption campaign
(c) Good governance
(d) Pay-offs and kickbacks

16. Press Council of India is located at
(a) Chennai (b) Mumbai
(c) Kolkata (d) Delhi

17. Adjusting the photo for publication by cutting is technically known as
(a) Photo cutting
(b) Photo bleeding
(c) Photo cropping
(d) Photo adjustment

18. Feedback of a message comes from
(a) Satellite (b) Media
(c) Audience (d) Communicator

19. Collection of information in advance before designing communication strategy is known as

(a) Feedback (b) Feed-forward
(c) Research study (d) Opinion poll

20. The aspect ratio of TV screen is
(a) 4:3 (b) 4:2
(c) 3:5 (d) 2:3

21. Which is the number that comes next in the sequence?
9, 8, 8, 8, 7, 8, 6, —
(a) 5 (b) 6
(c) 8 (d) 4

22. If in a certain language PUNCTUAL is coded as 16598623, how would ACTUPULN be coded?
(a) 834536 (b) 29861635
(c) 834530 (d) 834539

23. The question to be answered by factorial analysis of the quantitative data does not explain one of the following
(a) Is 'X' related to 'Y'?
(b) How is 'X' related to 'Y'?
(c) How does 'X' affect the dependent variable 'Y' at different levels of another independent variable 'K' or 'M'?
(d) How is 'X' by 'K' related to 'M'?

24. January 12, 1980 was Saturday, what day was January 12, 1979?
(a) Saturday (b) Friday
(c) Sunday (d) Thursday

25. How many Mondays are there in a particular month of a particular year, if the month ends on Wednesday?
(a) 5 (b) 4
(c) 3 (d) None of these

26. From the given four statements, select the two which cannot be true but yet both can be false. Choose the right pair.
1. All men are mortal
2. Some men are mortal
3. No man is mortal
4. Some men are not mortal

(a) 1 and 2 (b) 3 and 4
(c) 1 and 3 (d) 2 and 4

27. A Syllogism must have
(a) Three terms (b) Four terms
(c) Six terms (d) Five terms

28. Copula is that part of proposition which denotes the relationship between
(a) Subject and predicate
(b) Known and unknown
(c) Major premise and minor premise
(d) Subject and object

29. "E" denotes
(a) Universal Negative Proposition
(b) Particular Affirmative Proposition
(c) Universal Affirmative Proposition
(d) Particular Negative Proposition

30. 'A' is the father of 'C' and 'D' is the son of 'B'. 'E' is the brother of 'A'. If 'C' is the sister of 'D' how is 'B' related to 'E'?
(a) Daughter (b) Husband
(c) Sister-in-law (d) Brother-in-law

31. Which of the following methods will you choose to prepare choropleth map of India showing urban density of population?
(a) Quartiles (b) Quintiles
(c) Mean and SD (d) Break-point

32. Which of the following methods is best suited to show on a map the types of crops being grown in a region?
(a) Choropleth (b) Chorochromatic
(c) Choroschematic (d) Isopleth

33. A ratio represents the relation between
(a) Part and Part
(b) Part and Whole
(c) Whole and Whole
(d) All of the above

34. Out of four numbers, the average of the first three numbers is thrice the fourth number. If the average of the four numbers is 5, the fourth number is

(a) 4.5 (b) 5
(c) 2 (d) 4

35. Circle graphs are used to show
(a) How various sections share in the whole
(b) How various parts are related to the whole
(c) How one whole is related to other wholes
(d) How one part is related to other parts

36. On the keyboard of computer each character has an "ASCII" value which stands for
(a) American Stock Code for Information Interchange
(b) American Standard Code for Information Interchange
(c) African Standard Code for Information Interchange
(d) Adaptable Standard Code for Information Change

37. Which part of the Central Processing Unit (CPU) performs calculation and makes decisions
(a) Arithmetic Logic Unit
(b) Alternating Logic Unit
(c) Alternate Local Unit
(d) American Logic Unit

38. "Dpi" stands for
(a) Dots per inch
(b) Digits per unit
(c) Dots pixel inch
(d) Diagrams per inch

39. The process of laying out a document with text, graphics, headlines and photographs is involved in
(a) Deck Top Publishing
(b) Desk Top Printing
(c) Desk Top Publishing
(d) Deck Top Printing

40. Transfer of data from one application to another line is known as
(a) Dynamic Disk Exchange
(b) Dodgy Data Exchange
(c) Dogmatic Data Exchange
(d) Dynamic Data Exchange

41. Tsunami occurs due to
(a) Mild earthquakes and landslides in the oceans
(b) Strong earthquakes and landslides in the oceans
(c) Strong earthquakes and landslides in mountains
(d) Strong earthquakes and landslides in deserts

42. Which of the natural hazards have big effect on Indian people each year?
(a) Cyclones (b) Floods
(c) Earthquakes (d) Landslides

43. Comparative Environment Impact Assessment study is to be conducted for
(a) the whole year
(b) three seasons excluding monsoon
(c) any three seasons
(d) the worst season

44. Sea level rise results primarily due to
(a) Heavy rainfall
(b) Melting of glaciers
(c) Submarine volcanism
(d) Seafloor spreading

45. The plume rise in a coal based power plant depends on
1. Buoyancy
2. Atmospheric stability
3. Momentum of exhaust gases

Identify the correct code

Codes:
(a) Both (1) and (2) (b) Both (2) and (3)
(c) Both (1) and (3) (d) (1), (2) and (3)

46. Value education makes a student
(a) Good citizen
(b) Successful businessman

(c) Popular teacher
(d) Efficient manager

47. Networking of libraries through electronic media is known as
(a) Inflibnet (b) Libinfnet
(c) Internet (d) HTML

48. The University which telecasts interactive educational programs through its own channel is
(a) B.R. Ambedkar Open University, Hyderabad
(b) I.G.N.O.U.
(c) University of Pune
(d) Annamalai University

49. The Government established the University Grants Commission by an Act of Parliament in the year
(a) 1980 (b) 1948
(c) 1950 (d) 1956

50. Universities having central campus for imparting education are called
(a) Central Universities
(b) Deemed Universities
(c) Residential Universities
(d) Open Universities

ANSWERS

1. (d)	2. (a)	3. (a)	4. (b)	5. (a)
6. (c)	7. (d)	8. (b)	9. (b)	10. (b)
11. (b)	12. (a)	13. (c)	14. (a)	15. (c)
16. (d)	17. (c)	18. (c)	19. (d)	20. (a)
21. (c)	22. (b)	23. (c)	24. (b)	25. (d)
26. (b)	27. (a)	28. (b)	29. (a)	30. (d)
31. (b)	32. (c)	33. (b)	34. (c)	35. (a)
36. (a)	37. (a)	38. (a)	39. (c)	40. (d)
41. (b)	42. (b)	43. (a)	44. (b)	45. (d)
46. (a)	47. (a)	48. (b)	49. (d)	50. (b)

PAPER–II

Note: This paper contains fifty (50) objective type questions, each question carrying two (2) marks. All questions are compulsory.

1. Which of the following is incorrect?
(a) Towards a new public administration and Minnowbrook perspective: Frank Marini
(b) Public Administration in a time of Turbulence: Dwight Waldo
(c) A Study of Public Administration: L. D. White
(d) Approaches to Public Administration: Elton Mayo

2. According to Paul Appleby the best quality of a good administrator is:
(a) Intelligence (b) Loyalty
(c) Integrity (d) Self-Confidence

3. How many channels of control are mentioned by Henry Fayol?
(a) Four (b) Two
(c) Three (d) Five

4. Which of the following are British legacies?
(1) District Administration
(2) Ministerial responsibility
(3) Planning commission
(4) Civil service
(a) 1 & 4 (b) 1 & 2
(c) 3 & 4 (d) All of the above

5. Kothari Committee 1976 has made suggestions for:
(a) Educational Reforms
(b) Political Reforms
(c) Training Reforms
(d) Recruitment Reforms

6. Which of the following politicians and civil servants is not correctly related?

(a) T.T. Krishnamachari - H.M. Patel
(b) Gulzari Lal Nanda - L.P. Singh
(c) K. Hanumanthaiya - B.C. Ganguli
(d) Rajiv Gandhi - R.S. Talwar

7. The creator of "Zero-Based Budgeting" is:
(a) U.S. defence department
(b) Hoover Commission
(c) Peter A. Phyrr
(d) Guy Peters

8. Which state first established the Lok Adalats?
(a) Orissa (b) Rajasthan
(c) Gujarat (d) Maharastra

9. Which one of the following is the most effective means of Executive control of the administration?
(a) Appointment and removal of top officials
(b) Subordinate legislation
(c) Financial Administration
(d) Political Direction

10. Which of the following is incorrect?
(a) Montagu-Chelmsford Reforms 1939
(b) Kothari Committee 1976
(c) Administrative Reform commission 1966-70
(d) West Bengal Document on Centre-State relations 1977

11. Establishment officer of the Government of India reports directly to:
(a) Cabinet Secretary
(b) Chief Secretary
(c) Home Secretary
(d) Finance Secretary

12. Who among the following is the head of the Indian Government?
(a) The President
(b) The Prime Minister
(c) Both A & B
(d) None

13. Consider the following statements about civil service in a developing society
(1) It should act as an agent of change
(2) It should have a concern for societal equity
(3) It should have a concern for vested interests
(4) It should be politically neutral
Which of the above are correct? Choose the correct answer from the codes given below:
(a) 1 & 2 (b) 1, 2 & 3
(c) 1, 2 & 4 (d) 2, 3 & 4

14. Which one is not the form of organisation of public undertaking in India?
(a) Commission
(b) Department
(c) Statutory Corporation
(d) Holding Company

15. Budget is an instrument of control by:
(a) The Judiciary (b) The Legislature
(c) The Government (d) The Executive

16. Which one of the following is not a measure of central tendency?
(a) Correlation (b) Mean
(c) Mode (d) Median

17. Which one of the following is not a part of Panchayati Raj?
(a) Zilla Parishad
(b) Town Area Committee
(c) Gram Sabha
(d) Panchayat Samiti

18. According to 73rd Amendment, which of the following is the Maximum period for a Panchayati Raj body to remain suspended?
(a) Six months (b) One year
(c) Three months (d) Two years

19. Who wrote these words: "Public Administration is that part of the science of Administration which has to do with the government and thus concerns itself,

primarily with the executive branch, where the work of the Government is done":

(a) Urwick (b) Luther Gullick
(c) Willoughby (d) Nigro

20. "The field of administration is a field of business. It is removed from the hurry and strife of politics".
This is stated by:
(a) Marshall E. Dimmock
(b) Woodrow Wilson
(c) L.D. White
(d) Dwight Waldo

Note 21 to 30: Given below are two statements, one labelled as Assertion (A) and the other labelled as Reason (R). In the context of the two statements write the correct answer from the codes given below:

21. **Assertion (A):** Public Administration provides a professional input for the formulation of the public policy.
Reason (R): The administrators exercise much more power in the formulation of public policy than the formal description of their responsibilities suggest.
Choose the correct answer from the following answer code:
Codes:
(a) Both (A) and (R) are correct and (R) is the correct explanation of (A)
(b) Both (A) and (R) are correct but (R) is not the correct explanation of (A)
(c) (A) is true but (R) is false
(d) (A) is false but (R) is true

22. **Assertion (A):** The line of communication should not be interrupted during the time when the organization is functioning.
Reason (R): Organizational decisions are best made when the channels of communication are known.
Choose the correct answer from the following answer code:
Codes:
(a) Both (A) and (R) are correct and (R) is the correct explanation of (A)
(b) Both (A) and (R) are correct but (R) is not the correct explanation of (A)
(c) (A) is true but (R) is false
(d) (A) is false but (R) is true

23. **Assertion (A):** Unity of Command cannot exist without Unity of Direction.
Reason (R): If Unity of Command is violated, authority is undermined.
Choose the correct answer from the following answer code:
Codes:
(a) Both (A) and (R) are correct and (R) is the correct explanation of (A)
(b) Both (A) and (R) are correct but (R) is not the correct explanation of (A)
(c) (A) is true but (R) is false
(d) (A) is false but (R) is true

24. **Assertion (A):** There is a tendency on the part of the Government to intervene even in the delegations given to the Heads in matters of postings and transfers.
Reason (R): It is observed that the officials themselves approach the political masters in order to secure a better position or a more **lucrative** job.
Choose the correct answer from the following answer code:
Codes:
(a) Both (A) and (R) are correct and (R) is the correct explanation of (A)
(b) Both (A) and (R) are correct but (R) is not the correct explanation of (A)
(c) (A) is true but (R) is false
(d) (A) is false but (R) is true

25. **Assertion (A):** Local government institutions have largely failed to meet the needs of growing urban population.
Reason (R): There are no effective and adequate training arrangements for the

elected representatives and the administrative personnel.

Choose the correct answer from the following answer code:

Codes:

(a) Both (A) and (R) are correct and (R) is the correct explanation of (A)
(b) Both (A) and (R) are correct but (R) is not the correct explanation of (A)
(c) (A) is true but (R) is false
(d) (A) is false but (R) is true

26. **Assertion (A):** The unionization of the lower level of bureaucracy has destroyed not only the work culture and discipline but also demoralized the higher levels of bureaucracy.

Reason (R): There is a symbiosis between the politicians and the bureaucrats in that both share power in pursuit of their self-interest ends.

Choose the correct answer from the following answer code:

Codes:

(a) Both (A) and (R) are correct and (R) is the correct explanation of (A)
(b) Both (A) and (R) are correct but (R) is not the correct explanation of (A)
(c) (A) is true but (R) is false
(d) (A) is false but (R) is true

27. **Assertion (A):** Rational policy making is not feasible in the public sector.

Reason (R): Human rationality is limited in terms of the existence of multiple values.

Choose the correct answer from the following answer code:

Codes:

(a) Both (A) and (R) are correct and (R) is the correct explanation of (A)
(b) Both (A) and (R) are correct but (R) is not correct explanation of (A)
(c) (A) is true but (R) is false
(d) (A) is false but (R) is true

28. **Assertion (A):** The state should abdicate its authority with a view to reducing disparities.

Reason (R): Reducing disparities is the crucial aspect of the political dimension of governance in the state.

Choose the correct answer from the following answer code:

Codes:

(a) Both (A) and (R) are correct and (R) is the correct explanation of (A)
(b) Both (A) and (R) are correct but (R) is not the correct explanation of (A)
(c) (A) is true but (R) is false
(d) (A) is false but (R) is true

29. **Assertion (A):** In Rigg's prismatic society nepotism and favouritism play a dominant role in the making of appointments to various administrative posts.

Reason (R): The behaviour and performance of the 'sala' officer are influenced by rational thinking and existing laws.

Choose the correct answer from the following answer code:

Codes:

(a) Both (A) and (R) are correct and (R) is the correct explanation of (A)
(b) Both (A) and (R) are correct but (R) is not the correct explanation of (A)
(c) (A) is true but (R) is false
(d) (A) is false but (R) is true

30. **Assertion (A):** Adequate scrutiny by Parliament of the rules and regulations makes delegated legislation grow into despotism.

Reason (R): In a democratic country like India, it is expedient to delegate law making authority to the ministries for making rules and regulations.

Choose the correct answer from the following answer code:

Codes:
(a) Both (A) and (R) are correct and (R) is the correct explanation of (A)
(b) Both (A) and (R) are correct but (R) is not the correct explanation of (A)
(c) (A) is true but (R) is false
(d) (A) is false but (R) is true

31. Arrange the following in order of their precedence.
    1. R.A. Gopalaswamy : Report on the Machinery of Government.
    2. V.T. Krishnamchari : Report on Indian and State Administrative Services.
    3. Satish Chandra : Report on the Recruitment of Civil Services.
    4. D.S. Kothari : Report on Recruitment Policy and Selection Methods.
    5. A.D. Gorwala : Report on Public Administration.

Codes:
(a) 1, 2, 3, 4, 5 (b) 5, 1, 2, 4, 3
(c) 5, 1, 3, 2, 4 (d) 1, 5, 2, 3, 4

32. Arrange following in the order of precedence:
    1. Minnowbrook Conference
    2. Hawthorne Experiment
    3. Setting up of Comparative Administrative Group (CAG)
    4. 73rd Amendment
    5. Right to Information

Codes:
(a) 1, 2, 3, 4, 5 (b) 2, 3, 1, 4, 5
(c) 4, 5, 1, 2, 3 (d) 1, 2, 4, 5, 3

33. Arrange these approaches to the study of Public Administration in the order of their precedence:
    1. Structural Approach
    2. Scientific Management Approach
    3. Behavioural Approach
    4. System Approach

Codes:
(a) 1, 2, 3, 4 (b) 1, 2, 4, 3
(c) 4, 3, 1, 2 (d) 1, 4, 2, 3

34. Arrange the following committee/ commissions in order of their submission of reports by writing first the committee which submitted its report first:
    1. Haldane Committee
    2. Masterman Committee
    3. Fulton Committee
    4. Northcote-Trevelyan Committee
    5. Aitchison Commission

Codes:
(a) 4, 5, 1, 2, 3 (b) 5, 4, 1, 3, 2
(c) 4, 5, 2, 3, 1 (d) 4, 5, 2, 1, 3

35. Arrange the following needs in accordance with Maslow's theory:
    1. Need for food
    2. Need to belong to a social group
    3. Need to be free from danger
    4. Need to prove his worth
    5. Need to get appreciation

Codes:
(a) 1, 2, 3, 4, 5 (b) 5, 4, 3, 2, 1
(c) 1, 3, 2, 5, 4 (d) 1, 2, 3, 5, 4

36. Match List I with List II and select the correct answer from the codes given below:

List I
(A) F.W. Taylor (B) Henri Fayol
(C) M.P. Follett (D) Max Weber

List II
(i) Ballot-Box Democracy
(ii) Legal-relation authority
(iii) 'Gangplank'
(iv) Functional foremanship

Codes:	**A**	**B**	**C**	**D**
(a)	(iv)	(iii)	(ii)	(i)
(b)	(iv)	(iii)	(i)	(ii)
(c)	(iii)	(iv)	(i)	(ii)
(d)	(iv)	(i)	(iii)	(ii)

37. Match List I with List II and select the correct answer from the codes given below:

List I

(A) Herbert Simon (B) Chester Barnard
(C) Dwight Waldo (D) Chris Argyris

List II

(i) The Administrative State
(ii) Models of Man
(iii) The Functions of the Executive
(iv) Personality and Organization

Codes:	**A**	**B**	**C**	**D**
(a)	(ii)	(iv)	(iii)	(i)
(b)	(i)	(iii)	(ii)	(iv)
(c)	(ii)	(iii)	(i)	(iv)
(d)	(iii)	(ii)	(iv)	(i)

38. Match List I and List II and select answer from the code given below:

List I	**List II**
(A) Additional Secretary	(i) Division
(B) Assistant	(ii) Department
(C) Director	(iii) Branch
(D) Under Secretary	(iv) Section
	(v) Wing

Codes:	**A**	**B**	**C**	**D**
(a)	(ii)	(i)	(iii)	(iv)
(b)	(i)	(ii)	(iv)	(iii)
(c)	(ii)	(iv)	(i)	(iii)
(d)	(i)	(iii)	(iv)	(ii)

39. Match List I and List II and select answer from the code given below:

List I

(A) Paul Appleby
(B) Woodrow Wilson
(C) M. Crozier
(D) H.G. Frederickson

List II

(i) The Bureaucratic Phenomenon
(ii) The study of administration
(iii) New Public Administration
(iv) Policy and Administration

Codes:	**A**	**B**	**C**	**D**
(a)	(iv)	(i)	(ii)	(iii)
(b)	(iv)	(ii)	(i)	(iii)
(c)	(ii)	(iv)	(iii)	(i)
(d)	(iv)	(iii)	(i)	(ii)

40. Match List I and List II and select answer from code given below.

List I

(A) Due process of law
(B) Two sets of courts
(C) Judicial review
(D) Rule of Law

List II

(i) India (ii) United Kingdom
(iii) France (iv) United States

Codes:	**A**	**B**	**C**	**D**
(a)	(iii)	(i)	(ii)	(iv)
(b)	(i)	(iii)	(ii)	(iv)
(c)	(i)	(iii)	(iv)	(ii)
(d)	(iv)	(iii)	(i)	(ii)

41. Match List I and List II and select the correct answer from code given below:

List I

(A) Herbert Simon (B) Charles Lindblow
(C) A. Etzioni (D) David Easton

List II

(i) Mixed-Scanning
(ii) Systems approach
(iii) Disjointed incrementalism
(iv) Programmed and non-programmed decision

Codes:	**A**	**B**	**C**	**D**
(a)	(iv)	(iii)	(i)	(ii)
(b)	(iii)	(iv)	(i)	(ii)
(c)	(iv)	(iii)	(ii)	(i)
(d)	(iii)	(ii)	(i)	(iv)

42. Match List I and List II and select correct answer from code given below:

List I

(A) Union Cabinet secretariat
(B) National Human Rights Commission
(C) National Planning Commission
(D) National Finance Commission

List II

(i) Assessing the material capital and human resources of the country
(ii) Governing grants-in-aid principles

(iii) Ensuring inter-ministerial coordination
(iv) Inquiring into violation of human rights

Codes:	A	B	C	D
(a)	(iii)	(iv)	(ii)	(i)
(b)	(iii)	(i)	(ii)	(iv)
(c)	(iii)	(iv)	(i)	(ii)
(d)	(iv)	(iii)	(i)	(ii)

43. Match List I and List II and select correct answer from code, given below:

List I

(A) Mary Follett (B) F. Taylor
(C) Rensis Likert (D) Henri Fayol

List II

(i) Interaction-influence system
(ii) Law of the situation
(iii) Wage-incentive system
(iv) Scalar Chain and gang plank

Codes:	A	B	C	D
(a)	(ii)	(i)	(iv)	(iii)
(b)	(ii)	(iii)	(iv)	(i)
(c)	(iii)	(iv)	(i)	(ii)
(d)	(ii)	(iii)	(i)	(iv)

44. Match List I and List II and select correct answer from codes given below:

List I

(A) Contingency theory
(B) Group theory
(C) Trait theory
(D) Socioeconomic theory

List II

(i) Environmental factors
(ii) Exchange process between leader and followers
(iii) Goals and structure of organization
(iv) Personality attributes of a leader

Codes:	A	B	C	D
(a)	(i)	(iv)	(ii)	(iii)
(b)	(iv)	(iii)	(i)	(ii)
(c)	(iv)	(i)	(ii)	(iii)
(d)	(i)	(ii)	(iv)	(iii)

45. Match List I and List II and select correct answer form codes given below:

List I

(A) Head of the State Secretariat Administration
(B) Head of the Revenue Administration
(C) Nominal Head of the State
(D) Real Head of the State Administration

List II

(i) Chief Minister (ii) Governor
(iii) Collector (iv) Chief Secretary

Code:	A	B	C	D
(a)	(iv)	(iii)	(i)	(ii)
(b)	(iv)	(i)	(ii)	(iii)
(c)	(iv)	(iii)	(ii)	(i)
(d)	(iii)	(iv)	(ii)	(i)

Read the passage below, and answer the questions that follow based on your understanding of the passage

The ARC recommended that the departments and ministries dealing with scientific and technical policies should appoint specialists on policy positions.

On the levels of decision-making in a ministry or department, the ARC recommended that, as a rule, there should be only two levels of considerations and decision below the minister. At the lower-middle level, a case may be considered by an under secretary or a deputy secretary and, at the higher level, by the Joint or additional secretary or the secretary. Beside, the commission argued for the adoption of the desk- officer system.

Though the Government of India has generally welcomed proposals for 'level-Jumping' and the desk-officer system in the decisional process, in practice, however, the conventional system of cases being handled at almost all levels seems to have taken deep roots. The need is to excercise greater rigour in applying the norms of efficiency in official systems. This would certainly require a commitment to the virtues of decentralization and delegation and reducing the intensity of centralizing behaviour of senior officials.

Regarding the desk-officer system, it may be noted that invincibility of, 'Babu bureaucracy' has not been questioned in any emphatic manner so far. The babus continue to initiate noting on files. They, in fact, have the advantage of official memory that is a requisite of decision-making. Though the role of the babu should not, and in fact, cannot, be eliminated in the decisional process, there remains, undoubtedly, a constant need for more intensive analysis and examination of issues at the higher echelons of administration.

46. The number of levels recommended by ARC for consideration under the Ministers were:
 (a) Three (b) Two
 (c) One (d) Four

47. Which of the following officials does not belong to the higher level?
 (a) Deputy Secretary
 (b) Joint Secretary
 (c) Additional Secretary
 (d) Secretary

48. Which of the following has not been recommended by the ARC?
 (a) Appointment of specialists on policy positions
 (b) Level Jumping
 (c) Desk-Officer System
 (d) Appointment of generalists on policy positions

49. Which of the following has become the most compelling feature of the administrative system?
 (a) Desk-Officer System
 (b) Babu Bureaucracy
 (c) Decision-Making
 (d) None of the above.

50. State the advantage of babus in administration:
 (a) Decentralisation
 (b) Delegation
 (c) Official Memory
 (d) Intensive Analysis

ANSWERS

1. (d)	2. (d)	3. (b)	4. (a)	5. (d)
6. (d)	7. (c)	8. (c)	9. (a)	10. (a)
11. (a)	12. (b)	13. (c)	14. (a)	15. (b)
16. (a)	17. (b)	18. (a)	19. (b)	20. (b)
21. (a)	22. (a)	23. (a)	24. (a)	25. (a)
26. (b)	27. (b)	28. (d)	29. (c)	30. (b)
31. (b)	32. (b)	33. (a)	34. (a)	35. (c)
36. (a)	37. (c)	38. (c)	39. (d)	40. (d)
41. (a)	42. (c)	43. (d)	44. (d)	45. (c)
46. (d)	47. (a)	48. (d)	49. (c)	50. (b)

DECEMBER–2006

Note: This paper contains fifty (50) objective type questions, each question carrying two (2) marks. All questions are compulsory.

PAPER–I

1. Which of the following is *not* instructional material?
   (a) Over Head Projector
   (b) Audio Casset
   (c) Printed Material
   (d) Transparency

2. Which of the following statement is *not* correct?
   (a) Lecture Method can develop reasoning
   (b) Lecture Method can develop knowledge
   (c) Lecture Method is one way process
   (d) During Lecture Method students are passive

3. The main objective of teaching at Higher Education Level is:
   (a) To prepare students to pass examination
   (b) To develop the capacity to take decisions
   (c) To give new information
   (d) To motivate students to ask questions during lecture

4. Which of the following statement is correct?
   (a) Reliability ensures validity
   (b) Validity ensures reliability
   (c) Reliability and validity are independent of each other
   (d) Reliability does not depend on objectivity

5. Which of the following indicates evaluation?
   (a) Ram got 45 marks out of 200
   (b) Mohan got 38 percent marks in English
   (c) Shyam got First Division in final examination
   (d) All the above

6. Research can be conducted by a person who:
   (a) has studied research methodology
   (b) holds a postgraduate degree
   (c) possesses thinking and reasoning ability
   (d) is a hard worker

7. Which of the following statements is correct ?
   (a) Objectives of research are stated in first chapter of the thesis
   (b) Researcher must possess analytical ability
   (c) Variability is the source of problem
   (d) All the above

8. Which of the following is *not* the Method of Research?
   (a) Observation (b) Historical
   (c) Survey (d) Philosophical

9. Research can be classified as:
   (a) Basic, Applied and Action Research
   (b) Quantitative and Qualitative Research
   (c) Philosophical, Historical, Survey and Experimental Research
   (d) All the above

10. The first step of research is :
    (a) Selecting a problem
    (b) Searching a problem
    (c) Finding a problem
    (d) Identifying a problem

Read the following passage and answer the question nos. 11 to 15:

After almost three decades of contemplating Swarovski-encrusted navels on increasing flat abs, the Mumbai film industry is on a discovery of India and itself. With budgets of over 30 crore each, four soon to be released movies by premier directors are exploring the idea of who we are and redefining who the other is. It is a fundamental question which the bling-bling, glam-sham and disham-disham tends to avoid. It is also a question which binds an audience when the lights go dim and the projector rolls : as a nation, who are we? As a people, where are we going?

The Germans coined a word for it, zeitgeist, which perhaps Yash Chopra would not care to pronounce. But at 72, he remains the person who can best capture it. After being the first to project the diasporic Indian on screen in Lamhe in 1991, he has returned to his roots in a new movie. Veer Zaara, set in 1986, where Pakistan, the traditional other, the part that got away, is the lover and the saviour. In Subhas Ghai's Kisna, set in 1947, the other is the English woman. She is not a memsahib, but a mehbooba. In Ketan Mehta's The Rising, the East India Englishman is not the evil oppressor of countless cardboard characterisations, which span the spectrum from Jewel in the Crown to Kranti, but an honourable friend.

This is Manoj Kumar's Desh Ki dharti with a difference : there is culture, not contentious politics; balle balle, not bombs : no dooriyan (distance), only nazdeekiyan (closeness).

All four films are heralding a new hero and heroine. The new hero is fallible and vulnerable, committed to his dharma, but also not afraid of failure - less of a boy and more of a man. He even has a grown up name : Veer Pratap Singh in Veer-Zaara and Mohan Bhargav in Swades. The new heroine is not a babe, but often a bebe, dressed in traditional Punjabi clothes, often with the stereotypical body type as well, as in Bride and Prejudice of Gurinder Chadha.

11. Which word Yash Chopra would not be able to pronounce?
    (a) Bling + bling (b) Zeitgeist
    (c) Montaz (d) Dooriyan

12. Who made Lamhe in 1991?
    (a) Subhash Ghai (b) Yash Chopra
    (c) Aditya Chopra (d) Sakti Samanta

13. Which movie is associated with Manoj Kumar?
    (a) Jewel in the Crown
    (b) Kisna
    (c) Zaara
    (d) Desh Ki dharti

14. Which is the latest film by Yash Chopra?
    (a) Deewar
    (b) Kabhi Kabhi
    (c) Dilwale Dulhaniya Le Jayenge
    (d) Veer Zaara

15. Which is the dress of the heroine in Veer-Zaara ?
    (a) Traditional Gujarati Clothes
    (b) Traditional Bengali Clothes
    (c) Traditional Punjabi Clothes
    (d) Traditional Madrasi Clothes

16. Which one of the following can be termed as verbal communication?
    (a) Prof. Sharma delivered the lecture in the class room.
    (b) Signal at the cross-road changed from green to orange.

(c) The child was crying to attract the attention of the mother.
(d) Dipak wrote a letter for leave application.

17. Which is the 24 hours English Business news channel in India?
(a) Zee News (b) NDTV 24×7
(c) CNBC (d) India News

18. Consider the following statements in communication:
(i) Hema Malini is the Chairperson of the Children's Film Society, India.
(ii) Yash Chopra is the Chairman of the Central Board of Film Certification of India.
(iii) Sharmila Tagore is the Chairperson of National Film Development Corporation.
(iv) Dilip Kumar, Raj Kapoor and Preeti Zinta have all been recipients of Dada Saheb Phalke Award.
Which of the statements given above is/are correct?
(a) (i) and (iii) (b) (ii) and (iii)
(c) (iv) only (d) (iii) only

19. Which of the following pair is *not* correctly matched?
(a) N. Ram : The Hindu
(b) Barkha Dutt : Zee News
(c) Pranay Roy : NDTV 24×7
(d) Prabhu Chawla : Aaj tak

20. "Because you deserve to know" is the punchline used by:
(a) The Times of India
(b) The Hindu
(c) Indian Express
(d) Hindustan Times

21. In the sequence of numbers 8, 24, 12, X, 18, 54 the missing number X is:
(a) 26 (b) 24
(c) 36 (d) 32

22. If A stands for 5, B for 6, C for 7, D for 8 and so on, then the following numbers stand for 17, 19, 20, 9 and 8:
(a) PLANE (b) MOPED
(c) MOTOR (d) TONGA

23. The letters in the first set have certain relationship. On the basis of this relationship what is the right choice for the second set?
AST : BRU : : NQV : ?
(a) ORW (b) MPU
(c) MRW (d) OPW

24. In a certain code, PAN is written as 31 and PAR as 35. In this code PAT is written as:
(a) 30 (b) 37
(c) 38 (d) 39

25. The sides of a triangle are in the ratio of $\frac{1}{2}:\frac{1}{3}:\frac{1}{4}$. If its perimeter is 52 cm, the length of the smallest side is:
(a) 9 cm (b) 10 cm
(c) 11 cm (d) 12 cm

26. Which one of the following statements is completely non-sensical?
(a) He was a bachelor, but he married recently.
(b) He is a bachelor, but he married recently.
(c) When he married, he was not a bachelor.
(d) When he was a bachelor, he was not married.

27. Which of the following statements are mutually contradictory?
(i) All flowers are not fragrant.
(ii) Most flowers are not fragrant.
(iii) None of the flowers is fragrant.
(iv) Most flowers are fragrant.
Choose the correct answer from the code given below:
Code:
(a) (i) and (ii) (b) (i) and (iii)
(c) (ii) and (iii) (d) (iii) and (iv)

28. Which of the following statements say the same thing?
    (i) "I am a teacher" (said by Arvind)
    (ii) "I am a teacher" (said by Binod)
    (iii) "My son is a teacher" (said by Binod's father)
    (iv) "My brother is a teacher" (said by Binod's sister)
    (v) "My brother is a teacher" (said by Binod's only sister)
    (vi) "My sole enemy is a teacher" (said by Binod's only enemy)

    Choose the correct answer from the code given below:

    Code:
    (a) (i) and (ii)
    (b) (ii), (iii), (iv) and (v)
    (c) (ii) and (vi)
    (d) (v) and (vi)

29. Which of the following are correct ways of arguing?
    (i) There can be no second husband without a second wife.
    (ii) Anil is a friend of Bob, Bob is a friend of Raj, hence Anil is a friend of Raj.
    (iii) A is equal to B, B is equal to C, hence A is equal to C.
    (iv) If everyone is a liar, then we cannot prove it.

    Choose the correct answer from the code given below:

    Code:
    (a) (iii) and (iv)
    (b) (i), (iii) and (iv)
    (c) (ii), (iii) and (iv)
    (d) (i), (ii), (iii) and (iv)

30. Which of the following statement/s are ALWAYS FALSE?
    (i) The sun will not rise in the East some day.
    (ii) A wooden table is not a table.
    (iii) Delhi city will be drowned under water.
    (iv) Cars run on water as fuel.

    Choose the correct answer from the code given below:

    Code:
    (a) (i), (iii) and (iv) (b) Only (iii)
    (c) (i), (ii) and (iii) (d) (ii) alone

Study the following graph and answer question numbers 31 to 33:

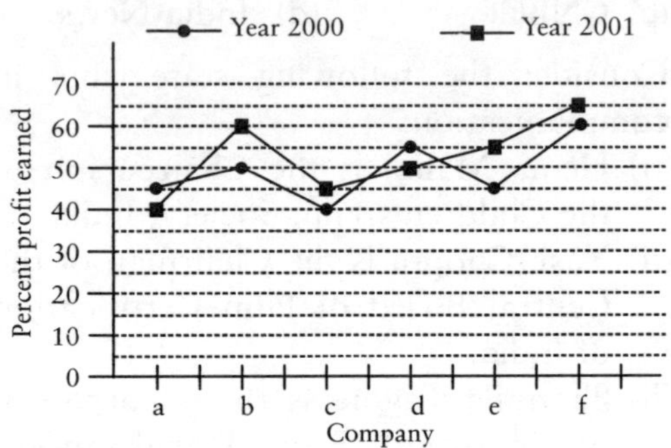

31. In the year 2000, which of the following Companies earned maximum percent profit?
    (a) a (b) b
    (c) d (d) f

32. In the year 2001, which of the following Companies earned minimum percent profit?
    (a) a (b) c
    (c) d (d) e

33. In the years 2000 and 2001, which of the following Companies earned maximum average percent profit?
    (a) f (b) e
    (c) d (d) b

34. Human Development Report for 'each' of the year at global level has been published by:
    (a) UNDP (b) WTO
    (c) IMF (d) World Bank

35. The number of students in four classes A, B, C, D and their respective mean marks obtained by each of the class are given below:

	Class A	Class B	Class C	Class D
Number of students	10	40	30	20
Arithmetic mean	20	30	50	15

The combined mean of the marks of four classes together will be:
(a) 32 (b) 50
(c) 20 (d) 15

36. LAN stands for:
(a) Local And National
(b) Local Area Network
(c) Large Area Network
(d) Live Area Network

37. Which of the following statement is correct?
(a) Modem is a software
(b) Modem helps in stabilizing the voltage
(c) Modem is the operating system
(d) Modem converts the analog signal into digital signal and vice-versa

38. Which of the following is the appropriate definition of a computer?
(a) Computer is a machine that can process information.
(b) Computer is an electronic device that can store, retrieve and process both qualitative and quantitative data quickly and accurately.
(c) Computer is an electronic device that can store, retrieve and quickly process only quantitative data.
(d) Computer is a machine that can store, retrieve and process quickly and accurately only qualitative information

39. Information and Communication Technology includes:
(a) On line learning
(b) Learning through the use of EDUSAT
(c) Web Based Learning
(d) All the above

40. Which of the following is the appropriate format of URL of e-mail?
(a) www_mail.com
(b) www@mail.com
(c) WWW@mail.com
(d) www.mail.com

41. The most significant impact of volcanic eruption has been felt in the form of:
(a) change in weather
(b) sinking of islands
(c) loss of vegetation
(d) extinction of animals

42. With absorption and decomposition of CO_2 in ocean water beyond desired level, there will be:
(a) decrease in temperature
(b) increase in salinity
(c) growth of phyto plankton
(d) rise in sea level

43. Arrange column II in proper sequence so as to match it with column I and choose the correct answer from the code given below:

Column I Water Quality	Column II pH Value
(A) Neutral	(i) 5
(B) Moderately acidic	(ii) 7
(C) Alkaline	(iii) 4
(D) Injurious	(iv) 8

Code:	(A)	(B)	(C)	(D)
(a)	(ii)	(iii)	(i)	(iv)
(b)	(i)	(iii)	(ii)	(iv)
(c)	(ii)	(i)	(iv)	(iii)
(d)	(iv)	(ii)	(iii)	(i)

44. The maximum emission of pollutants from fuel sources in India is caused by:
(a) Coal
(b) Firewood
(c) Refuse burning
(d) Vegetable waste product

45. The urbanisation process accounts for the wind in the urban centres during nights to remain:
(a) faster than that in rural areas
(b) slower than that in rural areas
(c) the same as that in rural areas
(d) cooler than that in rural areas

46. The University Grants Commission was constituted on the recommendation of:
(a) Dr. Sarvapalli Radhakrishnan Commission
(b) Mudaliar Commission
(c) Sargent Commission
(d) Kothari Commission

47. Which one of the following Articles of the Constitution of India safeguards the rights of Minorities to establish and run educational institutions of their own liking?
(a) Article 19 (b) Article 29
(c) Article 30 (d) Article 31

48. Match List I (Institutions) with List II (Functions) and select the correct answer by using the code given below:
List I (Institutions)
(A) Parliament
(B) C. & A.G.
(C) Ministry of Finance
(D) Executing Departments
List II (Functions)
(i) Formulation of Budget
(ii) Enactment of Budget
(iii) Implementation of Budget
(iv) Legality of expenditure
(v) Justification of Income

Code:	(A)	(B)	(C)	(D)
(a)	(iii)	(iv)	(ii)	(i)
(b)	(ii)	(iv)	(i)	(iii)
(c)	(v)	(iii)	(iv)	(ii)
(d)	(iv)	(ii)	(iii)	(v)

49. Foundation training to the newly recruited IAS (Probationers) is imparted by:
(a) Indian Institute of Public Administration
(b) Administrative Staff College of India
(c) L.B.S. National Academy of Administration
(d) Centre for Advanced Studies

50. Electoral disputes arising out of Presidential and Vice-Presidential Elections are settled by:
(a) Election Commission of India
(b) Joint Committee of Parliament
(c) Supreme Court of India
(d) Central Election Tribunal

ANSWERS

1. (d)	2. (a)	3. (b)	4. (b)	5. (d)
6. (c)	7. (d)	8. (b)	9. (d)	10. (b)
11. (b)	12. (b)	13. (d)	14. (d)	15. (c)
16. (c)	17. (c)	18. (d)	19. (b)	20. (d)
21. (c)	22. (b)	23. (d)	24. (b)	25. (d)
26. (b)	27. (b)	28. (b)	29. (a)	30. (d)
31. (d)	32. (a)	33. (a)	34. (a)	35. (a)
36. (b)	37. (d)	38. (b)	39. (d)	40. (b)
41. (a)	42. (c)	43. (c)	44. (c)	45. (b)
46. (a)	47. (c)	48. (b)	49. (c)	50. (c)

PAPER–II

1. Which one of the following does not come within the ambit of classical theory?
(a) Scientific management theory
(b) Bureaucratic theory
(c) Formal organisation theory
(d) Systems theory

2. The letter 'CO' in 'POSDCORB' stands for:
(a) Cooperation (b) Coordination
(c) Control (d) Contribution

3. Who among the following developed the sociometric theory of leadership?
(a) Keith Davis (b) Jacob Moreno
(c) Helen Jenings (d) Max Weber

4. Which of the following are the principles of organisation?
(i) Staffing (ii) Budgeting
(iii) Hierarch (iv) Span of Control
Select the correct answer from the codes given below:
Codes:
(a) (ii) and (iii) (b) (i) and (iv)
(c) (iii) and (iv) (d) (ii) and (iv)

5. Who among the following is the main critic of the concept of 'Bounded Rationality'?
(a) Herbert Simon
(b) Charles Lindblom
(c) David Easton
(d) Waldo

6. Delegation could be:
(i) General (ii) Written
(iii) Downwards (iv) Upwards
Select the correct answer from the codes given below:
Codes:
(a) (i), (ii) and (iv) (b) (i), (ii) and (iii)
(c) (ii), (iii) and (iv) (d) (i), (iii) and (iv)

7. The concept of 'Charismatic Authority' was put forward by:
(a) Fredrick Taylor
(b) Herbert Simon
(c) Max Weber
(d) Fred Riggs

8. Who among the following advocated a shift in focus from Bureaucratic and Wilsonian models to a dispersed service-delivery system?
(a) Vincent Ostrom
(b) H. Frederickson
(c) Dwight Waldo
(d) Nicholas Henry

9. Which one of the following is not a staff agency in the U.S.A.?
(a) National Security Council
(b) Office of Budget and Management
(c) State Department
(d) The White House Office

10. Prior to 1971, the British Civil Service was divided into the following classes:
(i) Clerical (ii) Executive
(iii) Ministerial (iv) Administrative
Select the correct answer from the codes given below:
Codes:
(a) (i), (ii) and (iii) (b) (ii), (iii) and (iv)
(c) (i), (ii) and (iv) (d) (i), (iii) and (iv)

11. According to Riggs which one of the following is not a characteristic of 'Prismatic-Sala'?
(a) Polyandry (b) Overlapping
(c) Formalism (d) Heterogeneity

12. Macaulay Report on Civil Service was submitted in the year:
(a) 1853 (b) 1854
(c) 1858 (d) 1861

13. Prime Minister is appointed by the President under Article:
(a) 73 (b) 74
(c) 75(1) (d) 76

14. Using the codes given below identify the correct statements.
President's rule in a state can be proclaimed if:
(i) The Governor of a state sends a report recommending to that effect.
(ii) The Governor fails to send any report to that effect.
(iii) The Governor fails to discharge his constitutional duties.
(iv) The Governor dies.
Codes:
(a) (i) and (ii) (b) (i) and (iv)
(c) (ii) and (iv) (d) (iii) and (iv)

15. In India, the President enjoys the right not to give assent to:
    (a) Non-money bills (b) Money bills
    (c) Both (a) and (b) (d) None of these
16. The first Comptroller and Auditor General appointed by the Government of India was:
    (a) Narahari Rao (b) Ashok Chanda
    (c) K.C. Neogy (d) K. Santhanam
17. 74th Constitutional Amendment Act provides for:
    (i) a constitutional status for municipalities
    (ii) ward committees
    (iii) direct election of chairperson of a municipality
    (iv) district planning committee
    Select the correct answer from the codes given below:
    (a) (i), (ii) and (iii) (b) (ii), (iii) and (iv)
    (c) (i), (iii) and (iv) (d) (i), (ii) and (iv)
18. Who among the following popularized the case study method for the students and practitioners of public administration?
    (a) E.A. Bock (b) W.J. Goode
    (c) Selltiz (d) Harold Stein
19. The term 'World Bank' is commonly used for the:
    (a) International Monetary Fund
    (b) International Bank for Reconstruction and Development
    (c) International Bank for the United Nations
    (d) International Bank for Economic and Social Affairs
20. The main sources of revenue for urban local bodies are:
    (i) Sales Tax (ii) Octroi
    (iii) Property Tax (iv) Toll Tax
    Select the correct answer from the codes given below:
    Codes:
    (a) (i), (ii) and (iii) (b) (i), (ii) and (iv)
    (c) (i), (iii) and (iv) (d) (ii), (iii) and (iv)

Given below are two statements, one labelled as Assertion (A) and the other labelled as Reason (R). Examine these two statements carefully and state if the Assertion (A) and the Reason (R) are individually true and if so, whether the Reason is a correct explanation of Assertion:

Select the correct answer from the codes given below the question.

21. **Assertion (A):** Hierarchy leads to rigidity and affects human relationships in administration.
    Reason (R): Hierarchy is a device to achieve coherence in the organisation.
    Codes:
    (a) Both (A) and (R) are correct and (R) is the correct explanation of (A)
    (b) Both (A) and (R) are correct, but (R) is not the correct explanation of (A)
    (c) (A) is true but (R) is false
    (d) (A) is false but (R) is true
22. **Assertion (A):** According to Herbert Simon, a decision is a choice between alternative courses of action.
    Reason (R): Every decision consists of a logical combination of fact and value propositions.
    Codes:
    (a) Both (A) and (R) are correct and (R) is the correct explanation of (A)
    (b) Both (A) and (R) are correct, but (R) is not the correct explanation of (A)
    (c) (A) is true but (R) is false
    (d) (A) is false but (R) is true
23. **Assertion (A):** According to Bernard, Informal organisation precedes formal organisation.
    Reason (R): Informal organisation plays an important role in harnessing the efforts of the Individuals.

Codes:
(a) Both (A) and (R) are correct and (R) is the correct explanation of (A)
(b) Both (A) and (R) are correct, but (R) is not the correct explanation of (A)
(c) (A) is true but (R) is false
(d) (A) is false but (R) is true

24. **Assertion (A):** UPSC is an independent organisation.
Reason (R): UPSC is created by an act of Parliament.
Codes:
(a) Both (A) and (R) are true and (R) is the correct explanation of (A)
(b) Both (A) and (R) are true but (R) is not the correct explanation of (A)
(c) (A) is true but (R) is false
(d) (A) is false but (R) is true

25. **Assertion (A):** Lok Sabha cannot make any change in the taxation proposals submitted to it.
Reasoning (R): All taxation proposals are prepared in the executive organ of the government.
Codes:
(a) Both (A) and (R) are correct but (R) is the correct explanation of (A)
(b) Both (A) and (R) are correct, but (R) is not the correct explanation of (A)
(c) (A) is true but (R) is false
(d) (A) is false but (R) is true

26. **Assertion (A):** The position of council of ministers in a state is similar to that of the council of ministers at the union level.
Reason (R): The position of the Chief Minister is similar to that of the Prime Minister.
Codes:
(a) Both (A) and (R) are correct and (R) is the correct explanation of (A)
(b) Both (A) and (R) are correct, but (R) is not the correct explanation of (A)
(c) (A) is true but (R) is false
(d) (A) is false but (R) is true

27. **Assertion (A):** The crux of Development administration is societal change in tune with modernity.
Reason (R): Its focus is essentially on indigenous development which is sustainable.
Codes:
(a) Both (A) and (R) are correct and (R) is the correct explanation of (A)
(b) Both (A) and (R) are correct, but (R) is not the correct explanation of (A)
(c) (A) is true but (R) is false
(d) (A) is false but (R) is true

28. **Assertion (A):** Participatory observation is not always a correct method of research.
Reason (R): There is a communication deficit between the researcher and the target group.
Codes:
(a) Both (A) and (R) are true and (R) is the correct explanation of (A)
(b) Both (A) and (R) are true but (R) is not the correct explanation of (A)
(c) (A) is true but (R) is false
(d) (A) is false but (R) is true

29. **Assertion (A):** Reservation policy in the public services is a mandate from the Indian Constitution.
Reason (R): Reservation policy is conducive to the promotion of social justice.
Codes:
(a) Both (A) and (R) are correct and (R) is the correct explanation of (A)
(b) Both (A) and (R) are correct, but (R) is not the correct explanation of (A)
(c) (A) is true but (R) is false
(d) (A) is false but (R) is true

30. Which one of the following is NOT correct regarding old Public Administration?
(a) Non-responsive
(b) Instrument for administrative reform

(c) Non-ethical
(d) Bureaucratic

31. Arrange the following Concepts/Theories in order in which they appeared. Use the code given below:
(i) Democratic Centralism.
(ii) Intelligence Activity.
(iii) Grapevine Communication.
(iv) Public Choice
Codes:
(a) (ii), (i), (iv), (iii) (b) (i), (iv), (iii), (ii)
(c) (i), (ii), (iv), (iii) (d) (i), (ii), (iii), (iv)

32. Arrange the following approaches to the study of Public Administration in the sequence in which they came in vogue:
(i) Human Relations approach
(ii) Classical approach
(iii) Public Choice approach
(iv) Behavioural approach
Codes:
(a) (ii), (i), (iv) and (iii)
(b) (i), (ii), (iii) and (iv)
(c) (ii), (iv), (i) and (iii)
(d) (i), (iii), (iv) and (ii)

33. Arrange the experiments conducted by Elton Mayo in a chronological order:
(i) Textile Mill experiments
(ii) Illumination experiments
(iii) Bank wiring observation study
(iv) Mass interview programme
Codes:
(a) (i), (ii), (iv), (iii) (b) (i), (ii), (iii), (iv)
(c) (i), (iii), (iv), (ii) (d) (i), (iii), (ii), (iv)

34. Arrange the following stages of Budget-making in the parliament in order:
(i) Passing of Appropriation Bill
(ii) Passing of Finance Bill
(iii) Voting on Demands
(iv) General discussions
Codes:
(a) (i), (ii), (iii), (iv) (b) (iv), (iii), (i), (ii)
(c) (ii), (iii), (iv), (i) (d) (iii), (ii), (i), (iv)

35. The following are involved in the preparation of Five year plans. Arrange them in the order of the stages of their involvement:
(i) Planning Commission
(ii) National Development Council
(iii) Central Cabinet
(iv) Parliament
Codes:
(a) (i), (iii), (ii), (iv) (b) (i), (ii), (iii), (iv)
(c) (iv), (iii), (ii), (i) (d) (iii), (ii), (i), (iv)

36. Arrange the following in a chronological sequence using the codes given below:
(i) Rural-Urban Relationship Committee
(ii) Local Finance Enquiry Committee
(iii) L.M. Singhvi Committee
(iv) Ashok Mehta Committee
Codes:
(a) (i), (iii), (iv) and (ii)
(b) (ii), (i), (iv) and (iii)
(c) (ii), (iv), (iii) and (i)
(d) (i), (ii), (iii) and (iv)

37. Arrange the following according to chronological sequence using the codes given below:
(i) Pendleton Act
(ii) First Hoover Commission Report
(iii) Fulton Committee Report
(iv) Vohra Committee Report
Codes:
(a) (ii), (i), (iii), (iv) (b) (iii), (iv), (ii), (i)
(c) (i), (ii), (iii), (iv) (d) (ii), (iv), (iii), (i)

38. Broad stages of Indian Planning are given below. Arrange them in order:
(i) Formulation of Guidelines
(ii) Perspective Targeting
(iii) Preparation of approach paper
(iv) Publication of the Draft plan
Codes:
(a) (i), (ii), (iii), (iv) (b) (ii), (i), (iii), (iv)
(c) (iii), (iv), (ii), (i) (d) (iv), (iii), (i), (ii)

39. Match List I with List II and select the correct answer from the codes given below:

List I (Approach)
(A) Bureaucratic (B) Behavioural
(C) General Systems (D) Ecological

List II (Characteristics)
(i) Agraria-Industria
(ii) Legal-Rational
(iii) Negative Feed-Back
(iv) Quantification

Codes:	A	B	C	D
(a)	(i)	(iii)	(ii)	(iv)
(b)	(i)	(ii)	(iv)	(iii)
(c)	(ii)	(iii)	(i)	(iv)
(d)	(ii)	(iv)	(iii)	(i)

40. Match List I with List II and select the correct answer from the codes given below:

List I
(A) Elton Mayo (B) Chester Barnard
(C) Max Weber (D) David Osborne

List II
(i) Market-oriented government
(ii) Domination Authority
(iii) Human Relations approach
(iv) Informal organization

Codes:	A	B	C	D
(a)	(iii)	(iv)	(i)	(ii)
(b)	(iii)	(i)	(ii)	(iv)
(c)	(iii)	(iv)	(ii)	(i)
(d)	(iv)	(iii)	(ii)	(i)

41. Match List I with List II and select the correct answer from the codes given below:

List I
(A) The head of revenue Administration in a state
(B) The head of Secretariat Administration in a State
(C) The constitutional-legal head of a State
(D) The real head of State Administration

List II
(i) Governor
(ii) Chief Secretary
(iii) Chief Minister
(iv) Member Board of Revenue/Revenue Commissioner

Codes:	A	B	C	D
(a)	(i)	(iv)	(iii)	(ii)
(b)	(ii)	(iii)	(iv)	(i)
(c)	(iv)	(ii)	(i)	(iii)
(d)	(iv)	(iii)	(ii)	(i)

42. Match List I with List II and select the correct answer:

List I
(A) France (B) Britain
(C) USA (D) USSR

List II
(i) Administrative Law
(ii) Committed Bureaucracy
(iii) Politically Neutral Bureaucracy
(iv) Regulatory Commissions

Codes:	A	B	C	D
(a)	(i)	(iii)	(iv)	(ii)
(b)	(ii)	(iv)	(iii)	(i)
(c)	(i)	(ii)	(iv)	(iii)
(d)	(iv)	(iii)	(i)	(ii)

43. Match List I with List II:

List I
(A) Classical Theory of Organisation
(B) Functional foremanship
(C) Span of Control
(D) Scalar Process

List II
(i) J.D. Mooney (ii) V.A. Graicunas
(iii) Henry Fayol (iv) F.W. Taylor

Codes:	A	B	C	D
(a)	(iii)	(iv)	(ii)	(i)
(b)	(iii)	(i)	(iv)	(ii)
(c)	(ii)	(i)	(iii)	(iv)
(d)	(i)	(iii)	(iv)	(ii)

44. Match List I with List II:

List I
(A) Human Relations
(B) Policy Science

(C) Politics-administration Separation
(D) Science of Management

List II

(i) Harold Lasswell
(ii) Elton Mayo
(iii) Woodrow Wilson
(iv) W.F. Willoughby

Codes:	A	B	C	D
(a)	(ii)	(i)	(iii)	(iv)
(b)	(i)	(iii)	(iv)	(ii)
(c)	(ii)	(iii)	(iv)	(i)
(d)	(iii)	(iv)	(i)	(ii)

45. Match the following:

List I

(A) A.D. Gorwala Report
(B) Krishnamachari Report
(C) Gopala Swamy Ayyangar Report
(D) D.S. Kothari Report

List II

(i) 1962 (ii) 1951
(iii) 1952 (iv) 1977

Codes:	A	B	C	D
(a)	(ii)	(i)	(iii)	(iv)
(b)	(iii)	(iv)	(i)	(ii)
(c)	(iv)	(iii)	(ii)	(i)
(d)	(i)	(ii)	(iii)	(iv)

Read the following passage below and answer the questions that follow, based on your understanding, of the passage:

Less attention has been paid in the literature to the variance in the power that state bureaucracies exert over and draw from society. Wealthy bureaucracies and/or bureaucracies with great control over policy are not necessarily bureaucracies that secure effective implementation of state policy. Relevant here may be the current distinction between 'weak' and 'strong' states. Weak states (in at least one acceptation of the term) may be those unable to collect taxes, enforce law and order, control borders, and in general assert and maintain statehood.

Even when states are strong enough to maintain sovereignty, their bureaucracies mobilize varying degrees of consent, trust and support from the population. Cultural variables seem important in explaining the differential capability of government bureaucracies, at similar levels of modernization, in securing citizen support and cooperation, in the implementation of government programs. (Almond and Verba 1963; Peters 1978; Pye and Verba 1965; Wildavsky 1986)

Studies of bureaucratic power tend to have two limitations. They tend to use reputational methods for identifying power patterns, and they tend to see power in Weberian terms, as 'Herrschaft' (domination) rather than in terms of collective empowerment (Public-Private Partnership).

46. Wealthy bureaucracies:
 (a) Don't always implement state policy effectively
 (b) Control society efficiently
 (c) Make weak state system
 (d) Create strong states

47. Weak States:
 (a) Maintain Statehood
 (b) Enforce Law and Order
 (c) Manage Borders
 (d) Fail to collect taxes

48. Cultural Variables are important for:
 (a) Securing citizen co-operation
 (b) Develop social sectors
 (c) To maintain law and order
 (d) To earn maximum revenue

49. Bureaucratic power has been studied by:
 (a) Marx (b) Lenin
 (c) Max Weber (d) Marini

50. Which one is not correct?
 (a) Citizen co-operation is required for implementation of government programmes
 (b) Strong states maintain sovereignty

(c) Bureaucracies have limitations
(d) Studies on bureaucracy do not use reputational methods

ANSWERS

1. (d)	2. (b)	3. (b)	4. (c)	5. (a)
6. (b)	7. (c)	8. (c)	9. (a)	10. (c)
11. (a)	12. (b)	13. (c)	14. (a)	15. (a)
16. (a)	17. (d)	18. (d)	19. (b)	20. (d)
21. (d)	22. (a)	23. (c)	24. (c)	25. (d)
26. (b)	27. (a)	28. (a)	29. (a)	30. (b)
31. (b)	32. (a)	33. (a)	34. (b)	35. (a)
36. (b)	37. (c)	38. (b)	39. (d)	40. (c)
41. (c)	42. (a)	43. (a)	44. (a)	45. (a)
46. (a)	47. (d)	48. (a)	49. (c)	50. (d)

JUNE–2006

Note: This paper contains fifty (50) objective type questions, each question carrying two (2) marks. All questions are compulsory.

PAPER–I

1. Which of the following comprise teaching skill:
   (a) Black Board writing
   (b) Questioning
   (c) Explaining
   (d) All the above

2. Which of the following statements is most appropriate?
   (a) Teachers can teach.
   (b) Teachers help can create in a student a desire to learn.
   (c) Lecture Method can be used for developing thinking.
   (d) Teachers are born.

3. The first Indian chronicler of Indian history was :
   (a) Megasthanese (b) Fahiyan
   (c) Huan Tsang (d) Kalhan

4. Which of the following statements is correct?
   (a) Syllabus is a part of curriculum.
   (b) Syllabus is an annexure to curriculum.
   (c) Curriculum is the same in all educational institutions affiliated to a particular university.
   (d) Syllabus is not the same in all educational institutions affiliated to a particular university.

5. Which of the two given options is of the level of understanding?
   (I) Define noun.
   (II) Define noun in your own words.
   (a) Only I (b) Only II
   (c) Both I and II (d) Neither I nor II

6. Which of the following options are the main tasks of research in modern society?
   (I) to keep pace with the advancement in knowledge.
   (II) to discover new things.
   (III) to write a critique on the earlier writings.
   (IV) to systematically examine and critically analyse the investigations/sources with objectivity.
   (a) IV, II and I (b) I, II and III
   (c) I and III (d) II, III and IV

7. Match List I (Interviews) with List II (Meaning) and select the correct answer from the code given below:

   List I (Interviews)
   (A) Structured interviews
   (B) Unstructured interviews
   (C) Focussed interviews
   (D) Clinical interviews

   List II (Meaning)
   (i) greater flexibility approach
   (ii) attention on the questions to be answered
   (iii) individual life experience
   (iv) Pre determined question
   (v) non-directive

Code:	A	B	C	D
(a)	(iv)	(i)	(ii)	(iii)
(b)	(ii)	(iv)	(i)	(iii)
(c)	(v)	(ii)	(iv)	(i)
(d)	(i)	(iii)	(v)	(iv)

8. What do you consider as the main aim of inter disciplinary research?
   (a) To bring out holistic approach to research.
   (b) To reduce the emphasis of single subject in research domain.
   (c) To over simplify the problem of research.
   (d) To create a new trend in research methodology.
9. One of the aims of the scientific method in research is to:
   (a) improve data interpretation
   (b) eliminate spurious relations
   (c) confirm triangulation
   (d) introduce new variables
10. The depth of any research can be judged by:
    (a) title of the research.
    (b) objectives of the research.
    (c) total expenditure on the research.
    (d) duration of the research.

Read the following passage and answer the questions 11 to 15:

The superintendence, direction and control of preparation of electoral rolls for, and the conduct of, elections to Parliament and State Legislatures and elections to the offices of the President and the Vice - President of India are vested in the Election Commission of India. It is an independent constitutional authority.

Independence of the Election Commission and its insulation from executive interference is ensured by a specific provision under Article 324 (5) of the Constitution that the chief Election Commissioner shall not be removed from his office except in like manner and on like grounds as a Judge of the Supreme Court and conditions of his service shall not be varied to his disadvantage after his appointment.

In C.W.P. No. 4912 of 1998 (Kushra Bharat Vs. Union of India and others), the Delhi High Court directed that information relating to Government dues owed by the candidates to the departments dealing with Government accommodation, electricity, water, telephone and transport etc. and any other dues should be furnished by the candidates and this information should be published by the election authorities under the commission.

11. The text of the passage reflects or raises certain questions:
    (a) The authority of the commission can not be challenged.
    (b) This would help in stopping the criminalization of Indian politics.
    (c) This would reduce substantially the number of contesting candidates.
    (d) This would ensure fair and free elections.
12. According to the passage, the Election Commission is an independent constitutional authority. This is under Article No.:
    (a) 324 (b) 356
    (c) 246 (d) 161
13. Independence of the Commission means :
    (a) have a constitutional status.
    (b) have legislative powers.
    (c) have judicial powers.
    (d) have political powers.
14. Fair and free election means:
    (a) transparency
    (b) to maintain law and order
    (c) regional considerations
    (d) role for pressure groups
15. The Chief Election Commissioner can be removed from his office under Article:
    (a) 125 (b) 352
    (c) 226 (d) 324
16. The function of mass communication of supplying information regarding the

processes, issues, events and societal developments is known as:
(a) content supply (b) surveillance
(c) gratification (d) correlation

17. The science of the study of feedback systems in humans, animals and machines is known as:
(a) cybernetics
(b) reverse communication
(c) selectivity study
(d) response analysis

18. Networked media exist in inter-connected:
(a) social environments
(b) economic environments
(c) political environments
(d) technological environments

19. The combination of computing, telecommunications and media in a digital atmosphere is referred to as:
(a) online communication
(b) integrated media
(c) digital combine
(d) convergence

20. A dialogue between a human-being and a computer programme that occurs simultaneously in various forms is described as:
(a) man-machine speak
(b) binary chat
(c) digital talk
(d) interactivity

21. Insert the missing number:

$\frac{16}{32}, \frac{15}{33}, \frac{17}{31}, \frac{14}{34}, ?$

(a) $\frac{19}{35}$ (b) $\frac{19}{30}$
(c) $\frac{18}{35}$ (d) $\frac{18}{30}$

22. Monday falls on 20th March 1995. What was the day on 3rd November 1994?
(a) Thursday (b) Sunday
(c) Tuesday (d) Saturday

23. The average of four consecutive even numbers is 27. The largest of these numbers is
(a) 36 (b) 32
(c) 30 (d) 28

24. In a certain code, FHQK means GIRL. How will WOMEN be written in the same code?
(a) VNLDM (b) FHQKN
(c) XPNFO (d) VLNDM

25. At what time between 4 and 5 O'Clock will the hands of a watch point in opposite directions?
(a) 45 min. past 4
(b) 40 min. past 4
(c) $50\frac{4}{11}$ min. past 4
(d) $54\frac{6}{11}$ min. past 4

26. Which of the following conclusions is logically valid based on statement given below ?

Statement: Most teachers are hard working.

Conclusions: (I) Some teachers are hard working.
(II) Some teachers are not hard working.

(a) Only (I) is implied
(b) Only (II) is implied
(c) Both (I) and (II) are implied
(d) Neither (I) nor (II) is implied

27. Who among the following can be asked to make a statement in Indian Parliament?
(a) Any MLA
(b) Chief of Army Staff
(c) Solicitor General of India
(d) Mayor of Delhi

28. Which of the following conclusions is logically valid based on statement given below ?

Statement : Most of the Indian states existed before independence.

Conclusions : (I) Some Indian States existed before independence.

(II) All Indian States did not exist before independence.

(a) only (I) is implied
(b) only (II) is implied
(c) Both (I) and (II) are implied
(d) Neither (I) nor (II) is implied

29. Water is always involved with landslides. This is because it:
(a) reduces the shear strength of rocks
(b) increases the weight of the overburden
(c) enhances chemical weathering
(d) is a universal solvent

30. Direction for this question:
Given below are two statements (A) and (B) followed by two conclusions (i) and (ii). Considering the statements to be true, indicate which of the following conclusions logically follow from the given statements by selecting one of the four response alternatives given below the conclusion:

Statements: (A) all businessmen are wealthy.

(B) all wealthy people are hard working.

Conclusions: (i) All businessmen are hard working.

(ii) All hardly working people are not wealthy

(a) Only (i) follows
(b) Only (ii) follows
(c) Only (i) and (ii) follows
(d) Neither (i) nor (ii) follows

31. Using websites to pour out one's grievances is called:
(a) cyberventing (b) cyber ranting
(c) web hate (d) **web plea**

32. In web search, finding a large number of documents with very little relevant information is termed:
(a) poor recall
(b) web crawl
(c) poor precision rate
(d) poor web response

33. The concept of connect intelligence is derived from:
(a) virtual reality
(b) fuzzy logic
(c) bluetooth technology
(d) value added networks

34. Use of an ordinary telephone as an Internet applicance is called :
(a) voicenet (b) voice telephone
(c) voice line (d) voice portal

35. Video transmission over the Internet that looks like delayed livecasting is called:
(a) virtual video
(b) direct broadcast
(c) video shift
(d) real-time video

36. Which is the smallest North-east State in India?
(a) Tripura (b) Meghalaya
(c) Mizoram (d) Manipur

37. Tamil Nadu coastal belt has drinking water shortage due to:
(a) high evaporation
(b) sea water flooding due to tsunami
(c) over exploitation of ground water by tubewells
(d) seepage of sea water

38. While all rivers of Peninsular India flow into the Bay of Bengal, Narmada and Tapti flow into the Arabian Sea because these two rivers:

(a) Follow the slope of these rift valleys
(b) The general slope of the Indian peninsula is from east to west
(c) The Indian peninsula north of the Satpura ranges, is tilted towards the west
(d) The Indian peninsula south of the Satpura ranges is tilted towards east

39. Soils in the Mahanadi delta are less fertile than those in the Godavari delta because of:
(a) erosion of top soils by annual floods
(b) inundation of land by sea water
(c) traditional agriculture practices
(d) the derivation of alluvial soil from red-soil hinterland

40. Which of the following institutions in the field of education is set up by the MHRD Government of India?
(a) Indian council of world Affair, New Delhi
(b) Mythic Society, Bangalore
(c) National Bal Bhawn, New Delhi
(d) India International Centre, New Delhi

41. **Assertion (A):** Aerosols have potential for modifying climate.
Reason (R): Aerosols interact with both short waves and radiation
(a) Both (A) and (R) are true, and (R) is the correct explanation of (A)
(b) Both (A) and (R) are true, but (R) is not the correct explanation of (A)
(c) (A) is true, but (R) is false
(d) (A) is false, but (R) is true

42. 'SITE' stands for:
(a) System for International technology and Engineering
(b) Satellite Instructional Television Experiment
(c) South Indian Trade Estate
(d) State Institute of Technology and Engineering

43. What is the name of the Research station established by the Indian Government for 'Conducting Research at Antarctic?
(a) Dakshin Gangotri
(b) Yamunotri
(c) Uttari Gangotri
(d) None of the above

44. Ministry of Human Resource Development (HRD) includes:
(a) Department of Elementary Education and Literacy
(b) Department of Secondary Education and Higher Education
(c) Department of Women and Child Development
(d) All the above

45. Parliament can legislate on matters listed in the State list:
(a) With the prior permission of the President.
(b) Only after the Constitution is amended suitably.
(c) In case of inconsistency among State legislatures.
(d) At the request of two or more States.

Q. No.: 46 to 50 NOT FOR VISUALLY HANDICAPPED CANDIDATES

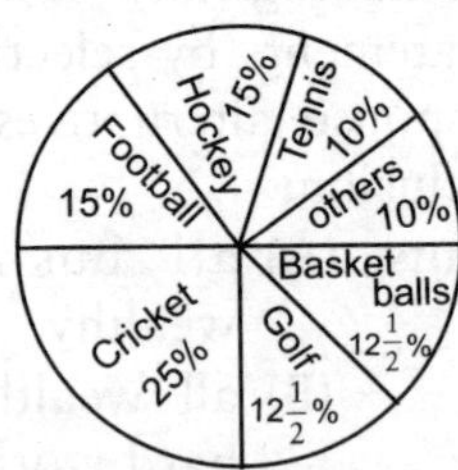

The following pie chart indicates the expenditure of a country on various sports during a particular year. Study the pie chart and answer Question Numbers 46 to 50.

46. The ratio of the total expenditure on football to that of expenditure on hockey is:

(a) 1 : 15 (b) 1 : 1
(c) 15 : 1 (d) 3 : 20

47. If the total expenditure on sports during the year was Rs. 1,20,000,00 how much was spent on basket ball?
(a) Rs. 9,50,000 (b) Rs. 10,00,000
(c) Rs. 12,00,000 (d) Rs. 15,00,000

48. The chart shows that the most popular game of the country is:
(a) Hockey (b) Football
(c) Cricket (d) Tennis

49. Out of the following country's expenditure is the same on:
(a) Hockey and Tennis
(b) Golf and Basket ball
(c) Cricket and Football
(d) Hockey and Golf

50. If the total expenditure on sport during the year was Rs. 1,50,00,000 the expenditure on cricket and hockey together was:
(a) Rs. 60,00,000 (b) Rs. 50,00,000
(c) Rs. 37,50,000 (d) Rs. 25,00,000

ANSWERS

1. (d)	2. (b)	3. (d)	4. (a)	5. (b)
6. (a)	7. (a)	8. (a)	9. (b)	10. (b)
11. (d)	12. (a)	13. (a)	14. (b)	15. (d)
16. (a)	17. (a)	18. (d)	19. (d)	20. (d)
21. (d)	22. (a)	23. (c)	24. (c)	25. (d)
26. (c)	27. (c)	28. (b)	29. (b)	30. (a)
31. (a)	32. (a)	33. (d)	34. (c)	35. (d)
36. (c)	37. (d)	38. (a)	39. (a)	40. (c)
41. (a)	42. (b)	43. (a)	44. (d)	45. (d)
46. (b)	47. (a)	48. (c)	49. (b)	50. (a)

PAPER–II

1. Who defines public administration as consisting of "all those operations having for their purpose the fulfilment or enforcement of public policy?
(a) Henry Fayol (b) L.D. White
(c) Urwick (d) Elton Mayo

2. Tick the correct answer from the codes given below:
Public Administration is associated with the activities of the:
(i) Central Government
(ii) State Government
(iii) Local Government
(iv) All of the above
(a) (i) (ii) (b) (ii) (iii)
(c) (i) (iii) (d) (iv)

3. Who among the following is the supporter of integral view of Administration?
(a) F.W. Taylor
(b) Max Weber
(c) L.D. White
(d) Woodrow Wilson

4. Which one of the following is not correct in regard to classical theory?
(a) Administrative Management
(b) Structured Management
(c) Formal organisation
(d) Functional Theory

5. Who among the following classified staff into three types — general staff, technical staff and auxiliary staff?
(a) Pfiffner and Presthus
(b) L.D. White
(c) J.D. Mooney
(d) Albert Lepawesky

6. Who divides the scope of public administration into administrative theory and applied administration?

(a) L.D. White
(b) H. Walker
(c) Paul H. Appleby
(d) Woodrow Wilson

7. Public Administration must scrupulously observe the principle of:
(a) Differential Treatment
(b) Consistency of Treatment
(c) Internal Financial Control
(d) Redressal of all grievances

8. Riggs ecological approach to the study of comparative Public Administration is based on his experience in:
(a) United States (b) Thailand
(c) Britain (d) Indonesia

9. Consider the following two statements and give the correct answer from the codes given below:
New thrust areas for analysis of a public Administration in the context of liberalisation and globalization consist of:
(i) study on citizens' character
(ii) disinvestment of public sector units
(iii) debureaucratization
(iv) Communitarianism
(a) (i) and (ii)
(b) (i) and (iii)
(c) (i) (ii) and (iii)
(d) (i) (ii) (iii) and (iv)

10. Which one of the following is an essential feature of Development Administration?
(a) Revenue Collection
(b) Law and Order
(c) Socio-economic transformation
(d) Women Empowerment

11. The definition of development administration as "an action-oriented and goal-oriented administrative system" is given by:
(a) Edward Weidner
(b) F.W. Riggs
(c) Goswami U.L.
(d) Mohit Bhattacharya

12. Who among the following said that the planning commission is an "Economic Cabinet"
(a) Santhanam (b) Ashok Chanda
(c) Raja Mannar (d) K. C. Neogy

13. Chairman of First Finance Commission is:
(a) K.C. Neogy (b) Raja Mannar
(c) Ashok Chanda (d) Santhanam

14. Kothari Commission was appointed in the year:
(a) 1974 (b) 1975
(c) 1976 (d) 1979

15. Which one of the following is not a pattern of management of public enterprises in India?
(a) Department
(b) Public Corporation
(c) Holding Company
(d) Operating Contract

16. Which of the following are true of the cabinet secretariat?
(i) It acts as the secretariat of the cabinet.
(ii) It acts as the originating department in union government.
(iii) The cabinet secretary presides over meetings of the secretaries.
(iv) It implements the decisions of the cabinet.
Select the correct one from the codes below:
(a) (i) and (iii) (b) (i) and (ii)
(c) (ii) and (iii) (d) (iii) and (iv)

17. Post independence Nagar Palika Bill was first introduced during the time of:
(a) V.P. Singh (b) Narasimha Rao
(c) Chandrashekhar (d) Rajiv Gandhi

18. Which one of the following is not the recommendation of the Ashoka Mehta committee:
(a) Creation of two tier system
(b) Creation of Nyaya Panchayats

(c) Open participation of political parties in panchayati election
(d) Creation of state finance commission

19. Which one of the following is not the limitation of the case study method?
(a) Analysis is essentially intuitive
(b) Interviewees object to the outcome of case analysis
(c) Case study is replicable and subject to verification through replication
(d) Case study is unable to support hypothesis testing

20. One of the following is not associated with Social Welfare:
(a) Empowerment of Women
(b) Reservation Policy
(c) Education Policy
(d) Irrigation Loans

21. Given below are two statements, one labelled as Assertion (A) and the other labelled as Reason (R). In the context of the two statements write the correct answer from the codes given below:
Assertion (A): The function of communication is not just to get something off the mind of the communicator.
Reason (R): Communication must create the desired impact at the receiving end
Codes:
(a) Both (A) and (R) are true and (R) is the correct explanation of (A)
(b) Both (A) and (R) are true but (R) is not the correct explanation of (A)
(c) (A) is true but (R) is false
(d) (A) is false but (R) is true

22. **Assertion (A):** Max Weber's bureaucratic model is based on hierarchy of offices.
Reason (R): There is a division of labour.
Select the correct answer from codes given below:
Codes:
(a) Both (A) and (R) are correct and (R) is the correct explanation of (A)
(b) Both (A) and (R) are correct but (R) is not the correct explanation of (A)
(c) (A) is true but (R) is false
(d) (A) is false but (R) is true

23. **Assertion (A):** Classical theorists did not take cognizance of the needs of individuals.
Reason (R): Classical theorists were basically formal in their approaches.
Choose the correct answer from the following answer codes:
Codes:
(a) (A) and (R) are true and (R) is the correct explanation of (A)
(b) Both (A) and (R) are true but (R) is not the correct explanation of (A)
(c) (A) is true (R) is false
(d) (A) is false (R) is true

24. **Assertion (A):** The prismatic society is characterized by a high degree of formalism.
Reason (R): Formalistic behaviour is caused by the lack of presure towards programme objectives and a great permissiveness for arbitrary administration.
Choose the correct answer from the following answer code:
Codes:
(a) Both (A) and (R) are correct and (R) is the correct explanation of (A)
(b) Both (A) and (R) are correct but (R) is not the correct explanation of (A)
(c) (A) is true but (R) is false
(d) (A) is false but (R) is true

25. **Assertion (A):** The concept of development administration is of recent origin.
Reason (R): Many countries became independent since world war II.
Choose the correct answer from the following answer code:

Codes:
(a) Both (A) and (R) are correct and (R) is the correct explanation of (A)
(b) Both (A) and (R) are correct but (R) is not the correct explanation of (A)
(c) (A) is true but (R) is false
(d) (A) is false but (R) is true

26. **Assertion (A):** There is a feeling that the institution of All India Services needs reconsideration.
Reason (R): Members of the All India Services foster national intergration as they are recruited from different parts of the country.
Choose the correct answer from codes given below:
Codes:
(a) Both (A) and (R) are true and (R) is the correct explanation of (A)
(b) Both (A) and (R) are true but (R) is not the correct explanation of (A)
(c) (A) is true but (R) is false
(d) (A) is false but (R) is true

27. **Assertion (A):** The cabinet is the main policy making body of the state government.
Reason (R): The cabinet is headed by the chief minister.
Choose the correct answer from codes given below:
Codes:
(a) Both (A) and (R) are correct and (R) is the correct explanation of (A)
(b) Both (A) and (R) are correct but (R) is not the correct explanation of (A)
(c) (A) is correct but (R) is false
(d) (A) is false but (R) is correct

28. **Assertion (A):** The central secretariat is a think-tank and vital treasure-hose of important information.
Reason (R): The central secretariat carries out a comprehensive and detailed scrutiny of every issue.
Choose the correct answer from codes given below:
Codes:
(a) Both (A) and (R) are true and (R) is the correct explanation of (A)
(b) Both (A) and (R) are true but (R) is not the correct explanation of (A)
(c) (A) is true (R) is false
(d) (A) is false (R) is true

29. **Assertion (A):** A member of the opposition can also be appointed as the chairman of the public accounts committee.
Reason (R): The reports of the public Accounts committee are quite often against the Government.
Choose the correct answer from codes given below:
Codes:
(a) Both (A) and (R) are correct and (R) is the correct explanation of (A)
(b) Both (A) and (R) are correct but (R) is not the correct explanation of (A)
(c) (A) is true (R) is false
(d) (A) is false (R) is true

30. **Assertion (A):** The 73rd Constitutional Amendment has heralded a new era for Panchayati Raj.
Reason (R): It opened doors for the political parties to contest the Panchayati Raj elections.
Choose the correct answer from codes given below:
Codes:
(a) Both (A) and (R) are correct and (R) is the correct explanation of (A)
(b) Both (A) and (R) are correct but (R) is not the correct explanation of (A)
(c) (A) is true (R) is false
(d) (A) is false (R) is true

31. What is the sequence of Morstein Marx's classification of bureaucracy given below:
(i) Merit (ii) Caste
(iii) Patronage (iv) Guardian

Select the correct answer from this codes:
(a) (i), (iii), (iv) and (ii)
(b) (iv), (ii), (iii) and (i)
(c) (ii), (iii), (iv) and (i)
(d) (iii), (iv), (ii) and (i)

32. What is the sequence of the following processes of formulating a rational policy?
(i) Consideration of alternative courses of action
(ii) Evaluation of consequences of each alternative course of action
(iii) Identification of societal values
(iv) Selection of one alternative in terms of most valued ends

Select the correct answer from codes given below:
(a) (iv), (iii), (ii) and (i)
(b) (ii), (iii), (i) and (iv)
(c) (iii), (i), (ii) and (iv)
(d) (i), (ii), (iv) and (iii)

33. What is the correct chronological sequence in the evolution of civil services in India?
(i) Lee Commission
(ii) Islington Commission
(iii) Macaulay's Report
(iv) Aitchison Commission

Select the correct code from the following:
(a) (iv), (ii), (i) and (iii)
(b) (iii), (i), (ii) and (iv)
(c) (iii), (iv), (ii) and (i)
(d) (ii), (iv), (i) and (iii)

34. Arrange the following offices in sequence of position:
(a) Special Secretary (b) Home Secretary
(c) Deputy Secretary (d) Director

Select correct answer from the code given below:

Codes:
(a) (ii), (i), (iv) and (iii)
(b) (i), (ii), (iii) and (iv)
(c) (ii), (i), (iii) and (iv)
(d) (ii), (iv), (i) and (iii)

35. What is the correct chronological sequence in which the following were set up:
(i) Establishment of the Federal Public Service Commission
(ii) Establishment of the Planning Commission
(iii) Establishment of National Commission for Women
(iv) Establishment of the National Development Council

Select the correct answer from the codes given below:

Codes:
(a) (iii), (iv), (ii) and (i)
(b) (i), (ii), (iii) and (iv)
(c) (i), (iii), (iv) and (ii)
(d) (i), (ii), (iv) and (iii)

36. Arrange the following according to chronological sequence:
(i) Ashok Mehta Committee
(ii) L.M. Singhvi Committee
(iii) Balwant Rai Mehta Committee
(iv) Community Development Programme

Select the correct code from the following:

Codes:
(a) (iv), (i), (iii) and (ii)
(b) (iv), (iii), (i) and (ii)
(c) (ii), (iv), (iii) and (i)
(d) (ii), (iv), (i) and (iii)

37. Arrange the following according to the sequence in which they appeared in the Constitution of India.
(i) Creation of All India Services
(ii) Finance Commission
(iii) Village Panchayats
(iv) Governor of a State

Answer with the help of the codes given below:

Codes:
(a) (i), (ii), (iii) and (iv)
(b) (iv), (i), (ii) and (iii)
(c) (iii), (iv), (ii) and (i)
(d) (ii), (iv), (iii) and (i)

38. In the evolution of Public Administration there has been a shift in emphasis during successive periods. In this context which of the following pairs are correctly matched?

List I	List II
(a) 1887-1926	(i) Crisis of Identity
(b) 1910-1920	(ii) Scientific Management
(c) 1920-1947	(iii) Human Relations
(d) 1948-1966	(iv) Behaviouralism

Codes:

(a) (b), (c) and (d) (b) (a), (b) and (c)
(c) (a), (c) and (d) (d) (a), (b) and (d)

39. Which of the following are correctly matched?

List I	List II
(i) Authority	It is accepted as legitimate
(ii) Power	Carrying out one's will despite resistance
(iii) Control	Ability to guide
(iv) Discretion	Choosing among alternatives causes of action

Answer with the help of following codes:

Codes:

(a) (i), (ii), (iii) and (iv)
(b) (ii) and (iv)
(c) (i), (ii) and (iv)
(d) (i) and (iii)

40. Match List I with List II and select the correct answer from the codes given below:

List I

(A) Fervel Heady (B) Herbert Simon
(C) Frank Marini (D) D. Waldo

List II

(i) Administrative Behavior
(ii) Public Administration a Comparative Perspective
(iii) Toward a New Public Administration
(iv) Ideas and Issues in public Administration

Codes:	A	B	C	D
(a)	(ii)	(i)	(iii)	(iv)
(b)	(iv)	(i)	(ii)	(iii)
(c)	(ii)	(iii)	(iv)	(i)
(d)	(iv)	(iii)	(i)	(ii)

41. Match List I with List II

List I	List II
(A) Rule of Law	(i) France
(B) Judicial Review	(ii) India
(C) Two sets of courts	(iii) U.K.
(D) Due process of Law	(iv) U.S.A.

Select the correct answer from the codes given below:

Codes:	A	B	C	D
(a)	(iii)	(ii)	(i)	(iv)
(b)	(iii)	(iv)	(ii)	(i)
(c)	(ii)	(i)	(iii)	(iv)
(d)	(iv)	(iii)	(i)	(ii)

42. Which one of the following is not correctly matched?

(a) Panchayati Raj introduced in Rajasthan in 1959
(b) National Development Council Set up in 1952
(c) Satish Chandra appointed Committee in 1988
(d) Sarkaria Commission submitted report in 1989

43. Match the following with the codes given below:

List I

(A) Balwant Rai Mehta
(B) Chester Barnard
(C) Gullick
(D) Woodrow Wilson

List II

(i) Principles of Organisation
(ii) Democratic Decentralisation
(iii) Study of Administration
(iv) Informal Organisations

Codes:	A	B	C	D
(a)	(i)	(ii)	(iv)	(iii)
(b)	(ii)	(iv)	(i)	(iii)
(c)	(iv)	(iii)	(i)	(ii)
(d)	(iii)	(iv)	(ii)	(i)

44. Match the following according to the codes given below:

List I

(A) Masterman Committee
(B) Assheton Committee
(C) Satish Chandra Committee
(D) Fulton Committee

List II

(i) Recruitment
(ii) Political Activities
(iii) Training
(iv) Professionalism

Codes:	A	B	C	D
(a)	(ii)	(iii)	(iv)	(i)
(b)	(iii)	(ii)	(i)	(iv)
(c)	(ii)	(iii)	(i)	(iv)
(d)	(iii)	(ii)	(iv)	(i)

45. Match List I with List II using the codes below:

List I

(a) Head of the Civil Service
(b) Head of the Indian State
(c) Head of the Union Government
(d) Head of the Accounts and Audit

List II

(i) Prime Minister in the central Government
(ii) Cabinet Secretary
(iii) Comptroller and Auditor General
(iv) President

Codes:	A	B	C	D
(a)	(i)	(iii)	(ii)	(iv)
(b)	(ii)	(iv)	(i)	(iii)
(c)	(iii)	(ii)	(i)	(iv)
(d)	(iv)	(iii)	(ii)	(i)

Read the following passage and answer the questions that follow on the basis of your understanding of the passage:

The modern version of political economy is now customarily referred to as either "non market economies" or the "Public Choice" approach. This body of knowledge is rich in tradition and intellectual rigor, but some what light in empirical evidence. Still, the public choice theorists are having and will continue to have an important influence on American Public Administration.

Vincent Ostrom (1973) has completed what is essentially a tying together of public choice logic, public administration history and theory, and political philosophy. In his book "The Intellectual crisis in American "Public Administration" he compares the perspective on public administration developed by Woodrow Wilson, which he labels bureaucratic theory, with the perspectives of the public choice theorist, which he labels a "paradigm of democratic administration". The Wilsonian perspective is, in Ostrom's judgement, a sharp departure from the Hamiltonian-Madisonian perspective on the nature of government. Both, however, trace more directly to the political philosophy of Hobbes.

46. What is the modern version of political economy?
(a) non market economies
(b) public choice
(c) both 'A and 'B
(d) None of the above

47. Who among the following tried to tie up public choice and Public Administration?
(a) Vincent Ostram (b) Wilson
(c) Hamilton (d) Madison

48. Perspectives of public choice theorists are labelled as
(a) Paradigm of Democratic Administration
(b) Public choice and Public Administration
(c) Perspectives on Public Administration
(d) Perspectives on Public Choice

49. In the Ostrom's judgement who has departed from whom on the nature of Government?
    (a) Wilson departed from Hamiltonal Modison
    (b) Hamiltan departed from Modison
    (c) Modison departed from Wilson
    (d) All of them expressed the same idea
50. The Book "The Intellectual Crisis in American Public Administration" is written by:
    (a) Vincent Ostrom
    (b) Woodrow Wilson
    (c) Hamilton
    (d) Modison

ANSWERS

1. (b)	2. (d)	3. (c)	4. (d)	5. (a)
6. (b)	7. (b)	8. (b)	9. (d)	10. (c)
11. (a)	12. (b)	13. (a)	14. (b)	15. (d)
16. (d)	17. (d)	18. (d)	19. (c)	20. (d)
21. (a)	22. (b)	23. (b)	24. (b)	25. (a)
26. (d)	27. (a)	28. (a)	29. (a)	30. (a)
31. (b)	32. (c)	33. (c)	34. (a)	35. (d)
36. (b)	37. (c)	38. (a)	39. (c)	40. (a)
41. (a)	42. (d)	43. (b)	44. (c)	45. (b)
46. (c)	47. (a)	48. (a)	49. (a)	50. (a)

DECEMBER–2005

Note: This paper contains fifty (50) objective type questions, each question carrying two (2) marks. All questions are compulsory.

PAPER–I

1. Team teaching has the potential to develop:
   (a) Competitive spirit
   (b) Cooperation
   (c) The habit of supplementing the teaching of each other
   (d) Highlighting the gaps in each other's teaching
2. Which of the following is the most important characteristic of Open Book Examination system?
   (a) Students become serious.
   (b) It improves attendance in the classroom.
   (c) It reduces examination anxiety amongst students.
   (d) It compels students to think.
3. Which of the following methods of teaching encourages the use of maximum senses?
   (a) Problem-solving method
   (b) Laboratory method
   (c) Self-study method
   (d) Team teaching method
4. Which of the following statement is correct?
   (a) Communicator should have fine senses
   (b) Communicator should have tolerance power
   (c) Communicator should be soft spoken
   (d) Communicator should have good personality
5. An effective teacher is one who can:
   (a) control the class
   (b) give more information in less time
   (c) motivate students to learn
   (d) correct the assignments carefully
6. One of the following is not a quality of researcher:
   (a) Unison with that of which he is in search
   (b) He must be of alert mind
   (c) Keenness in enquiry
   (d) His assertion to outstrip the evidence
7. A satisfactory statistical quantitative method should not possess one of the following qualities:
   (a) Appropriateness (b) Measurability
   (c) Comparability (d) Flexibility
8. Books and records are the primary sources of data in:
   (a) historical research
   (b) participatory research
   (c) clinical research
   (d) laboratory research
9. Which of the following statement is correct?
   (a) objectives should be pin-pointed
   (b) objectives can be written in statement or question form
   (c) another word for problem is variable
   (d) all the above
10. The important pre-requisites of a researcher in sciences, social sciences and humanities are:

(a) laboratory skills, records, supervisor, topic
(b) Supervisor, topic, critical analysis, patience
(c) archives, supervisor, topic, flexibility in thinking
(d) topic, supervisor, good temperament, pre-conceived notions

Read the following passage and answer the questions 11 to 15:

Knowledge creation in many cases requires creativity and idea generation. This is especially important in generating alternative decision support solutions. Some people believe that an individual's creative ability stems primarily from personality traits such as inventiveness, independence, individuality, enthusiasm, and flexibility. However, several studies have found that creativity is not so much a function of individual traits as was once believed, and that individual creativity can be learned and improved. This understanding has led innovative companies to recognise that the key to fostering creativity may be the development of an idea-nurturing work environment. Idea-generation methods and techniques, to be used by individuals or in groups, are consequently being developed. Manual methods for supporting idea generation, such as brainstorming in a group, can be very successful in certain situations. However, in other situations, such an approach is either not economically feasible or not possible. For example, manual methods in group creativity sessions will not work or will not be effective when : (1) there is no time to conduct a proper idea-generation session; (2) there is a poor facilitator (or no facilitator at all); (3) it is too expensive to conduct an idea-generation session; (4) the subject matter is too sensitive for a face-to-face session; or (5) there are not enough participants, the mix of participants is not optimal, or there is no climate for idea generation. In such cases, computerised idea-generation methods have been tried, with frequent success.

Idea-generation software is designed to help stimulate a single user or a group to produce new ideas, options and choices. The user does all the work, but the software encourages and pushes, something like a personal trainer. Although idea-generation software is still relatively new, there are several packages on the market. Various approaches are used by idea-generating software to increase the flow of ideas to the user. Idea Fisher, for example, has an associate lexicon of the English language that cross-references words and phrases. These associative links, based on analogies and metaphors, make it easy for the user to be fed words related to a given theme. Some software packages use questions to prompt the user towards new, unexplored patterns of thought. This helps users to break out of cyclical thinking patterns, conquer mental blocks, or deal with bouts of procrastination.

11. The author, in this passage has focussed on
(a) knowledge creation
(b) idea-generation
(c) creativity
(d) individual traits

12. Fostering creativity needs an environment of
(a) decision support systems
(b) idea-nurturing
(c) decision support solutions
(d) alternative individual factors

13. Manual methods for the support of idea-generation, in certain occasions,
(a) are alternatively effective
(b) can be less expensive
(c) do not need a facilitator
(d) require a mix of optimal participants

14. Idea-generation software works as if it is a:
(a) stimulant
(b) knowledge package
(c) user-friendly trainer
(d) climate creator

15. Mental blocks, bouts of procrastination and cyclical thinking patterns can be won when:
(a) innovative companies employ electronic thinking methods
(b) idea-generation software prompts questions
(c) manual methods are removed
(d) individuals acquire a neutral attitude towards the software

16. Level C of the effectiveness of communication is defined as:
(a) channel noise
(b) semantic noise
(c) psychological noise
(d) source noise

17. Recording a television programme on a VCR is an example of:
(a) time-shifting
(b) content reference
(c) mechanical clarity
(d) media synchronisation

18. A good communicator is the one who offers to his audience:
(a) plentiful of information
(b) a good amount of statistics
(c) concise proof
(d) repetition of facts

19. The largest number of newspapers in India is published from the state of:
(a) Kerala (b) Maharashtra
(c) West Bengal (d) Uttar Pradesh

20. Insert the missing number:
8 24 1 2 ? 18 54
(a) 26 (b) 24
(c) 36 (d) 3 2

21. January 1, 1995 was Sunday. What day of the week lies on January 1, 1996?
(a) Sunday (b) Monday
(c) Saturday (d) None of these

22. The sum of a positive number and its reciprocal is twice the difference of the number and its reciprocal. The number is:
(a) $\sqrt{2}$ (b) $\frac{1}{\sqrt{2}}$
(c) $\sqrt{3}$ (d) $\frac{1}{\sqrt{3}}$

23. In a certain code, ROUNDS is written as RONUDS. How will PLEASE will be written in the same code:
(a) LPAESE (b) PLAESE
(c) LPAEES (d) PLASEE

24. At what time between 5.30 and 6.00 will the hands of a clock be at right angles?
(a) $43\frac{5}{11}$ min. past 5
(b) $43\frac{7}{11}$ min. past 5
(c) 40 min. past 5
(d) 45 min past 5

25. **Statements:** I All students are ambitious
II All ambitious persons are hard working
Conclusions: (i) All students are hard-working
(ii) All hardly working people are not ambitious
Which of the following is correct?
(a) Only (i) is correct
(b) Only (ii) is correct
(c) Both (i) and (ii) are correct
(d) Neither (i) nor (ii) is correct

26. **Statement:** Most students are intelligent
Conclusions: (i) Some students are intelligent
(ii) All students are not intelligent

Which of the following is implied?
(a) Only (i) is implied
(b) Only (ii) is implied
(c) Both (i) and (ii) are implied
(d) Neither (i) nor (ii) is implied

27. **Statement:** Most labourers are poor
Conclusions: (i) Some labourers are poor
(ii) All labourers are not poor

Which of the following is implied?
(a) Only (i) is implied
(b) Only (ii) is implied
(c) Both (i) and (ii) are implied
(d) Neither (i) nor (ii) is implied

28. Line access and avoidance of collision are the main functions of:
(a) the CPU
(b) the monitor
(c) network protocols
(d) wide area networks

29. In the hypermedia database, information bits are stored in the form of:
(a) signals (b) cubes
(c) nodes (d) symbols

30. Communications bandwidth that has the highest capacity and is used by microwave, cable and fibre optics lines is known as:
(a) hyper-link (b) broadband
(c) bus width (d) carrier wave

31. An electronic bill board that has a short text or graphical advertising message is referred to as:
(a) bulletin (b) strap
(c) bridge line (d) banner

32. Which of the following is not the characteristic of a computer?
(a) computer is an electrical machine
(b) computer cannot think of its own
(c) computer processes information error free
(d) computer can hold data for any length of time

33. Bitumen is obtained from:
(a) Forests and Plants
(b) Kerosene oil
(c) Crude oil
(d) Underground mines

34. Malaria is caused by:
(a) bacterial infection
(b) viral infection
(c) parasitic infection
(d) fungal infection

35. The cloudy nights are warmer compared to clear nights (without clouds) during winter days. This is because:
(a) clouds radiate heat towards the earth
(b) clouds prevent cold wave from the sky, descend on earth
(c) clouds prevent escaping of the heat radiation from the earth
(d) clouds being at great heights from earth absorb heat from the sun and send towards the earth

36. Largest soil group of India is:
(a) Red soil (b) Black soil
(c) Sandy soil (d) Mountain soil

37. Main pollutant of the Indian coastal water is:
(a) oil spill
(b) municipal sewage
(c) industrial effluents
(d) aerosols

38. Human ear is most sensitive to noise in the following frequency ranges:
(a) 1-2 KHz (b) 100-500 Hz
(c) 10-12 KHz (d) None of these

39. Which species of chromium is toxic in water:

(a) Cr + 2 (b) Cr + 3
(c) Cr + 6 (d) Cr is non-toxic element

40. Match List I (Dams) with List II (River) in the following:

List I (Dams)	List II (River)
(A) Bhakra	(i) Krishna
(B) Nagarjunasagar	(ii) Damodar
(C) Panchet	(iii) Sutlej
(D) Hirakud	(iv) Bhagirathi
(E) Tehri	(v) Mahanadi

Codes:	A	B	C	D	E
(a)	v	iii	iv	ii	i
(b)	iii	i	ii	v	iv
(c)	i	ii	iv	iii	v
(d)	ii	iii	iv	i	v

41. A negative reaction to a mediated communication is described as:
(a) flak
(b) fragmented feedback
(c) passive response
(d) non-conformity

42. The launch of satellite channel by IGNOU on 26th January 2003 for technological education for the growth and development of distance education is:
(a) Eklavya channel
(b) Gyandarshan channel
(c) Rajrishi channel
(d) None of these

43. Match List I with List II and select the correct answer from the code given below:

List I (Institutions)
(A) The Indian Council of Historical Reasearch (ICHR)
(B) The Indian Institute of Advanced Studies (IIAS)
(C) The Indian Council of Philosophical Research (ICPR)
(D) The Central Institute of Coastal Engineering for fisheries

List II (Locations)
(i) Shimla (ii) New Delhi
(iii) Bangalore (iv) Lucknow

Codes:	A	B	C	D
(a)	ii	i	iv	iii
(b)	i	ii	iii	iv
(c)	ii	iv	i	iii
(d)	iv	iii	ii	i

44. Which of the following is not a Fundamental Right?
(a) Right to equality
(b) Right against exploitation
(c) Right to freedom of speech and expression
(d) Right of free compulsory education of all children upto the age of 14

45. The Lok-Sabha can be dissolved before the expiry of its normal five year term by:
(a) The Prime Minister
(b) The Speaker of Lok Sabha
(c) The President on the recommendation of the Prime Minister
(d) None of the above

Q.No.: 46 to 50 NOT FOR VISUALLY HANDICAPPED CANDIDATES

Study the following graph carefully and answer Q.No. 46 to 50 given below it:

EXPORT OF TINS

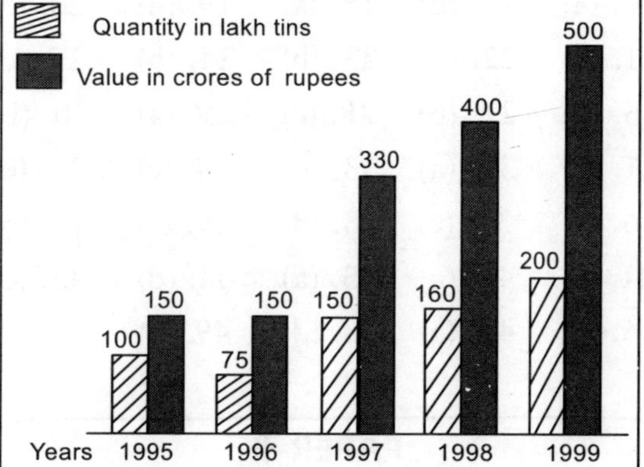

46. In which year the value per tin was minimum?
(a) 1995 (b) 1996
(c) 1998 (d) 1999

47. What was the difference between the tins exported in 1997 and 1998?
(a) 1 0 (b) 1000
(c) 100000 (d) 1000000

48. What was the approximate percentage increase in export value from 1995 to 1999?
(a) 350 (b) 330.3
(c) 433.3 (d) None of these

49. What was the percentage drop in export quantity from 1995 to 1996?
(a) 75 (b) 50
(c) 25 (d) None of these

50. If in 1998, the tins were exported at the same rate per tin as that in 1997, what would be the value (in crores of rupees) of export in 1998?
(a) 400 (b) 375
(c) 352 (d) 330

ANSWERS

1. (c)	2. (d)	3. (b)	4. (a)	5. (c)
6. (d)	7. (d)	8. (a)	9. (a)	10. (b)
11. (a)	12. (b)	13. (a)	14. (a)	15. (b)
16. (a)	17. (d)	18. (a)	19. (d)	20. (c)
21. (b)	22. (d)	23. (b)	24. (b)	25. (c)
26. (b)	27. (b)	28. (c)	29. (a)	30. (b)
31. (b)	32. (a)	33. (d)	34. (c)	35. (c)
36. (a)	37. (c)	38. (d)	39. (c)	40. (b)
41. (c)	42. (a)	43. (a)	44. (d)	45. (c)
46. (a)	47. (a)	48. (d)	49. (c)	50. (c)

PAPER–II

1. "Like Physics or Chemistry, administration is governed by principles" said by:
(a) Gullick (b) Urwick
(c) L.D. White (d) J.D. Mooney

2. One of the following is regarded as the father of the discipline of Public Administration:
(a) Gullick
(b) Urwick
(c) L.D. White
(d) Woodrow Wilson

3. Which is not correct about advantages of hierarchical form of organisation?
(a) It ensures proper division
(b) It ensures accountability of functionaries
(c) It is the only way of inculcating a sense of discipline in the organisation
(d) It can be used to create centres of decision making if required

4. Which one of the following pairs is correctly matched?

(a) Human Relation Approach	1. Formal Organisation Theory
(b) System approach	2. Input - Output Theory
(c) Structural - Functional approach	3. Decision - Making Theory
(d) Classical Approach	4. Development Theory

5. Which one of the following is the goal of Scientific Management?
(a) Maximisation of Social Welfare
(b) Maximisation of Employment
(c) Welfare of the Workers
(d) Higher Industrial efficiency

6. In the view of Edward Widner the development should have the following:
(a) Directional growth
(b) Planning
(c) Systems change
(d) All the above

7. Who observed that Weber's ideal model of Bureaucracy is not particularly relevant to the study of development societies?

(a) H. Simon (b) Fred Riggs
(c) Chester Barnad (d) R.K. Metan

8. Which one of the following is a draw back in Max Webers' bureaucratic model?
   (a) Lack of normative factors as guiding action
   (b) Lack of legal rational principles
   (c) Lack of a theoretically integrated total system of action
   (d) Lack of rule of law upon the functioning of bureaucratic organisation

9. Which of the following are points of criticism made by critics of Mayo?
   1. He ignored theory
   2. He neglected empiricism
   3. He was not pro - management
   4. He passed the way for workers manipulation

   (a) 1 and 2 (b) 2 and 3
   (c) 3 and 4 (d) 1 and 4

10. Who defined "Leadership is the activity of influencing people to strive willingly for group objectives"?
    (a) Terry (b) Weschler
    (c) Fred Massarik (d) Rensis Likert

11. The first conference on comparative Public Administration was held at:
    (a) Princeton University
    (b) Maxwell Graduate School
    (c) Harvard University
    (d) Cambridge University

12. Which one of the following is not a characteristic of a prismatic society?
    (a) Heterogencity (b) Formalism
    (c) Integrity (d) Over lapping

13. 'Development administration is an action - oriented and goal-oriented administrative system'. Who said this
    (a) Edward Weidner (b) F.W. Riggs
    (c) Ferrel Heady (d) Montegomery

14. Which one of the following is not a characteristic feature of British administrative system?
    (a) Open Recruitment
    (b) Centralised Administration
    (c) Administrative Law
    (d) Rule of Law

15. Who observed that "planning introduced not only a political complexion in the relationship between the Union and States but enabled the union to tighten its financial grip over the State"?
    (a) K.M. Munshi (b) K.M. Pannikar
    (c) K. Subha Rao (d) H.M. Patel

16. The Prime Minister's office occupies the status of the department of the Government of India under the:
    (a) Allocation of Business Rules 1961
    (b) Office Allocation Act 1965
    (c) Office Act 1965
    (d) Presidential order

17. In which year, the National integration council was created to deal with welfare measures for the minorities on an All India basis?
    (a) 1985 (b) 1986
    (c) 1987 (d) 1988

18. A case study method means:
    (a) An exploratory research method designed to study indepth one or few situations which are consistent with the researcher's original problem.
    (b) The method by which research problem is approached on case by case basis
    (c) The method of data collection
    (d) The process of understanding variables

19. Functions of Central Social Welfare Board are:
    1. Women welfare and development
    2. Financial assistance to NGOs

3. Enter into bilateral agreements
4. Distant education

Select the correct answer from code given below:

(a) 1 and 3 (b) 1 and 2
(c) 1, 2 and 4 (d) 1, 2, 3 and 4

20. The chairman and the members of the State Finance Commission are appointed by:

(a) President (b) Prime Minister
(c) Governor (d) Chief Minister

21. **Assertion (A):** Public Administration is a field of systemic study.

Reason (R): It developed as a discipline through a succession of fine overlaping paradigms.

Choose the correct answer from the following:

(a) Both (A) and (R) are correct and (R) is the correct explanation of (A)
(b) Both (A) and (R) are correct but (R) is not the correct explanation of (A)
(c) (A) is true but (R) is false
(d) (A) is false but (R) is true

22. **Assertion (A):** Judicial Review means the power of the Courts to declare the laws and orders of the Government as invalid if they are against the Constitution.

Reason (R): The failure of the Executive and Legislative has given rise to Judicial activism.

Choose the correct answer from the following:

(a) Both (A) and (R) are correct and (R) is the correct explanation of (A)
(b) Both (A) and (R) are correct but (R) is not the correct explanation of (A)
(c) (A) is true but (R) is false
(d) (A) is false but (R) is true

23. **Assertion (A):** Under the classical theory of organisation the whole is bound together by the lines of authority.

Reason (R): One of the principles of organisation is unity of command.

Choose the correct answer from the following:

(a) Both (A) and (R) are correct and (R) is the correct explanation of (A)
(b) Both (A) and (R) are correct but (R) is not the correct explanation of (A)
(c) (A) is true but (R) is false
(d) (A) is false but (R) is true

24. **Assertion (A):** Practical application of unity of command is not always possible.

Reason (R): Administrative and Technical tasks require different kinds of supervision.

Choose the correct answer from the following:

(a) Both (A) and (R) are correct and (R) is the correct explanation of (A)
(b) Both (A) and (R) are correct but (R) is not the correct explanation of (A)
(c) (A) is true but (R) is false
(d) (A) is false but (R) is true

25. **Assertion (A):** The Civil Service in India are divided into superior generalists class and sub-ordinate specialists class.

Reason (R): The origin of such a dichotomy in India can be traced to the Macaulay Committee Report.

Choose the correct answer from the following:

(a) Both (A) and (R) are correct and (R) is the correct explanation of (A)
(b) Both (A) and (R) are correct but (R) is not the correct explanation of (A)
(c) (A) is true but (R) is false
(d) (A) is false but (R) is true

26. **Assertion (A):** Hawthonic investigations lacked scientific base.

Reason (R): The evidence obtained from the experiments does not support conclusions.

Choose the correct answer from the following:
(a) Both (A) and (R) are correct and (R) is the correct explanation of (A)
(b) Both (A) and (R) are correct but (R) is not the correct explanation of (A)
(c) (A) is true but (R) is false
(d) (A) is false but (R) is true

27. **Assertion (A):** France is more unitary than Britain.
Reason (R): In Britain Local Governments enjoy a certain degree of Autonomy.
Choose the correct answer from the following using the code:
(a) Both (A) and (R) are correct and (R) is the correct explanation of (A)
(b) Both (aA) and (R) are correct but (R) is not the correct explanation of (A)
(c) (A) is true but (R) is false
(d) (A) is false but (R) is true

28. **Assertion (A):** The initial thrust was towards professionalization almost echoing the old sentiment of Dwight Waldo.
Reason (R): Efficiency in administration should, no doubt, have top priority in a country wedded to socio-economic reconstruction through direct state intervention.
Choose the correct answer from the following:
(a) Both (A) and (R) are correct and (R) is the correct explanation of (A)
(b) Both (A) and (R) are correct but (R) is not the correct explanation of (A)
(c) (A) is true but (R) is false
(d) (A) is false but (R) is true

29. **Assertion (A):** The New Public Management conforms to the Neo-Taylorist prescription to a large extent.
Reason (R): It does not mention the political agenda of Neo-Taylorism.
Choose the correct answer from the following using the code:
(a) Both (A) and (R) are correct and (R) is the correct explanation of (A)
(b) Both (A) and (R) are correct but (R) is not the correct explanation of (A)
(c) (A) is true but (R) is false
(d) (A) is false but (R) is true

30. **Assertion (A):** The issues underlying liberalisation are not trivial.
Reason (R): The basic philosophy of liberalisation leads to privatisation.
Choose the correct answer from the following using the code:
(a) Both (A) and (R) are correct and (R) is the correct explanation of (A)
(b) Both (A) and (R) are correct but (R) is not the correct explanation of (A)
(c) (A) is true but (R) is false
(d) (A) is false but (R) is true

31. We have now four committees appointed by the Government of India. Identify the correct order:
1. Second Pay Commission
2. Committee on the prevention of corruption
3. Administrative Reforms Commission
4. Balwant Roy Mehta Committee
(a) 1, 2, 3, 4 (b) 2, 1, 3, 4
(c) 1, 3, 4, 2 (d) 2, 1, 4, 3

32. Arrange the following Articles/Books in chronological order. Use the code given below:
1. The study of Administration
2. Politics and Administration
3. Introduction to the study of Public Administration.
4. The Principles of Public Administration.
(a) 1, 2, 3, 4 (b) 2, 1, 3, 4
(c) 3, 4, 2, 1 (d) 4, 3, 2, 1

33. We have the contents of Preamble of the Indian Constitution. Identify the correct

order in which they appear in the Indian Constitution:
(a) Sovereign, Secular, Socialist, Democratic Republic
(b) Sovereign, Socialist, Democratic Secular Republic
(c) Sovereign, Democratic, Socialist, Secular Republic
(d) Sovereign, Democratic, Secular, Socialistic Republic

34. Elton Mayo conducted following experiments to study human behaviour. Put them in chronological order.
1. Relay-Assembly Test Room Experiment
2. Bank-Wiring Experiment
3. Illumination Experiment
4. Mass Interviewing Programme

Codes:
(a) 1, 4, 2, 3 (b) 1, 4, 3, 2
(c) 3, 1, 4, 2 (d) 4, 2, 1, 3

35. Identify the correct order:
1. Budget speech
2. Finance Bill
3. Appropriation Bill
4. Voting of Demands

Codes:
(a) 1, 4, 3, 2 (b) 1, 3, 2, 4
(c) 2, 1, 3, 4 (d) 4, 3, 2, 1

36. Fayol has mentioned the following basic administrative activities. Put them in correct order.
1. Coordination 2. Organising
3. Command 4. Planning
5. Control

Codes:
(a) 1, 2, 3, 4, 5 (b) 2, 4, 1, 5, 3
(c) 4, 2, 3, 1, 5 (d) 3, 1, 2, 5, 4

37. Place in ascending order the types of bureaucrats.
1. Zealots 2. Conservers
3. Statesman 4. Climbers

Codes:
(a) 1, 2, 3, 4 (b) 2, 3, 1, 4
(c) 4, 2, 3, 1 (d) 4, 2, 1, 3

38. Identify the correct order from the list given below:
1. Department 2. Division
3. Branch 4. Wing

Codes:
(a) 1, 4, 2, 3 (b) 1, 2, 3, 4
(c) 1, 2, 4, 3 (d) 1, 3, 2, 4

39. Match List I with List II and select the correct answer from the codes given below:

List I
(A) County Borough (B) Parish
(C) Borough (D) County

List II
(i) Local Village Administration
(ii) Small City Local Administration
(iii) Largest Unit of Local Government
(iv) District Governing Body

Codes:	A	B	C	D
(a)	(iv)	(i)	(ii)	(iii)
(b)	(ii)	(iv)	(iii)	(i)
(c)	(ii)	(iii)	(i)	(iv)
(d)	(iv)	(ii)	(i)	(iii)

40. Match List I with List II and select the correct answer from the codes given below:

List I
(A) Gossip Grapevine
(B) Cluster Grapevine
(C) Single Strand Grapevine
(D) Probability Grapevine

List II
(i) Information passes selectivity
(ii) Non-selective communication
(iii) Information passes randomly
(iv) Information from one member to another

Codes:	A	B	C	D
(a)	(iii)	(ii)	(iv)	(i)
(b)	(iii)	(iv)	(ii)	(i)
(c)	(ii)	(i)	(iv)	(iii)
(d)	(ii)	(iii)	(iv)	(i)

41. Match List I with List II and select the correct answer from the code given below:

List I

(A) Sixth Schedule (B) Second Schedule
(C) Twelfth Schedule (D) Fifth Schedule

List II

(i) Administration and control of Scheduled areas and Scheduled tribes
(ii) Administration of tribal areas in State of Assam, Meghalaya, Tripura and Mizoram
(iii) Provisions regarding Speakers of State Legislative Assemblies
(iv) Powers of municipalities

Codes:	**A**	**B**	**C**	**D**
(a)	(i)	(iii)	(iv)	(ii)
(b)	(i)	(iv)	(ii)	(iii)
(c)	(ii)	(iii)	(iv)	(i)
(d)	(ii)	(iv)	(i)	(iii)

42. Match List I with List II and select the correct answer from the codes given below:

List I

(A) Comptroller and Auditor General
(B) Annual Financial Statement
(C) Appropriation Bill
(D) Vote on Account

List II

(i) Article 112 (ii) Article 114
(iii) Article 116 (iv) Article 148

Codes:	**A**	**B**	**C**	**D**
(a)	(iii)	(iv)	(i)	(ii)
(b)	(iv)	(i)	(iii)	(ii)
(c)	(iv)	(i)	(ii)	(iii)
(d)	(ii)	(iii)	(i)	(iv)

43. Match List I with List II and select the correct answer from codes given below:

List I	**List II**
(A) Theory of Neutrality	(i) France
(B) Deconcentration	(ii) England
(C) Decentralization	(iii) India
(D) City Manager Plan	(iv) USA

Codes:	**A**	**B**	**C**	**D**
(a)	(ii)	(iii)	(i)	(iv)
(b)	(iii)	(ii)	(iv)	(i)
(c)	(i)	(ii)	(iii)	(iv)
(d)	(ii)	(i)	(iii)	(iv)

44. Match List I with List II and select the correct answer from codes given below:

List I	**List II**
(A) G.V.K. Rao Committee	(i) 1985
(B) L.M. Singhvi Committee	(ii) 1986
(C) Master man Committee	(iii) 1949
(D) Brown low Committee	(iv) 1937

Codes:	**A**	**B**	**C**	**D**
(a)	(i)	(ii)	(iii)	(iv)
(b)	(iii)	(ii)	(i)	(iv)
(c)	(iii)	(i)	(iv)	(ii)
(d)	(iv)	(ii)	(iii)	(i)

45. Match List I with List II and select the correct answer from the codes given below:

List I

(A) Central Secretariat
(B) Cabinet Secretariat
(C) Planning Commission
(D) Finance Commission

List II

(i) Grants in aid
(ii) Coordination
(iii) Policy formulation
(iv) Allocation of resources

Codes:	**A**	**B**	**C**	**D**
(a)	(iii)	(ii)	(i)	(iv)
(b)	(ii)	(iii)	(iv)	(i)
(c)	(i)	(ii)	(iii)	(iv)
(d)	(iv)	(i)	(iii)	(ii)

Read the following passage below and answer the questions that follow based on your understanding of the passage

Riggs liberally coined new words to explain his concepts. In addition he also gave different meanings to a number of words already in use. But free use of new words and words used with different meanings may create confusion instead of clarifying the concepts. He borrowed most of his terminology from physical sciences to give scientific temper to his models. Han Been Lee doubts the utility of the prismatic and sala models in view of the development administrations focus on social change. He considers Rigg's model as equilibrium models. The equilibrium-models would facilitate very much in preserving the system but not introducing any change in the system. Therefore the models of Riggs are not useful when the objective of administration is to change the system rather than maintenance of the system.

The proposed fused and diffracted societies are imaginary, all the societies are to be classified as prismatic at various levels of low, middle and high. But when the scales to measure the levels of prismatism are lacking, the low, middle and high words have no relevance. Since there is no empirical evidence to these assumptions, the validity of such assumptions are highly questionable. Lack of international perspective in his approach is another limitation of his concept. Prismatic model mainly describes developing societies; but fails to explain the place administration in the society. Arona opines that overlapping exists equally in prismatic societies as in diffracted societies. Although his administrative models are difficult to findout in practice, they help us in understanding the realities, his models may deepen our insight into some of the underlying problems of Public Administration in transitional societies. Rigg's models may be considered as more sophisticated tools for describing and diagnosing administrative systems.

46. Which one of the following is not concerned with Riggs' approach?
    (a) New words are coined
    (b) Different meanings of words are given
    (c) It creates confusion
    (d) It gives clarification

47. Which one of the following is not true of 'Prismatic Society'?
    (a) Borrowed the words from Physical Sciences
    (b) Borrowed the words from Biological Sciences
    (c) Gives scientific temper
    (d) Utility of prismatic sala model to development is doubtful

48. Han-Been-Lee considers Riggs' model as:
    1. Facilitates preservation of the system
    2. Facilitates change in the system
    3. Does not facilitate any change in the system
    4. Not useful

    Codes:
    (a) 1, 3, 4 (b) 1, 2, 3
    (c) 2, 3, 4 (d) 1, 2, 4

49. The limitation of Riggs' concept are:
    1. No empirical evidence to the assumptions
    2. Validity of assumptions is questionable
    3. Lacking international perspective
    4. Describes developing societies

    (a) 1, 2, 3 (b) 1, 2, 4
    (c) 2, 3, 4 (d) 1, 3, 4

50. Riggs model:
    (a) Does not help us in understanding realities
    (b) Does not deepen our insight into the problems of Public Administration in transitional of societies
    (c) Fails to explain in the place of administration in the society
    (d) Does not provide sophisticated tools

ANSWERS

1. (a)	2. (d)	3. (c)	4. (b)	5. (d)
6. (d)	7. (b)	8. (c)	9. (d)	10. (a)
11. (a)	12. (c)	13. (a)	14. (c)	15. (c)
16. (a)	17. (b)	18. (a)	19. (b)	20. (c)
21. (a)	22. (a)	23. (b)	24. (a)	25. (a)
26. (c)	27. (a)	28. (b)	29. (c)	30. (b)
31. (d)	32. (a)	33. (b)	34. (c)	35. (b)
36. (c)	37. (d)	38. (a)	39. (a)	40. (c)
41. (c)	42. (c)	43. (d)	44. (a)	45. (b)
46. (d)	47. (d)	48. (a)	49. (b)	50. (c)

JUNE–2005

Note: This paper contains fifty (50) objective type questions, each question carrying two (2) marks. All questions are compulsory.

PAPER–II

1. The word 'Public Administration' was first used by:
   (a) Hamilton
   (b) Lord Brice
   (c) Woodrow Wilson
   (d) L.D. White
2. The word 'Bureau Pathology' was created by:
   (a) Max Weber
   (b) Robert Morten
   (c) Victor Thompson
   (d) Karl Marx
3. Who defined organisation as a system of consciously coordinated activities of two or more persons?
   (a) Taylor (b) Chester Barnard
   (c) Simon (d) Likert
4. Which one of the following statement is connected with the managerial view of administration?
   (a) every particular application of law is an act of administration
   (b) public administration is directed by the Chief Executive as the General Manager
   (c) Administration is not doing things but getting things done
   (d) Public Administration is concerned with the ends of the state
5. Which of the following is not correct about behaviour of organisation as a system?
   (a) It seeks equilibrium
   (b) It seeks equilibrium with environment
   (c) It does not change once adapted to the needs of the environment
   (d) the equilibrium sought is a dynamic equilibrium
6. The 'one best way' in scientific management means:
   (a) Equal division of work
   (b) Mental Revolution in workers and management
   (c) Standardisation of work methods
   (d) Intensive analysis of work processes
7. Which of the following is not a feature of ideal type of bureaucracy?
   (a) Officials may appropriate the post
   (b) Salary is graded according to position
   (c) Officials are subject to unified control
   (d) Functions are clearly specified
8. Motivation has been expressed as:
   (a) Valency × Expectancy
   (b) Valency × Ability
   (c) Expectancy × knowledge
   (d) Expectancy × skill
9. In an informal organisation the authority always flows:
   (a) downwards
   (b) upwards
   (c) across and downwards
   (d) upwards and across
10. Grehman theory of leadership led to the rise of:
    (a) The behavioural theory of leadership
    (b) The Trait theory of leadership

(c) The situational theory of leadership
(d) Democratic theory of leadership

11. Middle range studies of comparative public administration focus on:
(a) Structures of bureaucracies of two or more nations
(b) Recruitment or training system of two or more administrative organizations
(c) Administrative systems of two or more countries
(d) Administrative systems in the same country

12. According to F.W. Riggs, the trends in comparative public administration are:
(i) Normative to empirical
(ii) Ideographic to Nomothetic
(iii) Empirical to normataive
(iv) Ecological to non-ecological
(v) Non-ecological to ecological
(a) i, ii, & iv (b) ii, iii, & v
(c) ii, iii, & iv (d) i, ii, & v

13. 'Development administration is an organised effort to carry out programmes and projects .... to serve development objectives: Who said this?
(a) Edward Weidner (b) F.W. Riggs
(c) Donald Stone (d) Montegomery

14. The Planning Commission is described as the "Economic Cabinet" by:
(a) P.P. Agarwal (b) Ashok Chanda
(c) D.R. Gadgil (d) Santhanam

15. The Budget system in India was first introduced by:
(a) Financial Resolution, 1860
(b) Govt. of India Act, 1919
(c) Lee Commission, 1923
(d) Constitution of India, 1950

16. Prime Ministers office is a:
(a) Constitutional body
(b) Part of the Secretariat
(c) Department under the Government of India, Business Rules, 1961
(d) Line agency

17. Hypothesis is:
(a) An acquired tendency on the part of the people
(b) A statement relating to expected relationship between two or more variables
(c) The procedure of systematically recording verbal and non-verbal behaviour
(d) A statement explaining the meaning of words

18. Which one of the following is not correct of the concept of social justice?
(a) It originates from the concept of human equality
(b) It believes in human freedom and dignity
(c) It is dynamic
(d) It is always co-extensive with social change

19. 73rd Constitutional amendment provided for:
(a) Constitutional status to rural and urban bodies
(b) Mandatory three tier system for all the states
(c) Audit of panchayat finances by C.A.G
(d) Direct elections of chairpersons and members of PRI at all levels

20. According to Fred. W. Riggs, the comparative Public Administration approach stands for a distintive orientation. Which one of the following is typical of that approach?
(a) Behavioural approach
(b) Public policy approach
(c) Ecological approach and Empirical approach
(d) Logical approach

21. **Assertion (A):** March and Simon have described Classical Theory as a Machine Model Theory.
Reason (R): Classical Theory emphasises on orderly structure, rationally, impersonality, efficiency and specialisation.
Choose the correct answer from the following answer code:
(a) Both (A) and (R) are correct, and (R) is the correct explanation of (A)
(b) Both (A) and (R) are correct, but (R) is not the correct explanation of (A)
(c) (A) is true but (R) is false
(d) (A) is false but (R) is true

22. **Assertion (A):** Judicial Review means the power of the courts to declare the laws and orders of the Government as invalid if they are against the Constitution.
Reason (R): The failure of the executive and legistature has given rise to judicial activism.
Choose the correct answer from the following answer code:
(a) Both (A) and (R) are correct, and (R) is the correct explanation of (A)
(b) Both (A) and (R) are correct, but (R) is not the correct explanation of (A)
(c) (A) is true but (R) is false
(d) (A) is false but (R) is true

23. **Assertion (A):** Delegation is a functional imperative for all types of organisations
Reason (R): The Chief Executive can provide effective leadership only when he has all the powers himself.
Choose the correct answer from the following answer code:
(a) Both (A) and (R) are correct, and (R) is the correct explanation of (A)
(b) Both (A) and (R) are correct, but (R) is not the correct explanation of (A)
(c) (A) is true but (R) is false
(d) (A) is false but (R) is true

24. **Assertion (A):** The behavioural approach stresses upon the informal relationship among the members of an organisation.
Reason (R): Behaviouralists employ integrated and interdisciplinary approach.
Choose the correct answer from the following answer code:
(a) Both (A) and (R) are correct, and (R) is the correct explanation of (A)
(b) Both (A) and (R) are correct, but (R) is not the correct explanation of (A)
(c) (A) is true but (R) is false.
(d) (A) is false but (R) is true.

25. **Assertion (A):** 73rd Constitutional Amendment Act is a significant land mark in the evolution of grass roots democratic institutions in India.
Reason (R): The act brought the Panchayat Raj institutions under the perview of justiciable part of the Constitution.
Choose the correct answer from the following answer code:
(a) Both (A) and (R) are correct, and (R) is the correct explanation of (A)
(b) Both (A) and (R) are correct, but (R) is not the correct explanation of (A)
(c) (A) is true but (R) is false
(d) (A) is false but (R) is true

26. **Assertion (A):** Although the workers were capable of producing more, the output was held down to maintain the uniform rate of output:
Reaason (R): They were highly integrated with their social structure and informal pressure was used to set right the erring members.
Choose the correct answer from the following answer code:
(a) Both (A) and (R) are correct, and (R) is the correct explanation of (A)
(b) Both (A) and (R) are correct, but (R) is not the correct explanation of (A)

(c) (A) is true but (R) is false
(d) (A) is false but (R) is true

27. **Assertion (A):** A decision is made within the guidelines established by policy.
Reason (R): It is moment in the process of policy formulation.
Choose the correct answer from the following answer code:
(a) Both (A) and (R) are correct, and (R) is the correct explanation of (A)
(b) Both (A) and (R) are correct, but (R) is not the correct explanation of (A)
(c) (A) is true but (R) is false
(d) (A) is false but (R) is true

28. **Assertion (A):** Municipal corporation enjoys a greater measure of autonomy than other forms of local government
Reason (R): A municipal corporation is set up under a special statute passed by the state legislature.
Choose the correct answer from the following answer code:
(a) Both (A) and (R) are correct, and (R) is the correct explanation of (A)
(b) Both (A) and (R) are correct, but (R) is not the correct explanation of (A)
(c) (A) is true but (R) is false
(d) (A) is false but (R) is true

29. **Assertion (A):** According to Paul H. Appleby, parliament is the chief citadel of opposition to delegation of powers, the need for which is the worst shortcoming of Indian Administration.
Reason (R): To him the parliament's reluctance to delegate its powers in detail, discourages ministers, secretaries, and managing directors from delegating their powers.
Choose the correct answer from the following answer code:
(a) Both (A) and (R) are correct, and (R) is the correct explanation of (A)
(b) Both (A) and (R) are correct, but (R) is not the correct explanation of (A)
(c) (A) is true but (R) is false
(d) (A) is false but (R) is true

30. **Assertion (A):** The Finance Ministry exercises financial control over all the administrative ministries.
Reason (R): It is responsible for the formulation and execution of the budget.
(a) Both (A) and (R) are correct, and (R) is the correct explanatin of (A)
(b) Both (A) and (R) are correct, but (R) is not the correct explanation of (A)
(c) (A) is true but (R) is false
(d) (A) is false but (R) is true

31. Likert has proposed following stages of organisational development. Put them in order:
(1) Correcting weaknesses concerning structure, leader behaviour etc.
(2) Analysing and interpreting scores based on their relationship to the ideal model
(3) Establishing the ideal model
(4) Preparing the action plan
Codes:
(a) 2, 3, 1, 4 (b) 3, 2, 1, 4
(c) 1, 4, 3, 2 (d) 4, 2, 3, 1

32. What is the correct sequence of the following land marks in the growth and emergence of New Public Administration?
(1) The Minnowbrook Conference
(2) The Honey Report on Higher Education for Public Service.
(3) The Philadelphia conference on the theory and practice of Public Admnistration
(4) Publication of 'Toward a New Public Administration the Minnowbrook perspective.
Codes:
(a) 4, 3, 2, 1 (b) 2, 3, 1, 4
(c) 2, 4, 1, 3 (d) 1, 2, 3, 4

33. We have now four stages in the evolution of Public Administration, identify the correct order:
(1) Principles approach
(2) American universities offering courses of instruction in public administration
(3) Human Relation School (or approach)
(4) Behavioural approach
Codes:
(a) 2, 1, 3, 4 (b) 4, 1, 2, 3
(c) 1, 2, 3, 4 (d) 3, 4, 2, 1

34. Arrange the following French local government units in order:
Use the code given below:
(1) Department (2) Arrondisement
(3) Canton (4) Commune
Codes:
(a) 1, 2, 3, 4 (b) 2, 1, 3, 4
(c) 3, 1, 2, 4 (d) 4, 3, 2, 1

35. Various programmes which are directly or indirectly designed for the amelioration of the socio-economic conditions of the rural poor are:
(1) Bhoodan Movement
(2) Community Development Programme
(3) Hill area development programme
(4) Tribal area development programme
Codes:
(a) 1, 2, 3, 4 (b) 2, 1, 3, 4
(c) 2, 1, 4, 3 (d) 3, 4, 1, 2

36. Taylor advocated the following steps to make management more systematic. Put them in correct order:
(1) Employees to be scientifically selected.
(2) Using methods of research experiments to formulate principles of standards
(3) A spirit of friendly co-operation.
(4) Imparting appropriate training
Codes:
(a) 2, 1, 3, 4 (b) 1, 3, 4, 2
(c) 3, 4, 2, 1 (d) 1, 2, 3, 4

37. The Bounded Rationality Model of Simon exhibits following activities. Put them in order:
(1) Establish level of aspiration
(2) Appraise aspiration-level attainment
(3) Identify feasible alternative
(4) Appraise alternative
Codes:
(a) 3, 2, 1, 4 (b) 4, 1, 2, 3
(c) 1, 3, 4, 2 (d) 2, 3, 4, 1

38. Arrange the following articles in order. Use the code given below:
(1) Principles of Public Administration
(2) Introduction to the study of Public Administration
(3) The study of Administration
(4) Politics and Administration
Codes:
(a) 3, 1, 2, 4 (b) 1, 2, 3, 4
(c) 2, 1, 3, 4 (d) 4, 3, 2, 1

39. Match the List I and List II and select the correct answer from the codes given below:
List I
(A) F.W. Taylor (B) Max Weber
(C) Chester Barnard (D) Elton Mayo
List II
(1) Domination Authority and legitimacy
(2) Human attitude and sentiments
(3) Organisation as a cooperative effort
(4) Functional foremanship

Codes:	**A**	**B**	**C**	**D**
(a)	4	3	2	1
(b)	4	1	3	2
(c)	1	2	3	4
(d)	3	2	1	4

40. Match the List I and List II and select the correct answer from the codes given below:
List I
(A) Proverbs of administration
(B) Principles of Management
(C) Functions of Executive
(D) Elements of Public Administration

List II

(1) Henry Fayol (2) Chester Barnard
(3) Herbert Simon (4) Moreisten Marx

Codes:	A	B	C	D
(a)	2	3	1	4
(b)	3	2	4	1
(c)	3	1	2	4
(d)	1	2	3	4

41. Match the List I and List II and select the correct answer from the codes given below:

List I

(A) Human problems of an industrial civilization
(B) The theory of organisation
(C) Scientific principles of organisation
(D) The administrative theory in the state

List II

(1) Gulick and Urwick
(2) Mayo
(3) Urwick
(4) Henry Fayol

Codes:	A	B	C	D
(a)	1	2	3	4
(b)	2	3	1	4
(c)	3	1	2	4
(d)	3	4	1	2

42. Match the List I and List II and select the correct answer from the codes given below:

List I

(A) Bureaucracy is an imperfect tool
(B) Bureaucracy is a participative decision making process
(C) Bureaucracy means work done in organisation in routine
(D) Bureaucracy is opposed to organisational ends

List II

(1) Victor Thompson (2) Warren Bennis
(3) Charles Perrow (4) Crozier

Codes:	A	B	C	D
(a)	2	3	1	4
(b)	1	2	3	4
(c)	3	2	4	1
(d)	4	1	3	2

43. Match the List I and List II and select the correct answer from the codes given below:

List I

(A) Economic subsystem
(B) Administrative subsystem
(C) Differentiated and integrated
(D) Differentiated and distintegrated

List II

(1) Sala model
(2) Diftracted society
(3) Prismatic society
(4) Bazar-canteen model

Codes:	A	B	C	D
(a)	1	3	2	4
(b)	2	3	1	4
(c)	4	1	2	3
(d)	4	2	3	1

44. Match the List I and List II and select the correct answer from the codes given below:

List I

(A) Frontiers of development adminstration
(B) Public Administration—a comparitive study
(C) Overcoming organisational defence
(D) The making of scientific management

List II

(1) Riggs (2) F. Heady
(3) Argyris (4) Urwick

Codes:	A	B	C	D
(a)	2	3	1	4
(b)	1	2	3	4
(c)	2	3	4	1
(d)	4	1	3	2

45. Match the List I and List II and select the correct answer from the codes given below:

List I	List II
(A) Vote on credit	(1) Contingency fund
(B) Vote on account	(2) Emergency
(C) Special grant	(3) Advanced grant
(D) Guillotine	(4) Vote without debate

Codes:	A	B	C	D
(a)	2	3	1	4
(b)	1	4	2	3
(c)	3	2	4	1
(d)	4	3	1	2

Read the passage below, and answer the questions that follow based on your understanding, of the passage.

Weberian formulation has been characterised as value-neutral; it simply provides a conceptualisation of a form of social organisation with certain characteristics. It can be examined from three different points of view which are not, of course, mutually exclusive. Firstly, bureaucracy can be viewed in terms of purely structural characteristics. In fact, the structural dimension has attracted the most attention in the discussions on bureaucracy. The features like division of work and hierarchy have been identified as important aspects of structure. Secondly, bureaucracy has been sought to be defined in terms of behavioural characteristics. Certain patterns of behaviour form an integral part of the conception. To quote Weber, "When fully developed, burreaucracy also stands in a specific sense under the principle of sine ira ac studio. Its specific nature, which is welcomed by capitalism, develops the more completely the more bureaucracy is 'dehumanised', the more completely it succeeds in eliminating from official business love, hatred, and all purely personal, irrational, and emotional elements which escape calculation. This is the specific nature of bureraucracy and its specific virtue".

Thirdly, bureaucracy has been looked at from the point of view of achievement of purpose. This is an instrumental view of bureaucracy. As per peter Blau suggests, it should be considered as an "organisation that maximises efficiency in administration or an institutionalised method of organised social conduct in the interests of administratiave efficiency".

All these approaches have their respective values, and the critics of Weber have often taken one or the other view as the starting point of their criticism.

In evaluating Weber, one has to understand that Weber wanted to construct an "ideal type" or a mental map of a "fully developed" bureaucracy. The ideal type is a mental construct that cannot be found in reality. It is an abstracation that exaggerates certain features and deemphasises certain others with a view to conveying an image or an idea.

In Weberian formulation, bureaucracy is not to be confused with the civil services. It refers to the sociological concept of rationalisation of collective activities. As a form or design of organisation it assures predictability of behaviour of the organisational members. The bureaucratic form, according to Weber, is the most efficient organisational form for large-scale , complex administration that has been developed in the modern world so far. It is superior to any other form in decision precision, stability, maintenance of discipline and reliability. For the heads of organisations, it makes possible a high degree of calculability of results. Bureaucracy compares to other forms or of organisation as does the machine with non-mechanical modes of production.

46. Weberian concept has been characterised by:
(a) value neutral
(b) value free
(c) value less
(d) value proportional

47. Webers bureaucracy cannot be viewed in terms of:
(a) Structural characteristics
(b) Division of work
(c) Hierarchy
(d) Social-psychological attributes

48. According to the author, bureaucracy can be examined from the point of view of:
    (a) Structural characteristics
    (b) Behavioural characteristics
    (c) Achievement of power
    (d) All of the above
49. The instrumental view of Bureaucracy refers to:
    (a) viewing it from achievement of purpose
    (b) viewing it in the context of value
    (c) viewing it as rationalisation of activities
    (d) viewing it in the context of its structure
50. According to Weber the bureaucratic form is the most efficient form for:
    (a) Large scale administration only
    (b) Complex administration only
    (c) Simple administration only
    (d) Both (a) and (b)

ANSWERS

1. (a)	2. (c)	3. (d)	4. (c)	5. (c)
6. (c)	7. (a)	8. (a)	9. (c)	10. (b)
11. (a)	12. (d)	13. (b)	14. (b)	15. (a)
16. (d)	17. (b)	18. (d)	19. (b)	20. (c)
21. (b)	22. (a)	23. (c)	24. (a)	25. (b)
26. (a)	27. (a)	28. (c)	29. (a)	30. (a)
31. (c)	32. (b)	33. (a)	34. (d)	35. (a)
36. (a)	37. (c)	38. (d)	39. (b)	40. (c)
41. (b)	42. (c)	43. (c)	44. (b)	45. (a)
46. (a)	47. (d)	48. (d)	49. (a)	50. (d)

PRACTICE PAPERS

MOCK TEST–1
PAPER–I

1. A teacher is called the leader of the class because
   (a) he is autocratic emperor of his class
   (b) he masters the art of oratory like a political leader
   (c) he is a maker of the future of his students
   (d) he belongs to a recognised teachers' union

2. The aim of introducing career courses in schools and colleges is to
   (a) increase G.K. in students
   (b) develop the ability to make the intelligent choice of jobs
   (c) provide professional knowledge to students
   (d) All of the above

3. The most effective attribute for a teacher is
   (a) Teaching skills (b) Knowledge
   (c) Feedback (d) Management

4. Those teachers are preferred most by students who
   (a) are themselves disciplined
   (b) give important questions before examination
   (c) dictate notes in the class
   (d) can clear their difficulties regarding subject-matter

5. The qualities of a teacher is/are:
   (i) He must not give any false promise
   (ii) He must not have any bad habits
   (iii) He should be mentally and physically fit
   (iv) He must not be superstitious about his class and students
   (a) Only (iii), (iv) and (ii)
   (b) Only (iv), (i) and (ii)
   (c) Only (i), (iii) and (iv)
   (d) All of the above

6. A teacher is more effective who can
   (a) motivate students to learn
   (b) control the class
   (c) correct the assignments carefully
   (d) give more information in less time

7. A teacher ought to know the problems prevalent in the field of education because
   (a) he can tell the government about it
   (b) with this knowledge, he can have information about education
   (c) he can tell about the same to another teacher
   (d) only he can do something about solving them

8. We can judge the quality of a research by the
   (a) experience of researcher
   (b) relevance of research
   (c) depth of the research
   (d) methodology followed in conducting the research

9. The theory or model developed through the fundamental research to the actual solution of the problems is applied in
   (a) educational research
   (b) action research
   (c) applied research
   (d) basic research

10. A write-up based on studies of the census data of a given area is called
    (a) Research paper (b) Article
    (c) Research report (d) Thesis

Direction: (11-16) Study the following passage and give answer to the questions based on it.

Knowledge creation in many cases requires creativity and idea generation. This is especially important in generating alternative decision support solutions. Some people believe that an individual's creative ability stems primarily from personality traits such as inventiveness, independence, individuality, enthusiasm, and flexibility. However, several studies have found that creativity is not so much a function of individual traits as was once believed, and that individual creativity can be learned and improved. This understanding has led innovative companies to recognise that the key to fostering creativity may be the development of an idea-nurturing work environment. Idea-generation methods and techniques, to be used by individuals or in groups, are consequently being developed. Manual methods for supporting idea generation, such as brain-storming in a group, can be very successful in certain situations. However, in other situations, such an approach is either not economically feasible or not possible. For example, manual methods in group creativity sessions will not work or will not be effective when: (a) there is no time to conduct a proper idea-generation session; (b) there is a poor facilitator (or no facilitator at all); (c) it is too expensive to conduct an idea-generation session; (d) the subject matter is too sensitive for a face-to-face session; or (e) there are not enough participants, the mix of participants is not optimal, or there is no climate for idea generation. In such cases, computerised idea-generation methods have been tried, with frequent success. Idea-generation software is designed to help stimulate a single user or a group to produce new ideas, options and choices. The user does all the work, but the software encourages and pushes, something like a personal trainer. Although idea-generation software is still relatively new, there are several packages on the market. Various approaches are used by idea-generating software to increase the flow of ideas to the user. Idea Fisher, for example, has an associate lexicon of the English language that cross-references words and phrases. These associative links, based on analogies and metaphors, make it easy for the user to be fed words related to a given theme. Some software packages use questions to prompt the user towards new, unexplored patterns of thought. This helps users to break out of cyclical thinking patterns, conquer mental blocks, or deal with bouts of procrastination.

11. The author, in this passage has focused on
    (a) individual traits
    (b) knowledge creation
    (c) creativity
    (d) idea-generation
12. Idea-generation software works as if it is a
    (a) user-friendly trainer
    (b) stimulant
    (c) climate creator
    (d) knowledge package
13. Which among the following personality traits is not believed to be a factor contributing to an individual's creative ability?
    (a) Flexibility (b) Individuality
    (c) Sophistication (d) Enthusiasm
14. In certain occasions, manual methods for the support of idea-generation
    (a) can be less expensive
    (b) do not need a facilitator
    (c) require a mix of optimal participants
    (d) are alternatively effective

15. Mental blocks, bouts of procrastination and cyclical thinking patterns can be won when
    (a) idea-generation software prompts questions
    (b) individuals acquire a neutral attitude towards the software
    (c) manual methods are removed
    (d) innovative companies employ electronic thinking methods

16. Fostering creativity needs an environment of
    (a) decision support systems
    (b) alternative individual factors
    (c) idea-nurturing
    (d) decision support solutions

17. For controlling noise in a classroom, the best method of communication is
    (a) remaining calm and just looking at student
    (b) saying 'don't talk'
    (c) continue teaching without caring for noise
    (d) raising one's voice above students voice

18. In India, Education TV was first introduced in the year
    (a) 1978 (b) 1959
    (c) 1987 (d) 1998

19. The failure of the teacher to communicate his ideas well to students may result into:
    I. Classroom indiscipline.
    II. Decrease in attendance in class.
    III. Loss of student's interest in class.
    (a) Only II (b) Only III
    (c) Only I (d) All of these

20. Visualisation in the instructional process cannot increase
    (a) curiosity and concentration
    (b) interest and motivation
    (c) stress and boredom
    (d) retention and adaptation

21. Communication helps in
    (a) entertainment
    (b) integration of country
    (c) cultural promotion
    (d) All of these

22. "Because you deserve to know" is the punchline used by
    (a) *Hindustan Times*
    (b) *The Telegraph*
    (c) *The Times of India*
    (d) *India Today*

23. Find the odd man out from the following groups of letters.
    (a) UlmnE (b) AbcdE
    (c) ApqrL (d) IfghO

24. The ambitious computerisation program of the Government of India aimed at connecting 60,000 government schools through internet is known as
    (a) Vidya Vahini (b) Gyan Vahini
    (c) Kalpana project (d) Vidya Vani

25. Find the wrong number in the following sequence.
    225, 336, 447, 557, 669, 771
    (a) 669 (b) 557
    (c) 336 (d) 771

26. In this question two words are given which have certain relationship followed by four paired lettered words. Select the paired words, that has the same relation as original pair.
    ROOF : FOUNDATION
    (a) Plateau : Valley
    (b) Peak : Valley
    (c) Mountain : Grassland
    (d) Hill : Mountain

27. "Communication is a verbal process by which we understand each other and reduce uncertainty through the use of symbol." Who is the author of this statement?

(a) David K. Barlo
(b) Dance
(c) P.S.K. Serichavenko
(d) K.J. Newman

28. Find out the missing number:
8 24 12 ? 18 54
(a) 28 (b) 32
(c) 36 (d) 38

29. A D C F
C F E H
O R ? ?
(a) JK (b) RN
(c) SU (d) QT

30. 3, 12, 27, 48, 75, (?), 147.
(a) 111 (b) 108
(c) 117 (d) 122

31. In this question four words have been given, out of which three are alike in some manner and the fourth one is different. Choose the odd one out.
(a) Epigraphy (b) Ecology
(c) Archaeology (d) Palaeontology

32. Which of the following figures will represent the right relationship between, societies, societies who run schools, DPS society.

(a) 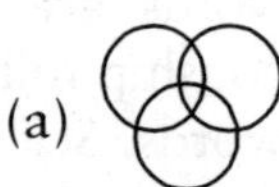 (b) 

(c) 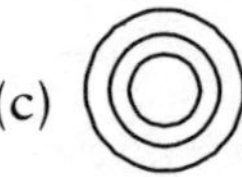 (d) 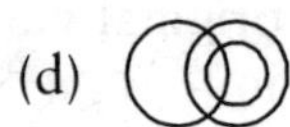

33. **Statements:**
I. All students are ambitious.
II. All ambitious persons are hard working.
Conclusions:
(i) All students are hard-working.
(ii) All hardly working people are not ambitious.
Which of the following is correct?
(a) Only (i) is correct
(b) Only (ii) is correct
(c) Both (i) and (ii) are correct
(d) Neither (i) nor (ii) is correct

34. In a certain code language:
'pit dit mit' means: 'Reena went to Delhi'.
'dit ket set' means: 'Delhi is closing'.
'mit set un' means: 'Reena' is educated.
Then what is the code for 'went'?
(a) dit (b) mit
(c) pit (d) None of these

35. EDITOR : MAGAZINE
Choose the pair from the answer choices that best expresses the relationship similar to that expressed by the question pair.
(a) Novel : Writer
(b) Director : Film
(c) Poem : Poet
(d) Chair : Carpenter

36. Should education in India be made free?
Arguments:
I. Yes, this is the only way to improve the level of literacy.
II. No, this would add already heavy burden on the exchequer.
(a) Only argument I is strong
(b) Only argument II is strong
(c) Both the arguments are strong
(d) None of these

Direction: (37-41) Study the table and answer the questions:

Export of Pulses and Import of Onion (in ₹ crores)

Year	Export of Pulses (in ₹ crores)	Import of Onion (in ₹ crores)
1998-99	44	58
1999-00	45	50
2000-01	60	54

2001-02	56	60
2002-03	92	68
2003-04	100	78
2004-05	68	60

37. During which year there was a maximum fall in export?
(a) 2004-05 (b) 2001-02
(c) 2003-04 (d) None of these

38. The percent of increase of imports in 2003-04 over 2002-03 is
(a) 14.9% (b) 14.7%
(c) 18.4% (d) 18.9%

39. In 1999-2000, the ratio of export to the import is
(a) 19:11 (b) 11:9
(c) 13:17 (d) 9:10

40. During which year there was maximum increase in import over its preceding year?
(a) 2003-04 (b) 2000-01
(c) 2001-02 (d) 2002-03

41. During which year there was minimum increase in import over its preceding year?
(a) 2003-04 (b) 2002-03
(c) 2001-02 (d) None of these

42. The sum of a positive number and its reciprocal is twice the difference of the number and its reciprocal. The number is:
(a) $\sqrt{3}$ (b) $\sqrt{2}$
(c) $\frac{1}{\sqrt{2}}$ (d) $\frac{1}{\sqrt{3}}$

43. Which one of the following states has the maximum number of Wildlife Sanctuaries (National Park and Sanctuaries)?
(a) Madhya Pradesh
(b) Rajasthan
(c) Uttar Pradesh
(d) West Bengal

Directions: (44-48) Answer the following questions based on the graph given below:

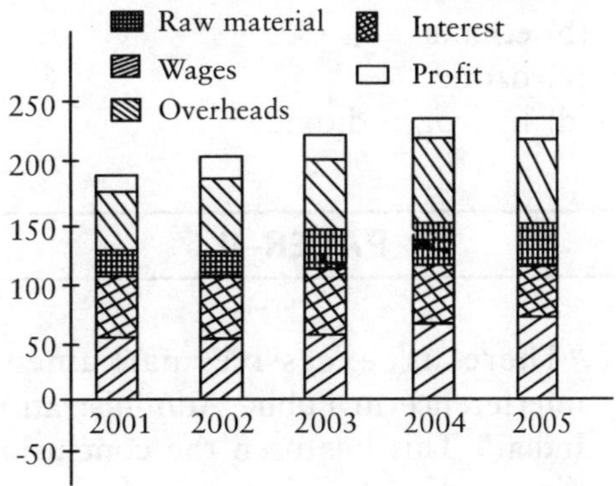

44. Which component of the cost of production has remained almost unchanged over the period 2001-2005?
(a) Wages (b) Interest
(c) Raw material (d) Overheads

45. In which year was the increase in raw material maximum?
(a) 2004 (b) 2002
(c) 2003 (d) 2001

46. What percent of costs did the profits form over the period?
(a) 7% (b) 5%
(c) 2% (d) 1%

47. In which period was the change in profit maximum?
(a) 2002-03 (b) 2001-02
(c) 2004-05 (d) 2003-04

48. If the interest component is not included in the total cost calculation, which year would show the maximum profit per unit cost?
(a) 2001 (b) 2002
(c) 2003 (d) 2005

49. How many types of emergencies have been envisaged by the Constitution?
(a) One (b) Two
(c) Three (d) Four

50. Photocopying and other electrical equipments produce
    (a) methane
    (b) ethane
    (c) ozone
    (d) hydrogen dioxide

PAPER–II

1. "There is excessive parliamentary interference in Public Administration of India." This has been the conclusion of the
    (a) Appleby Report
    (b) Boothalingam Committee Report
    (c) Raja Chelliah Committee Report
    (d) Hanumanthaiya Commission Report
2. The Law of Probability is applied in
    (a) Non-random sampling
    (b) Geometry
    (c) Random sampling
    (d) None of the above
3. The Sixth Schedule to the Constitution of India makes special administrative provisions in regard to the tribal areas in
    (a) Meghalaya, Assam, Nagaland and Manipur
    (b) Assam, Meghalaya, Tripura and Mizoram
    (c) Arunachal Pradesh, Nagaland, Assam and Tripura
    (d) Tripura, Manipur, Mizoram and Meghalaya
4. Harmonic mean of a series of data is
    (a) always ill-defined.
    (b) the reciprocal of the arithmetic average of the values of various items.
    (c) the reciprocal of the arithmetic average of the reciprocal values of its various items.
    (d) None of the above.
5. What could be termed as the destructive effect of British colonialism in India?
    (a) It led to the division of India into small units.
    (b) It led to systematic exploitation of India.
    (c) It promoted divisive forces to keep itself in power.
    (d) Both (b) and (c).
6. Which of the following management thinkers is to be credited for advancing the idea of making planning an independent function?
    (a) F.W. Taylor (b) Elton Mayo
    (c) Henri Fayol (d) Max Weber
7. Health Insurance Business is with:
    (a) LIC
    (b) UTI associated
    (c) GIC
    (d) State Trading Corporation
8. Profit motive is no longer the sole driving force in
    (a) Private Administration
    (b) Public Administration
    (c) Both Public and Private Administrations
    (d) Neither Public Administration nor Private Administration
9. Railway Budget was separated from the General Budget in
    (a) 1911 (b) 1921
    (c) 1931 (d) 1951
10. The success of efficient and honest Public Administration is
    (a) indirectly related to political environment.
    (b) partially related to political environment.
    (c) directly related to political environment.
    (d) None of the above.

11. Find the median of the following data: 160, 180, 200, 280, 300, 320, 400.
(a) 180 (b) 280
(c) 320 (d) 400

12. For doing external criticism (for establishing the authenticity of data) a researcher must verify
(a) the signature and handwriting of the author.
(b) style of prose writing of that period.
(c) the paper and ink used in that period which is under study.
(d) All of the above.

13. Which of the following are the important contributions to both political and administrative issues and ideas of the Western world?
(a) Ramayana and Mahabharata
(b) Roumean's Discourse
(c) *Arms and the Man*
(d) Aristotle's *Politics*

14. The classification of services in India is governed by the
(a) Civil Services Rules, *1950*.
(b) Civil Services Rules, 1960.
(c) Civil Services Rules, 1987.
(d) Civil Services Rules, 1990.

15. Which of the following is the basic thesis to make public administration an effective instrument for ushering in the democratic welfare state?
(a) Administration is a moral act and administrator is a moral agent.
(b) Constitutional promises.
(c) Basic principles of the political party in power.
(d) Calibre of public servants.

16. The administrative system of France is called 'classic' because
(a) French bureaucracy conforms most closely to the Weberian model.
(b) France adopted different administrative orientations.
(c) France has had remarkable administrative and bureaucratic continuity.
(d) administrative change in France has been abrupt, drastic and frequent.

17. "The future of civilised government and even, I think, of civilisation itself, rests upon our ability to develop a service and philosophy and a practice of administration competent to discharge the public functions of a civilised society." Who said this?
(a) Charles Beard
(b) Eisenstadt and Diamant
(c) Gabriel Almond
(d) Ordway Tead

18. Which one of the following is not true of Line activity?
(a) It stands for thought and facilitation.
(b) It has operational abilities.
(c) It has authority.
(d) It decides the organisational goals.

19. The Office of General Services Administration was set up in the USA on the recommendation of
(a) Brownlow Committee
(b) First Hoover Commission
(c) Second Hoover Commission
(d) Ramspeck Report

20. The greatest limitation of this approach is that one cannot get a true picture of how an organization functions in practice. Which of this is the approach?
(a) Institutional structural approach
(b) Behavioural approach
(c) Historical approach
(d) Philosophical approach

21. "It is being felt growingly over the last twenty or thirty years that the amount of expertise, which is available on the government side is so out of proportion to the amount of expert knowledge which

an M.P. normally gets hold of, that the critical role of Parliament is losing in its effectiveness .... "Who said this"?

(a) Clement Attlee
(b) Hugh Gaitskell
(c) Shriram Maheshwari
(d) Morris Jones

22. The Scientific Management Approach developed during
(a) 18th century
(b) 19th century
(c) early 20th century
(d) late 20th century

23. The Independent Regulatory Commissions are called
(a) Islands of autonomy
(b) the arms of the Congress
(c) President's branch of Government
(d) the arms of the Congress and Presidents branch of Government

24. Which one of the following statements about the systems approach to organisation is not correct?
(a) It studies the organisation as a whole in relation to its environment.
(b) It is derived from the general systems theory.
(c) It views the organisation and its environment as interdependent for inputs and resources.
(d) It leads to certain fundamental principles of organisation.

25. Which of these are correct, in common parlance, about administration?
1. A synonym of cabinet
2. A branch of learning
3. The art of management
4. Sum-total of the activities undertaken to implement public policy/policies.

Codes:
(a) 2 and 3 (b) 3 and 4
(c) 1, 3 and 4 (d) 1, 2, 3 and 4

26. Esteem needs include the desire for
1. Achievement
2. Adequacy
3. Strength
4. Mastery and competence
5. Independence and freedom

Codes:
(a) 1, 2 and 3 (b) 2, 3 and 4
(c) 3, 4 and 5 (d) All of these

27. Which of the following did Herbert Simon emphasize?
1. Value-fact dichotomy
2. Means-ends relationship
3. Composite decision-making
4. Illusion of final authority

Codes:
(a) 1 and 2 (b) 1, 2 and 3
(c) 1, 3 and 4 (d) 2, 3 and 4

28. In the evolution of Public Administration there has been a shift in emphasis during successive periods. In this context which of the following pairs are correctly matched?
1. 1887-26 : Crisis of Identity
2. 1910-20 : Scientific Management
3. 1920-47 : Human Relations
4. 1948-66 : Behaviouralism

Codes:
(a) 1, 2 and 3 (b) 1, 2 and 4
(c) 1, 3 and 4 (d) 2, 3 and 4

29. The basic similarity between the Public Administration and the Private Administration is that
1. Many of the managerial techniques are common to both.
2. Some of the practices in vogue in private Administration have been influencing Public Administration, and are even assimilated by the latter.
3. The responsibility of the government official as of his counterpart in the private business is the same in as

much as each aims at achieving results in his assigned field of work by getting things done.
4. Public and Private Administration function in the same environment.

Codes:
(a) 1 and 2 (b) 1 and 3
(c) 1, 2 and 3 (d) 1, 2, 3 and 4

30. Which of the following statements are correct in respect of cameralists?
1. They did much for the training of administrators.
2. They were a group of French Scholars.
3. The foremost among them was G. Zinck E.
4. They combined professional posts with public service.

Codes:
(a) 1 and 3 (b) 2 and 4
(c) 1, 3 and 4 (d) 1, 2, 3 and 4

31. **List I**
A. Abandonment of the political development concept
B. Development as an Ideal type
C. Political authority and competition Eckstein for politically allocated values
D. Political culture and development

List II
1. F.W. Riggs 2. Hans. S. Park
3. Harry 4. Almond

Codes:	A	B	C	D
(a)	2	1	4	3
(b)	1	2	3	4
(c)	4	3	2	1
(d)	3	1	4	2

32. **List I (Person)**
A. Lord Wellesley
B. Warren Hastings
C. William Bentinck
D. Lord Cornwallis

List II (Act)
1. Created the post of Civil Judge.
2. Created the office of Chief Secretary.
3. Created the office of District Collector.
4. Created the post of Deputy Collector.

Codes:	A	B	C	D
(a)	2	4	3	1
(b)	1	3	4	2
(c)	2	3	4	1
(d)	1	4	3	2

33. **List I**
A. Psychological and behavioural factors in organisational analysis.
B. Long range planning and human relations in industry and Government.
C. Rejected classical principles of administration and politics administration dichotomy.
D. Challenged public administration as sctence.

List II
1. Herbert Simon 2. Peter Drucker
3. Chester Barnard 4. Robert Dahl

Codes:	A	B	C	D
(a)	3	2	1	4
(b)	2	1	3	4
(c)	4	1	2	3
(d)	3	2	4	1

34. **List I**
A. Government of India Act
B. Indian Councils Act
C. Minto-Morley Reforms
D. Montague-Chelmsford Report

List II
1. 1909 2. 1861
3. 1858 4. 1919

Codes:	A	B	C	D
(a)	3	2	4	1
(b)	2	3	1	4
(c)	2	3	4	1
(d)	3	2	1	4

35. **List I**
   A. Vincent Ostrom
   B. J. Habermas
   C. Amitai Etzioni
   D. H.G. Frederickson
   List II
   1. Complex Organizations
   2. New Public Administration
   3. Public Choice School
   4. Critical Theory
   5. New Public Management

Codes:	**A**	**B**	**C**	**D**
(a)	4	3	1	2
(b)	3	4	2	5
(c)	4	3	2	5
(d)	3	4	1	2

36. **List I**
   A. Blake and Mouton
   B. Scandinavian studies
   C. Fiedler model
   D. Hersey and Blanchard
   List II
   1. Development-oriented behaviour
   2. Least preferred co-worker questionnaire
   3. Situational theory
   4. Managerial grid

Codes:	**A**	**B**	**C**	**D**
(a)	2	3	4	1
(b)	1	4	2	3
(c)	4	1	2	3
(d)	4	1	3	2

37. **List I**
   A. The Tribal areas of the State of Assam, Meghalaya, Tripura and Mizoram
   B. All India Services
   C. Control of Scheduled Areas and Scheduled Tribes
   D. Comptroller and Auditor General of India
   List II
   1. Third Schedule 2. Fifth Schedule
   3. Sixth Schedule 4. Seventh Schedule
   5. Eighth Schedule

Codes:	**A**	**B**	**C**	**D**
(a)	3	5	2	1
(b)	1	3	4	5
(c)	3	4	2	1
(d)	4	3	1	2

38. **Assertion (A):** The new Public Administration postulates that public officials should drop the facade of neutrality.
   Reason (R): They should use their discretion in administering social and other programmes to protecr and advance the interests of the less privileged groups in society.
   (a) Both (A) and (R) are true and (R) is the correct explanation of (A).
   (b) Both (A) and (R) are true but (R) is not the correct explanation of (A).
   (c) (A) is true but (R) is false.
   (d) (A) is false but (R) is true.

39. **Assertion (A):** Early writers in Public Administration did make a distinction between policy and administration.
   Reason (R): They were anxious to keep politics out of administration.
   (a) Both (A) and (R) are true and (R) is the correct explanation of (A).
   (b) Both (A) and (R) are true but (R) is not the correct explanation of (A).
   (c) (A) is true but (R) is false.
   (d) (A) is false but (R) is true.

40. **Assertion (A):** The basic nature of an advisory relationship characterises the nature of staff authoriry.
   Reason (R): Staff is sometimes prone to step into the position of directing the lower Line elements without following down full chain of command.
   (a) Both (A) and (R) are true and (R) is the correct explanation of (A).
   (b) Both (A) and (R) are true but (R) is not the correct explanation of (A).

(c) (A) is true but (R) is false.
(d) (A) is false but (R) is true.

41. **Assertion (A):** A hierarchical organisation does not necessarily involve superior subordinate relationship.
Reason (R): Delegation of authoriry is possible in hierarchial organisation.
(a) Both (A) and (R) are true and (R) is the correct explanation of (A).
(b) Both (A) and (R) are true but (R) is not the correct explanation of (A).
(c) (A) is true but (R) is false.
(d) (A) is false but (R) is true.

42. **Assertion (A):** Most developing countries in which there is a combination of traditional agricultural (fused) and modern industrial (diffracted) characteristics exists side by side and is prismatic.
Reason (R): The fused and diffracted models should be taken as polar types on a scale, with an indefinitely large number of intermediate types in-between.
(a) Both (A) and (R) are true and (R) is the correct explanation of (A).
(b) Both (A) and (R) are true but (R) is not the correct explanation of (A).
(c) (A) is true but (R) is false.
(d) (A) is false but (R) is true.

43. **Assertion (A):** Restrictions on political activities of public employees are in their own interests.
Reason (R): Neutrality of civil servants ensures that all of them are treated alike.
(a) Both (A) and (R) are true and (R) is the correct explanation of (A).
(b) Both (A) and (R) are true but (R) is not the correct explanation of (A).
(c) (A) is true but (R) is false.
(d) (A) is false but (R) is true.

44. **Assertion (A):** In India, Public Administration is the integration among the executive, legislature and judiciary.
Reason (R): Therefore, Public Administration must be defined in narrower terms.
(a) Both (A) and (R) are true and (R) is the correct explanation of (A).
(b) Both (A) and (R) are true but (R) is not the correct explanation of (A).
(c) (A) is true but (R) is false.
(d) (A) is false but (R) is true.

45. **Assertion (A):** The entire administrative machinery comes under the potential control of the legislature.
Reason (R): This is because every action may provoke a question, every question an adjournment debate, and every adjournment, a full-dress debate.
(a) Both (A) and (R) are true and (R) is the correct explanation of (A).
(b) Both (A) and (R) are true but (R) is not the correct explanation of (A).
(c) (A) is true but (R) is false.
(d) (A) is false but (R) is true.

46. Which of the following refers to the degree of discrepancy or congruence between the formally prescribed and the effectively practised norms and relatives?
(a) Formalism (b) Overlapping
(c) Nepotism (d) Heterogeneity

47. *General and Industrial Management* has been authored by
(a) Henri Fayol (c) L.F. Urwick
(b) Ernest Dale (d) J.D. Mooney

48. The view that there ought to be greater emphasis on normative concerns in Public Administration is held by
(a) Frank Marini (b) Ferrel Heady
(c) Fred Riggs (d) Herbert Simon

49. Which of the following is correct about Woodrow Wilson's concept of public administration?
(a) Systematic execution of public policy.
(b) Systematic form of administrative structure.

(c) Detailed and systematic execution of public law.
(d) Politics-administration dichotomy.

50. The letter 'R' in POSDCORB stands for
(a) Retirement (b) Revenue
(c) Reporting (d) Risk

PAPER–III

1. Which one of the following is the correct sequence in which the following approaches to the study of Public Administration as a discipline evolved?
(a) Classical Approach, Policy Approach, Behavioural Approach, Human Relations Approach.
(b) Classical Approach, Human Relations Approach, Policy Approach, Behavioural Approach.
(c) Classical Approach, Human Relations Approach, Behavioural Approach, Policy Approach.
(d) Classical Approach, Behavioural Approach, Human Relations Approach, Policy Approach.

2. Organisations can be understood with reference to their
(a) operational modes
(b) objectives
(c) human context
(d) All of the above

3. The American Political Science Association published a report, which discussed the objectives of the teaching of political science in the year
(a) 1911 (b) 1912
(c) 1914 (d) 1916

4. Defined in a narrow sense, Public Administration restricts it to the operations of
(a) Judiciary (b) Legislature
(c) Executive (d) All of the above

5. It is that gives public administration its special character.
(a) pressure group
(b) political direction
(c) private companies
(d) peer group

6. About some of the classical "Principles", Simon's conclusion was that these were
(a) scientifically derived and are of great value.
(b) unscientifically derived and were no more than proverbs.
(c) obsolete principles.
(d) None of the above.

7. "It is not the business of the enterprise to create happiness among workers. Who observed this?
(a) Peter Drucker
(b) Harold Leavitt
(c) Frederick Herzberg
(d) Douglas McGregor

8. What did the Bhore Committee deal with?
(a) Technical education in India
(b) Public health in India
(c) Development of airports in India
(d) Development of ports in India

9. The Jawahar Rojgar Yojana was launched to:
(a) give employment to people in most backward districts.
(b) give food to people in backward districts.
(c) give employment to women in backward districts.
(d) provide basic facilities to people in rural areas.

10. If both the variables are varying in the same direction it is called
(a) Multiple correlation
(b) Negative correlation
(c) Positive correlation
(d) None of the above

11. Attributes of objects, events or things which can be measured are called
(a) Qualitative measure
(b) Variables
(c) Data
(d) None of the above

12. In order to review the intellectual development of public administration, who among the following used the belief of locus and focus?
(a) Woodrow Wilson
(b) Frank J. Goodnow
(c) Nicholas Henry
(d) Leonard D. White

13. When the delegated assignments and the accompanying authority for each delegate are spelt out on a piece of paper, it is known as
(a) Informal delegation
(b) Formal delegation
(c) General delegation
(d) Specific delegation

14. Which one of the following does not relate to inspection of administration?
(a) Inspection work and investigation work mostly go together.
(b) Inspection of some kind or the other has been an integral part of Public Administration.
(c) To acquaint top management with the operating problems faced at the subordinate levels.
(d) The purpose of inspection is to acquire information.

15. The Hawthorne experiments pioneered a movement which came to be known as the Human Relations Approach to Management, marking the ____ stage of evolution of administrative thought.
(a) final (b) fourth
(c) third (d) second

16. The traditional literature on 'comparative government' focused on
(a) Election machinery
(b) Pressure groups
(c) Foreign relations
(d) All of the above

17. The role of Public Administration is to execute the
(a) programmes of political parties
(b) will of the states
(c) will of the people
(d) policies of the government

18. If 4 or 6 or 8 years moving average is secured to draw a trend line it is called
(a) Sampling Method
(b) Even period of moving averages
(c) Semi Average Method
(d) None of the above

19. Each employee engaged in a staff function creates work for his colleagues. This phenomenon has been described by
(a) Graicunas (b) Lyndall Urwick
(c) Parkinson (d) Creep

20. The centre of administration are
(a) the Governors
(b) people
(c) the President
(d) the administrators

21. The process not needed in experimental researches is
(a) Observation
(b) Controlling
(c) Reference collection
(d) Manipulation and replication

22. Which of the following was the first to draw attention to the fact that informal organisations are necessary to the operation of formal organisations?
(a) William W. Haynes
(b) Joseph L. Massie
(c) Chester Barnard
(d) None of the above

23. Which of the following is/are a staff agency of India?

(a) Vigilance division in the Home Ministry
(b) Planning Commission
(c) Cabinet Committee
(d) All of the above

24. The theory of Economic Maturity emphasizes that
(a) population growth is faster in modern times than it was in the 19th century.
(b) entrepreneurs must be encouraged by the state.
(c) conditions of the 19th century were more conducive to development than the 20th century.
(d) there is greater scope for shifting of the farm frontiers in the 20th century than there was in the 19th century.

25. The entrepreneur theory of development in which the entrepreneur has a central role to play, is associated with
(a) Georges Sorel (b) Sidoey Webb
(c) David Ricardo (d) J. Schumpeter

26. The American concept of civil service neutrality was described by the
(a) Hatch Act
(b) US Congress
(c) Hoover Commission
(d) Masterman Committee

27. Woodrow Wilson, the pioneer of Public Administration, as a subject of study called it as the
(a) Science of Public Administration
(b) Art of Public Administration
(c) Both science and art
(d) None of the above

28. The scope of public administration includes which of the following?
1. Administrative theory
2. Application of administrative theory in various fields
3. Administrative organisation
4. Ecology of administrative systems in different countries

Codes:
(a) 2 and 3 (b) 1, 2 and 3
(c) 1, 2 and 4 (d) 1, 3 and 4

29. Which of the following statements about Public Administration are correct?
1. It is concerned with the affairs of the state.
2. It is concerned with the welfare of the people.
3. It serves the extra interests of politicians.
4. It is concerned with all three branches of government.

Codes:
(a) 1 and 2 (b) 2 and 4
(c) 1, 2 and 4 (d) 2, 3 and 4

30. Taylor's scientific management covers which of the following?
1. Differential piecework plan.
2. Separation of planning and execution.
3. Time study.
4. Assuming worker as machine.

Codes:
(a) 2 and 3 (b) 1, 2 and 4
(c) 1, 3 and 4 (d) 1, 2, 3 and 4

31. Taylor advocated the following steps to make management more systematic. Put them in correct order:
1. Employees to be scientifically selected.
2. Using methods of research experiments to formulate principles of standards
3. A spirit of friendly co-operation.
4. Imparting appropriate training

Codes:
(a) 2, 1, 4, 3 (b) 1, 3, 4, 2
(c) 3, 4, 2, 1 (d) 1, 2, 3, 4

32. The 'great illumination' experiment led to the discovery, that for higher productivity of an organisation,
1. relations between workers and supervisors are important.
2. relations between the workers are important.

3. working conditions are important.
4. social security is important.

Codes:

(a) 1 and 2 (b) 1, 2 and 3
(c) 1, 2 and 4 (d) 2, 3 and 4

33. Who among the following have advocated the public policy aspect of Public Administration?
 1. H. Walker 2. M.E. Dimock
 3. F.A. Nigro 4. J.W. Fesler

Codes:

(a) 2, 3 and 4 (b) 1, 2 and 3
(c) 2 and 4 (d) 1, 3 and 4

34. In democracy, a civil servant must be committed to the
 1. goal of the Constitution.
 2. common good.
 3. ruling party's ideology.
 4. execution of public policy.

Codes:

(a) 1, 2 and 3 (b) 1, 2 and 4
(c) 1, 3 and 4 (d) 2, 3 and 4

35. Which of the following are the objectives of the Community Development Programme?
 1. Agricultural development
 2. Economic development
 3. Development of free and compulsory education
 4. Provision facilities

Codes:

(a) 1, 2, and 3
(b) 1, 2 and 4
(c) 2, 3 and 4 of proper health care
(d) 1, 2, 3 and 4

36. **List I (Writer)**
 A. L.D. White
 B. E.N. Gladden
 C. Pfiffner and Presthus
 D. John. A. Vieg

List II (Statement)
 1. Administration is a long and slightly pompous word but it has a humble meaning.
 2. Administration is the direction, coordination and control of many persons to achieve some purpose or objective.
 3. Administration is a determined action taken in pursuit of a conscious purpose.
 4. Administration is the organization and direction of human and material resources to achieve desired ends.

Codes:	A	B	C	D
(a)	3	4	2	1
(b)	1	3	4	2
(c)	2	1	4	3
(d)	2	4	1	3

37. **List I**
 A. Models of man
 B. The new science of management decision
 C. Administrative behaviour
 D. Administrative man

List II
 1. Decisions are made at every level within an organisation.
 2. Mathematical models of programme feasibility within bounded rationality.
 3. Decision-making process broken into intelligence, design and choice activities.
 4. Satisficing.

Codes:	A	B	C	D
(a)	3	4	2	1
(b)	4	3	1	2
(c)	2	4	3	1
(d)	3	4	1	2

38. **List I**
 A. Scope for bias in decision-making.
 B. Helps to narrow down the alternatives.
 C. Slow changes due to consensus-approach in decision-making.
 D. Socio-economic environment of an organisation.

List II

1. Fact and Value 2. Incrementalism
3. Non-programmed 4. MIS

Codes:	A	B	C	D
(a)	3	4	2	1
(b)	3	4	1	2
(c)	4	3	1	2
(d)	4	3	2	1

39. **List I (Terms)**

A. Social equity
B. Formalism
C. Democratic administration
D. Action-oriented administration

List II (Associated with)

1. V. Ostrom 2. E. Weidner
3. H.G. Fredrickson 4. F.W. Riggs
5. J. Habermas

Codes:	A	B	C	D
(a)	5	4	2	3
(b)	4	3	2	5
(c)	3	4	1	5
(d)	3	4	5	2

40. **List I (Book)**

A. How Britain is governed
B. The Administrative State
C. Ethics in Government
D. Civil Service Neutrality

List II (Author)

1. Ramsay Muir 2. Paul H. Douglas
3. S. Lall 4. Rensis Likert
5. F.M. Marx

Codes:	A	B	C	D
(a)	1	4	2	5
(b)	1	5	2	3
(c)	5	4	2	1
(d)	1	3	4	5

41. **List I**

A. Tenure System
B. Simon Commission
C. Maxwell Committee
D. Central Government announced the introduction of the Desk-Officer in its Ministries

List II

1. 1930 2. 1937
3. 1905 4. 1970
5. 1973

Codes:	A	B	C	D
(a)	3	1	2	5
(b)	4	2	3	5
(c)	2	1	3	4
(d)	1	2	3	4

42. **Assertion (A):** The New Public Management is a mere extension of New Public Administration.
Reason (R): The Second Minnowbrook Conference followed the First Minnowbrook Conference after twenty years.
(a) Both (A) and (R) are true and (R) is the correct explanation of (A).
(b) Both (A) and (R) are true but (R) is not the correct explanation of (A).
(c) (A) is true but (R) is false.
(d) (A) is false but (R) is true.

43. **Assertion (A):** Max Weber's bureaucratic model is based on hierarchy of offices.
Reason (R): There is a division of labour.
(a) Both (A) and (R) are true and (R) is the correct explanation of (A).
(b) Both (A) and (R) are true but (R) is not the correct explanation of (A).
(c) (A) is true but (R) is false.
(d) (A) is false but (R) is true

44. **Assertion (A):** Under the classical theory of organisation the whole is bound together by the lines of authority.
Reason (R): One of the principles of organisation is unity of command.
(a) Both (A) and (R) are true and (R) is the correct explanation of (A).
(b) Both (A) and (R) are true but (R) is not the correct explanation of (A).
(c) (A) is true but (R) is false.
(d) (A) is false but (R) is true.

45. **Assertion (A):** The Behavioural approach stresses upon the informal relationship among the members of an organisation.
Reason (R): Behaviouralists employ integrated interdisciplinary approach.
(a) Both (A) and (R) are true and (R) is the correct explanation of (A).
(b) Both (A) and (R) are true but (R) is not the correct explanation of (A).
(c) (A) is true but (R) is false.
(d) (A) is false but (R) is true.

46. **Assertion (A):** Hawthorne investigations lacked scientific base.
Reason (R): The evidence obtained from the experiments does not support conclusions.
(a) Both (A) and (R) are true and (R) is the correct explanation of (A).
(b) Both (A) and (R) are true but (R) is not the correct explanation of (A).
(c) (A) is true but (R) is false.
(d) (A) is false but (R) is true

47. **Assertion (A):** The New Public Management conforms to the Neo-Taylorist prescription to a large extent.
Reason (R): It does not mention the political agenda of Neo-Taylorism.
(a) Both (A) and (R) are true and (R) is the correct explanation of (A).
(b) Both (A) and (R) are true but (R) is not the correct explanation of (A).
(c) (A) is true but (R) is false.
(d) (A) is false but (R) is true.

48. A researcher selects a probability sample of 100 out of the total population. It is a
(a) Random sample
(b) Cluster sample
(c) Stratified sample
(d) Systematic sample

49. Lord Hewart has characterised the power and authority of bureaucracy as
(a) New despotism
(b) Self-aggrandisement
(c) Empire building
(d) Elite rule

50. Which of the following sampling techniques would be appropriate if sample is drawn from a heterogeneous population?
(a) Random
(b) Purposive
(c) Multi-Stage Sampling
(d) Stratified

ANSWER SHEET

PAPER—I

1. (c)	2. (c)	3. (a)	4. (d)	5. (d)
6. (a)	7. (d)	8. (b)	9. (c)	10. (b)
11. (d)	12. (a)	13. (c)	14. (c)	15. (a)
16. (c)	17. (a)	18. (b)	19. (a)	20. (c)
21. (d)	22. (a)	23. (c)	24. (a)	25. (b)
26. (b)	27. (b)	28. (c)	29. (d)	30. (b)
31. (b)	32. (c)	33. (a)	34. (c)	35. (b)
36. (b)	37. (a)	38. (b)	39. (d)	40. (a)
41. (d)	42. (c)	43. (a)	44. (b)	45. (c)
46. (b)	47. (d)	48. (b)	49. (c)	50. (c)

PAPER—II

1. (a)	2. (c)	3. (b)	4. (c)	5. (d)
6. (a)	7. (c)	8. (a)	9. (b)	10. (c)
11. (b)	12. (d)	13. (d)	14. (a)	15. (a)
16. (a)	17. (a)	18. (a)	19. (b)	20. (a)
21. (d)	22. (c)	23. (a)	24. (c)	25. (d)
26. (d)	27. (c)	28. (d)	29. (c)	30. (a)
31. (b)	32. (c)	33. (a)	34. (d)	35. (d)
36. (c)	37. (a)	38. (a)	39. (a)	40. (b)
41. (d)	42. (b)	43. (a)	44. (c)	45. (a)
46. (a)	47. (a)	48. (a)	49. (c)	50. (c)

PAPER—III

1. (c)	2. (d)	3. (c)	4. (c)	5. (b)
6. (b)	7. (a)	8. (b)	9. (a)	10. (c)
11. (b)	12. (c)	13. (b)	14. (d)	15. (c)
16. (d)	17. (c)	18. (b)	19. (c)	20. (b)
21. (c)	22. (c)	23. (d)	24. (c)	25. (d)
26. (c)	27. (a)	28. (b)	29. (c)	30. (d)
31. (a)	32. (b)	33. (a)	34. (b)	35. (d)
36. (c)	37. (d)	38. (a)	39. (d)	40. (b)
41. (a)	42. (d)	43. (b)	44. (b)	45. (b)
46. (b)	47. (c)	48. (a)	49. (a)	50. (d)

MOCK TEST–2
PAPER–I

1. Minimum program of guidance includes
   (a) occupational information service
   (b) data collector service
   (c) counselling service
   (d) All of these
2. If majority of students in a class is weak, a teacher should
   (a) not care about intelligent students
   (b) keep his speed of teaching fast so that students comprehension level may increase
   (c) keep his teaching slow which can also be helpful-to bright students
   (d) keep his teaching slow along with some extra guidance to bright students
3. If the principal of your institution is not satisfied with your performance and charge you with the act of negligence of duties, how would you behave with him?
   (a) You would neglect him
   (b) You would take revenge by giving physical and mental agony to him
   (c) You would keep yourself alert and make his efforts unfruitful
   (d) You would take a tough stand against the charges
4. What makes people to undertake research?
   (a) Desire to get intellectual joy of doing some creative work
   (b) Desire to get a research degree along with its consequential benefits
   (c) Desire to face the challenge in solving the unsolved problems
   (d) All of these
5. Which of the following aims at probing into the phenomenon to formulate a more precise research problem or to develop a new hypothesis?
   (a) Descriptive research
   (b) Conclusive research
   (c) Diagnostic research
   (d) Exploratory research
6. Which of the following is not instructional material?
   (a) Transparency
   (b) Overhead projector
   (c) Printed material
   (d) Audio cassette
7. Of great importance in determining the amount of transference that occurs in the process of learning is the
   (a) knowledge of the teacher
   (b) IQ of the teacher
   (c) presence of identical elements
   (d) use of appropriate elements
8. The characteristic(s) of hypothesis is/are:
   I. It can be tested.
   II. It must consist of known facts.
   III. It must be objective and specific.
   (a) Only I and III (b) Only I and II
   (c) Only I (d) All of these
9. The guide for the research requires which of the following qualities?

(a) Interdisciplinary expertise
(b) Subject matter expertise
(c) Methodological expertise
(d) All of these

10. Which of the following indicates evaluation?
(a) Seema got 195 marks out of 200
(b) Sapna got 72 percent marks in English
(c) Asha got First Division in final examination
(d) All of the above

Direction: (11-16) Study the following passage and give answer to the questions based on it.

Much of the theoretical literature of archeology in the 1980s devotes considerable energy to bashing the 1970s, and the target often turns out to be the so-called New or Processual Archeology. While many of the attacks come from recent theorists who are attempting to replace it with post-processual archeology, some criticism comes from within what was New Archeology even from the hand of its original champion, Lewis Binford. If scholars from both outside and inside the theoretical developments of the 1970s are rejecting the New Archeology, why am I defending its importance to us today? The answer is very simple...for better or worse, it is us! As Alison Whylie has recently said the New Archeology of the 1960s quickly became everybody's archeology in the 1970s. Most of today's faculty members and senior archeologists were the people who, in one way or another, adopted the teachings of New Archeology. Although most archeologists did not claim to agree with all aspects of New Archeology nor could more than two or three people agree on what it was, virtually one rejected it outright. Typically, each one presented her or his version, often using a New Archeology text as a starting point for pedagogical purposes. Few wanted to be left out of the exciting new theoretical movement of those years, and New Archeology was passed on to the succeeding generation of students who reached maturity in the 1980s and are today's young professionals.

Criticisms now leveled against the New Archeology of the seventies do have merit, but by discounting that era as misguided, critics have overlooked its crucial importance. New Archeology has an important historical rôle in the developments of the field we have today and it has continuing importance because it is still guiding archeology's trajectory into the future. Equally troubling is that some critics ask us to reject the basic tenets of New Archeology and to replace them with a system often called post processualist archeology. I believe this is rhetoric that not only misrepresents the achievements of the New Archeology of the seventies, but also does not successfully articulate the potential contributions of its own position.

To put the New Archeology of the seventies into perspective, it is important to review the decades leading up to its development. In the first years following World War II, archeology was still a small field, but by the fifties and the sixties, it was expanding rapidly and taking itself quite seriously. Since the launching of Sputnik in 1957 there had emerged a frenzy in the United States to make all disciplines more scientific. Great strides were made in bringing science into archeology through new dating techniques a multidisciplinary approach, early experiments with the use of statistics, and devoting substantial attention to increasing the precision of artifact classification. The sixties provided the nation with both the optimistic Kennedy years, with an emphasis on science and the conviction that we were capable of accomplishing wondrous; things, and the cynical Vietnam era. Coming on the heels of a decade of civil rights unrest, the widespread dissatisfaction with the Vietnam conflict in the late sixties molded a generation of young Americans who were distrustful of established authority. In academic life, there was an increasing emphasis on environment, other cultures, and people oriented disciplines. Anthropology and archeology grew markedly because of these trends. Archeologists were urged to become concerned with sociological issues—the people behind the artifacts.

It was during these decades of rapid change that many of the core concepts of the New Archeology entered the literature. However, they were not, at first, assembled into a program for action that attracted a solid following. Water Taylor advocated the conjuctive approach with little effect, while Leslie White's evolutionism and Julian Styeward's cultural ecology attracted some attention, but largely among cultural anthropologists. Albert Spaulding led a one-man campaign to bring science and statistics into archeology. But the individual whose work catalyzed the New Archeology movement was Lewis Binford, who incorporated these earlier lines of thinking together with an explicit concern for scientific methods and field research designs. Much of Binford's thinking probably crystallised while he was at the University of Michigan, but was during his relatively few years at the University of Chicago that he changed the direction of modern archeology.

11. New Archeology refers to
   (a) newer techniques used in Archeology
   (b) newer inventions used in Archeology
   (c) newer theoretical foundations in Archeology
   (d) None of these

12. The author defends the Archeology of the 1970's because
   (a) he has a nostalgic feeling about it
   (b) it has research value
   (c) it paved way for newer traditions
   (d) it has historical value

13. The author suggests that
   (a) We should respect new Archeology as a movement in Archeology
   (b) We should go back to the tenets of processual Archeology
   (c) We should treat tenets of new Archeology with respect
   (d) All of the above

14. The importance of Archeology arose from
   (a) the end of World War II
   (b) an increasing scientific outlook
   (c) the launch of Sputnik in 1957
   (d) All of these

15. Which one of the following is not an area of focus for archeologist?
   (a) Study the interaction of people of small group
   (b) Studying cultures of other people
   (c) Study the social structure of the past societies
   (d) Study the man-environment relationship in the past

16. An archeologist is concerned with
   (a) classification of artefacts
   (b) maintenance of museums
   (c) digging of ancient cities
   (d) All of these

17. Rhetorics means
   (a) study of the technique and rules for using language effectively
   (b) using language effectively to please or persuade
   (c) excessive use of verbal ornamentation
   (d) All of the above

18. If a receiver replying on 'hmm-mm' or 'I see'. This type of reply is known as
   (a) positive feedback
   (b) ambiguous feedback
   (c) negative feedback
   (d) None of these

19. Which of the following FM radio stations is owned by the Times of India group?

(a) AIR
(b) Radio Rainbow
(c) Radio Mirchi
(d) Red FM

20. Find the next number in the following sequence:
9, 8, 25, 12, 49, 18, 121, 26, ??
(a) 142, 36 (b) 169, 36
(c) 225, 36 (d) 196, 36

21. **Statement:** Should there be complete ban on pouched tobacco products (like Gutka) in India?
Arguments:
(i) Yes, it is the most important cause of mouth cancer and mouth ulcer in our country.
(ii) No, there are many people employed in this industry right from manufacturing to retailing. This ban will hamper their livelihood.
(a) Only argument (i) is strong
(b) Only argument (ii) is strong
(c) Both the arguments (i) and (ii) are strong
(d) Neither (i) nor (ii) is strong

22. The relationship between Animal, Cows, Dogs can be shown by

(a) 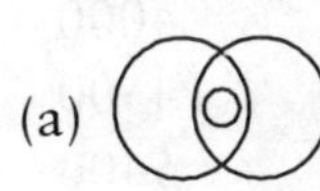 (b) 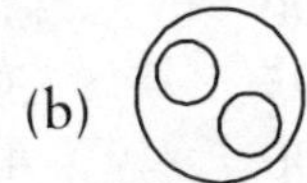

(c) 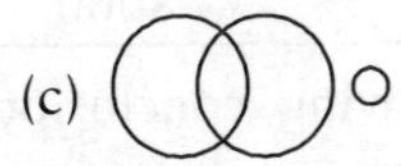 (d) 

23. If in a certain code:
'nso prt kli chn' means 'sharma gets marriage gift'.
'pit lnm wop chn' means 'wife gives marriage gift'. 'tti wop nhi' means 'he gives nothing'. What would mean gives:
(a) kli (b) tti
(c) wop (d) lnm

24. Characteristics of all informal and formal communications are
(a) Same (b) Structured
(c) Different (d) None of these

25. Three of the following four are alike in a certain way and so form a group. Find the one which doesn't belong to that group?
(a) Dog (b) Tiger
(c) Horse (d) Lion

26. What is research design?
(a) The methods used in analysis and finding the final conclusion is known as research design
(b) A researcher needs to prepare a plan of action for his study which is known as research design
(c) The presentation of final data is known as research design
(d) None of these

27. Recording a television program on a Set Top Box is an example of
(a) content reference
(b) time-shifting
(c) media synchronisation
(d) mechanical clarity

28. Which of the following statements say the same thing?
(i) "I am a teacher" (said by Arvind)
(ii) "I am a teacher" (said by Binod)
(iii) "My son is a teacher" (said by Binod's father)
(iv) "My brother is a teacher" (said by Binod's sister)
(v) "My brother is a teacher" (said by Binod's only sister)
(vi) "My sole enemy is a teacher" (said by Binod's only enemy)
Choose the correct answer from the codes given below:
Codes:
(a) (v) and (vi)
(b) (i) and (ii)

(c) (ii) and (vi)
(d) (ii), (iii), (iv) and (v)

29. In this question there are two statements followed by four conclusions numbered I, II, III and IV.

Statements:
A. All books are trees.
B. All trees are lions.

Conclusions:
I. All books are lions.
II. All lions are books.
III. All trees are books.
IV. Some lions are books.

Choose the correct answer.
(a) Only I and IV follow
(b) Only II and III follow
(c) None of conclusions follow
(d) All conclusion follows

Directions: (30-34) Answer the questions based on following table.

Machines X and Y can independently produce either product P or product Q. The time taken by machines X and Y (in minutes) to produce one unit of product P and Q are given in the table below. (Each machine works 8 hours per day.)

Product	X	Y
P	10	8
Q	6	6

30. If the number of units of P is to be three times that of Q, what is the maximum idle time to maximise total units manufactured?
(a) 8 minutes (b) 0 minute
(c) 12 minutes (d) None of these

31. If X works at half its normal efficiency, what is the maximum number of units produced, if at least one unit of each must be produced?
(a) 119 (b) 135
(c) 127 (d) 136

32. What is the maximum number of units that can be manufactured in one day?
(a) 250 (b) 160
(c) 270 (d) 195

33. If equal quantities of both are to be produced, then out of four choice given below the least efficient way would be
(a) 59 of each with 8 min. idle
(b) 71 of each with 9 min. idle
(c) 53 of each with 10 min. idle
(d) 48 of each with 4 min. idle

34. What is the least number of machine hours required to produce 30 pieces of P and 25 pieces of Q respectively?
(a) 6 hr 30 min. (b) 9 hr 30 min.
(c) 6 hr 40 min. (d) 8 hr 30 min.

35. Telematic is a combination of
(a) Telecommunication and computer
(b) Telecommunication and information
(c) Television and computer
(d) All of the above

36. Following is a part of balance sheet of Timas Pvt. Ltd. Study the table and give answer to the question given below:

(All values in ₹ crore)

Year	Expenditure	Income
1990	3400	4000
1995	3800	4500
2000	4500	5400
2005	6400	8000

Which of the following conclusions is not true?
(a) There has been a steady growth in % profit of the company
(b) There is around 90% increase in expenditure of the firm from 1990 to 2005
(c) Income of the company is doubled in 15 years
(d) Percentage profit in 2000 was 18%

37. If EFGHUK is coded as VUTSRQ then LIMIT can be coded as
(a) KNRNC (b) ORNRG
(c) JKOKG (d) RSTSG

38. The more is 'Resolution Power' of a printer better is its
(a) Speed (b) Colour
(c) Memory (d) Quality

39. Laterite soil develops due to
(a) deposits of alluvial
(b) deposition of loess
(c) leaching
(d) continued vegetation cover

40. Line access and avoidance of collision are the main functions of
(a) network protocols
(b) wide area networks
(c) the CPU
(d) the monitor

41. Communication satellites are placed in
(a) Geostationary Orbit
(b) Polar Orbit
(c) Both (a) and (b)
(d) None of these

42. DLL stands for
(a) Data Deriving Language
(b) Data Definition Language
(c) Data Design Language
(d) All of the above

43. Transistors were first used in
(a) 2nd generation computers
(b) 3rd generation computers
(c) 4th generation computers
(d) None of these

44. Which of the following is not provided in the constitution?
(a) Planning Commission
(b) Election Commission
(c) Finance Commission
(d) Public Service Commission

45. The 1st satellite launched in space was
(a) Early Bird (b) Sputnik-1
(c) Skylab (d) Aryabhatta-1

46. At what time between 5.30 and 6.00 will the hands of a clock be at right angles?
(a) 45 minutes past 5
(b) $43\frac{5}{11}$ minutes past 5
(c) $43\frac{7}{11}$ minutes past 5
(d) 40 minutes past 5

47. A person can be a member of Council of Ministers without being a member of Parliament for a maximum period of
(a) 45 days (b) 90 days
(c) 180 days (d) one year

48. Many engineers and architects use a different type of pen called a
(a) Pointer pen (b) Computer pen
(c) Light pen (d) Logical pen

49. Which of the following are wrongly matched?

Name of Volcano	Country
(a) Mt. Spur	USA
(b) Mt. Fuego	Guatemala
(c) Mt. Ag'ung	Indonesia
(d) Mt. Lascor	Equador

50. How many types of emergency can be declared by the President of India?
(a) 1 (b) 2
(c) 3 (d) 4

PAPER–II

1. "Too often, we try to solve human problems with non-human tools and in terms of non-human data. It is my simple thesis that a human problem requires a human solution. First, we have to learn to recognise a human problem when we

see one; and second, upon recognising it, we have to learn to deal with it as such and not as it were something else. A human problem to be brought to a human solution requires human data and human tools." Who said this?
(a) F.J. Roethlisberger
(b) Max Weber
(c) L.D. White
(d) F.W. Taylor

2. To conclude the argument of the critics, public administration cannot be called a science until main conditions are fulfilled
(a) three (b) six
(c) seven (d) eight

3. The approach which traces its ancestry to the European tradition is the
(a) Case-method approach
(b) Philosophical approach
(c) Legal approach
(d) Historical approach

4. The positive welfare state must
(a) take only positive but not negative action to maintain social welfare.
(b) be natural regarding the clashing interests of its citizens.
(c) see that people obtain freedom from restraints of regulations and planning.
(d) take both positive and negative action to balance the welfare of its citizens.

5. The validity and reliability of a research will be at stake when the
(a) author who is the source of information is biased, incompetent or dishonest.
(b) researcher himself is not competent enough to draw logical conclusions.
(c) incident was reported after a long period of time from that of its occurrence.
(d) All of the above.

6. The principles of Scientific Management developed by F.W. Taylor did not include
(a) division of responsibility.
(b) scientific selection and training.
(c) mental revolution.
(d) esprit de corps.

7. In ancient days, Public Administration was confined itself to
(a) some philanthropic functions
(b) judicial functions
(c) police functions
(d) All of the above

8. Who among the following said that Public Administration is different from Personal Administration?
(a) Mary P. Follett (b) Paul H. Appleby
(c) Luther Gulick (d) Henry Fayol

9. What important role does the bureaucracy play in the field of legislation?
(a) Formulating rules and regulations under skeleton laws passed by Parliament.
(b) Preparing most of the bills.
(c) Both (a) and (b).
(d) Controlling the finances.

10. The policy of neutrality of the Indian Civil Service is mainly a legacy of
(a) Historical traditions
(b) the British rule
(c) the National Movement
(d) Cultural heritage

11. While comparing Akbar's revenue administrative system to Ripon's local government system, how would you define this comparison?
(a) Cross-institutional and cross-cultural
(b) Cross-processual and cross-institutional
(c) Cross-territorial and cross-temporal
(d) Cross-institutional and cross-temporal

12. "Bureaucracy is the core of modern governments"? This is the quote of
(a) Max Weber (b) Carl Friedrich
(c) Harold Laski (d) None of these

13. Who among the following introduced the Indianisation of Civil Services in the Country?
(a) Lord Lytton (b) Warren Hastings
(c) Lord Cornwallis (d) Lord Clive

14. Civil servants play an important role in the formulation of policy by
(a) tendering necessary advice to ministers and other executives.
(b) supplying necessary information.
(c) Both (a) and (b).
(d) None of the above.

15. Which of the following is not advocated by the New Public Administration?
(a) Decentralisation of delegation
(b) Behaviouralism
(c) Pluralism
(d) Humanism

16. As per New Public Administration, administration should be
(a) fact oriented
(b) value oriented
(c) not fact oriented
(d) not value oriented

17. Which of the following defined power as "the ability to make things happen, to be a causal agent, to initiate change"?
(a) Henri Fayol
(b) Mary Parker Follett
(c) Max Weber
(d) None of the above

18. Which of the following statements regarding the two conferences, Minnowbrook I (1968) and Minnowbrook II (1988) is correct?
(a) The former was concerned with social equity and the latter was not.
(b) The former was more pragmatic and less radical in thought.
(c) Both the conferences highlighted the debt between normative and behaviouralist perspectives with emphasis on epistemo-logical questions.
(d) Both the conferences reaffirmed democratic values with special focus on ethics, accountability and administrative leadership.

19. "A fully developed bureaucratic administration stands in the same relationship to non-bureaucratic forms as machinery to non-mechanical modes of production". This was the observation of
(a) Henri Fayol (b) Max Weber
(c) Elton Mayo (d) Peter Balu

20. Who of the following has described authority as the "Supreme coordinating power"?
(a) Mooney and Reiley
(b) Barnard
(c) Weber
(d) Fayol

21. Which one among the following is not a characteristic of "Organised Society"?
(a) Attainment value
(b) Attribution
(c) Particularism
(d) Functional diffusion

22. Advocates of basic human needs approach have argued that the trickle-down effects predicted by classical economic development theory have failed to materialise because of
(a) lack of foreign aid from the World Bank.
(b) corruption and other barriers to growth caused by the ruling elites of the Third World.
(c) socialist pattern of society.
(d) mixed economy model.

23. The study of Public Administration started as an independent science in
(a) Britain (b) USA
(c) India (d) West Germany

24. Louis Brandeis used the term Scientific Management for the first time in the year
(a) 1910 (b) 1925
(c) 1930 (d) 1935

25. Simon regards organisations as systems in which means are
(a) Tools
(b) Cog in the wheel
(c) Decision-making mechanisms
(d) None of the above

26. "A good deal of circumvention of formal procedures is essential to make the transaction of business possible." This is the observation of
(a) Terry (b) Millett
(c) Follett (d) Appleby

27. Middle range studies of comparative public administration focus on
(a) structures of bmeaucracies of two or more nations.
(b) recruitment or training system of two or more administrative organizations.
(c) administrative systems of two or more countries.
(d) administrative systems in the same country.

28. Woodrow Wilson laid the foundation for the study of Public Administration by his emphasis on
1. a science of administration.
2. a more businesslike administration.
3. efficiency, economy and effectiveness as lasting values of administration.
4. the need to study human behaviour, attitudes and actions.

Codes:
(a) 1 and 2 (b) 2 and 3
(c) 1, 2 and 3 (d) 1, 3 and 4

29. Which of the following statements were suggested by Robert Dahl?
1. Science is value free but administration is not.
2. Universal principle cannot be based on limited examples.
3. Administration involves human beings.
4. Social framework does not differ from country to country.

Codes:
(a) 1, 2 and 3 (b) 1, 2 and 4
(c) 1, 3 and 4 (d) 2, 3 and 4

30. Which of the following statements are correct about Public Choice School?
1. Followers of classical economic theory.
2. Replacement of bureaucratic administration by democratic administration.
3. Deals with institutional particularism
4. Preferences to consumers.

Codes:
(a) 1, 2 and 3 (b) 1, 2 and 4
(c) 1, 3 and 4 (d) 2, 3 and 4

31. Which of the following are features of piece rate system of wage payment?
1. Observation and analysis of work through the time study to set the standard.
2. Differential rate system of piece work.
3. Preferable work method with consideration to raw materials, tools and equipments.
4. Paying men and not positions.

Codes:
(a) 2, 3 and 4 (b) 1, 2 and 4
(c) 1, 3 and 4 (d) 1, 2 and 3

32. According to Fred Riggs in his study of Comparative Public Administration,
1. ideographic orientation concentrates on an approach of generalization.
2. nomothetic orientation concentrates on unique case studies.

Codes:
(a) 1 only (b) 2 only
(c) Both 1 and 2 (d) Neither 1 nor 2

33. The Civil Service Reform Act, 1978 of the United States introduced
   1. performance-budgeting system.
   2. performance bonus for members of the senior executive service.
   3. merit pay provision for middle managerial personnel.
   4. performance appraisal system.
   5. office of personnel management.

   Codes:
   (a) 2, 3 and 4 (b) 1, 2 and 3
   (c) 1, 4 and 5 (d) 2, 3 and 5

34. One or more of the following may act as a dynamic instrument of change according to the Structural-Functional perspective of Political Development.
   1. Scientists 2. Political Leaders
   3. Agronomists 4. Technocrats

   Codes:
   (a) 2 only (b) 2 and 4
   (c) 1, 2 and 3 (d) All of these

35. Which of the statements given below is/are correct?
   1. New literatures related with public organisations have the hypothesis that task environment is more influential and critical in private organisation than in public organisation.
   2. During 1970's the normative definition of public administration did not focus on the governmental agencies but on those events which affected the welfare of the public.

   Codes:
   (a) 1 only (b) 2 only
   (c) Both 1 and 2 (d) Neither 1 nor 2

36. **Assertion (A):** Efficiency and economy are the watch words of Public Administration.
   Reason (R): The book Introduction to the Study of Public Administration deals with politics-administration dichotomy.
   (a) Both (A) and (R) are true and (R) is the correct explanation of (A).
   (b) Both (A) and (R) are true but (R) is not the correct explanation of (A).
   (c) (A) is true but (R) is false.
   (d) (A) is false but (R) is true.

37. **Assertion (A):** In a classification plan, the highest unit is a position.
   Reason (R): Position is the work consisting of duties and responsibilities given to an employee.
   (a) Both (A) and (R) are true and (R) is the correct explanation of (A).
   (b) Both (A) and (R) are true but (R) is not the correct explanation of (A).
   (c) (A) is true but (R) is false.
   (d) (A) is false but (R) is true.

38. **Assertion (A):** In the United States, there is no machinery analogous to the Whitley Councils in England.
   Reason (R): The system of Whitley Councils has been in existence in the civil service of the UK since 1919.
   (a) Both (A) and (R) are true and (R) is the correct explanation of (A).
   (b) Both (A) and (R) are true but (R) is not the correct explanation of (A).
   (c) (A) is true but (R) is false.
   (d) (A) is false but (R) is true.

39. **Assertion (A):** The President of India occupies almost the same position as the king or Queen of England.
   Reason (R): The President is ultimately bound to act in accordance with the advice given by the Council of Ministers.
   (a) Both (A) and (R) are true and (R) is the correct explanation of (A).
   (b) Both (A) and (R) are true but (R) is not the correct explanation of (A).
   (c) (A) is true but (R) is false.
   (d) (A) is false but (R) is true.

40. **Assertion (A):** Public Administration provides stability in the society.

Reason (R): Public Administration is responsible for bringing socio-economic change in the society.
(a) Both (A) and (R) are true and (R) is the correct explanation of (A).
(b) Both (A) and (R) are true but (R) is not the correct explanation of (A).
(c) (A) is true but (R) is false.
(d) (A) is false but (R) is true.

41. **Assertion (A):** The exercise of authority is always based on rules.
Reason (R): Rules and regulations help to check arbitrary action.
(a) Both (A) and (R) are true and (R) is the correct explanation of (A).
(b) Both (A) and (R) are true but (R) is not the correct explanation of (A).
(c) (A) is true but (R) is false.
(d) (A) is false but (R) is true.

42. **List I**
A. Situationist, Traitist and Elementalist
B. Four Qualities for a leader
C. Gresham's law of planning
D. Bounded Rationality
List II
1. Chester Barnard
2. Koontz and O'Donnell
3. James March
4. John Millett
5. Herbert Simon

Codes:	A	B	C	D
(a)	2	3	4	5
(b)	2	1	4	5
(c)	2	1	3	5
(d)	1	4	5	3

43. **List I (Book)**
A. Administrative State
B. The Golden Book of Management
C. Organisation and Management
D. Bureaucracy
List II (Author)
1. Max Weber
2. Mortin Albrow
3. Dwight Waldo
4. Seckler-Hudson
5. Lyndall F. Urwick

Codes:	A	B	C	D
(a)	3	5	1	4
(b)	3	5	4	2
(c)	1	3	5	4
(d)	1	3	4	2

44. **List I**
A. Thomas Carlyle
B. Vincent de Gournay
C. Michel Crozier
D. Gaetano Mosca
List II
1. The Ruling Class
2. The Bureaucratic Phenomenon
3. Bureaucracy as Continental Nuisance
4. Bureaucracy

Codes:	A	B	C	D
(a)	3	4	2	1
(b)	3	2	1	4
(c)	2	3	4	1
(d)	1	3	2	1

45. **List I**
A. Trait Theory
B. Sociometric Theory
C. Group Theory
D. Contingency Theory
List II
1. Exchange process between leaders and followers.
2. Personality characteristic of a leader.
3. Environmental factors.
4. Goals and structure of an organisation.
5. Facts and values.

Codes:	A	B	C	D
(a)	2	4	1	3
(b)	1	2	3	4
(c)	3	2	5	4
(d)	3	4	5	1

46. **List I (Approach)** **List II (Characteristics)**
A. Bureaucratic — 1. Agraria-Industria
B. Behavioural — 2. Legal-Rational

C. General Systems 3. Negative Feed-Back

D. Ecological 4. Quantification

Codes:	A	B	C	D
(a)	1	3	2	4
(b)	1	2	4	3
(c)	2	3	1	4
(d)	2	4	3	1

47. List I

A. Distinction between obedience and acceptance.

B. Distinction between 'Economic man' and 'Administrative man'.

C. Distinction between 'charismatic', 'traditional' and 'legal rational' authority.

D. Distinction between 'principles' and 'mechanics of management'.

List II

1. Herbert A. Simon
2. Chester Barnard
3. F.W. Taylor
4. Max Weber
5. Henri Fayol

Codes:	A	B	C	D
(a)	1	3	5	2
(b)	2	1	4	3
(c)	1	3	2	5
(d)	2	3	4	1

48. Find the coefficient of concurrent deviations from the following data. No. of pairs of observation = 96, No. of pairs of concurrent deviations = 36.

(a) 0.577 (b) –0.482
(c) –0.577 (d) 0.482

49. Mayo made out a case for skills that are

(a) Social and adaptive
(b) Human and interactive
(c) Technical and empirical
(d) Scientific and normative

50. The lowest and the highest values that can be included in a class are called

(a) Frequency table
(b) Class interval
(c) Class limit
(d) None of the above

PAPER–III

1. "Administration is a moral act and an administrator is a moral agent". This statement is credited to whom among the following?

(a) L.D. White (b) F.A. Nigro
(c) O. Tead (d) C. Merriam

2. Taylor's concept of mental revolutions stands for

(a) cooperation, harmony and restricted output.
(b) harmony and cooperation.
(c) economy, cooperation and restricted output.
(d) restricted output and cooperation.

3. Which of the following is not true about the third phase of Public Administration?

(a) It reacted against mechanical approach of scientific management.
(b) Social and psychological factors emerged in work situation.
(c) Politics and administration could not be separated.
(d) Attention was given to formal organisation in informal set-ups.

4. The code of conduct was maintained for group solidarity and informal pressure was used to set right the erring members of the group during the Hawthrone experiments. It did not include one being a

(a) 'squealer' (b) 'rate-buster'
(c) 'recluse' (d) 'chiseler'

5. The systems approach to administrative analysis has enriched our understanding

of administrative processes by focusing mainly on
(a) management's crucial role in efficient coordination.
(b) interpersonal relations in an organisation and human behaviour.
(c) systematic analysis of organisational structure and functioning.
(d) open nature of organisation and its relationship with the environment.

6. According to classical school, 'the Science of Public Administration' was based on
(a) presence of codified principles and techniques.
(b) absence of ethical or normative values.
(c) presence of empirical exact knowledge.
(d) presence of scientific principles and methods of universal application.

7. Who among the following authors attached more importance to the structure rather than persons in organisation?
(a) Elton Mayo
(b) Luther Gulick
(c) Mary Parker Follett
(d) Chester Barnard

8. According to Abraham Maslow, one should try to understand behaviour in administration through
(a) Psychoanalysis
(b) Group activity
(c) Human relations
(d) Mass behaviour

9. Whose view is in sharp contrast to the Weberian conception of bureaucracy as rationalisation of organisation?
(a) Claus Offe (b) Robert Merton
(c) Karl Marx (d) Robert Michels

10. Which of the following thinkers has written the book *Toward a Philosophy of Administration*?
(a) Charles Bayard
(b) Hodgkinson
(c) Herbert Simon
(d) Johann Bluntschli

11. Who wrote these words: "Public Administration is a detailed and systematic application of Law."
(a) L.D. White
(b) Woodrow Wilson
(c) Pfiffner
(d) Herbert Simon

12. The one method which satisfies the "time reversal test" under price index numbers is
(a) Laspeyres Method
(b) Fisher's Ideal Method
(c) Paasche's Method
(d) None of the above

13. In the opinion of Simon, which of the following will reduce the size of the middle-link managerial personnel and simultaneously increase the centralisation of decision-making?
(a) Programmed decision
(b) Authority
(c) Bounded rationality
(d) Unprogrammed decision

14. Which one of the following statements is not correct?
(a) Before dissolving the Parliament, the President of France is required to consult the Presidents of the two chambers of Parliament and the Prime Minister.
(b) The President of France has the power to dissolve the Parliament.
(c) The President of France cannot dissolve the Parliament more than once in twelve months.
(d) While dissolving the Parliament, the President of France is required to follow the advice of the Prime Minister and the Presidents of the two chambers.

15. In the USA, the merit system was introduced in the year
(a) 1847 (b) 1877
(c) 1887 (d) 1917

16. Which one of the following approaches to decision-making is referred to as the 'with or without principle'?
(a) Factor analysis
(b) Cost-benefit analysis
(c) Marginal analysis
(d) Differential analysis

17. Which one of the following is not correct?
(a) Informal organizations are customary and social.
(b) Informal organizations are spontaneous and sentimental.
(c) Informal organizations are personal and emotional.
(d) Informal organizations are legal and rational.

18. A symmetrical distribution is one where
(a) Median = Mode
(b) Mean = Median
(c) Mean = Mode
(d) Mean = Median = Mode

19. Which of the following patterns reveals an unstructured informal type of organisational style?
(a) The chain pattern
(b) The wheel pattern
(c) Circular pattern
(d) Y-pattern

20. Which one of the following is not a traditional characteristic of the Japanese workforce and practices?
(a) Slow promotions
(b) Lifetime employment
(c) Top-down communications
(d) Informal organization structure

21. The 'Collegial' type of executive can be found in which one of the following countries?
(a) Japan (b) France
(c) Switzerland (d) Great Britain

22. 'Development Administration is an organised effort to carry out programmes and projects to serve development objectives: Who said this?
(a) Edward Weidner
(b) F.W. Riggs
(c) Donald Stone
(d) Montegomery

23. Which one of the following is not a traditional characteristic of the Japanese workforce and practices?
(a) Slow promotions
(b) Lifetime employment
(c) Top-down communications
(d) Informal organization structure

24. The constitution provides for supplimentary budget in Article:
(a) 110 (b) 114
(c) 120 (d) 314

25. Which of the following are positional averages?
(a) Arithmetic mean (b) Harmonic mean
(c) Geometric mean (d) Median

26. The average age of 10 students in a class is 17 years. If one of them who is 26 years old leaves the school, the average age will be
(a) 15 years (b) 16 years
(c) 17 years (d) 18 years

27. 'Development Administration is an organised effort to carry out programmes and projects to serve development objectives: Who said this?
(a) Edward Weidner (b) F.W. Riggs
(c) Donald Stone (d) Montegomery

28. 'Unity of Command' does not
(a) mean that a subordinate will have only one superior.
(b) mean that one subordinate will receive only one order.

(c) result into a shrinking apex of an organisation.
(d) mean that all units are put under one head.

29. Survey study aims at
 1. knowing facts about the existing situation.
 2. comparing the present status with the standard norms.
 3. criticising the existing situation.
 4. identifying the means of improving the existing situation.

Codes:
(a) 2 and 3 (b) 1, 2 and 3
(c) 1, 3 and 4 (d) 2, 3 and 4

30. Human diseconomies from increasing work specialization beyond a surface in the form of
 1. stress.
 2. poor quality of output.
 3. increased absenteeism.
 4. higher job turnover.

Codes:
(a) 1 only (b) 1 and 4
(c) 2 and 3 (d) 1, 2, 3 and 4

31. Who among the following are writers in whose writings efficiency is a dependent variable?
 1. Gulick and Urwick
 2. Fred Riggs
 3. Max Weber
 4. Herbert Simon

Codes:
(a) 2 and 4 (b) 3 and 4
(c) 1 and 2 (d) 1 and 3

32. Which of the following are the defining features of Public Administration according to Sir Josiah Stamp?
 1. Uniformity of rules
 2. Political accountability
 3. Lack of ethics in business practices
 4. Matrix structure of organizations

Codes:
(a) 1 and 2 (b) 3 and 4
(c) 1, 2 and 3 (d) 2, 3 and 4

33. McGregor's Theory Y provides for which of the following?
 1. Shared responsibility.
 2. Imposed direction and control.
 3. Self-direction and self-control.

Codes:
(a) 2 only (b) 3 only
(c) 1 and 2 (d) 1 and 3

34. Which of the following will help reduce rivalry and rancour in Line-Staff relationship?
 1. Opportunities to exchange roles.
 2. Training to Line people in Staff work and vice versa.
 3. Special pay to Line people.
 4. Departmentalism.

Codes:
(a) 1 and 2 (b) 1 and 4
(c) 2 and 3 (d) 3 and 4

35. Which of the following statements regarding behavioural approach are correct?
 1. It is more deductive than inductive.
 2. It is less macro and more micro.
 3. It is inter-disciplinary in nature.
 4. It is more descriptive and less empirical.

Codes:
(a) 1 and 2 (b) 1, 2 and 3
(c) 1, 3 and 4 (d) 2, 3 and 4

36. What is the correct sequence of the following characteristics of political development?
 1. Capacity 2. Equality
 3. Differentiation

Codes:
(a) 3, 1, 2 (b) 3, 2, 1
(c) 1, 2, 3 (d) 2, 1, 3

37. **List I**
 A. Parkinson Law
 B. Rule of Law

C. Legal Rational Authority
D. Committed Bureaucracy

List II

1. Rising pyramid of bureaucrats
2. Indira Gandhi
3. Max Weber
4. A.V. Dicey
5. Jawaharlal Nehru

Codes:	A	B	C	D
(a)	1	4	3	2
(b)	1	2	5	4
(c)	4	1	3	2
(d)	1	4	3	5

38. **List I**

A. Herbert Simon
B. Charles Lindblom
C. Chester Barnard
D. Amitai Etzioni

List II

1. Positive and negative decisions
2. Logical Positivism
3. Mixed -scanning
4. Incrementalism
5. One best way

Codes:	A	B	C	D
(a)	1	4	3	5
(b)	1	2	3	4
(c)	2	1	4	3
(d)	2	4	1	3

39. **List I**

A. Santhanam Committee
B. Mudaliar Committee
C. Kothari Committee
D. Fulcan Committee

List II

1. Recruitment Policy and Selection Methods
2. Reorganisation of the British Civil Service
3. Prevention of Corruption
4. Public Services (qualifications for recruitment)
5. Training of Civil Servants

Codes:	A	B	C	D
(a)	1	4	3	2
(b)	5	3	1	4
(c)	3	5	2	1
(d)	3	4	1	2

40. **List I (Name of Local Body)**

A. Janpad Panchayat
B. Mandai Praja Parishad
C. Mandai Panchayat
D. Taluka Panchayat

List II (State)

1. Andhra Pradesh 2. Karnataka
3. Madhya Pradesh 4. Gujarat

Codes:	A	B	C	D
(a)	4	2	1	3
(b)	3	1	2	4
(c)	4	1	2	3
(d)	3	2	1	4

41. **List I**

A. Panchayati Raj Elections
B. Democratic Decentralization
C. Nagar Panchayats
D. Block Committees

List II

1. 74th Amendment
2. 73rd Amendment
3. B.R. Mehta Committee
4. Intermediate level
5. Ashok Mehta Committee

Codes:	A	B	C	D
(a)	2	3	1	4
(b)	1	5	2	4
(c)	2	1	5	3
(d)	1	5	4	3

42. **List I (Committees)**

A. G.V.K. Rao Committee
B. Balwant Rai Mehta Committee
C. L.M. Singhvi Committee
D. Ashok Mehta Committee

List II (Set up on)

1. Panchayati Raj Institutions.
2. Revitalisation of PR is for democracy and development.

3. Existing administrative arrangements for rural development and poverty alleviation programmes.
4. Community Development Programme and National Extension Service.
5. Panchayati Raj Elections.

Codes:	A	B	C	D
(a)	4	3	2	1
(b)	4	5	1	2
(c)	3	5	1	2
(d)	3	4	2	1

43. **Assertion (A):** After the World War II, the concept of Public Administration expanded.
Reason (R): The formal lines of authority were replaced by much broader focus.
(a) Both (A) and (R) are true and (R) is the correct explanation of (A).
(b) Both (A) and (R) are true but (R) is not the correct explanation of (A).
(c) (A) is true but (R) is false.
(d) (A) is false but (R) is true.

44. **Assertion (A):** Public Administration provides a professional input for the formulation of the public policy.
Reason (R): The administrators exercise much more power in the formulation of pnblic policy than the formal description of their responsibilities suggest.
(a) Both (A) and (R) are true and (R) is the correct explanation of (A).
(b) Both (A) and (R) are true but (R) is not the correct explanation of (A).
(c) (A) is true but (R) is false.
(d) (A) is false but (R) is true

45. **Assertion (A):** The principal objective of Scientific Management is to secure maximum prosperity for the employer, coupled with maximum prosperity for employees.
Reason (R): The philosophy of scientific management is that there is no inherent conflict in the interests of the employer, workers and consumers.
(a) Both (A) and (R) are true and (R) is the correct explanation of (A).
(b) Both (A) and (R) are true but (R) is not the correct explanation of (A).
(c) (A) is true but (R) is false.
(d) (A) is false but (R) is true.

46. **Assertion (A):** According to Herbert Simon, a decision is a choice between alternative courses of action.
Reason (R): Every decision consists of a logical combination of fact and value propositions.
(a) Both (A) and (R) are true and (R) is the correct explanation of (A).
(b) Both (A) and (R) are true but (R) is not the correct explanation of (A).
(c) (A) is true but (R) is false.
(d) (A) is false but (R) is true.

47. **Assertion (A):** In every modern state increasing administration has focussed attention on the urgent need for unity in administration.
Reason (R): Integration and coordination have, therefore, become *sine qua non* of a good administrative system today.
(a) Both (A) and (R) are true and (R) is the correct explanation of (A).
(b) Both (A) and (R) are true but (R) is not the correct explanation of (A).
(c) (A) is true but (R) is false.
(d) (A) is false but (R) is true.

48. **Assertion (A):** Leadership is a continuous process of influencing behaviour.
Reason (R): Leaders must show a genuine human concern for subordinates.
(a) Both (A) and (R) are true and (R) is the correct explanation of (A).
(b) Both (A) and (R) are true but (R) is not the correct explanation of (A).
(c) (A) is true but (R) is false.
(d) (A) is false but (R) is true.

49. **Assertion (A):** The concept of development Administration is of recent origin.
    Reason (R): Many countries became independent since World War II.
    (a) Both (A) and (R) are true and (R) is the correct explanation of (A).
    (b) Both (A) and (R) are true but (R) is not the correct explanation of (A).
    (c) (A) is true but (R) is false.
    (d) (A) is false but (R) is true.

50. **Assertion (A):** The legislatures are well equipped and mature enough to effectively control the rapidly expanding administration.
    Reason (R): The work of the administration has been phenomenally on the increase both in volume and complexity.
    (a) Both (A) and are true and (R) is the correct explanation of (A).
    (b) Both (A) and (R) are true but (R) is not the correct explanation of (A).
    (c) (A) is true but (R) is false.
    (d) (A) is false but (R) is true.

ANSWER SHEET

PAPER—I

1. (d)	2. (d)	3. (c)	4. (d)	5. (d)
6. (a)	7. (b)	8. (d)	9. (d)	10. (d)
11. (d)	12. (c)	13. (c)	14. (b)	15. (a)
16. (d)	17. (d)	18. (b)	19. (c)	20. (b)
21. (a)	22. (b)	23. (c)	24. (c)	25. (c)
26. (b)	27. (b)	28. (c)	29. (b)	30. (b)
31. (a)	32. (b)	33. (c)	34. (a)	35. (b)
36. (d)	37. (b)	38. (d)	39. (c)	40. (a)
41. (a)	42. (b)	43. (a)	44. (a)	45. (b)
46. (c)	47. (c)	48. (c)	49. (d)	50. (c)

PAPER—II

1. (a)	2. (a)	3. (c)	4. (d)	5. (d)
6. (d)	7. (a)	8. (b)	9. (c)	10. (b)
11. (a)	12. (b)	13. (a)	14. (c)	15. (b)
16. (b)	17. (b)	18. (d)	19. (b)	20. (a)
21. (b)	22. (b)	23. (b)	24. (a)	25. (c)
26. (d)	27. (d)	28. (c)	29. (d)	30. (b)
31. (b)	32. (a)	33. (d)	34. (a)	35. (c)
36. (b)	37. (d)	38. (b)	39. (a)	40. (b)
41. (d)	42. (c)	43. (b)	44. (a)	45. (a)
46. (d)	47. (b)	48. (c)	49. (b)	50. (c)

PAPER—III

1. (c)	2. (b)	3. (d)	4. (c)	5. (d)
6. (d)	7. (b)	8. (a)	9. (c)	10. (b)
11. (b)	12. (b)	13. (a)	14. (d)	15. (c)
16. (c)	17. (d)	18. (d)	19. (c)	20. (a)
21. (c)	22. (b)	23. (a)	24. (b)	25. (d)
26. (b)	27. (b)	28. (b)	29. (b)	30. (d)
31. (d)	32. (a)	33. (b)	34. (a)	35. (b)
36. (c)	37. (a)	38. (c)	39. (d)	40. (b)
41. (a)	42. (d)	43. (d)	44. (b)	45. (a)
46. (a)	47. (a)	48. (b)	49. (b)	50. (d)

MOCK TEST–3
PAPER–I

1. Which among the following gives more freedom to the learner to interact?
   (a) Small group discussion
   (b) Lectures by experts
   (c) Use of film
   (d) Viewing country-wide classroom program on TV

2. While designing communication strategy feed-forward studies are conducted by
   (a) Media (b) Audience
   (c) Communicator (d) Satellite
3. A theory is correct because
   (a) its derivations match with most observations
   (b) its advocate has written a big volume to establish it
   (c) it is supported by a large number of scholars
   (d) it has a large number of followers
4. Which of the following are true about the concepts?
   I. Concepts have different meanings in different contents.
   II. Concepts are the blocks from which theories are built.
   III. Concepts are ideas, abstractions, that do not have meaning in themselves.
   (a) Only II (b) I and III
   (c) I and II (d) All of these
5. The most sensible idea about teaching and research is that
   (a) they interfere with each other
   (b) they are two entirely different kinds of activities
   (c) they cannot go together
   (d) they are two sides of the same coin
6. Which of the following is quality of a teacher?
   (a) He should know the child psychology
   (b) He should evoke curiosity of the pupils by presenting the subject matter in an effective manner with clear explaining leading to better understanding of the matter
   (c) He should be trained in various teaching methodologies
   (d) All of these
7. Which of the following is/are true about research?
   (i) Gives emphasis to the development of theories, principles and generalisation, which are very helpful in accurate prediction regarding the variable understudy.
   (ii) It is always directed towards the solution of a problem.
   (iii) It is always based upon empirical or observable evidences.
   (a) Both (i) and (ii)
   (b) Both (i) and (iii)
   (c) Both (ii) and (iii)
   (d) All of the above
8. Which of the following methods of teaching encourages the use of maximum senses?
   (a) Team teaching method
   (b) Problem-solving method
   (c) Laboratory method
   (d) Self-study method
9. A non-fictional literary composition that forms an independent part of a publication, as a newspaper or magazine is known as
   (a) Symposium (b) Paper
   (c) Article (d) None of these
10. Photo bleeding means
    (a) Photo placement
    (b) Photo cropping
    (c) Photo colour adjustment
    (d) Photo cutting
11. Attitudes, concepts, skills and knowledge are products of
    (a) Explanation (b) Learning
    (c) Research (d) Heredity
12. To study the relationship of family size with income a researcher classifies his population into different income slabs and then takes a random sample from each slab. Which technique of sampling does he adopt?
    (a) Systematic Sampling
    (b) Random Sampling

(c) Stratified Random Sampling
(d) Cluster Sampling

13. In business communication, the major obstacles arise because of the
(a) psychological barriers
(b) physical barriers
(c) organisational barriers
(d) mechanical barriers

14. The most important question that a researcher is interested to use statistical techniques in his problem then he has to see
(a) whether worthwhile inferences could be drawn
(b) whether the data could be quantified
(c) whether appropriate statistical techniques are available
(d) whether analysis of data would be possible

15. How can the objectivity of the research be enhanced?
(a) Through its validity
(b) Through its impartiality
(c) Through its reliability
(d) All of these

16. Which one of the following is not correct? A belief becomes a scientific truth when it
(a) can be replicated
(b) is established experimentally
(c) is arrived by logically
(d) is accepted by many people

17. **Statements:** All cars are ducks. All ducks are birds.
Conclusions:
(i) All birds are cars.
(ii) All cars are birds.
Choose the correct one.
(a) Only conclusion (i) follows
(b) Only conclusion (ii) follows
(c) Both (i) and (ii) follow
(d) Neither (i) nor (ii) follows

18. Research can be conducted by a person who
(a) is a hard worker
(b) has studied research methodology
(c) holds a postgraduate degree
(d) possesses thinking and reasoning ability

19. Action-research is
(a) A longitudinal research
(b) An applied research
(c) A research carried out to solve immediate problems
(d) All of the above

Read the following passage and answer the questions 20 to 24:

The genesis of service tax emanates from the ongoing structural transformation of the Indian economy, whereby presently more than one-half of GDP originates from the services sector. Despite the growing presence of the services sector in the Indian economy it remained out of the tax net prior to 1994-95, leading to a steady deterioration in tax-GDP ratio. The service tax was introduced in 1994-95 on a select category of services at a low rate of five percent. While the service tax rate and the coverage of services being taxed have increased ever since, the combined tax-GDP ratio of the Centre and States, nevertheless, deteriorated from 16.4 percent in 1985-86 to 14.1 percent in 1999-2000. It may be noted that between 1990-91 and 1998-99, the share of industrial sector in GDP dropped by 6.4 percentage points whereas almost 64 percent of the tax revenue was generated by indirect taxes for which industrial sector continues to be the principal tax base. On the other hand, during the same period, the share of services sector in GDP has increased by 10 percentage points and this sector has still remained poorly taxed.

The rationale for service tax, therefore, lies not only in arresting the falling tax-GDP ratio but also in *ipso facto* improving allocative efficiency in the economy as well as promoting equity. Against this backdrop, the service tax needs to be designed taking into account the fact that (i) the share of services in GDP is expanding; (ii) failure to tax services distorts consumer choices and encourages spending on services at the expense of goods; (iii) untaxed service traders are unable to claim Value Added Tax (VAT) on service inputs, which encourages businesses to develop in-house services, creating further distortions; and (iv) most services that are likely to become taxable are positively correlated with expenditure of high-income households and, therefore, service tax improves equity.

In the Indian context, taxation of services assumes importance in the wake of the need for improving the revenue system, ensuring a measure of neutrality in taxation between goods and services and eventually helping to evolve an efficient system of domestic trade taxes, both at the Central and the State levels.

20. What, according to the passage, was the impact of exclusion of service tax till the first half of the last decade of the past century?
    (a) Service sector used to flourish exorbitantly
    (b) There was no impact as there was no service tax
    (c) There was a steady deterioration in the GDP
    (d) Tax-GDP ratio had steadily and gradually aggravated
21. Levying service tax is most likely to achieve which of the following?
    (i) Promoting equity.
    (ii) Check on reducing tax-GDP ratio.
    (iii) Enhancement in allocative efficiency.
    (a) Both (ii) and (iii)
    (b) Both (i) and (iii)
    (c) Both (i) and (ii)
    (d) All the three
22. The origin of service tax is attributed to
    (a) metamorphosis of our country's economy
    (b) increase in Gross Domestic Product (GDP)
    (c) existence of service sector
    (d) tax of the future
23. Which of the following factors helps service tax to improve fairness across different economic strata of society?
    (a) It improves revenue system
    (b) Taxable services are mostly those that are utilised by the rich
    (c) Untaxed service traders are prevented from claiming value added tax
    (d) Encouragement to in-house services is effected
24. Which of the following is most likely to provide neutrality to various economic activities?
    (a) Consistency in tax structure and revenue buoyancy
    (b) Increase in revenue buoyancy
    (c) fairness in tax administration
    (d) Equity and efficiency in various activities
25. Which of the following is classified in the category of the developmental research?
    (a) Descriptive research
    (b) Philosophical research
    (c) Action research
    (d) All the above
26. The education aims at the fullest realisation of all the potentialities of children. It implies that
    I. it is necessary that their attitudes are helpful, encouraging and sympathetic.
    II. teacher and parents must know what children are capable of and what potentialities they possess.

III. they should provide suitable opportunities and favourable environmental facilities which are conducive to the maximum growth of children.

Choose the correct one.
(a) II and III (b) I and III
(c) I and II (d) All of them

27. How many times has the preamble of Indian constitution been amended so far?
(a) Once (b) Twice
(c) Thrice (d) Never

28. The relationship between earth, mountains and forests can be represented as

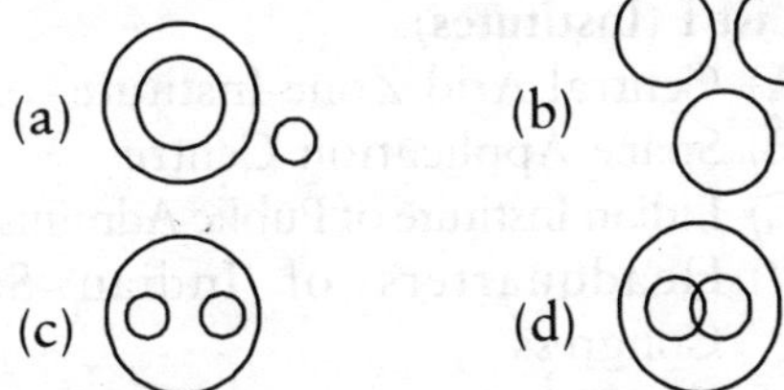

29. Central Fuel Research Institute is situated in
(a) Pune (b) Jadugoda
(c) Lucknow (d) Kolkata

30. The letters in the first set have certain relationship. On the basis of this relationship what is the right choice for the second set?
AST : BRU :: NQV : ?
(a) OPW (b) ORW
(c) MPU (d) MRW

31. The number of students in four classes A, B, C, D and their respective mean marks obtained by each of the class are given below:

	Class A	Class B	Class C	Class D
Number of students	10	40	30	20
Arithmetic mean	20	30	50	15

The combined mean of the marks of four classes together will be
(a) 15 (b) 32
(c) 50 (d) 20

32. Communication with oneself is known as
(a) Organisational communication
(b) Interpersonal communication
(c) Intrapersonal communication
(d) Grapevine communication

33. The number system which is not a positional notation system is
(a) Binary (b) Octal
(c) Roman (d) Decimal

34. Which of the following options will complete the series?
AZ, GT, MN, ?, YB.
(a) TS (b) KF
(c) RX (d) SH

35. If '367' means 'I am happy'; '748' means 'You are sad' and '469' means 'Happy and sad' in a given code, then which of the following represents 'and' in that code?
(a) 4 (b) 6
(c) 3 (d) 9

36. What is the excess 3 code?
(a) self-algebraic code
(b) cyclic complimenting code
(c) cyclic algebraic code
(d) self-complimenting code

37. Which of the following is not created by the Act of Parliament?
(a) Railway Board
(b) Atomic Energy Commission
(c) Backward Class Commission
(d) University Grants Commission

38. Which of the following is radioactive pollutant?
(a) Nickel (b) Iron
(c) Chlorine (d) Thorium

39. The first Indian experimental geostationary communication satellite was
(a) Skylab (b) Apple
(c) INSAT-1A (d) INSAT-1B

40. Which one of the following is a research tool?
(a) Diagram (b) Questionnaire
(c) Graph (d) Illustration

41. Which article of the Constitution provides safeguards to Naga Customary and their social practices against any act of Parliament?
(a) Article 371 B (b) Article 371 A
(c) Article 263 (d) Article 371 C

42. **Statement:** Although the city was under kneedeep water for a week in this monsoon, there is no outbreak of any water borne disease.
Assumptions:
(i) Waterborne disease usually spreads in monsoon.
(ii) Water concentration at a place leads to waterborne disease.
Choose the correct option.
(a) Only assumption (i) is implicit
(b) Only assumption (ii) is implicit
(c) Both (i) and (ii) are implicit
(d) Neither (i) nor (ii) is implicit

43. Books and records are the primary sources of data in
(a) laboratory research
(b) historical research
(c) participatory research
(d) clinical research

44. The Kothari Commission's report was entitled on
(a) Learning to be adventure
(b) Education and National Development
(c) Education and socialisation in democracy
(d) Diversification of Education

45. What is the term used for a half byte?
(a) word (b) bit
(c) nibble (d) bug

46. C-band transponder in satellites uses the frequency range
(a) 12 GHz to 14 GHz
(b) 4 GHz to 6 GHz
(c) 2 GHz to 4 GHz
(d) None of these.

47. Which of the following water pollutants is the cause of sterility in human beings?
(a) Manganese (b) Mercury
(c) Arsenic (d) None of these

48. Match List I with List II and select the correct answer using the codes given below.
List I (Institutes)
(A) Central Arid Zone Institute
(B) Space Application Centre
(C) Indian Institute of Public Administration
(D) Headquarters of Indian Science Congress
List II (Cities)
(1) Kolkata (2) New Delhi
(3) Ahmedabad (4) Jodhpur

Codes:	A	B	C	D
(a)	4	3	2	1
(b)	4	2	1	3
(c)	3	1	2	4
(d)	1	2	4	3

The total CO_2 emissions from various sectors are 5 mmt. In the Pie Chart given below, the percentage contribution to CO_2 emissions from various sectors is indicated.

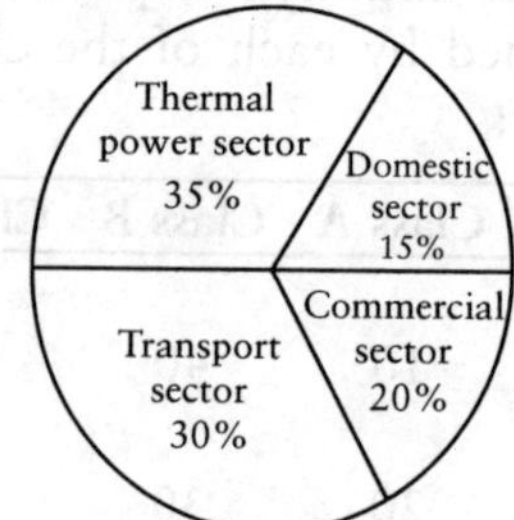

49. What is the absolute CO_2 emission from domestic sector?
(a) 1.75 mmt (b) 0.75 mmt
(c) 1.5 mmt (d) 2.5 mmt

50. What is the absolute CO_2 emission for combined thermal power and transport sectors?
(a) 1.5 mmt (b) 3.25 mmt
(c) 4 mmt (d) 2.5 mmt

PAPER–II

1. The classic "Three Es" of Public Administration are
(a) Economy, Efficiency, Effectiveness
(b) Equity, Ecology, Environment
(c) Equity, Efficiency, Effectiveness
(d) Efficiency, Ecology, Economy

2. Herbert Simon is not associated with which one of the following?
(a) Fact and value premises
(b) Satisficing
(c) Logical positivism
(d) Science of muddling through

3. The concept of satisfying behaviour comes close to the economic concept of
(a) Optimum output
(b) Maximising output
(c) Easily achievable output
(d) Best output

4. Herbert Simon's model of decision-making is known as
(a) Policy science
(b) Behaviour alternative
(c) Disjointed incrementalism
(d) Mixed scanning

5. Who among the following further developed the Politics-Administration dichotomy-a fairly constant line of thought at the initial stages of the evolution of Public Administration?
(a) H. Fayol (b) L. Gulick
(c) L. Urwick (d) F. Goodnow

6. "We are no longer confronted with several administrative sciences but with one which can be applied equally well to public and private affairs". The above statement is by:
(a) Henry Fayol (b) Luther Gulick
(c) L. Urwick (d) M.P. Follett

7. Which is not the right statement? Weber's bureaucracy model is criticised because it emphasises on
(a) absolute implementation of Hierarchy theory.
(b) keeping of written documents.
(c) increase in efficiency owing to structure.
(d) approving informal organisations in a formal organisation.

8. Which writer claimed that technological advancement could be used by the capitalist class to defend itself against the rising wages?
(a) Marshall (b) Keynes
(c) Malthus (d) Ricardo

9. The US Public Service Commission was established by Congress in 1883 through an Act passed by
(a) Office of Personnel Management
(b) Merit System Protection Board
(c) Federal Labour Relation Authority
(d) Civil Service Department

10. Traditionally, managers and executive leaders have been
(a) 'made' rather than 'born.'
(b) 'born' rather than 'made'.
(c) both 'made' and 'born'.
(d) None of the above.

11. In the Ohio State Leadership Model, the per se perception of the Leadership style by the leader himself was systematised through the use of

(a) Leader behaviour description questionnaire
(b) Leader opinion questionnaire
(c) Group behaviour questionnaire
(d) Initiating structure questionnaire

12. Administrative morality is
(a) is an isolated concept.
(b) is a wide ranging term.
(c) doesn't exist at all.
(d) is a narrow term.

13. Most of the Third World States are
(a) linguistically homogeneous.
(b) ethnically and culturally divided.
(c) economically self-reliant.
(d) rich in natural resources.

14. The average marks secured by 30 students are 60. If two more students join the class, the average comes down to 56.25. The total marks secured by these two students were
(a) 0 (b) 10
(c) 20 (d) 30

15. Which of the following is not a basic characteristic of Sala Model?
(a) Heterogeneity (b) Overlapping
(c) Formalism (d) Achievement

16. Which of the following is not correct about local administration?
(a) Panchayats have Constitutional responsibility that they work in self administration form.
(b) Constitution lays responsibility on State governments for local self administration.
(c) State governments have the Constitutional responsibility that they constitute a finance commission which will decide on the financial transactions of the municipality.
(d) Municipal institutions have the Constitutional responsibility that they implement the projects of the public distribution system.

17. Open participation of political parties in Panchayati Raj affairs was a major recommendation of which of the following committees?
(a) Balwant Rai Mehta
(b) Ashok Mehta
(c) G.V.K. Rao
(d) L.M. Singhvi

18. Mechanical devices or even electric test scoring machines can be used to screen out the correct answers in this type of examination. It is
(a) Essay type examination
(b) Written examinations
(c) Oral examination
(d) Short answer tests

19. The basic objective of an interview is to assess the candidate's
(a) General knowledge
(b) Intellectual capacity
(c) Power of expression
(d) Personal qualities

20. If σ is –22.5, mean is 45, median is 48, the coefficient of skewness will be:
(a) –0.5 (b) –0.4
(c) –0.3 (d) –0.2

21. How many functions have been assigned to municipal bodies in India under the 74th Constitution Amendment Act?
(a) 33 (b) 18
(c) 29 (d) 12

22. 73rd Constitutional amendment provided for
(a) Constitutional status to rural and urban bodies.
(b) mandatory three-tier system for all the states.
(c) audit of panchayat finances by CAG.
(d) direct elections of chairpersons and members of PRI at all levels.

23. Which of the following is a committee on block-level planning?

(a) Hanumantha Rao Committee
(b) Dantewala Committee
(c) G.V.K. Rao Committee
(d) L.M. Singhvi Committee

24. Which eminent personality observed, "there is a saying that all politics is local. But increasingly, all local politics has global consequences. And those global consequences, in turn, affect the quality of local life everywhere". (1998)?
(a) Bill Clinton
(b) James Gustave Speth
(c) Jiang Zemin
(d) Kofi Annan

25. Which of the following statement about civil service in a developing society are correct?
1. It should act as an agent of change.
2. It should have a concern for societal equity.
3. It should have a concern for vested interests.
4. It should be politically neutral.

Codes:
(a) 1 and 2 (b) 1, 2 and 3
(c) 1, 2 and 4 (d) 2, 3 and 4

26. Which of the statements given below is/ are correct?
1. Shri Jagjivan Ram was appointed as the Chairman of the Central Social Welfare Board when it was set up in 1953.
2. The National Commission for Women was set up as a national apex statutory body in 1992.
3. The National Institute of Public Cooperation and Child Development is an autonomous body and functions under the aegis of the Ministry of Health and Family Welfare.

Codes:
(a) 2 only (b) 3 only
(c) 1 and 2 (d) 2 and 3

27. Which of the following statements regarding civil services in Japan is/are correct?
1. The NPA and MCA are its principal controlling and coordinating agencies.
2. The Japanese higher civil service is elitist.

Codes:
(a) 1 only (b) 2 only
(c) Both 1 and 2 (d) Neither 1 nor 2

28. The political activities of civil servants in the USA are regulated by
1. The Pendleton Act of 1883
2. The Hatch Act of 1939
3. Ramspeck Act of 1940
4. Taft Hartley Act of 1947

Codes:
(a) 1 and 2 (b) 1, 2 and 3
(c) 1, 3 and 4 (d) 2, 3 and 4

29. Which of the following were outlined by Max Weber as key characteristics of bureaucracy?
1. System of supervision and subordination
2. Unity of Command
3. Training in job requirement and skills

Codes:
(a) 1 and 2 (b) 1 and 3
(c) 2 and 3 (d) 1, 2 and 3

30. What is the correct sequence of the following landmarks in the growth and emergence of new public administration?
1. The Minnowbrook Conference
2. The Honey Report on Higher Education for Public Service
3. The Philadelphia Conference on the theory and practice of Public Administration
4. Publication of *Toward a New Public* Administration: The Minnowbrook Perspective.

Codes:
(a) 4, 3, 2, 1 (b) 2, 3, 1, 4
(c) 2, 4, 1, 3 (d) 1, 2, 3, 4

31. Which of the statements given below are correct?
   1. In an open control system in organizations, managers actively intervene to make decisions.
   2. Establishing standards is not a constituent step of the control process of an organization.
   3. Most statistical control procedures have strong post-action elements.

Codes:
(a) 1 and 2 (b) 1 and 3
(c) 2 and 3 (d) 1, 2 and 3

32. In every organization the need for coordination rests upon which of the following factors?
   1. The need to avoid overlapping and confusion in the organization.
   2. The need to prevent lopsided concentration on one aspect of work to the exclusion of other aspects.
   3. The need firstly to avoid conflict and secondly to resolve the conflicts whenever these may arise.

Codes:
(a) 1 and 2 (b) 1 and 3
(c) 2 and 3 (d) 1, 2 and 3

33. **List I**
A. Human Relations
B. Policy Science
C. Politics Administration Separation
D. Science of Management

List II
1. Harold Lasswell
2. Elton Mayo
3. Woodrow Wilson
4. W.F. Willoughby

Codes:	**A**	**B**	**C**	**D**
(a)	2	1	3	4
(b)	1	3	4	2
(c)	2	3	4	1
(d)	3	4	1	2

34. **List I**
A. Bureaucracy
B. Closed system
C. Normative Control structure
D. Scalar chain

List II
1. Generation of moral involvement.
2. Vertical differentiation.
3. Facts and values.
4. Entropy and disorganisation.
5. Administration by appointed officials.

Codes:	**A**	**B**	**C**	**D**
(a)	4	3	1	2
(b)	5	4	1	2
(c)	4	1	2	3
(d)	5	4	3	1

35. **List I**
A. Henri Fayol B. Herbert Simon
C. Shannon-Weaver D. Norbert Wiener

List II
1. Grapevine 2. Cybernetics
3. Gangplank 4. Noise

Codes:	**A**	**B**	**C**	**D**
(a)	3	1	4	2
(b)	3	4	2	1
(c)	3	4	1	2
(d)	3	2	4	1

36. **List I**
A. Short duration discussion
B. Calling attention notice
C. Zero Hour
D. Committee on Public Undertakings

List II
1. 1964 2. 1962
3. 1953 4. 1954

Codes:	**A**	**B**	**C**	**D**
(a)	3	4	2	1
(b)	4	3	1	2
(c)	3	2	4	1
(d)	4	2	1	3

37. **List I (Committees)**
A. G.V.K. Rao Committee
B. Balwant Rai Mehta Committee

C. L.M. Singhvi Committee
D. Ashok Mehta Committee
List II (Set up on)
1. Panchayati Raj Institutions.
2. Revitalisation of PR is for democracy and development.
3. Existing administrative arrangements for rural development and poverty alleviation programmes.
4. Community Development Programme and National Extension Service.
5. Panchayati Raj Elections.

Codes:	A	B	C	D
(a)	4	3	2	1
(b)	4	5	1	2
(c)	3	5	1	2
(d)	3	4	2	1

38. **List I**
A. Panchayati Raj Elections
B. Democratic Decentralization
C. Nagar Panchayats
D. Block Committees
List II
1. 74th Amendment
2. 73rd AJnendment
3. B.R. Mehta Committee
4. Intermediate level
5. Ashok Mehta Committee

Codes:	A	B	C	D
(a)	2	3	1	4
(b)	1	5	2	4
(c)	2	1	5	3
(d)	1	5	4	3

39. **Assertion (A):** F.W. Taylor is known as the Father of 'Scientific Management.'
Reason (R): It was he who used the term 'Scientific Management' for the first time.
(a) Both (A) and (R) are true and (R) is the correct explanation of (A).
(b) Both (A) and (R) are true but (R) is not the correct explanation of (A).
(c) (A) is true but (R) is false.
(d) (A) is false but (R) is true.

40. **Assertion (A):** Henri Fayol identified five elements as the primary functions of management activity.
Reason (R): According to him, knowledge of administration, rather than technical knowledge, is needed at higher levels of an organisation.
(a) Both (A) and (R) are true and (R) is the correct explanation of (A).
(b) Both (A) and (R) are true but (R) is not the correct explanation of (A).
(c) (A) is true but (R) is false.
(d) (A) is false but (R) is true

41. **Assertion (A):** The prismatic society is characterized by a high degree of formalism.
Reason (R): Formalistic behaviour is caused by the lack of presure towards programme objectives and a great permissiveness for arbitrary administration.
(a) Both (A) and (R) are true and (R) is the correct explanation of (A).
(b) Both (A) and (R) are true but (R) is not the correct explanation of (A).
(c) (A) is true but (R) is false.
(d) (A) is false but (R) is true.

42. **Assertion (A):** Public Administration is an action oriented applied social science because it is engaged in the task of implementing public policies.
Reason (R): The need to adopt management science and techniques for improving the skills of Public Administrators can hardly be over emphasized.
(a) Both (A) and (R) are true and (R) is the correct explanation of (A).
(b) Both (A) and (R) are true but (R) is not the correct explanation of (A).
(c) (A) is true but (R) is false.
(d) (A) is false but (R) is true.

43. **Assertion (A):** In a democracy, the functioning of bureaucracy is confined by the operation of party system.

Reason (R): Where the party system is unable to produce a stable government, bureaucracy acquires a special position.
(a) Both (A) and are true and (R) is the correct explanation of (A).
(b) Both (A) and (R) are true but (R) is not the correct explanation of (A).
(c) (A) is true but (R) is false.
(d) (A) is false but (R) is true.

44. **Assertion (A):** A tenet of scientific management is cooperation and harmony between workers and managers by human relations.
Reason (R): Taylor did not believe in participative management.
(a) Both (A) and (R) are true and (R) is the correct explanation of (A).
(b) Both (A) and (R) are true but (R) is not the correct explanation of (A).
(c) (A) is true but (R) is false.
(d) (A) is false but (R) is true.

45. **Assertion (A):** Nowadays the length of span of control has increased.
Reason (R): Increasing automation in administration, information revolution and role of specialists are the major reasons for change.
(a) Both (A) and (R) are true and (R) is the correct explanation of (A).
(b) Both (A) and (R) are true but (R) is not the correct explanation of (A).
(c) (A) is true but (R) is false.
(d) (A) is false but (R) is true.

46. **Assertion (A):** In the USA, the President's men are political appointees.
Reason (R): Their spoils system is the recruitment method.
(a) Both (A) and (R) are true and (R) is the correct explanation of (A).
(b) Both (A) and (R) are true but (R) is not the correct explanation of (A).
(c) (A) is true but (R) is false.
(d) (A) is false but (R) is true.

47. The situational variables identified by Fieldler were
(a) Position power
(b) Leader-member relation
(c) Task structure
(d) All of the above

48. Which of the following writers rejected the neo-classical theory which believed in the gradual and harmonious growth of the economy?
(a) David Ricardo (b) Adam Smith
(c) J.M. Keynes (d) Schumpeter

49. Who among the following said that leadership and authority are plural because of involvement of many people?
(a) Chester Barnard
(b) Ordway Tead
(c) Marshall Dimock
(d) Mary Parker Follett

50. Who among the following is the author of History of the United States Civil Service?
(a) John W. Burgess
(b) Woodrow Wilson
(c) Paul P. Van Riper
(d) Leonard D. White

PAPER–III

1. "Administration should have a scientific system which can make its function easy, can make its function less unskilled, can strengthen and dean its organisation, and through its help the government can perform its duty sincerely." Whose statement is this?
(a) Frank J. Goodnow
(b) Peter F. Drucker
(c) R.H. Hodel
(d) Woodrow Wilson

2. Which one of the following is not a part of Mary Parker Follett's thought?

(a) Integration must follow the law of the situation.
(b) Power is self-developing capacity.
(c) Authority relates to the job.
(d) Human behaviour is linear.

3. Which one of the following is not the characteristic of Max Weber's model of bureaucracy?
(a) Offices are arranged in the form of a hierarchy.
(b) All organizational members are to be selected on the basis of technical qualifications.
(c) Control in the bureaucratic organization is based on personally applied rules.
(d) Officials pursue their careers within the organization.

4. The systems approach is mainly based on the work of which one of the following?
(a) Chris Argyris
(b) Chester Barnard
(c) Ludwing Bertalanffy
(d) Amitai Etzioni

5. This method brings into the service persons without previous administrative experience and therefore prolonged training has to be given to them before they can be entrusted with the responsibilities of a substantive post. The reference is to
(a) Temporary recruitment
(b) Ordinary recruitment
(c) Direct recruitment
(d) Recruitment by promotion

6. Which of the following does not affect the area of control?
(a) Nature of work.
(b) Kind of Employees.
(c) Geographical considerations of employees.
(d) Service tenure and training of employees.

7. The centre point of Taylor's Scientific Management Principle was:
(a) Production
(b) Economic status of workers
(c) Relation between workers and management
(d) None of the above

8. In plotting a frequency polygon, it is important to see that
(a) Mid point of all class intervals are joined together.
(b) The mid point of an interval is always taken to represent the entire interval.
(c) Each class interval is represented by a separate rectangle.
(d) None of the above

9. In a week the prices of a bag of rice were 350, 280, 340, 290, 320, 310, 300. The range is
(a) 60 (b) 70
(c) 80 (d) 100

10. Which one of the following is the correct chronological order of the Committee/Commission Reports?
(a) Macaulay-Aitchison-Lee-Fulton-Islington
(b) Aitchison-Macaulay-Fulton-Islington-Lee
(c) Macaulay-Aitchison-Islington-Lee-Fulton
(d) Islington-Aitchison-Lee-Fulton-Macaulay

11. Which of the following States first adopted the Panchayati form of rural local government?
(a) Rajasthan and Kerala
(b) Rajasthan and Gujarat
(c) Andhra Pradesh and Maharashtra
(d) Rajasthan and Andhra Pradesh

12. Jawahar Gram Samridhi Yojana (JGSY) is implemented entirely at the level of
(a) Intermediate Panchayat
(b) District Panchayat

(c) Nagar Panchayat
(d) Village Panchayat

13. What decides the reservation for women in Panchayati Raj?
(a) Economic welfare of women and children.
(b) Gender equality in rural society.
(c) Participation of women in public life.
(d) Empowerment of women.

14. In which one of the following Schedules of the Constitution of India is Urban Local Self Government mentioned?
(a) Sixth (b) Ninth
(c) Eleventh (d) Twelfth

15. A beginning of local government may be said to have been made in
(a) 1687 (b) 1787
(c) 1859 (d) 1950

16. Which committee was the first to recommend a Constitutional status to Gram Pancbayats?
(a) Balwant Rai Mehta Committee
(b) Ashok Mehta Committee
(c) G.V.K. Rao Committee
(d) L.M. Shinghvi Committee

17. Which international organisation defines globalization as "the increasingly close international integration of markets both for goods and services, and for capital"?
(a) UNDP (b) UNO
(c) IMF (d) World Bank

18. The World Bank supports the efforts of developing country governments to
(a) build schools and health centres.
(b) provide water and electricity.
(c) fight disease and protect the environment.
(d) All of the above.

19. The WTO Ministerial Decision on procedures for the facilitation of solutions to non-tariff barriers is also known as
(a) Vertical mechanism
(b) Horizontal mechanism
(c) Export-related mechanism
(d) None of the above

20. The most popular form of city Government in USA is the
(a) Mayor-Administrator Plan
(b) Mayor-Council Plan
(c) City-Manager Plan
(d) Commission Plan

21. What could be termed as the destructive effect of British colonialism in India?
(a) It led to the division of India into small units.
(b) It led to systematic exploitation of India.
(c) It promoted divisive forces to keep itself in power.
(d) Both (b) and (c).

22. What did the Covenanted Civil Service denote?
(a) Indian Civil Service
(b) Provincial Civil Service
(c) British Civil Service
(d) Subordinate Civil Service

23. The 'Classification of Services' in India is governed by the Civil Services Rules of:
(a) 1930 (b) 1950
(c) 1960 (d) 1987

24. Which one of the following statements about design-stage in decision-making process is correct?
(a) Finding occasions calling for a decision.
(b) Inventing, developing and analysing possible courses of action.
(c) Carrying out the decision.
(d) Selecting a particular course of action.

25. Which one of the following streams of thought could not *be* labelled under 'situational design theory'?

(a) Behavioural approach
(b) Neo-classical approach
(c) Contingency approach
(d) Bureaucratic model

26. The State legislature of Jammu and Kashmir is authorised to confer special rights and privileges upon persons permanently resident in the State with respect to
(a) settlement in the State.
(b) acquisition of immovable property in the State.
(c) employment under the State government.
(d) All of the above.

27. Which of the following States have the institution of Revenue Tribunal instead of the Board of Revenue?
(a) Maharashtra and Gujarat
(b) Maharashtra and Punjab
(c) Haryana and Tamil Nadu
(d) Punjab and Himachal Pradesh

28. Which one among the following is not the function of the State Secretariat?
(a) To act as a channel of communication between one Government and another.
(b) To assist the Minister in the formulation of policy.
(c) To assist the legislature in its secretarial work.
(d) To prepare drafts of legislation to be introduced in the Assembly.

29. Fulton Committee recommended for:
1. Communism
2. Integrated structuralism
3. Elitism
4. Commercialism

Codes:
(a) 1 and 2 (b) 1 and 3
(c) 2 and 3 (d) 2, 3 and 4

30. Which of the statements given below are correct?
1. The determination of policies and objectives in an administration is related to the establishment of appropriate organisation, etc.
2. Administration is the execution of policies.
3. Administration and management have been used as synonyms.
4. Administration and management are appropriate for government and private sector, respectively.

Codes:
(a) 1 and 4 (b) 2 and 3
(c) 2, 3 and 4 (d) 1, 2, 3 and 4

31. The following programmes were launched for the improvement of the socio-economic conditions of rural population. Put them in chronological order
1. Bhoodan Movement
2. Gramdan Movement
3. Applied Nutrition Programme
4. Community Development

Codes:
(a) 1, 2, 4, 3 (b) 1, 3, 4, 2
(c) 1, 2, 3, 4 (d) 4, 3, 2, 1

32. Weber used the Greek word ‘charisma’ to mean
1. Inherited qualities
2. Supernatural qualities
3. Superhuman qualities
4. Exceptional qualities

Codes:
(a) 1, 2 and 3 (b) 1, 3 and 4
(c) 2, 3 and 4 (d) 1, 2, 3 and 4

33. The powers/functions of the Chief Minister of a State in India include
1. Appointing ministers and allocating portfolios to them
2. Presiding over the meetings of the Cabinet
3. Resolving conflicts between ministers
4. Communicating with the Governor

Codes:

(a) 1 and 4 (b) 1, 2 and 3
(c) 2, 3 and 4 (d) 1, 2, 3 and 4

34. Which of the statements about the behavioural approach are correct?
 1. It is concerned with the scientific study of human behaviour.
 2. It was started by Chester Barnard and later on developed by Herbert Simon.
 3. Its literature is mostly descriptive and not perspective.
 4. It stresses on informal relations and communication patterns.

Codes:

(a) 1 and 2 (b) 2 and 4
(c) 1, 2 and 3 (d) 1, 3 and 4

35. Which of the following are British legacies?
 1. District Administration
 2. Ministerial responsibility
 3. Planning commission
 4. Civil service

(a) 1 and 4 (b) 1 and 2
(c) 3 and 4 (d) All of the above

36. **List I**
 A. Government of India Act
 B. Indian Councils Act
 C. Minto-Morley Reforms
 D. Montague-Chelmsford Report

List II
 1. 1909 2. 1861
 3. 1858 4. 1919

Codes:	A	B	C	D
(a)	3	2	4	1
(b)	2	3	1	4
(c)	2	3	4	1
(d)	3	2	1	4

37. **List I**
 A. France B. USA
 C. India D. Britain

List II
 1. Constitutional monarchy
 2. Constitutional republic
 3. Mixture of presidential and parliamentary democracy
 4. True constitutional federal republic
 5. Quasi-federal republic

Codes:	A	B	C	D
(a)	3	4	2	1
(b)	2	4	5	3
(c)	3	4	1	2
(d)	2	5	4	3

38. **List I**
 A. Tenure System
 B. Simon Commission
 C. Maxwell Committee
 D. Central Government announced the introduction of the Desk-Officer in its Ministries

List II
 1. 1930 2. 1937
 3. 1905 4. 1970
 5. 1973

Codes:	A	B	C	D
(a)	3	1	2	5
(b)	4	2	3	5
(c)	2	1	3	4
(d)	1	2	3	4

39. **List I**
 A. Coordination B. Control
 C. Supervision D. Planning

List II
 1. Integration of several parts into an orderly whole to achieve the purpose.
 2. Ensuring compliance by staff with laws, orders and directions.
 3. Overseeing the work of subordinates.
 4. Collection of relevant information.
 5. Devising ways and means for resolution of problems.

Codes:	A	B	C	D
(a)	2	3	4	1
(b)	1	2	3	5
(c)	3	2	1	5
(d)	1	4	3	2

40. **List I**
   A. Masterman Committee
   B. Assheton Committee
   C. Satish Chandra Committee
   D. Fulton Committee
   List II
   1. Recruitment
   2. Political Activities
   3. Training
   4. Professionalism

Codes:	**A**	**B**	**C**	**D**
(a)	2	3	1	4
(b)	2	3	4	1
(c)	3	2	4	1
(d)	3	2	1	4

41. **List I (Country)**
   A. USA B. Great Britain
   C. France D. Japan
   List II (Features of Civil Service)
   1. Tradition of administrative centralisation is undergoing change.
   2. The office of Personnel Management is an independent agency under the President.
   3. 'Next Steps' programmes sought to transform structure of management of the civil service.
   4. Bureaucratic elitism is reinforced by educational and employment system.

Codes:	**A**	**B**	**C**	**D**
(a)	2	3	1	4
(b)	4	1	3	2
(c)	2	1	3	4
(d)	4	3	1	2

42. **Assertion (A):** The Union Home Ministry is the advisory and coordinating body in the field of law and order administration.
   Reason (R): The main responsibility for law and order lie with States.
   (a) Both (A) and (R) are true and (R) is the correct explanation of (A).
   (b) Both (A) and (R) are true but (R) is not the correct explanation of (A).
   (c) (A) is true but (R) is false.
   (d) (A) is false but (R) is true.

43. **Assertion (A):** The Internal emergency prevailed in India from 26 June 1975 to 23 March 1977.
   Reason (R): The Parliament can become captive under the authoritarian regime like this.
   (a) Both (A) and (R) are true and (R) is the correct explanation of (A).
   (b) Both (A) and (R) are true but (R) is not the correct explanation of (A).
   (c) (A) is true but (R) is false.
   (d) (A) is false but (R) is true.

44. **Assertion (A):** The Prime Minister of India occupies a superior position than the British Prime Minister.
   Reason (R): The office of the Prime Minister of India has been created by the Constitution.
   (a) Both (A) and (R) are true and (R) is the correct explanation of (A).
   (b) Both (A) and (R) are true but (R) is not the correct explanation of (A).
   (c) (A) is true but (R) is false.
   (d) (A) is false but (R) is true.

45. **Assertion (A):** Reservation policy in the public services is a mandate from the Indian Constitution.
   Reason (R): Reservation policy is conducive to the promotion of social justice.
   (a) Both (A) and (R) are true and (R) is the correct explanation of (A).
   (b) Both (A) and (R) are true but (R) is not the correct explanation of (A).
   (c) (A) is true but (R) is false.
   (d) (A) is false but (R) is true.

46. **Assertion (A):** There shall be a council of ministers with the Chief Minister at the head to aid and advise the Governor in the exercise of his functions, except in so

far as he is bound by or under the Constitution required to exercise his functions, or any of them in his discretion.
Reason (R): The Chief Minister shall be appointed by the Governor and other ministers shall be appointed by the Governor on the advice of the Chief Minister.
(a) Both (A) and (R) are true and (R) is the correct explanation of (A).
(b) Both (A) and (R) are true but (R) is not the correct explanation of (A).
(c) (A) is true but (R) is false.
(d) (A) is false but (R) is true.

47. **Assertion (A):** The tendency of hierarchy is to make the organisation tall.
Reason (R): Men at the top lose touch with the men at the bottom.
(a) Both (A) and (R) are true and (R) is the correct explanation of (A).
(b) Both (A) and (R) are true but (R) is not the correct explanation of (A).
(c) (A) is true but (R) is false.
(d) (A) is false but (R) is true.

48. Who among the following authors saw organisation in the form of basic design process and realized that, the lack of design makes an organisation illogical, rigid, extravagant and inefficient?
(a) Luther Gulick (b) Lyndall Urwick
(c) Henri Fayol (d) James Mooney

49. The Department of Jammu and Kashmir Affairs was created in 1994 and was then attached to the:
(a) Ministry of Defence
(b) PMO
(c) Ministty of External Affairs
(d) Ministty of Home Affairs

50. If the Karl Pearson's coefficient of correlation between x and y is 0.3, then the coefficient of correlation between –x and 2y is:
(a) –0.6 (b) –0.3
(c) 0.3 (d) 0.5

ANSWER SHEET

PAPER—I

1. (a)	2. (c)	3. (a)	4. (d)	5. (d)
6. (d)	7. (d)	8. (c)	9. (b)	10. (c)
11. (b)	12. (c)	13. (c)	14. (b)	15. (d)
16. (b)	17. (a)	18. (d)	19. (c)	20. (d)
21. (d)	22. (a)	23. (b)	24. (a)	25. (d)
26. (d)	27. (a)	28. (d)	29. (b)	30. (a)
31. (b)	32. (c)	33. (c)	34. (d)	35. (d)
36. (d)	37. (a)	38. (d)	39. (b)	40. (b)
41. (b)	42. (c)	43. (b)	44. (b)	45. (c)
46. (b)	47. (a)	48. (a)	49. (b)	50. (b)

PAPER—II

1. (a)	2. (a)	3. (a)	4. (b)	5. (d)
6. (b)	7. (c)	8. (d)	9. (d)	10. (b)
11. (b)	12. (b)	13. (b)	14. (a)	15. (b)
16. (d)	17. (b)	18. (d)	19. (d)	20. (b)
21. (b)	22. (b)	23. (b)	24. (d)	25. (c)
26. (a)	27. (c)	28. (a)	29. (a)	30. (b)
31. (c)	32. (d)	33. (a)	34. (b)	35. (a)
36. (a)	37. (d)	38. (a)	39. (c)	40. (b)
41. (a)	42. (b)	43. (b)	44. (d)	45. (a)
46. (b)	47. (d)	48. (d)	49. (d)	50. (a)

PAPER—III

1. (b)	2. (c)	3. (c)	4. (c)	5. (c)
6. (c)	7. (b)	8. (a)	9. (b)	10. (c)

11. (d)	12. (d)	13. (c)	14. (d)	15. (a)	31. (a)	32. (c)	33. (c)	34. (d)	35. (a)
16. (b)	17. (c)	18. (d)	19. (b)	20. (b)	36. (d)	37. (a)	38. (a)	39. (b)	40. (a)
21. (d)	22. (a)	23. (a)	24. (a)	25. (d)	41. (a)	42. (a)	43. (b)	44. (a)	45. (a)
26. (d)	27. (a)	28. (c)	29. (c)	30. (d)	46. (b)	47. (a)	48. (b)	49. (d)	50. (c)